Political Correctness

THE LANGUAGE LIBRARY

Series editor: David Crystal

The Language Library was created in 1952 by Eric Partridge, the great etymologist and lexicographer, who from 1966 to 1976 was assisted by his coeditor Simeon Potter. Together they commissioned volumes on the traditional themes of language study, with particular emphasis on the history of the English language and on the individual linguistic styles of major English authors. In 1977 David Crystal took over as editor, and *The Language Library* now includes titles in many areas of linguistic enquiry.

The most recently published titles in the series include:

Political Correctness

Geoffrey Hughes

A History of Semantics and Culture

A John Wiley & Sons, Ltd., Publication

This edition first published 2010
© 2010 Geoffrey Hughes

Blackwell Publishing was acquired by John Wiley & Sons in February 2007. Blackwell's publishing
program has been merged with Wiley's global Scientific, Technical, and Medical business to form
Wiley-Blackwell.

Registered Office
John Wiley & Sons Ltd, The Atrium, Southern Gate, Chichester, West Sussex, PO19 8SQ,
United Kingdom

Editorial Offices
350 Main Street, Malden, MA 02148-5020, USA
9600 Garsington Road, Oxford, OX4 2DQ, UK
The Atrium, Southern Gate, Chichester, West Sussex, PO19 8SQ, UK

For details of our global editorial offices, for customer services, and for information about how
to apply for permission to reuse the copyright material in this book please see our website at
www.wiley.com/wiley-blackwell.

The right of Geoffrey Hughes to be identified as the author of this work has been asserted in
accordance with the Copyright, Designs and Patents Act 1988.

Library of Congress Cataloging-in-Publication Data

Hughes, Geoffrey.
Political correctness : a history of semantics and culture / Geoffrey Hughes.
    p. cm. — (The language library)
  Includes bibliographical references and index.
  ISBN 978-1-4051-5278-5 (hardcover : alk. paper) — ISBN 978-1-4051-5279-2
(pbk. : alk. paper) 1. Political correctness. 2. Communication and culture.
3. Semantics. I. Title.
  BD175.5.P65H84 2009
  306.01—dc22
                                                                    2009012681

A catalogue record for this book is available from the British Library.

Set in 10/12.5pt Sabon by Graphicraft Limited, Hong Kong
Printed in Singapore by Ho Printing Singapore Pte Ltd

1   2010

*To the memory of George Orwell,
who understood political correctness
in so many guises*

Contents

Preface

This book aims to do three things. It studies the origins, progress, content and style of political correctness from the opening salvos of the academic debate in the United States to its recent global manifestations. These have proved to be protean, some would say "hydra-headed," covering all manner of agendas and linguistically embedded prejudices. For readers now familiar with these often dour semantic battles, I thought it would be interesting to bring in other dimensions. One is to show that political correctness of one sort or another has been a feature of English society for centuries, certainly since the English Reformation. The other is, broadly, to introduce the stimulating and varied evidence of culture, literature, thought, and images from "the absorbing past," as Lord Acton called it.

The campus debate showed academics with their gloves off, some of them defending unexpected corners. As the proposals for sanitizing the language, and therefore by implication the public mind, took on a Swiftian earnestness, a new (or supposedly new) species, the "public intellectual" emerged from the Ivory Tower to engage in, variously, the Battle of the Books, the Culture Wars, and the nature, function, and soul of the university. Several of these issues had, of course, been raised and debated by those Victorian sages Matthew Arnold, John Stuart Mill, Cardinal Newman, and Thomas Carlyle. But now institutions of higher learning formulated speech codes, designed to suppress or inhibit offensive language. Contrary codes were also at work, in stigmatizing acronyms like the recycled *WASP* and the newer *DWEM* (standing for "dead white European male," thus both racist and sexist). Their currency remained unchecked. Double standards proliferated, especially in the matter of "difference": it was acceptable to publish research findings demonstrating racial differences in health or sporting ability, but not in IQ scores and college admissions. What was increasingly called "PC" seemed to be the kind of social engineering which springs from the best of intentions, but can bring out less healthy Puritanical impulses in a society, as did Prohibition, the Communist witch-hunt and the abortion issue.

Who started it? Some, notably Doris Lessing, saw political correctness as the natural continuum of the Communist party line. Others saw "political correctness" as a label systematically deployed by those on the right to discredit views challenging the status quo. Who was right? Or were both right? Even more mysterious than the source was the efficacy and the acceptance of political correctness. Comparisons with "Orwellian" thought control and semantic engineering were made from the start, but where was the Politburo? Artificial formulas like *physically challenged, differently abled, sex worker*, and numerous other oddities, some being bureaucratic coinages, gained a certain official currency but proved unsustainable in normal discourse. Most strangely, even from the early 1990s when the debate was in full swing, virtually everybody disowned political correctness. It had become a code language without a visible champion. Since then it has been heavily criticized as "The most powerful mental tyranny in what we call the free world" (Lessing, 2004). Is this an overstatement by Lessing or a wise warning from an experienced combatant?

What about the world before it was "free"? Literature illuminates the topic in many fascinating ways. Our greatest dramatist wrote some plays which uphold traditional ideas of authority, but others which interrogate and even subvert this notion. "Family values" proves another highly problematic concept in his work, for his insights into sibling rivalry are deeply disturbing. Many of the agendas of political correctness surface in his plays, notably prejudice against the most conspicuous outsiders, Jews, blacks, the disabled, even the Puritans. A good case can be made for the view that from about 1600 Shakespeare seems intentionally to have written plays which deal with irresolvable moral and political problems. Nor was he alone: "I think hell's a fable" was just one provocative notion floated by Marlowe in *Dr Faustus*. The focus of criticism has also changed from the personal to the political: increasing emphasis on colonialism has radically reinterpreted plays like *Othello* and *The Tempest*. A recent production had the final words of Prospero's Epilogue, "As you from crimes would pardoned be, / Let your indulgence set me free," addressed not to the audience, as the context indicates, but to Caliban.

The time line and the global range can be extended. Two centuries before Shakespeare, Chaucer's *The Canterbury Tales*, which was created in a supposedly harmonious social setting of "quiet hierarchies" (Robertson, 1963, p. 51), contains typical expressions of xenophobia, racism, sexism, ageism and lookism, even vestiges of the class struggle. A century after Shakespeare's death, Alexander Pope boldly criticized "The right divine of

kings to govern wrong," while Jonathan Swift satirized all manner of institutions. They have had many distinguished followers. The structure of the
book accordingly accommodates these historical and literary dimensions.
In addition, South Africa required some coverage, because the nation has
been in a unique political and social time warp, only recently emerging from
apartheid to deal with the issues of democracy, national identity, affirmative action and various forms of empowerment in a multicultural society.

Is the world "free" now, in terms of reasonable people without a clear
political agenda being able to speak their minds on matters of public importance? Or has the notion of what is "offensive" or "unacceptable" or "inappropriate" or "racist" now taken on such broad and intrusive dimensions
that open debate on contentious issues is an impossibility? Has political
correctness succeeded in redefining morality by the introduction of the new
concept of "ethical living"? Has it succeeded in eliminating prejudice? Or
has it enabled some to be quicker to "take offense" where none was intended,
forcing others into elaborate stratagems to avoid "giving offense"?

Political correctness is a serious matter, grounded in suffering, prejudice,
and difference, and has certainly made everyone consider the plight of
others, giving a new emphasis to respect. But it has also provoked a great
deal of satire, irony, and humor, which have their place in a study of this
kind. Some of it is unexpected: we have become used to Jews and blacks
telling jokes about themselves and reclaiming ethnic slurs; but now we have
jokes being told about cripples, by cripples who insist on using that designation. Consequently, the earlier tendency to see things in dichotomous
terms of plain black and white is increasingly complicated.

The problem of finishing the book was similar to those faced in my
previous attempts at a history of swearing, since history does not stop
(obviously), and political correctness continues to influence our behavior
in manifold ways, virtually every week bringing some new episode or
outrage. I began to feel the force of Lytton Strachey's brilliant paradox in
the Preface to *Eminent Victorians*: "The history of the Victorian Age will
never be written: we know too much about it." Furthermore, mine was a
"hot topic." Of previous books people would say, "How interesting!" Now
several asked, "Will it get you into trouble?"

There was also the problem of what to call it. Most of the early PC titles
were melodramatic, relying on "War" and "Police," words which have been
rather overdone. Among many suggestions were: "The Rise and Fall of
Meaning," "Shifting Agendas," "Conflicting Agendas," "Exploring the
Unacceptable," "Zones of Controversy," "Mere Words," "Verbal Mine-
fields," and "What Can One Say?" In the end a simple descriptive title
seemed best.

I must express my gratitude to several people who helped shape the work. David Crystal shrewdly perceived a structure that was lacking in the somewhat inchoate first draft. Danielle Descoteaux has been an ideal editor, supportive, enthusiastic, but tactfully critical. Also in the Boston team, Julia Kirk gave excellent editorial support. The final text was greatly improved by the meticulous and sensitive editing of Jenny Roberts. I was greatly assisted by my good friend and colleague Peter Knox-Shaw, who read the first draft and made valuable suggestions; by the assistance of the indefatigable Tanya Barben of the Rare Books Department at the University of Cape Town Library; and by my dear son Conrad, who enlightened me in unfamiliar areas of popular culture. My beloved wife Letitia has, as always, been an endlessly patient reader and partner.

Geoffrey Hughes

Acknowledgments

The author and publisher would like to thank the following persons and institutions for permission to reproduce copyright material: Professor Bernth Lindfors for the image of the Hottentot "Apron"; AKG-Images for the film poster for D. W. Griffith's *Birth of a Nation*; Zapiro (Jonathan Shapiro) for the "African Renaissance Gallery"; the German National Museum, Nürnberg for the image of Five Opponents of Martin Luther; Steve Bell for the cartoon of Tony Blair and David Blunkett.

Epigraphs

Let her [Truth] and falsehood grapple; who ever knew Truth put to the worse, in a free and open encounter? (John Milton, *Areopagitica*, 1644)

He nevere yet no vileyne ne sayde,
In al his lyf unto no maner wight.
(He had never in his life said anything
Disrespectful to any kind of person.)
               (Chaucer, *Prologue to the Canterbury Tales*, ll. 70–2)

MARIA:	Sometimes he [Malvolio] is a kind of Puritan.
SIR ANDREW AGUECHEEK:	O, if I thought that I'd beat him like a dog.
SIR TOBY BELCH:	What! For being a Puritan? Thy exquisite reason, dear knight?

               (Shakespeare, *Twelfth Night*, II, 3, ll. 153–5)

He was the great Hieroglyphick of Jesuitism, Puritanism, Quaqerism [sic] and of all the Isms from Schism. ("Hercalio Democritus," *Vision of Purgatory*, 1680)

Let us dare to read, think, speak, and write . . . Let every sluice of knowledge be opened and set a-flowing. (John Adams, *Liberty and Knowledge*, 1765)

Clear your mind of cant. (Dr Johnson, Boswell's *Life of Johnson*, 1791)

. . . the principle of free thought – not free thought for those who agree with us, but freedom for the thought that we hate. (Justice Holmes, *United States v. Schwimmer*, 1929)

The most powerful mental tyranny in what we call the free world is Political Correctness. (Doris Lessing, "Censorship," 2004)

True literature can exist only where it is created not by diligent and trustworthy officials, but by madmen, hermits, heretics, dreamers, rebels and sceptics. (Yevgeny Zamyatin, "I am Afraid," 1921)

Part I

Political Correctness and its Origins

Chapter 1
Defining Political Correctness

Preamble and Rationale: Words and Ideas, Norms and Values

Political correctness became part of the modern lexicon and, many would say, part of the modern mind-set, as a consequence of the wide-ranging public debate which started on campuses in the United States from the late 1980s. Since nearly 50 percent of Americans go to college, the impact of the controversy was widespread. It was out of this ferment that most of the new vocabulary was generated or became current. However, political correctness is not one thing and does not have a simple history. As a concept it predates the debate and is a complex, discontinuous, and protean phenomenon which has changed radically, even over the past two decades. During just that time it has ramified from its initial concerns with education and the curriculum into numerous agendas, reforms, and issues concerning race, culture, gender, disability, the environment, and animal rights.

Linguistically it started as a basically idealistic, decent-minded, but slightly Puritanical intervention to sanitize the language by suppressing some of its uglier prejudicial features, thereby undoing some past injustices or "leveling the playing fields" with the hope of improving social relations. It is now increasingly evident in two opposing ways. The first is the expanding currency of various key words (to be listed shortly), some of a programmatic nature, such as *diversity*, *organic*, and *multiculturalism*. Contrariwise, it has also manifested itself in speech codes which suppress prejudicial language, disguising or avoiding certain old and new taboo topics. Most recently it has appeared in behavioral prohibitions concerning the environment and violations of animal rights. As a result of these transitions it has become a misnomer, being concerned with neither *politics* nor *correctness* as those terms are generally understood.

Political correctness inculcates a sense of obligation or conformity in areas which should be (or are) matters of choice. Nevertheless, it has had a major influence on what is regarded as "acceptable" or "appropriate" in language, ideas, behavioral norms, and values. But "doing the right thing" is, of course, an oversimplification. There is an antithesis at the core of political correctness, since it is liberal in its aims but often illiberal in its practices: hence it generates contradictions like *positive discrimination* and *liberal orthodoxy*. In addition, it has surprising historical and literary antecedents, surfacing in different forms and phases in Anglo-Saxon and global culture.

Although this book is called a "history," it is not really possible to write a conventional sequential history incorporating all these themes, of which there are basically six: political, literary, educational, gender, cultural, and behavioral. This is a large, interesting, but unwieldy package. The choice of "semantics" in the title rather than the broader and more familiar "language" is intentional, mainly because much of the debate was and continues to be about the changing of names, what are commonly known as "Orwellian" substitutions, and many of the practices which – rightly or wrongly – have given "semantics" a questionable name in popular parlance. Semantics (the study of meaning) is, of course, a respectable branch of linguistics unassociated with this practice, and much of the book is taken up with analyzing the semantic changes undergone by individual terms and in the evolution of word-fields.

Any discussion of political correctness necessarily involves its inseparable obverse, political incorrectness, just as "A History of Manners" would perforce involve bad manners, and "A History of Propaganda" would involve not only the techniques employed by propagandists, but the reactions of those being influenced and the strategies of counterpropaganda. For, just as people are suspicious of propaganda and resist it, so the institution of new taboos, especially against referring to personal features of size, color, addiction, and so on invokes feelings, even charges of censorship. These pressures provoke a counterreaction of satire, opportunistic defiance, and outrages, especially in popular culture. These reactions are covered in chapter 8. For all these reasons, the topic cannot be simply reduced to the standard template of "a definition," a "story," and a "conclusion." This complexity in part explains this book's structure.

The origins are in many ways the strangest feature. "Political Correctness is the natural continuum of the party line. What we are seeing once again is a self-appointed group of vigilantes imposing their views on others. It is a heritage of communism, but they don't seem to see this." So wrote Doris Lessing in the *Sunday Times* (May 10, 1992), continuing in this vein in her trenchant essay "Censorship" (2004), which is quoted among the epigraphs above. She was unambiguous and certainly right: political correctness first emerged in the diktats of Mao Tse-Tung, then chairman of the Chinese Soviet Republic, in the 1930s. But over half a century later it had mutated, rematerializing in a totally different environment, in an advanced secular capitalist society in which freedom of speech had been underwritten by the Constitution for two centuries, and in American universities, of all places. As Christopher Hitchens acutely observed: "For the first time in American history, those who call for an extension of rights are also calling for an abridgement of speech" (in Dunant, 1994, pp. 137–8).

Far from being a storm in an academic inkwell, political correctness became a major public issue engaged in by a whole variety of participants including President George Bush (briefly), public intellectuals, major academics, and journalists of all hues and persuasions. Some claim that the debate was a manufactured rather than a natural phenomenon, and that political correctness started as a chimera or imaginary monster invented by those on the Right of the political spectrum to discredit those who wished to change the status quo. These matters are taken up in chapter 2 "The Origins and the Debate." The fact is that the debate certainly took place. Exchanges were often acrimonious, focusing on numerous general issues of politics, ideology, race, gender, sexual orientation, culture, the curriculum, freedom of expression and its curtailment and so on. All of these will be discussed and developed.

This work attempts a detailed semantic analysis of how the resources of the language have been deployed, especially in forms of semantic engineering and the exploitation of different registers, both to formulate the new agendas, values, and key words of political correctness and to subvert them. A whole new semantic environment has come into being, through creation, invention, co-option, borrowing, and publicity: a representative sample of this new world of words includes *lookism, phallocratic, other, significant other, sex worker, multicultural, herstory, disadvantaged, homophobic, waitron, wimmin, differently abled, to Bork, physically challenged, substance abuse, fattist, Eurocentric, Afrocentric, demographics, issue, carbon footprint, glass ceiling, pink plateau,* and *first people,* as well as code abbreviations like *DWEM, PWA, HN,* and *neo-con.*

These are not simply new words, in the way that Shakespeare's *incarnadine, procreant, exsufflicate, be-all and end-all, unmanned, assassination,* and *yesterdays* were original forms four centuries ago. They are more like Orwell's artificial coinages in Newspeak, for instance, *thoughtcrime, joycamp,* and *doublethink.* Many are of a completely different order of novelty, opaqueness, and oddity, several of a character aptly described by the doughty Dr Johnson two centuries ago as "scarce English." The reaction of the uninitiated, and many of the educated, to this strange new galaxy of word formations or, some would say, deformations, is like that described by Edward Phillips in his *New World of Words*: "Some people if they spy but a hard word are as much amazed as if they had met with a Hobgoblin" (cited in Baugh, 1951, p. 260). That was in 1658, when new words of classical origin were still not welcomed as potential denizens, but rather regarded with suspicion as dubious immigrants disturbing "the King's English" (as it has been called since 1553).

Language theoretically belongs to all, but is often changed by only a few, many of them anonymous. Resentment at interference or sudden changes in the language has a long history. It started in the sixteenth century with the Inkhorn Controversy, a contretemps about the introduction of alien classical vocabulary, or hostility at semantic innovation of the kind Phillips satirized. In the long run most of these "hard words" as they were originally called, have been accepted. But it has been a very long run. Political correctness is still a relatively new phenomenon, and the serious or general acceptance of these words is still a matter of debate.

Let us briefly consider a fairly recent focused linguistic intervention, the attempt by feminists to alter or enlarge the stock of personal pronouns and to feminize agent nouns like *chairman* in order to diminish the dominance of the male gender, traditionally upheld in the grammatical dictum that "the male subsumes the female." Proposals for forms such as *s/he* were successful in raising consciousness, but produced few long-term survivals. Forms like *wimmin* and *herstory* became objects of satire, while the extensive replacement of *man* by *person* aroused some strong reactions: "I resent this ideological intrusion and its insolent dealings with our mother (perhaps I should say 'parent') tongue," wrote Roger Scruton (1990, p. 118). Scruton's mocking parody "parent tongue" is a response we shall see replicated many times in reactions to politically correct language. Nevertheless, some new forms like *chairperson* and *spokesperson* have managed to establish themselves.

Another comparison can be made with radical political discourse. Communism attempted to establish a whole new ideological discourse by means of neologisms like *proletariate*, semantic extensions like *bourgeois*, and by co-opting words like *imperialist* and *surplus*. Hard-line Communists still call each other "comrade" and refer to "the workers," "the collective," "capital," and the "party line," terms which are regarded by outsiders (who now form the majority) with irony and humor. For the days and locales when Communists could impose semantic norms on populations have long disappeared.

There are three characteristics which make political correctness a unique sociolinguistic phenomenon. Unlike previous forms of orthodoxy, both religious and political, it is not imposed by some recognized authority like the Papacy, the Politburo, or the Crown, but is a form of semantic engineering and censorship not derivable from one recognized or definable source, but a variety. There is no specific ideology, although it focuses on certain inequalities and disadvantaged people in society and on correcting prejudicial attitudes, more especially on the demeaning words which express them. Politically correct language is the product and formulation of a militant minority which remains mysteriously unlocatable. It is not the spontaneous creation of the speech community, least of all any particular deprived sector of it. Disadvantaged groups, such as the deaf, the blind, or the crippled (to use the traditional vocabulary), do not speak for themselves, but are championed by other influential public voices.

In these respects political correctness has a very different dynamic from the earlier high-profile advocates of, say, feminism or black consciousness in the USA. The feminists of the second wave, such as Germaine Greer, Betty Friedan, Kate Millett, Gloria Steinem, and Susan Sontag, were highly articulate, individual, and outspoken controversialists who did not always agree with each other, characteristics shared by Martin Luther King, Eldridge Cleaver, and Malcolm X. By contrast, the anonymous agenda-manipulators of political correctness are more difficult to identify. These features make the conformity to political correctness the more mysterious.

Paradoxically, political correctness manifested itself rapidly and most strongly, not in political parties, but on university campuses; not in the closed societies of Eastern Europe, but in free Western societies, especially in America, the only country in the world where freedom of speech is a constitutional right. Much play was accordingly made about the rights enshrined in the First Amendment, their "ownership" and their proper application.

In addition to these contemporary issues, it is important to recognize both a historical and a moral dimension, that is, to be aware that political correctness is not an exclusively modern manifestation. Accordingly, it is enlightening to consider some earlier forms of changing orthodoxies and their semantic correlatives, as well as the moral imperatives which these changing orthodoxies have generated. In many ways there has been a continuing dialectic between political orthodoxy and dissent since the sixteenth century, virtually since the invention of printing. Reflection shows that political correctness of one sort or another has been a feature of English society for centuries, certainly since the English Reformation, the first major political change which was not an invasion.

Furthermore, literature illuminates the topic in many fascinating ways. Our greatest dramatist, for instance, wrote some plays which uphold traditional ideas of authority and the Divine Right, but others which interrogate this notion. "Family values" proves another highly problematic concept in his work, for his insights into sibling rivalry are deeply disturbing. Very few love relationships are free of hostility, jealousy, or tragic interference. A good case can be made for the view that from about 1600 Shakespeare seems intentionally to have written plays which deal with irresolvable moral and political problems. Major issues are not buried in the subplot or in speeches of minor characters. No audience could fail to be disturbed or provoked by a whole series of resounding utterances, such as Hamlet's misogynist generalization "Frailty, thy name is woman," or Shylock's question "Hath not a Jew eyes?," or Falstaff's cynical view that "honor" is "a mere word," or by the bastard Edmund's dismissive comment on heredity: "fine word, legitimate!" A mere century later Alexander Pope was to mock "the right divine of kings to govern wrong," while two centuries before Shakespeare, Chaucer's *Canterbury Tales*, created in a supposedly harmonious medieval social setting, contains biting satires of the ecclesiastical establishment and many unexpected expressions of xenophobia, racism, sexism, ageism, and lookism, even vestiges of the class struggle. Part IV accordingly seeks to accommodate these historical and literary dimensions.

In addition, the new South Africa offers a fruitful example of the semantic and social problems of "normalization" after the iniquities of apartheid. The nation has been in a political and social time warp, only recently emerging from the agendas of colonialism, white domination, and racial separation to deal with the issues of democracy, national identity, affirmative action, and various forms of empowerment in a multicultural society. These aspects are covered in this chapter, in chapter 5, and in the Conclusion.

What is Political Correctness?

This fundamental question has become increasingly difficult to answer as new agendas have materialized. Most people would frame answers along the lines of "It means not using words like *nigger, queer,* or *cripple*," or "It means showing respect to all," or "It means accepting and promoting diversity." These answers are adequate, but cover only the main issues, by means of proscription (the first) or prescription (the second and third). The emphases on offensive language, prejudiced attitudes, and insulting behavior towards the marginalized are central. The question is less easily answered in a comprehensive way, as the historical précis has suggested. Specific answers are supplied by verbal definition, by identifying role models, by description of approved or bad practices, or assumptions about proper and improper behavior.

Leaving aside the theoretical and social aspects for the time being, let us briefly consider the epigraphs at the beginning of the book. It is striking that the oldest, from Chaucer's portrait of a medieval nobleman, describes a role model, an ideal of behavior (that of never saying anything disrespectful to anyone, regardless of status) which conforms with the best notions of political correctness. Chaucer evidently regards this aspect of his "verray, parfit gentil knyght" as both admirable and unusual. The exchange from Shakespeare's *Twelfth Night* shows us two very different knights, one idiotic, the other decadent. Although the comedy is set in Illyria, the issue is highly relevant. Sir Andrew Aguecheek's antagonism towards Malvolio as a suspected Puritan ("I'd beat him like a dog") has a contemporary edge of intolerance, which Sir Toby Belch's critical reproof rightly shows to be mindless: "For being a Puritan? Thy exquisite reason, dear knight?" Being tolerant towards the Puritans, who wished to impose their strict religious régime on all, who hated the theaters and eventually succeeded in closing them, required an act of considerable charity. But Sir Toby, for all his faults, has a balanced, *laissez faire* attitude. The kind of sectarian extremism which lay ahead is shown in the scathing references to "Jesuitism, Puritanism and Quaqerism [Quakerism] and of all the Isms from Schism" in the remarkable quotation from 1680. From a different perspective, the quotations from Milton, John Adams, and Justice Holmes show a faith, indeed an insistence, on open debate and in "the principle of free thought," attitudes which are often lacking from modern political and educational forums, a point which Doris Lessing argues strongly. Indeed "free thought" and "free speech" are often seen to be curtailed by political correctness. Dr Johnson's famous dictum reminds us that though "cant" is now largely obsolete as a word, the plausible hypocrisy which it denotes still thrives, and is too often encountered.

The question could be put another way: what do speech codes, Chairman Mao, eating foie gras, the letters of Philip Larkin, *Tintin in the Congo*, George Orwell's *1984*, wearing fur, shock jocks, McCarthyism, Borat, AIDS jokes, Christmas cards, the films of Spike Lee, ethnic slurs, and *The Simpsons* have in common? At first sight, not much. Discussion of these topics will show that political correctness and its obverse, political incorrectness, are more easily recognized than defined, and that both appear in manifold forms.

Yet even this list is by no means exhaustive. A survey of instances culled from the British National Corpus (BNC) shows the phrase being applied to an extraordinary variety of entities, namely to individuals, culture, children's literature, musical bands, the mixture of ethnic groups, even a lasagne, as well as to language. Many of the quotations come from press reports and analyses, some from book reviews, from novels and interviews. "Politically Correct movies are fairy tales" was an early comment in 1984 by Joel Schumacher, a film producer, in *The Scotsman*. Most of the quotations in the BNC date from the early 1990s, for instance references to "Glenda Jackson, the Politically Correct actress" and to "Politically Correct feminism" (both from the *Daily Telegraph*, 1992). Another report comments: "Politically Correct language was the order of the day at the BASW [British Association of Social Workers] conference as the debates centred on gender issues" (*Community Care*, 1993). An interviewee in the *Daily Express* comments: "I have a very good Politically Correct feminist side and a very glamour-oriented attention-getting whorey side, and they clash." These last three quotations show an equation of political correctness with feminism, an identification we shall encounter frequently. There is also, in British politics, an assumption that political correctness is a feature of the Left, seen in many quotations, such as: "Labour would preside over the entrenching of Political Correctness in the classroom" (*Daily Telegraph*, 1992). Many similar comments are recorded from 1992, the year of a general election. Socialist assumptions certainly seem to lie behind this item: "Another ruled that a grassy lawn was politically incorrect on the grounds that not all children have gardens" (*The Scotsman*).

Environmental issues appear, but in unexpected places: "Complaining that a recent photograph showed him with an unrecyclable styrofoam coffee cup, he denounced it as 'politically incorrect'" (*Daily Telegraph*, 1992). Benny Hill is described as "the politically incorrect comedian" (*Punch*, 1992), while an observation is made that "The culture is politically incorrect, so violence gets cheered" (*The Scotsman*). A comment from *Pilot* magazine concludes: "but you have to be politically correct these days!" (1992). Others are less concessive: "Terms such as 'faggot' may be unacceptable to polite society, in this age of Political Correctness, but clearly nothing has altered what goes on the privacy of the popular conscience" (*Daily Telegraph*, 1992). In similar tone: "Even in an era of 'Political Correctness', and hypersensitivity over racial slights, Eskimo Pie has retained its name and its logo" (*Daily Telegraph*, 1992).

Two reports, both from *The Scotsman* in 1992, relate to children's literature: "A survey of children's authors by the writers' group PEN suggests that publishers are not content merely with encouraging writers to be politically correct, but are actually censoring anything they feel to be politically incorrect." The second reports: "Indeed publishers told PEN they were under pressure from schools, libraries and local authorities to be politically correct." This aspect is discussed further under the "Censorship" section below. Fiction is a frequent candidate. "*The First Wives Club* is a very American book . . . in its fashionable Political Correctness: having taken revenge on their rich, white, middle aged husbands, the ex-wives find true love with, variously, a lesbian, an impoverished Puerto Rican lawyer, and a younger man" (*Daily Telegraph*, 1992). This last comment contains a clearly ironic observation on the "rich, white" husbands getting their just desserts, since the betrayed wives seek adventurous lives outside the bourgeois norms.

These topics are related to the previously listed aspects, namely: political, literary, educational, cultural, gender, and behavioral. Perhaps because many of the instances come from the early 1990s, they do not put much emphasis on later key aspects of political correctness, namely animal rights, colonialism, the environment, and AIDS. Many quotations identify an aspect of political correctness without defining it. It is merely asserted, for example, that various groups ". . . want a Labour win in order to impose Political Correctness" (*Daily Telegraph*, 1992). This practice clearly assumes that even then political correctness was recognizable in some way. We also notice that in all the early instances both "political" and "correctness" are capitalized.

What constitutes politically incorrect behavior? The characterization is not as simple as one would imagine, as the following table of "inappropriate" activities shows. These range from the serious to the trivial, covering linguistic modes, behavioral patterns, and lifestyle choices, and are designated by means of the symbols ✓ (yes) or ✗ (no) or ? (uncertain):

Inappropriate activities	Politically incorrect
using ethnic slurs	✓
religious swearing	✗
sexual swearing	?
pedophilia	✗
rape	✓
chauvinism	✓
sexism	✓
homophobia	✓
pornography	?
blasphemy	✗
racism	✓
domestic violence	?
cruelty to animals	✓
smoking cigarettes	✓
smoking cannabis	✗
wearing fur	✓
eating veal	✓
eating beef	✗

Even granted that the simple categorization of "yes" or "no" is obviously somewhat crude, and that not everybody would agree with all the allocations, the degree of inconsistency is extraordinary. It shows a feature which we shall encounter in different categories and locales, that of double or variable standards. Thus in the category of swearing, only ethnic slurs qualify unambiguously. Religious swearing generally does not: a recent survey showed that the name of Jesus was familiar to the majority of British children, but as a swearword. Sexual swearing is divided along gender lines: *bitch*, *cow*, and *cunt* definitely qualify, although not in all cases, while *fucker*, *bugger*, and *prick* do not. Indeed, the British celebrity chefs Jamie Oliver and Gordon Ramsay, especially notorious for his copious use of the word *fuck*, have achieved royal recognition. Feminists regard pornography as demeaning to women; most males do not. Under the category of blasphemy, *The Life of Brian* (1979) and *Jerry Springer: The Opera* (2005), grossly satirizing the life of Jesus, provoked protests, but not banning. Rejecting a subsequent appeal by Christian Voice against the Springer show, the Law Lords ruled that the appeal "does not raise an arguable point of law of general public importance" (*The Times*, March 5, 2008). Less comprehensible was the attempt to invoke the blasphemy law against Salman Rushdie's *The Satanic Verses* (1989), discussed further in chapter 5 under "Islam." It failed on the grounds that the law covers only Christianity, its personages and articles of belief. While it is understandable that homophobia should be regarded as politically incorrect, it seems extraordinary that pedophilia is not, certainly not with the same detestation. And where to place treason? Who knows?

A number of the listed "inappropriate activities" are illegal; some are merely bad manners. But their correlation with what is regarded as politically incorrect is not simple. Thus smoking in nondesignated areas or using ethnic slurs are punishable by law. Similarly, religious swearing or farting in company are unacceptable breaches of manners or decorum. Political correctness occupies a behavioral space between the two. As has been mentioned, it inculcates a sense of obligation to conform in some areas (such as chauvinism or wearing fur) which, some would argue, should be matters of choice. This creates problems in a free society. At the same time, no one is obliged to be politically correct. Consequently, charges of censorship or fascism, which are often made, have to be analyzed closely.

Definitions

It is customary to answer the broader question with a definition. Here is a selection:

Conformity to a body of liberal or radical opinion on social matters, characterized by the advocacy of approved views and the rejection of language and behaviour considered discriminatory or offensive. (*Oxford Dictionary of New Words*, 1997)

The most powerful mental tyranny in what we call the free world is Political Correctness, which is both immediately evident, and to be seen everywhere, and as invisible as a kind of poison gas, for its influences are often far from the source, manifesting as a general intolerance. (Doris Lessing, 2004)

Political Correctness is a concept invented by hard-rightwing forces to defend their right to be racist, to treat women in a degrading way and to be truly vile about gay people. They invent these people who are Politically Correct, with a rigid, monstrous attitude to life so they can attack them. But we have all had to learn to modify our language. That's all part of being a human being. (Clare Short, *Guardian*, February 18, 1995)

As we can see here, and will see further in the argument, especially in chapter 2 and in Part II, there are various modes of definition. The first of these is authoritative and neutral, while the second and third are combative or tactical. Simply in terms of semantics, the first authority gives a balanced, referential account, using the key term "conformity," while the second and third use the rhetorical strategy of highly emotive terms like "powerful mental tyranny," "a kind of poison gas," "hard-rightwing forces," "truly vile," and so on. Their subtext is of a war going on. Yet on closer examination, the first definition fudges the issue in various ways, by using "liberal or radical," which have very different meanings, particularly in Britain and America; it also contains a series of begged questions arising from the terms *conformity*, *approved*, and *considered* – without identifying by whom.

Ideologically, the second and third explanations are, of course, diametrically opposed. Lessing derives political correctness from left-wing conformity which has bred "tyranny" and "general intolerance"; Short from a cynical right-wing stalking horse, "invented" to discredit liberal attitudes (*liberal* in the British sense of broad-minded, unprejudiced). But neither can truly identify the source, what Lessing in her previously cited quotation called "the party" and the "vigilantes" or what Short calls the "hard-rightwing forces," to whom they attribute this curious sociolinguistic phenomenon.

The two explanations are not, however, mutually exclusive, in that a strict form of orthodoxy may be initially acceptable to its hard-line followers, then be satirized by outsiders, and finally come to be denounced by the majority as an intolerant infringement of personal liberty. Thus Puritanism, often compared with political correctness, began as a worthy reformist spiritual and doctrinal position within Christianity, before it became increasingly intolerant, satirized, and even regarded as un-Christian. Of many ironic quotations, this by the American Finley Peter Dunne on Thanksgiving (from *Mr Dooley's Opinions*, 1901) is one of the sharpest: "'Twas founded be [by] the Puritans to give thanks f'r being presarved fr'm the Indyans, and we keep it to give thanks we are presarved fr'm the Puritans." Lessing traces the development of political correctness as being similar to that of Puritanism:

> This began as a sensitive, honest and laudable attempt to remove the racial and sexual biases encoded in language, but it was at once taken over by the political hysterics, who made of it another dogma. . . . There could hardly be a conversation without it, and PC was used as often as the Victorians used "It isn't done", meaning socially improper, or to bolster the orthodoxies of "received opinion", or even to criticise the eccentric. (Lessing, 2004, p. 76)

"Fascism" has followed the same semantic pattern, being transformed from its strict Italian political origins to its broader sense of dictatorship and conformity. Roger Scruton has a notable essay on the topic in *Untimely Tracts* (1987). Today both "Puritan" and "Fascist" are, of course, highly critical terms. Paul Johnson defined political correctness as "liberal fascism" (cited in Kramer and Kimball, 1995, p. xii).

How adequate are the definitions so far offered? They are accurate, but only up to a point. What is obviously noteworthy about all of them is their lack of reference to what is really the most obvious semantic fact about political correctness, namely the emergence of a whole new series of artificial substitutions, some of them already listed, terms such as *abled*, *herstory*, *lookism*, *phallocentric*, *waitron*, and *wimmin*. Many other established terms, such as *challenged*, *Eurocentric*, *gay*, *homophobic*, *patriarchy*, and *person* have been given new meanings in the furtherance of particular agendas. Typically, politically correct language avoids judgmental terms, preferring an artificial currency of polysyllabic abstract euphemistic substitutions. Thus *drug addiction* is avoided, the preferred opaque formula being *substance dependence*; *visually impaired* is preferred to *blind*, while *sex worker* is the politically correct term for *prostitute*. Although *cripple* and *spastic* have become taboo, some formulas, such as *differently abled* for *disabled* have proved too artificial to gain real currency.

What is characteristic about the language? A detailed semantic analysis of the word field is to be found in chapter 4, while individual topics and forms are discussed under the various relevant headings in Part III. But in essence the language is unfamiliar and abstract, using high register classical elements (*phallocratic, heterosexism*) to an unusual degree and comparatively few native Anglo-Saxon terms. Even these appear in odd combinations like *fattist* and *lookism*. In essence it is a code language, with most of the forms, both the new (*herstory,* to *Bork*) and even the apparently familiar (*disadvantaged, challenged*) requiring translation and explanation of their agenda.

In addition to the semantic problems, the grammatical structure is noteworthy for its oddness. William Safire rightly observed that the most frequently used linguistic form was the "adverbially premodified adjectival lexical unit" (*New York Times,* May 5, 1991). This slightly cumbersome but accurate description perhaps contains a tinge of irony. A great number of the formulas of political correctness (e.g., *politically correct* itself, *physically challenged, visually impaired,* and *differently abled*) follow the same grammatical structure. Most seem unnatural for various reasons: they are abstract, imprecise, and euphemistic. However, the structure itself is not unusual: thus "financially sound" is an established phrase describing a company or institution. But *financially underprivileged* is problematic because there is a semantic mismatch: *underprivileged* does not normally qualify a financial situation. There is also the literal implication that being rich is a privilege, which is not valid, being true only of those who inherit wealth. The phrase has come about simply as one of the many euphemisms for "poor." Similarly, *physically strong* describes a person in ordinary terms, but *differently abled* is logically an absurdity and a tautology, since people obviously differ in ability. Here the problem is compounded by unfamiliarity: *differently* is not normally used as a premodifier, and *abled* is a comparative neologism, recorded only from 1981.

What do these formulas mean? The real problem with all of them, as with most euphemisms, is that we do not know how disabled or poor these unfortunate people are, let alone what they feel about being called "abled," "challenged," and so on. This kind of semantic innovation is not truly traditional or idiomatic, thereby provoking objections and satire. We shall be returning to the issues of euphemism and satire in due course.

The Semantic Problems of Political Correctness

In essence, the political correctness debate has been about naming, or rather renaming. Typically outsiders are named and labeled, whether they be foreigners, the colonized, minorities, homosexuals, cripples, or the mad, to use the older vocabulary. The primary intentions of the interventions of political correctness were laudable, as all agree, namely to change

:d prejudicial attitudes and their semantic correlatives by the intro-
of new, neutral, and unfamiliar lexical forms. In tandem there were
_____ to denounce and diminish the currency of established demeaning vocabulary. These worthy initiatives were obviously not expressed on a *tabula
rasa*, since, as many studies have shown, in crucial respects language is
not neutral, but a reflection of dominant ideologies, unhealthy prejudices,
and limited notions of normality. Centuries of bias have become established,
even entrenched, in prejudicial and stereotypical language evident in terms
for women, as well as the groups mentioned above. The more insulting of
these terms are demotic and low in register: *bitch*, *queer*, *wog*, *loony*, and
spastic are just some examples. Over time these have gained established
currencies in the ordinary language of the street, in some literature, and in
dictionary entries.

The attempt to reformulate such expressions in more neutral language
of a higher register appropriate to public discourse, admirable though the
motives were, has not received wholesale endorsement. After a period of
initial acceptance, reactions ranged from measured criticism to outright hostility, ironic parody, and scornful rejection. There have simultaneously
emerged various genres and figures in popular culture, notably rappers
and "shock jocks," who in various ways express views and use language
which is blatant in its political incorrectness. In addition there have
appeared semiserious and quite substantial anthologies of common and
uncommon insults, such as Jonathon Green's *Big Book of Being Rude* (2000),
which focuses on personal insults, and Julian L'Estrange's *Big Book of Insults*
(2002) which contains a wealth of xenophobic (and anti-British) material.
Whether these contrary tendencies are phases in a cultural model of thesis
and antithesis remains to be seen. But the reaction of those whom Stanley
Fish calls "the backlashers" (1994, p. 11) is disturbing, and can be
explained by the model discussed below under the subsection "Semantic
frameworks."

The principal topics involved in renaming are dealt with in Part III. Here
we are concerned with the formula *political correctness* itself, rather than
the historical dimension of earlier regimes requiring conformity and orthodoxy. The formulation is fairly modern. As with many formulas, *political
correctness* originally had quite a clear literal sense in a limited context,
referring to the orthodox Communist party political line. Since then it has
broadened in its applications and has also acquired meanings that are different from those of its individual component terms. These developments
are not surprising in themselves. Let us compare two other set phrases of
a social character, namely *free enterprise* and *industrial action*. We note that
although *enterprise* and *free* have a wider range of meanings, *free enterprise*

generally means what it says, within its capitalist framework. By contrast *industrial action*, in the UK, means something quite different from the general meanings of *industrial* and *action*: it is a euphemism or code term for *strike*.

We have seen earlier in the discussion that even serviceable definitions, such as that in the *Oxford Dictionary of New Words* (1997) turn out to be problematic or inadequate. In essence this is because the formula *political correctness* is an inherently problematic semantic construct. In the first place, there is no such thing as a "correct political attitude," for various reasons. *Politics* is by any definition a diversified term covering a wide spectrum of activities going far beyond affairs of state and government to include local politics, office politics, family politics, marital politics, sexual politics, identity politics, and so on. We are virtually in the realm of the Marxist interpretation which sees politics in everything. Furthermore, outside the confines of totalitarian societies, no one political system or party can claim to be "correct." Even within major political parties, there are "moderates," "hardliners," and "extremists." *Correctness*, by contrast, denotes conformity to certain agreed standards or practices. Consequently, *political correctness* does not have an agreed, clear literal meaning, in the way that *grammatical correctness* or *political corruption* do.

The origins and evolution of these three formulas essentially reflect the degree of their accepted meanings in the speech community. *Free enterprise* has been in the language for over two centuries, but it took about a century for the modern capitalist sense to emerge. Since its meaning has developed naturally and gradually by consensus in the public domain, it is largely undisputed, even though there may be arguments about the desirable degrees of freedom within capitalism. *Industrial action*, on the other hand, is an artificial bureaucratic coinage dating from only around 1971, designed largely as a substitute formula to avoid the negative connotations of *strike*, the natural and common word. It is not only a euphemism; it is a misnomer, meaning essentially, industrial inaction. Consequently, although it has an official currency, it is generally regarded as an example of cynical double-speak and is thus seldom used in ordinary discourse. One cannot imagine a man saying to his mate in the pub: "We can't go to the cricket because of the industrial action on the trains." It is also essentially British in currency: foreigners and visitors would need a translation.

The history of *political correctness* is more complex, first emerging in Communist terminology as a policy concept denoting the orthodox party line of Chinese Communism as enunciated by Mao Tse-Tung in the 1930s. This we may call the hard political or literal sense. It was then borrowed by the American New Left in the 1960s, but with a more rhetorical than strictly programmatic sense, before becoming adopted and current in Britain. It is essentially a modern coinage by a minority, deriving from *politically correct*, dating from about 1970. The semantic history is treated in detail in chapter 2 in the section "Origins of the Phrase."

Euphemisms: traditional, institutional and contrived

Euphemism is clearly the closest semantic relation, since all the classic formulations of political correctness show avoidance of direct reference to some embarrassing topic or condition. These go far beyond the traditional topics and modes of euphemism including, for example, *disadvantaged, substance abuse, demographics, differently abled*, and *vertically challenged*. Euphemism and other forms of verbal sanitization have a long history and typically take two semantic forms: the metaphorical use of root terms (*pass water* instead of *piss* and *break wind* instead of *fart*), or the substitution of so-called "Anglo-Saxon" words by polysyllabic abstract formulations using classical vocabulary, well described by Edward Gibbon as "the decent obscurity of a learned language" (*Decline and Fall*, chap. 30). Examples range from *terminated pregnancy* instead of *abortion, erectile dysfunction* for *impotence*, through to *liquidate, neutralize*, or *terminate with extreme prejudice* instead of *kill*. While the first examples are natural and have a long history in the speech community, the latter are more institutional, recent, unfamiliar, and "Orwellian" in the sense of disguising the violence and ugliness of war by means of bland abstraction. Some, like *pacification* for "subject to new tyranny" (an actual Orwellian coinage) show the added refinement of meaning virtually the opposite of their apparent sense, a feature we have noted in *industrial action*.

Significantly, Michel Bréal, the founding figure of semantics, noted in his seminal work over a century ago that words often "come to possess a disagreeable sense as a result of euphemism" (1900, p. 100). This is, of course, an ironic outcome, since the intention of euphemism is precisely to avoid "the disagreeable sense." The point is that euphemisms seldom remain euphemisms over time, but become tainted by association with what they seek to disguise. Otto Jespersen, another great historian of the language, observed in 1905: "This is the usual destiny of euphemisms; in order to avoid the real name of what is thought indecent or improper, people use some innocent word. But when that becomes habitual in this sense it becomes just as objectionable as the word it has ousted and now is rejected in its turn" (1962, p. 230). Bréal also presciently perceived the results of "false delicacy" in sensitive areas:

We remember what a noble signification *amant* and *maîtresse* still possessed in Corneille [1606–84]. But they are dethroned, as was *Buhle* in German. Here we see the inevitable results of false delicacy; honourable names are dishonoured by being given to things which are dishonourable. (Bréal, 1900, p. 101)

This perception was taken further by the semanticist Stephen Ullmann, who argued that "the notorious deterioration which has affected various words for 'girl' or 'woman' . . . was no doubt due to genuine or pseudo-euphemism" (1964, pp. 90–1). Ullmann's valuable term *pseudo-euphemism* is a more technical version of Bréal's "false delicacy." They can be seen in copious examples, such as *lady of the night* or *fille de joie* for "prostitute," the more poetic antecedents of the politically correct industrial term *sex-worker*. Indeed, both "false delicacy" and "pseudo-euphemism" are very apt descriptions of much of the terminology of political correctness.

Euphemism is a genuine collective attempt to avoid an embarrassing topic that often becomes undermined by association, whereas pseudo-euphemism typically betrays certain elements of humorous connivance and irony. Thus to say "Snooks is a bit slow on the uptake" is a euphemism, whereas to say "Snooks is two cards short of a full house" is a pseudo-euphemism. Pseudo-euphemism draws attention to itself by being maliciously clever: thus "slow on the uptake" is an established phrase, a variation of "slow-witted," whereas "two cards short of a full house" is a creative variation of a fertile new idiom discussed further under "Disability" in chapter 6.

Both modes are well established. Thus the ironic phrase "lick [i.e., touch] of the tar brush" is included by Francis Grose in his inimitable slang dictionary, *A Classical Dictionary of the Vulgar Tongue* (1785), explaining another euphemism, *blue skin*: "A person begotten on a black woman by a white man." Also in Grose are *love begotten child*: a bastard, *mother*: a prostitute, *mother of all saints*: the monosyllable (a code word for *cunt*), *unfortunate women*: prostitutes, and *a lady of easy virtue*. *Sapphic* was an early pseudo-euphemism for *lesbian*; it has now become institutionalized. However, all euphemisms, precisely because they are not literal, are code terms or phrases depending on tacit or mutual understandings. An outsider will not grasp all the nuances: hence there is always a possibility of confusion. This increases when euphemisms are contrived artificially and given a new, limited currency by a particular pressure group, as has happened with political correctness.

The focus of euphemisms has, of course, changed from universals such as death, disease, sex, bodily functions, madness, the names of God and the Devil, to being crippled, being poor, being fired, being fat, or having a humble occupation. As this list shows, euphemisms cannot be entirely avoided, since *bodily functions* and *having a humble occupation* are euphemisms in themselves. Some readers will feel that *crippled* should be replaced by *disabled*. Race is a burgeoning new area of euphemism: political commentators and journalists increasingly prefer general terms like *demographic change, immigrant, minority, origin,* or *background* to specific markers like *black* or *Asian*. It is significant that a fairly comprehensive *Dictionary of Euphemisms* (1983) by Neaman and Silver covered all the traditional topics, including "Bureaucratese" and "The Game of War," but not race. Today some journalistic codes and house rules forbid the mention of race in news stories about crime or violence. The number of euphemisms which grows up round a particular topic is an obvious indication of its power to embarrass: thus there are no euphemisms for "color," only for "people of color." The issue of race is taken up in more detail in Part III.

Long ago H. L. Mencken, the frank but controversial authority on what he called *The American Language* (1919–36), observed the American habit of dignifying menial occupations by means of grand titles: "The American seldom believes that the trade he follows is quite worthy of his virtues and talents . . . and even invents a sonorous name to set himself off from the herd" (1963, p. 339). His numerous examples included *exterminating engineer* and *rodent operative* for *rat-catcher*. Although Mencken called these "Occupational Euphemisms," and like most observers treated these restylings with his typical ironic humor, they are not typical euphemisms in the manner of *excrement, intimacy,* and *molest*, since in many cases the object or calling is not unpleasant or embarrassing as such. They can be seen in another light, as attempts by those in the lower echelons of trade to be regarded with egalitarian dignity. Equality and dignity are, of course, two key watchwords of political correctness, and it is thus not surprising that this semantic tendency has become so highly developed in the United States.

Today we are used to Orwellian substitutions such as ministries of war being called ministries of peace, ministries of labour being restyled ministries of productivity, and so on. In some cases the new politically correct names are justified: perhaps "correctional services" is a more accurate name for the enterprise than plain old gloomy "prisons." Yet historically the substitution of names as a bureaucratic subterfuge is not new. In the Prologue to an ancient morality play the figure of Avarice announces: "I will my name disguise; And call my name Policy instead of Covetise." The point is that *policy* was and is a respectable, albeit vague term, while *covetise* was the name of a deadly sin, archaically known as Covetousness. The play was *Respublica*, dated 1553. Semantic substitutions were not entirely new even then, as the history of *purveyor* reveals. In the fourteenth century purveyors became notorious for not paying for goods commandeered in the king's name. The solution was simple: a statute of 1360 required them to pay up on delivery and changed their designation, so that "the odious title of purveyor shall be changed and styled purchaser" ("le heignous noun de pourveyour soit chaungé & nomé achatour").

These are extreme and cynical examples. In general, euphemisms come from many sources, but in essence they have grown up spontaneously in the speech community. They remind us of the complex relationship between *politics* and *politeness*, in that while to do what is *politic* or *expedient* may involve a questionable or even detestable compromise in the public domain, it may be the right thing to do in personal, family, or group relations. When Aristotle defined Man as being "a political animal," he meant essentially that he lives in a society or social organism, the *polis*, not solitary like a wild animal. Euphemisms obviously exist in great numbers and in many varieties. But fundamentally and naturally they spring from an impulse not to embarrass, which could be claimed as a prime motivation for political correctness.

Ideals, Ideology, and Practice

Political correctness is based on various idealistic assumptions on how society should be run, and how people should behave towards each other. However, a society is necessarily made up of individuals and groups, with different histories, manners, cultures, needs, and expectations. Furthermore, the two societies with which we are mainly concerned, the United States and Britain, are essentially multicultural, as opposed to say, Japan. America was multicultural from the beginning, although the political history has generally emphasized the interests of the white race. The British Isles previously contained the Anglo-Saxon heptarchy and the kingdoms of the Picts, the Scots, and the Irish, subsequently evolving into four independent nations: although the political concept of "Great Britain," dating from 1704, gave a nominal sense of national unity, there were numerous minorities. The arrival of Commonwealth immigrants from the late 1950s was the beginning of a radical social change. In many ways the impulse behind political correctness in its essential sense of respect derives from an awareness of multiculturalism.

The primary idealistic assumption is that of equality. This is stronger in the American ideology, underpinned by the proposition that "All men are created equal" (in the Declaration of Independence, 1776) than in the British political scheme, which has no written constitution; accommodates monarchy, ranks of nobility, and a class system, admits deference, accepting the more realistic and practical notion that all are equal before the law. A major problem, as always, is how to achieve "equality," that is, to redress historical inequalities, at a particular moment in time.

Yet historical fact and ideology do not always square. Thus slavery was entrenched at the time of Independence (there were already some 500,000 slaves in America), but the word *slave* is not mentioned in the Declaration or the Constitution. The institution remained in force until 1865, having become a major cause of the ruinous Civil War. The iniquity of slavery, discussed further in Part III, obviously has its legacy in the continuing inequalities in the status of American blacks, creating problems of rectification, reparation, and so on. Furthermore, those who are now called Native Americans were characterized in the Declaration as "the merciless Indian Savages."

Another governing assumption is that of representativity in gender and race, in administration, in major public forums, even in national sporting teams. This may lead to contrived forms of social engineering such as tokenism and quotas. In some cases, such as in South Africa, these and other measures are designed to compensate for the social engineering of apartheid. Problematically, assumptions of representativity militate against both the criteria of democratic choice in politics and that of talent or merit in business, administration, and sport. Arguments such as "It's time America had a woman/black president" are grounded in the assumption of representativity. Few would argue on the same basis: "It's time America had a truly representative basketball team," that is, with four white players and one black. However, in South Africa such arguments are commonly retailed in politics and in those sports historically dominated by the white minority, such as rugby and cricket. Quotas have become a highly contentious issue. Programs of affirmative action obviously derive from the ideals of representativity and reparations for historical disadvantage, but are problematic in their implementation, since they are often seen as "reverse discrimination."

Most problematic are assumptions of conformity, since political correctness seeks to establish new norms in dignified address and to suppress established prejudicial practices. This is an understandable and entirely worthy enterprise, especially in its aim to confer at least dignity on all. The treatment of the individual with respect is relatively easy to manage; the problem arises when conformity is expected in political matters. Even such rituals as the oath of allegiance in the United States have provoked objections. Furthermore, norms turn out to be historically unstable, in view of social, political, and religious changes in societies. Assumptions of conformity are tenable only in highly regulated or totalitarian societies, being inimical to free democracies, even for the best of motives.

Revealingly, the modern field of entertainment proves to be highly complex in terms of representativity. In the US a double standard generally prevails. Thus American television police series are commonly politically correct in that detective teams are invariably representative, with broad quotas both in terms of race and gender. So, in the main, are hospital series and soap operas. Sitcoms, on the other hand, are commonly uniracial, appealing to a particular group. *Cosby, Two and Half Men, Jamie Foxx, George Lopez*, and *Sex and the City* are the most obvious examples. The same is true of drama series such as *Desperate Housewives* and *The Orange County*. In the UK, by contrast, most entertainment, being aimed at a predominantly white audience, has had a predominance of white actors and preoccupations. Differences are based more on class and region. The list includes *Coronation Street, EastEnders, Porridge, Absolutely Fabulous, Class Act, One Foot in the Grave, Yes Minister, Yes Prime Minister* and *Men Behaving Badly*. In recent years there have been some attempts to introduce elements of multiculturalism. However, racial exclusivity does not prevent some series from being politically incorrect. An apparent exception like *The Kumars at No 42* actually trades on the cast's Indian origins as well as their assimilation and difference from the white mainstream. Alternative US cartoon series such *The Simpsons* and *South Park* and adult UK printed comics like *Viz* are most daringly politically incorrect. These issues are dealt with more fully under the section on "Popular Culture" in chapter 8.

Once the issue of awards arises, arguments of representativity often emerge with force, especially in America. Thus for many years there has been pressurizing publicity that it was time for black actors to win Oscars, even though the issue was supposedly one of merit, decided by the members of the Motion Picture Academy of America. The Booker Prize, on the other hand, open to British and Commonwealth authors, has provoked no such controversy, with winners of all hues and backgrounds over the years. The Nobel Prize for Literature has often been criticized in recent decades for making awards considered politically correct in the sense of favoring authors critical of repressive regimes. The complex relationship between Literature and Ideology is covered in chapter 8.

Orthodoxy in Religion and Politics

Political correctness can be related to much earlier kinds of conformity engineered by pressure groups requiring compliance to particular values or definitions. As we have seen, linguistically it is a form of *euphemism* rooted in various social agendas, while politically it can be seen as a new form of *orthodoxy*, a term which has its roots in ethics and religion. Indeed, the *Random House Webster's College Dictionary* (1991) defined *political correctness* as "marked by or adhering to a typically progressive orthodoxy on issues involving especially race, gender, sexual affinity, or ecology." This is an excellent definition, but both *orthodox* and *orthodoxy* are traditionally and almost by definition conservative in meaning, and thus the conjunction with *progressive* is unusual. Furthermore, in cultural matters political correctness has involved not just seeking to establish a new orthodoxy, but in jettisoning and stigmatizing established cultural norms and "the canon" as Eurocentric, outdated, elitist, and chauvinist. These developments have provoked controversy and opposition to what has been called "liberal orthodoxy" (Kramer and Kimball, 1995, p. xii).

Historically, societies typically evolve through cycles whereby one orthodoxy becomes dominant, then declines through being discredited or contaminated, before being replaced by another. Both Vico and Oswald Spengler demonstrated this thesis at length. The ecclesiastical history of England in all its complexity and confusion shows such oscillations of values in eras of conformity and denunciation, as different power groups have established their authority. Oscillations of régime and values obviously make political correctness a highly relative notion. Thus what was politically correct in England in 1640 (under Charles I, leading up to the crisis of the Civil War) changed entirely in 1650 (under the Cromwellian or Puritan Commonwealth) and changed again in 1660 with the Restoration of the monarchy under Charles II. The English Civil War was described by the Earl of Clarendon, a royalist, from his semantic perspective as *The History of the Great Rebellion in England* (1704–7). Similarly, in the US the Civil War was also known as the War of Rebellion (the Southerners being the rebels) and the War of Secession. Günter Grass's *The Tin Drum* (1959) is a searingly ironic view of oscillating loyalties in wartime Germany.

A key concept in this topic is dogma. As de Tocqueville shrewdly observed: "Catholicism is like an absolute monarchy" (*Democracy in America*, 1835, chapter xvii). Political correctness evolved in a highly dogmatic political system, that of Chinese Communism. In general Communism set out to destroy its great rival, dogmatic religion, by discrediting it as "the opium of the people" and setting up its own hierarchy and belief system. Thus Lenin or Chairman Mao became the equivalent of the Pope, the Politburo became the equivalent of the College of Cardinals, dissident elements were subjected to inquisitions, excommunicated, or purged as "counter-revolutionaries," while those who made extreme sacrifices were elevated to the level of secular saints: they were the Stakhanovites, who excelled not by faith, but by extraordinary feats of productivity.

Often orthodoxies are established by means of various code words, which in turn have become mere shibboleths. The semantic history of *shibboleth* itself forms a revealing footnote. It was originally a password mentioned in the Old Testament (Judges 12: 4–6) whereby the Gileadites could identify themselves and especially target the Ephraimites, outsiders who could not pronounce the sound *sh*. In that context it was a matter of life and death. It has since come to mean a passé code word, phrase, or entrenched formula regarded as identifying or betraying a person's social background or political allegiance. The sense of a test word, watchword, or slogan of a political party, class, and so on dates from as far back as 1638.

Protestantism and Puritanism are two important movements in English political and ecclesiastical history that are illuminating and germane to the development of political correctness. English Protestantism initially offered liberation from papal authority, but then assumed a form of enforced political correctness in the form of an oath of loyalty to Henry VIII. The crisis of conscience created by this requirement is treated further under the section on "The Reformation" in chapter 7. Oaths of allegiance are still required of British Members of Parliament to the Queen and by American citizens to the United States and to the national flag.

Puritanism, which has had a longer history in America than in Britain, has considerable and enduring relevance to political correctness, since it encapsulates strictness in morality with a Pharisaic attitude of being "holier than thou," combined with an unhealthy curiosity, even an inquisitiveness or inquisitorial attitude concerning the "lapses" and "nonconformity" of others. Not for nothing has political correctness been stigmatized as the New Puritanism. It was this mind-set which Judge Louis D. Brandeis had in mind when he commented that "The greatest dangers to liberty lurk in insidious encroachment by men of zeal, well-meaning but without understanding" (quoted in Ravitch, 2003, p. 3). The mental attitude can be seen in this personal advertisement: "Professor Leftist . . . but tired of clichés, sloppy thinking and PC holier-than thou-ism" (*New York Review of Books*, March 27, 1995). Here one senses that genuine Puritan fervor has been diluted to posturing and attitudinizing.

The Founding Fathers (to use the traditional chauvinist formula) wisely enacted prohibitions against religious orthodoxy, seeking to avoid the fanaticism and its consequent horrors which Massachusetts had suffered in the Salem witch hunt. Yet an enlightened Constitution did not prevent the evil of slavery, the essentially Puritan social control of alcohol by Prohibition, or the fanaticism of the Communist witch hunt.

Semantic and Lexical Changes

Symbiotic, mediated and "Orwellian" changes

We have seen that political correctness is expressed by both a range of new terms and new meanings applied to established words. Putting these developments in historical context, *semantic change* refers to the change of meaning undergone by words over time, while *lexical change* refers to alterations in the word stock of the language. Because of the complex social history of England, both kinds of change are widely evident in the evolution of the vocabulary. Comparatively few words have shown no change of denotation or connotation over time. However, the reasons for the changes have themselves shifted from being originally symbiotic, then mediated, and finally Orwellian. There are hundreds of such changes, many of them treated in my study *Words in Time* (1988).

Symbiotic change refers to semantic and lexical changes that reflect changed realities, such as conquests, or changes in values. Thus as the feudal class structure broke down, so imported French terms like *gentle* and *noble*, which originally meant "well-born" and were thus class-bound, became less exclusive. The secularization of society is also reflected in words like *office* and *sanction*, both originally ecclesiastical, becoming generalized. The evolution of capitalism is reflected in *fee* and *purchase*, both originally general in meaning, becoming exclusively monetary terms. Four centuries ago when monarchy was well established, *democracy* and *politician* had negative senses, while *aristocracy* literally meant "rule by the best." With the change to the democratic ethos, *democracy* and *politician* have clearly ameliorated, the first more than the second, while *aristocracy* has deteriorated. Prior to the Reform Bill in 1832, both *radical* and *reform* were largely negative terms: on July 17, 1819 George Cruikshank produced a savage cartoon depicting Reform as a monster with the caption "Universal Suffrage or the Scum Uppermost." The little word *cell* has managed to traverse an amazing range of meanings over the past millennium, reflecting different power structures: monastic, punitive, correctional, scientific, political, and technical. All these changes were essentially spontaneous, not organized.

Mediated changes are brought about by vested interests exploiting the power of the media to introduce new words or new meanings. Thus soon after its invention the printing press was brought into play in the controversies of the Reformation, generating multitudinous pamphlets, many attacking Catholics and Catholicism, using terms such as *papist*, *popery*, *papistical*, *popeling*, and *popestant*. These critical terms were coined in a mere 40 years, between 1521 and 1561: the last three did not outlive this period of sectarian abuse. Semantic interventions and coinages by interest groups like political parties also generated stigmatic terms like *Whig* and *Tory* (both from c. 1646), followed by the more respectable labels *Conservative* (1832) and *Labour* (1900).

Orwellian changes are the most drastic, achieved by using the whole propaganda machinery of the modern state to generate new terms or to impose new meanings on words. These changes have the least relation to reality. A prime example is *liberation*, which in its "Orwellian" senses means the opposite of its accepted sense. Although "Orwellian" is usually equated with "totalitarian," since *Nineteen Eighty-Four* (1949) was a dystopia clearly based on Communism, Orwellian semantic changes are also found in the free world. Thus in the context of the Vietnam War, *pacification* came to be defined as "a process (usually a military operation) designed to secure the peaceful co-operation of a population" (*OED*). In the same military context, *air support* became a standard euphemism for "bombing."

However, there is a complicating development whereby positive value terms can surface when the social quality they describe is perceived to be passing away. Thus the value of the family as a social institution has been an obvious feature in nearly all societies, regardless of how *family* is defined. Indeed, the value of the family is so obvious that one cannot imagine, let alone find, instances in, say, Defoe or Dickens extolling *family values* in those terms. But the formula is in fact a recent sociosemantic development, recorded from about 1916, and its currency, predominantly American, has increased precisely over a period when the model of the traditional close family unit or "nuclear family" has actually been in decline, together with its assumed qualities of maintaining moral standards and discipline. In addition, *family values* has become a code political term implying a conservative political outlook.

Where do the semantic and lexical changes of political correctness fit in to this tripartite scheme? Virtually all of them are mediated: words like *abled*, *waitron*, and *wimmin* had no semantic history prior to their induction into the vocabulary of political correctness; others like *multicultural*, *homophobic*, and *challenged* were recycled in new senses. Furthermore, words like *addict*, *alcoholic*, and *cripple*, which had developed negative symbiotic changes, were suppressed and replaced by euphemisms. The following sections show further examples of mediated changes.

Semantic frameworks

From a social and political perspective, the initiatives of political correctness can be compared in broad terms with previous systemic attempts to change social attitudes and values. For instance, Protestantism involved accepting a new politicoreligious hierarchy, its values and keywords, while rejecting, ridiculing, or outlawing those of Catholicism. A similar dynamic can be seen in relation to the adoption of Communism and feminism. However, once Protestantism was espoused and championed by Henry VIII, it became essentially an institutional or "top-down" innovation, whereas the other initiatives derived from pressure groups. Consequently, the mediated semantic innovations of Protestantism were accepted and became institutionalized, while in tandem hostile terms relating to Catholicism became entrenched. By contrast, the degree of acceptance of the other programs and their keywords has varied in the wider community.

National attitudes towards Communism have varied radically since 1848, the "year of revolutions" in Europe, which also saw the publication of the *Communist Manifesto* by Marx and Engels. The philosophy became acceptable in much of Europe and politically obligatory in Russia, but it has never been accepted in Britain. The American Communist Party was founded in 1919, but was essentially outlawed by a variety of legislation, leading to the great McCarthyite Communist witch hunt. In the meantime Moral Re-Armament, the revivalist spiritual organization founded by Frank Buchman in 1938, had developed an anti-Communist agenda publicized by the slogan "Godless Communism."

In the build-up to World War II, Communism was increasingly regarded as unpatriotic in America, where both *Communist* and *commie* took on the senses of "enemy" and "traitor." The odd stereotypic idiom "to see Commies under the bed" is recorded in a letter of 1940. But much earlier, in 1933, Jack Warner denounced leaders of the striking Hollywood Screen Writers Guild as "communists" and "radical bastards" while his brother Harry chimed in with "You goddamn Communist bastards!" (Behlmer, 1985, pp. 9–10). Semantic correlatives included *fellow traveler* from 1936 and *card-carrying* from 1948: "The most dangerous Communists . . . today are not the open, avowed, card-carrying party members," claimed Bert Andrews (1948, p. 96). Whereas *sympathy* and *sympathetic* are positive terms, *sympathizer* has always been used for politically incorrect activities, such as in *Communist sympathizer* and *Nazi sympathizer*. Thus in capitalist societies it makes no sense to call someone a *capitalist sympathizer*, although the designation could be used ironically of one who is supposed to be a socialist, as in "Tony Blair is a capitalist sympathizer."

The frameworks set out in Tables 1.1 and 1.2 also seek to illustrate the dynamic concerning social outsiders, conceived or constructed from religious, racial, or sexual perspectives. The general trend in their case is of

Table 1.1 Macro View of Social Change and Lexical Innovation

	Action	*Reactions*	
		Positive	*Negative*
Program	*Lexical innovation*	*Acceptance*	*Satire, Parody*
Protestantism	*Anglican*	>	*Romish*
Communism (UK)	*Proletarian*	✗	*prole*
Communism (US)	*Communist*	✗	*red*
Feminism	*Feminist*	>	*feminazi*
Disability	*physically challenged*	✗	*vertically challenged*
Blacks	*African Americans*	>	*darkies*
Mexicans	*Hispanics*	>	*wetbacks*
Homosexuals	*Urnings* (original coinage)	✗	*queers*

Table 1.2 Individual Semantic Change

A: Neutral/descriptive >	*B: Emotive* >	*C: Insult/taboo* ↔	*D: Reclamation*
Bougre	bugger	bugger	✓
Jewe	Jew	Jew	✗
Dago	dago	dago	✗
Hottentot	Hottentot	Hottentot	✗
Hun	Hun	Hun	✗
Queer	queer	queer	✓
Lesbian	lesbian	lesbian	✓
Negar (original form)	Nigger	nigger	✓

semantic deterioration or pejoration, that is, the words develop negative denotations or connotations.

The frameworks give two semantic perspectives, a *macro* or wider view (Table 1.1), showing the new words, and the more detailed focus of *individual semantic change* (Table 1.2). The first framework traces the lexical consequences of the new programs in terms of *action* (lexical innovation) and of subsequent *reaction*, which may be positive or negative. The symbol > indicates acceptance, essentially in public discourse, while ✗ indicates rejection. In either case there are some negative reactions, leading to satire or parody, usually in slang or underground usages, shown in the last column.

Concerning *individual semantic change*, in a number of key words for outgroups, three phases can be detected, set out in Table 1.2 as A, B, and C.

These show a pattern of deterioration from *neutrality* through negative *emotive* uses to *insult*. However, a fourth phase (D, *reclamation*) is also a feature of political correctness occurring in some cases, marked ✓; those cases where it does not occur are marked ✗.

Prime examples of the three-phase pattern (A–C) are the semantic deterioration undergone by *bugger, Jew, dago, hottentot,* and *hun*. Reclamation (D) is seen in recent developments concerning *queer, lesbian,* and *nigger*. Some of these changes, discussed in more detail in Part III, have been spontaneous; others are the result of intervention by pressure groups. However, there is the important rider that the pattern of deterioration through A, B, and C is recorded in the whole speech community, while D (reclamation) is current only in the target group. Thus *nigger* remains a term of insult when used by whites of blacks (as it was originally), the reclamation usage being current only among some blacks. This dynamic highlights one of the complex features of politically incorrect language: context and user become as important as the word itself in assessing meaning and impact. Terms which show reclamation thus have split currency, being used in various ways, according to context. Thus *queer* can be used as an insult ("bloody queers!"), or ironically ("what a queer fellow!"), or humorously ("there's nothing as queer as folk"), or officially ("the latest book on Queer Theory").

Historically, the role of pressure groups is obviously important, but the degree of their success depends essentially on their institutionalization or access to public media. Thus *Anglican* became current because of its official status. On the other hand, *Quaker* is a name that the Quakers themselves have always resisted, regarding it as a nickname and preferring the Society of Friends. But, being a minority, they have not succeeded in changing public currency. In recent decades, under the aegis of political correctness, semantic "successes" have been achieved by feminists, homosexuals, and environmentalists, amongst others. On the other hand, semantic makeovers for the disabled, prostitutes, drug addicts, and others have been only partial or marginal.

Semantic engineering

Semantic engineering involves interventions in the existing semantic market by two principal means: the claiming of new meanings for established words and the creation of new lexical forms. With both types the intention is to shift the agenda and highlight the change by the tactic of unfamiliarity. Notable instances concerning feminism were the extended use of *sister*, the creation of *herstory*, and the great number of forms in which the suffix *–man* has been replaced by *–person*. Another controversial instance concerning attitudes towards homosexuals was the co-option of *gay* in the 1970s. These are discussed further in Part III.

Linguistic substitutions of "natural" or traditional terms and the generation of new artificial formulations commonly derive from some authoritarian intervention in the semantic market. In the previous subsection we noted the semantic successes achieved by Protestantism. In modern mediated and totalitarian societies the Orwellian model of *Nineteen Eighty-Four* (1949) has proved so powerful that it is now a truism to observe that language is manipulated by semantic engineering to persuade or coerce the populace, or to disguise and redefine reality, usually for propaganda purposes designed by some political oligarchy.

The basic assumption of semantic engineering is that the redefinition of conditions, roles, and programs will change individual and social attitudes. This practice is obviously more effective in a closed society, where there is no free press or competition between rival vested interests in the semantic marketplace. Typically, such definitions derive from a normative agency such as the Communist Party Politburo or equivalent. These are evident in the embedded clichés of communist rhetoric and propaganda, such as *bourgeois individualism, counterrevolutionary, imperialist lackeys*, and *capitalist warmongers*. In the totalitarian or closed society in which the state has a monopoly over the media, such manipulation is simple. The Communist formulas just quoted were essentially public and propagandist: it is hard to imagine ordinary Russians or Poles using them in daily mealtime conversation. (See, in this respect, the discussion of Julian Konstantinov's paper "The breakdown of Newspeak in an Eastern European country" in Cameron, 1995, pp. 152–5.)

In a similar development during the apartheid era in South Africa (1948 to about 1990), the ruling white Nationalist Party generated factitious legal definitions establishing the contrived ideological use of *immorality* to mean "miscegenation" and of *homelands* to denote "reservations for the natives." The semantic engineering of the apartheid forms was not subtle but effective, instilling in the white electorate the racially skewed notions that "immorality" or "sex across the color line" (a standard formula of the time) was a crime, already defined by the Immorality Act of 1927 as "illicit carnal intercourse between Europeans and natives." Likewise, the "homelands" became legislated as places where the indigenous populations naturally and properly belonged, not in the "white" areas.

It would be naïve, however, to see such ideological manipulation as being confined to totalitarianism. Five years after the publication of *Animal Farm*, George Orwell's satire on Communism, Senator Joseph McCarthy stunned America with his unsubstantiated allegations of a Communist conspiracy within the government bureaucracy and began his infamous witch hunt. Communism became much more than an alien and irreligious political system: it became unpatriotic and had to be rooted out. A number of studies, including David Caute's *The Great Fear* (1978), have explored the ramifications of this hysterical phase of American politics. It is, furthermore, something of a historical irony that in the McCarthyite era only some universities and a few academics protested vigorously against the anti-Communist inquisition, although it was a fundamental threat to academic freedom, civil liberties, and the American way of life. As Mary McCarthy wrote at the time: "When Arthur Miller, author of *Death of a Salesman*, was indicted for contempt of Congress this February [1957], the American liberal public was not aroused" (McCarthy, 1962, p. 147). Called before the House Committee for Un-American Activities, Miller declined to give the names of people he had seen at Communist-sponsored meetings. His contemporary play *The Crucible* (1953) remains a devastating parable of this political purge.

In her role as novelist, McCarthy set her contemporary academic satire, *The Groves of Academe* (1953) in this paranoid and conformist period. But her fictional establishment is not omnipotent. By an ironic reversal, an apparently vulnerable Marxist academic shrewdly succeeds in manipulating his pending dismissal into a case of political victimization *because* of his Communist associations, thereby becoming a *cause célèbre*. By threatening to expose the university's questionable treatment of him to every liberal newspaper and magazine in the country, he survives; it is the president of the university, the author of "The Witch Hunt in Our Universities," who resigns.

Two significant semantic correlatives were *McCarthyism* (coined by Herbert Block, the *Washington Post* cartoonist on March 29, 1950) and the insidious *un-American*, which became especially current from 1953, but was in fact a revival from 1938, when the House Committee for Un-American Activities was originally set up. In a notable riposte during the proceedings, Paul Robeson told the committee curtly "You are un-American," while Lionel Stander, another actor, used more elaborate sarcasm (Ross, 2002, p. 202). The Alabaman Representative Joe Starnes asked Hallie Flanagan, an avant-garde theatrical producer, if Christopher Marlowe was a Communist.

Although *McCarthyism* is now a historical term denouncing inquisitorial methods, *un-American*, a unique nationalist epithet quintessentially expressing political correctness, retains its disturbing currency. It implies a special loyalty of the citizen to the American state manifestly not endorsed by other national adjectival forms such as *un-French*, *un-British* or *un-Italian*. The semantic history of *un-American* is surprisingly long: it was used in 1887 by James Cardinal Gibbons, Archbishop of Baltimore: "The accusation of being 'un-American,' that is to say alien to our national spirit, is the most powerful weapon the enemies of the Church know how to use against her" (in Boorstin, 1966, p. 486). Furthermore, virtually every US administration since World War II has invoked the formula of *national security* to justify a range of drastic military measures from the invasion of neighboring states down to the Patriot Act (2001).

Communism and apartheid were extreme cases of social-*cum*-semantic engineering. Both were based on rigorous ideologies and comprehensive methods of enforcement. During its Communist phase *political correctness* had the status of a literal meaning, setting out the party line. This is, of course, no longer the case, so that the basic assumption is weakened, particularly when redefinitions and new agendas appear virtually overnight and apparently from nowhere.

We may consider two prime instances. The first derived from Mahatma Gandhi, obviously an inspirational and politically innovative leader of the first order. For the hereditary caste of the Indian untouchables, who formed such an affront to humanity and democracy, he proposed in 1931 the name *harijan*, derived from Sanskrit and meaning "people of God." In 1949 the new democratic government outlawed the term *untouchable*: the people were reclassified as "scheduled castes." However, two decades later the *Times* reported that "In spite of Gandhi's dream . . . and the government's enlightened policy over the past 22 years, *Harijans* must still draw water from different taps" (October 13, 1969). Since then attitudes have changed, to the point that some untouchables have become prominent figures. The second argument comes from Robert Hughes in his polemical commentary on America, *Culture of Complaint*:

> We want to create a sort of linguistic Lourdes, where evil and misfortune are dispelled by a dip in the waters of euphemism. Does the cripple rise from his wheelchair, or feel better about being stuck in it, because someone . . . decided that, for official purposes, he was "physically challenged"? (Hughes, 1993, pp. 18–19)

Gandhi's proposal and Hughes's question go right to the heart of the problem. These two instances could be considered examples of benign semantic engineering, in that the intentions are good and the means are not totalitarian in nature.

Semantic changes in the New South Africa

The history of South Africa provides many examples of semantic engineering reflecting its colonial past and its recent liberation. Racial separation of various degrees of formality existed between the colonizers and the colonized for centuries, prior to apartheid becoming systematized by the Afrikaner nationalists after their watershed election victory in 1948. As it faced increasing international opposition, apartheid was recycled in new semantic outfits in classic Orwellian style, first as *separate development* from 1955, then *multinationalism* from 1971, then *plural democracy* from 1978, then *vertical differentiation* from 1985. It was officially declared dead in about 1990, although the term has resurfaced to designate forms of organized social separation in the wider world.

The New South Africa was essentially embodied and symbolized by the tolerance of Nelson Mandela of the liberation movements and the political rapprochement with F. W. de Klerk of the Afrikaner Nationalist regime. The new order was memorably called "the Rainbow Nation" by Archbishop Desmond Tutu and the phrase was used by President Mandela in his Inauguration address on May 10, 1994. The old apartheid politics of race and its bureaucratic terminology became taboo from 1994, officially at any rate, and new political keywords became current in the process of normalization.

Among the early positive slogans were *nation building* and its African equivalent *Masakhane*. These embodied both an ideological sense of unifying the nation after decades of racial separation and a physical sense of equitable reconstruction. At the same time, *delivery* took on the more specific and urgent sense of the provision of basic services to communities disadvantaged by apartheid. In the aftermath of the violence and terror of the apartheid system, *reconciliation* became a new key word, embodied in the *Truth and Reconciliation Commission* or *TRC*, founded in 1997. There were obvious counterclaims over the primacy of *truth* and its judicial consequences vis à vis *reconciliation*, leading to a different outcome, problems which have not entirely been solved; nor have those concerning *reparation* for those who suffered or were dispossessed.

There are other keywords with global currencies, which in their South African usage show semantic stress caused by ideological pressure. These are: *transformation, forum, empowerment, disadvantaged, informal,* and *quota*. In essence, all have become racialized.

Shortly after the 1994 election, the general sense of the term *transformation* in global English of "a sudden change" was given a new racialized political sense, namely the alteration of the profile of personnel in charge of an institution (government, business, university, etc.) by means of affirmative action to reflect the demographics of the nation. Since, as a consequence of the inequalities of apartheid, there was a general shortage of black expertise in many fields, transformation could not be literal and has perforce been slow. Simultaneously and consequently, the definition of black has become a highly controversial issue, especially in relation to the Coloured community, who form the majority of the voting population of the Western Cape and about 9 percent nationally. Under the old regime Coloureds were classified "Non-White," now they are not officially subsumed under "Black," but classified as separate from "African." Within the population group, some regard themselves as "Black," others as "Coloured." The ironic saying "not White enough, not Black enough" sums up feelings of continued political exclusion or marginalization, and is the title of Mohamed Adhikari's book, discussed in chapter 5. Rhoda Kadalie, a Human Rights activist, commented trenchantly in a national newspaper:

> In common political parlance, "transformation" has come to mean: is the organization black enough? One is never sure that black "enough" includes coloured and Indian. . . . When we talk about the transformation of the judiciary, it should be more than just a racial head-count . . . The increase in black appointments has not improved the situation; if anything it has worsened it because black arrivals often lack skills and qualifications . . . (*Business Day*, March 17, 2005)

The journalist Rian Malan's analysis of the South African situation in the *Spectator* (October 14, 2006) took a similarly pessimistic view.

The South African academic journal *Transformation* (which has as its design logo a chameleon) is devoted to research into all aspects of this social issue. One article, "Beyond apartheid: race, transformation and governance in Kwa-Zulu-Natal cricket," raises the major issues of race, affirmative action, quotas, and management with convenient clarity. In this province the two major groups of "nonwhites" are the Zulus and the Indians. Under the ironic heading "Too many Indians are chiefs," the article explains:

> Racial tension in post-apartheid sport is no longer an issue of black and white. New and more complex "patterns of prejudice" have surfaced. The meaning of "black" is now contested, and struggles have emerged between Africans, Indians and Coloureds over power and opportunity. The nomenclature "black African" in the Transformation Charter is a source of concern for many Indians and Coloureds as it excludes them . . . (*Transformation*, 61, 2006, p. 82)

The racial balance of national sporting teams has become a perennial source of major controversy, with merit (preferred by the players) being set against representativity (preferred by the administrators). Those selected by quota are resentful at the slight; those excluded are bitter at the perceived injustice. An uproar was created by the proposal in April 2007 of Mr Butana Komphela, Chairman of the Parliamentary Sports Portfolio Committee, that if the Springbok rugby squad for the World Cup did not match transformation quotas, the passports of white players and administrators should be withheld. In May 2008 Charl Langeveldt withdrew from the national cricket team since he felt that he had been included, not on merit, but because he was Coloured.

In 2008 the election for the President of the South African Rugby Union resulted in a narrow win for Mr Oregon Hoskins, a Coloured man, over Mr Mike Stofile, a Black man. Speaking to the national press, Mr Stofile said: "For the past four years there is no place for Black people in South African Rugby. Today was the final nail for [them]." Mr Hoskins responded: "I did not know that I am not a Black person. I did not know that I am not African and born in Africa." Hoskins also pointed out that two months previously, when the Union appointed Mr Peter de Villiers, a Coloured man, as the new Springbok coach, Mr Stofile had championed him because "he was a Black person" (*Weekend Argus*, March 28, 2008, p. 1).

Transformation has also come to serve a similar purpose to the older term *rationalization*. The original Freudian senses of giving plausible reasons which disguise real motives generated, from the 1960s, institutional meanings justifying more efficient economic production. However, it was often "used as a euphemistic camouflage for reducing the size of an operation, firing employees, etc." (Ayto, 1999). In the South African context both J. M. Coetzee's *Disgrace* (1999) and André Brink's *Rights of Desire* (2000) allude to this process as their white academic narrators lose their jobs: "'Rationalisation' it was called, an abuse of language. There's nothing rational about it. A whole new vocabulary is proliferating around us" (Brink, 2000, p. 13).

In many instances *transformation* has taken on the characteristics of the older and now discredited term *Africanization*, defined by the *OED* as "to give an African character to; to make African; to subject to the influence or domination of Black Africans." As African states achieved independence, the sense became apparent, as in this instance from the Gold Coast Government, Accra: "Statement on the Programme of the Africanisation of the Public Service" (1954). A quotation from the *Listener* (September 29, 1960) gave a more cynical view: "The 'Africanization' to which so many firms have had to bow, by promoting their messengers and office boys into managing directors and retaining their Europeans merely as 'advisers'."

Forum refers, not to a general discussion group like the World Economic Forum, but to racially exclusive power groups such as the Black Editors' Forum, the Black Managers' Forum, and the Black Officers' Forum in the South African Defence Force. *Empowerment* has become a key term in attempts to redress the economic imbalances that existed in the new South Africa, since the settlement prior to the 1994 election was essentially political, not economic. The formula *Black Economic Empowerment* is widely used and increasingly abbreviated to *BEE*. The process became controversial on two grounds: it favored only a few, and there were the familiar problems with the definition of "Black." There has been a revealing resuscitation of *non-Black*, originally an ironic coinage of 1953, parodying the apartheid *non-White*. An article in the *Weekly Mail & Guardian* asked the question concerning invitations to a conference on "the African Renaissance": "Will non Blacks be welcome?" (October 9, 1998, p. 24).

As the New South Africa came into being, the formula *previously disadvantaged* became a code word to refer to the nonwhite population. Obviously under apartheid the majority of the population was genuinely disadvantaged. However, programs of affirmative action and empowerment, being targeted at these population groups, have had the effect of improving the status of many to the point that *disadvantaged* has become a misnomer: in fact in some cases individuals are now privileged. The issue was raised in a very public forum by Professor David Benatar of the University of Cape Town in his inaugural lecture, "Justice, Diversity and Affirmative Action" in April 2008 criticizing the university's employment policies. The key question he raised was "Why use 'race' as a proxy for disadvantage when one can focus directly on disadvantage"?

Informal has also become a code euphemism for activities outside the normal social and economic structures. Thus *informal sector* was used from about 1980 for Black hawkers and street traders, while *informal settlement* has become the established euphemism for a shanty town or squatter camp. The definition in the *Dictionary of South African English* (1989) runs: "erected in an unregulated and unplanned manner upon unproclaimed land with no infrastructure provided by the local authority." It notes that in 1989 the Urban Foundation "estimated that 7 million people lived in informal settlements." The term *Mandela Town* for an imitation shanty town erected in protest by students in the US and the UK is recorded from 1986.

Norms and Normality

Political correctness is fundamentally concerned with changing norms in behavior and language. Norms are not cultural universals, but socially conditioned forms and expectations of correct social behavior. Even the most abhorrent practices, such as cannibalism and incest, are sanctioned in certain societies and classes. In the ancient English tradition, Anglo-Saxon society was largely "androcentric" or male-centered, in many ways reminiscent of Sparta, the dominant ideal being embodied in the heroic code whereby a man was expected to have absolute loyalty to the regional lord and his followers or *cynn* when faced with a common martial threat. The Anglo-Saxon poem *The Battle of Maldon* celebrates the heroism and condemns the cowardice of the men of Maldon in Essex in the actual conflict against the marauding Vikings in 991. The androcentric norm is the essence of the warrior phase of the culture, excluding and preceding the romantic.

Thus there is no love interest in Anglo-Saxon poetry, least of all in the great epic poem *Beowulf*, the hero being exclusively engaged in titanic struggles against the cannibalistic monster Grendel (who represents the Anglo-Saxon "Other"), his formidable mother (the first "single parent"), and finally and fatally, against a dragon. The only significant woman in the poem is Wealtheow, Queen of the Scyldings, the Danish people who are the victims of Grendel. Her role is entirely ceremonial and diplomatic. This chaste ancient text had to await the glorious emergence of Hollywood, in the form of Angelina Jolie, to be subjected to the artificial modern norm of romance.

The great medieval romances, notably *Tristan and Isolde* and the *Morte d'Arthur*, are essentially concerned with the conflict between the cohesive heroic ideal of martial loyalty and that of romantic passion, which is socially disruptive. Both end tragically. The heroic code seemingly petered out in the fictions of the Far West and in war films. However, Leslie A. Fiedler's controversial study *Love and Death in the American Novel* (1966) shows that, surprisingly, strong bonded relationships between males have been and continue to be a staple in American fiction.

Romance is a classic example of a socially conditioned behavior, since obviously irrational conventions such as "love at first sight," "falling in love," being "lovesick," and the extreme form of "dying for love" would make little sense to Anglo-Saxons, Africans, or Polynesians. It is learnt, furthermore, from books. Yet romance continues to thrive as a global industry. This divertissement could be extended to include other norms of social behavior such as politeness, table manners, and attitudes towards death.

Thorstein Veblen's acerbic classic *Theory of the Leisure Class* (1899) sur-veyed a number of such artificial behavioral models. Today one of the effects of globalization and mass marketing is to create a conflict between sup-posed global norms or standards and actual local customs.

Norms can, of course, be reinforced by legislation, sometimes in unpre-dictable ways. Thus the liberal US Constitution essentially underwrites freedom of speech and enshrines the right of all citizens to bear arms, but according to the 18th Amendment, in a clear survival of the original spirit of Puritanism, it denied citizens the right to possess alcohol from 1919 to 1933. Furthermore, Communism has never been prohibited in Britain, but failed to gain a foothold there. But in America it was essentially outlawed by a variety of legislation, including the Smith Act (1940), the McCarran Act (1950), and the Communist Control Act (1954), leading to the great Communist witch hunt.

Conformity is strongest in modern mediated societies with a powerful political ideology, for example Nazi Germany and the former Soviet bloc, or nations with strong religious values, such as Puritan England, many Catholic countries, and those with a strong sense of racial identity. Apartheid South Africa combined all three cohesive factors (albeit only in the white popu-lation). In some modern secular societies there are still anomalies. For instance, Turkey retains in its penal code Article 301, an offence termed "insulting Turkishness," carrying a penalty of six months to three years imprison-ment for explicitly insulting "being a Turk, the Republic, or the Turkish Grand National Assembly." According to the *New Statesman*, "Around 60 writers, publishers and journalists have been before the courts in the past year" (May 8, 2006). Among the high-profile victims are Nazim Hikmet, Turkey's greatest poet, who died in exile in Moscow, and the novelists Orhan Pamuk and Perihan Magden.

However, it would be naïve to see patriotic conformity as exclusive to societies where individual human rights are not upheld. Thus the Pledge of Allegiance in the United States is a requirement almost universally enacted by schoolchildren, and it required a legal challenge by a particular parent (*Newdow v. United States Congress 2002*) to express conscientious objection. Recently two less substantial cases concerning conformity surfaced in the New South Africa. During a cricket test match series in March 2007, it was noticed that a major South African player, Jacques Kallis, was not singing the national anthem. This occasioned much press coverage and comment, but virtually no support for Kallis, even on the grounds that this was a private matter. Prior to Workers Day (May 1, 2007) a number of labor leaders stressed that it was inappropriate for the public to regard this as an ordinary holiday, and that they should instead go to political rallies.

Although *normal* is, as one would logically expect, derived from *norm*, the two forms have diverged semantically. *Norm* is in origin a Latin term for a carpenter's square and its early senses were a pattern or rule, which provides the revealing cognates *rule* and *ruler*. It has since become a sociological term meaning a model or pattern of behavior (dating from c. 1820) arrived at on the basis of research. However, *normal* has steadily moved away from denoting behavior analyzed by strict criteria, and now essentially reflects popular notions of what is "normal." In other words, it is a misnomer. It can also be misleading, since popular notions of normality, being based on folklore and prejudice, are often erroneous, fickle, and superficial. Thus the popular and traditional notion of sexual normality was that heterosexuality was the norm, while homosexuality was "abnormal," "aberrant," "deviant," and so on. The findings of the Kinsey Report (1947) and its successors revealed a spectrum of sexual behavior, not a dominant norm, showing that many practices regarded as "perversions," such as fellatio, proved to be widespread. Although meticulously researched, the report was not received as providing new light on an obscure subject, but generally provoked incredulity and outrage.

Many notions of normality have become semantically embedded or impacted. Among them are "law and order," "right and proper," "For King and Country," the relationship between heterosexual "straight" vis à vis homosexual "bent" or "queer," and that between "deviant" and "devious," to mention a few. Several of the initiatives of political correctness have been concerned with publicizing research showing the erroneousness of many notions of what is "normal," as well as the reclamation of negative labels, topics which are taken up in Part III.

Stereotypes and Etymology

A great deal of political correctness is concerned with changing ingrained attitudes and language based on offensive stereotypes deriving from collective prejudices, folklore, and ignorance. Prejudice derives, as the term suggests, from "judging in advance" of facts or knowledge of an individual or the true situation. It is the natural consequence of stereotypical thinking. Although prejudice is most apparent in negative stereotypes and attitudes, it can appear in unwarranted positive assumptions. As the section on "Xenophobia and Antisemitism" in chapter 5 shows, many stereotypes are centuries old. Originally *stereotype* was a printing term recorded from 1798 and its earliest sense was technical, that of a stereotyped phrase or formula set in a readymade block of type. (*Cliché* has the same origin.)

The modern sense of a "preconceived and oversimplified idea of the characteristics which typify a person or situation" is recorded only from 1922 in Walter Lippman's classic pioneering study, *Public Opinion*, where he observed that "A stereotype may be so consistently and authoritatively transferred from each generation from parent to child that it seems almost like a biological fact" (cited in *OED*). The sociological-cum-psychological sense was well defined in 1948 by Krech and Crutchfield in their *Theory and Problems of Social Psychology*: "The concept of stereotype refers to two different things: (1) a tendency for a given belief to be widespread in a given society; (2) a tendency for a belief to be oversimplified in content and unresponsive to the objective facts" (cited in *OED*).

Stereotypes are generally based on prejudice. Usually the "home" nationality sees itself in positive terms, stereotyping outsiders and foreigners by negative characterizations such as idleness, dirtiness, inefficiency, stupidity, meanness, cowardice, aggressiveness, drunkenness, sexual promiscuity, and perversion. These qualities are attributed to groups and by extension to individuals, which is manifestly absurd and offensive. Typically based on ethnic, racial, and gender considerations, these prejudicial notions often develop into what are known as *blasons populaires*, that is to say, attributions of group or national characteristics, such as "the Scots are mean," "the Irish are stupid," and so on. A *blason populaire* is literally a popular emblem or badge, but one given to a group by outsiders, not worn spontaneously by them. These stereotypes tend to originate in xenophobia and prove to be surprisingly tenacious, being exacerbated in times of economic hardship, competition, or war.

There are also national stereotypes, such as John Bull, originally the literary creation of Dr John Arbuthnot in 1712, a positive and aggressive representation of the national character, later usually accompanied by a bulldog. Both thrived up to World War II, but are now considered somewhat passé. The American stereotype of Uncle Sam originated verbally as an ironic interpretation of "U.S." on soldiers' uniforms by opponents of the War of 1812. The cartoon figure appeared first in 1832, but not in the recognizable modern form, which is attributed to Thomas Nast in 1868 (Flexner, 1976, p. 363). The French national symbol, naturally feminine, of Marianne dates from just after the Revolution, in 1792. The negative propaganda image of the French frog first appeared in an English cartoon of 1799. The semantic link dates from 1778, when Fanny Burney used it memorably in *Evelina*: "Hark you Mrs Frog . . . you may lie in the mud until some of your monsieurs come to help you out of it." But *frog* had been long used generally of enemies, applied in 1652 to the Dutch, and previously in 1629 (in Lewis Owen's, *Speculum Jesuiticum*) to a religious sect: "These infernall frogs [Jesuits] are crept into the West and East Indyes."

The more obvious stereotypes are linguistically embedded in clichés such as "to turn Turk" (to betray), the supposed English "stiff upper lip," or the *mañana* attitude of the Spanish. Some, such as "Beware Greeks bearing gifts" and "The only good Indian is a dead Indian," actually started as quotations, but have become embedded as stereotypical proverbs. (The first is from Virgil's *Æneid* II, l. 48: *"timeo Danaos dona ferentes"*; the second is attributed to Captain Philip Sheridan at Fort Cobb, Oklahoma, January 1869.) Many appear in the great collections of proverbs such as those of B. J. Whiting (1968) and M. P. Tilley (1950). Some develop into what are known technically as *ethnophaulisms*, or more transparently, as ethnic slurs or opprobrious nicknames. These include *yid*, *kraut*, *nigger*, and *wop*, often with allusions to backwardness, such as *bogtrotter*, or to dubious origins, such as *wetback*.

Research into the origins of nicknames shows the tenacity of what is known as *folk etymology* in the face of genuine etymology. (*Folk etymology* is an appealing but essentially fanciful explanation for the origin of a word, usually with the assistance of a tall story.) Thus *wop* is genuinely derived from Neapolitan and Sicilian *guappo* meaning "a dude, a swell, or a bold showy ruffian." However, prejudicial folk etymology derives the term from a supposed acronym used by US immigration officials for some Italians, namely "without passport" or "without papers." Myth continues to triumph over logic, as is shown in a number of studies, such as Irving Lewis Allen's *The Language of Ethnic Conflict* (1983).

However, actual etymologies can also be revealing. Thus one of the meanings of Anglo-Saxon *wæpen*, "weapon" is "penis," a suggestive root. *Bugger* derives from *Bulgarian*, from the prejudicial notion that the people subscribed to the Albigensian heresy and were sodomites. The medieval form *bougre* meant "heretic" from the fourteenth century and "sodomite" from the sixteenth. The attribution of "unnatural" sexual practices to heathens, deviant religious sects, or traditional enemies is a common source of stereotypical prejudice. This theme is developed further in "Xenophobia" in chapter 5.

Reliance on etymology can, however, lead to what is known as the "etymological fallacy." Thus *hysteria* derives from Greek *hystera*, meaning "womb," as in *hysterectomy*. On this genuine etymological foundation the false notion developed that only women could be *hysterical*. When Freud discovered hysterical symptoms in men, he had great difficulty in persuading his colleagues, who continued to be bound by the "etymological fallacy" and the misleading stereotype of female hysteria. Ironically, a classic study of male hysteria is to be found in the protagonist of Shakespeare's *King Lear* (Act II, scene iv, "O! how this mother swells up toward my heart; *Hysterica passio!* down, thou climbing sorrow!").

Etymology can also be an original indicator of physical difference:

> Campbell is from a Gaelic word meaning wry or crooked mouth . . . Cameron has the meaning also of deformity in a physical sense, meaning a crooked or hooked nose. It is strange that nicknames of this type, which are distinctly opprobrious, should have stuck to the remote descendants. Yet four great houses – Campbell, Cameron, Scrope and Giffard – are marked in this way. (Pine, 1965, pp. 112–31)

(Scrope is thought to be derived from the Norse word for a crab.) Commenting on the prevalence of nicknames, Pine observes that "at worst it is a symptom of the more vicious bent of the human mind" (1965, p. 13). In his study on the subject, Ernest Weekley added Kennedy, meaning "ugly head" in the course of a whole chapter devoted to nicknames (1914, p. 216). Less judgmental in his comments, Weekley observed simply that "It may seem strange that the nickname, conferred essentially on the individual, and often of a very offensive character, should have persisted and become hereditary" (1914, p. 191).

Nicknames for historical figures have varied from Edward Longshanks and William Rufus to those in a contemptuous rhyme satirizing the reign of Richard III:

> The Cat, the Rat and Lovell the Dog
> Rule all England under the Hog.

Recorded by Edward Hall in his *Chronicle* for 1483, this alludes to Catesby, Ratcliffe, and Lovell, "the Hog" referring to the boar, Richard's emblem. The rhyme qualifies as an early piece of graffiti, one of several apparently published on the door of St Paul's Cathedral. There is also an ironic medieval word-play on the name *Dominican* to mean *domini canes*, "the dogs of God." They were authorized to carry out the Inquisition as a consequence of the Papal Bull *Ad Extirpanda* published in 1252.

While the origins of these names may be regarded as footnotes, etymologies can also be revealing of attitudes. Thus *ugly* is rooted in the Norse word for "fear," and "horrid" in a Latin word meaning "to make one's hair stand on end." As is noted in chapter 5, the Old English word for "beautiful" was *fæger*, now "fair," a color term. In the word field for "beautiful" is the synonym "attractive," while among those for "ugly" is "repulsive." These indicate primal responses. It is also worth noting that the etymological root of *belief* lies in Anglo-Saxon *leof*, meaning "dear" or "close to one's heart."

Difference

Historically, difference has been a major factor in social definition and identity, focusing on features of race, complexion, appearance, dress, diet, language, and religion, any or all of which can become the source of discrimination and xenophobia. Essential or superficial points of difference have also become the basis of *ethnophaulisms* or ethnic nicknames, such as the following:

Complexion: *yellow belly, slant-eye, slant, pale face, pale male, darkie, spade, schwartze*;
Appearance: *squarehead, pongo, hairyback, hooknose, thicklips*;
Dress: *towel head*;
Diet: *limey, kipper, frog, kraut, macaroni, spaghetti, chilli-eater, bagel, porker*;
Language: *hottentot, wi-wi, palaver*;
Religion: *bugger, kaffir, Mahounde, mammet, Pope Day, Christ killer*;
War: *Hun, Tojo*;
Backwardness: *bogtrotter, camel jockey*;
Immigrant status: *wetback*;
Politics: *Whig, Tory, carpet-bagger*;
Physical curiosities: *Hottentot apron* (discussed in chapter 5).

Also falling within the ambit of difference is the vexed issue of tribalism. Although tribal divisions exist historically as natural manifestations of differences of language, culture, and territory, colonial policy emphasized these differences and stressed racial categorization as part of a policy of divide and rule. But the end of colonialism did not bring liberation for all. According to Van den Berghe:

> A neat semantic trick of mislabeling took place with the nearly universal cooperation of Western social scientists. All states were declared to be nation-states. The real nations within these artificial multinational creations of European colonialism were proclaimed to be mere "tribes" and any genuine nationalism that might develop within them was stigmatized as "tribalism." (1981, p. 3)

In postcolonial discourse, nationalism is emphasized and tribalism becomes taboo. In the South African context, in his Steve Bantu Biko Memorial Lecture

(September 26, 2006) Archbishop Tutu warned that the rulers should "hear the complaint of those who complain about an Nguni-ocracy and even of a Xhosa-ocracy," while the conservative commentator Dan Roodt was more contemptuous about "the Gucci set known as La Xhosa Nostra." Sarah Britten includes this last in a list of 22 ethnic and tribal slurs (2006, p. 12).

One of the aims of political correctness is, of course, to remove or attempt to suppress from public discourse semantically impacted aspects of cultural difference which have become objects of prejudice or hurtful language. As Wolfgang Mieder observes: "Many of today's stereotypes and prejudices date back to medieval times, and their longevity is a clear indication of the task that still lies ahead to free the world of such preconceived and ill-founded notions" (Mieder, 2000, p. 105). However, the topic is not without problems, as the Preface of *Stereotype Accuracy* comments:

> It is not easy to do research on stereotype accuracy, for both scientific and political reasons. . . . The intellectual content of this book commits multiple heresies. First, research on any type of accuracy in social perception was all but unthinkable until the 1980s. . . . Second, the idea that stereotypes may sometimes have some degree of accuracy is apparently anathema to many social scientists and laypeople. Those who document accuracy run the risk of being seen as racists, sexists, or worse. (Lee, Jussim, and McCauley, 1995, p. xiii)

As we shall see in the following section, these comments on the pressures of political correctness are not as paranoid as they might seem.

Taboo

Taboos exist in all societies, from the most "primitive" to the most modern, and at all levels of society, covering a wide range of behavior. Many now fall under the rubric variously found in "not in front of the children," "not in front of the audience," "not in front of the ladies," "not over the airwaves," and so on, which are general rather than absolute prohibitions. Although behavioral taboos are very ancient, the term *taboo* was brought into English by Captain Cook in 1777 from his voyages in the Pacific. Freud pointed out in *Totem and Taboo* (first published in 1913) that "Taboo is a Polynesian word, the translation of which provides difficulties for us because we no longer possess the idea it connotes" (1950, p. 18). This is because the term traditionally denoted religious topics which were considered so holy that they could not be spoken of, or practices such as incest, cannibalism, or necrophilia that are considered disgusting or depraved.

Taboo has now become mainly semantic, referring to words which are unmentionable in polite company, such as gross religious swearwords, obscenities, racial insults, and terms like *cripple* and *spastic*. However, in this discussion *taboo* is used in its broad modern sense of "highly inappropriate" rather than the traditional sense of "strictly forbidden." A revealing instance of the modern double standard concerning taboo language is found in this comment by Deborah Cameron: "In Scandinavia the taboo words are to do with the devil. Here [in Britain] they're fuck or cunt" (*Guardian*, July 12, 2006). Obviously the fact that Professor Cameron can say the words in an interview and that they are printed in a national newspaper shows that they are no longer strictly taboo. There are still survivals of prissiness: a recent semantic study appeared under the title of *The F-Word: The Complete History of the Word in all its Robust and Various Uses* (Sheidlower, 1995). The front cover announced "the word" as f***.

Despite such anomalies, the broader sense of taboo has, of course, been apparent for some time. In recent decades there have even appeared dictionaries of taboo language, such as James McDonald's *Dictionary of Obscenity, Taboo and Euphemism* (1988) and *Forbidden American English: A Serious Compilation of Taboo American English* (1990) by Richard A. Spears. In the course of his 200-page study Spears includes mild terms like *boob*, *horny*, and *one night stand*, comparatively unfamiliar codes like *b.m.* for "bowel movement," and more provocative ethnic slurs like *dothead*, *towelhead*, *Christ killer*, *gook*, and *jew-boy*. This indiscriminacy shows the problem of where to draw the line, but Spears partly corrects this breadth by using a series of cautionary usage notes, especially in relation to "racial, national, ethnic and religious slurs" (1990, p. 205). A simpler, more drastic designation was employed by Robert L. Chapman in his *New Dictionary of American Slang* (1986) which employed the symbol △ for obscene words but ▲ for taboo terms "never to be used".

Political correctness can be seen as an endeavor to extend the boundaries of its progressive orthodoxy to make taboo many areas which previously involved prejudicial attitudes and stigmatizing language. Socially it is thus something of an anomaly, since in modern Western society virtually nothing is "strictly forbidden." Similarly, in modern times *obscenity* has lost its earlier strong senses of "abominable, disgusting, filthy, or lewd," while *indecent*, which previously sustained some of the same meanings, has become almost obsolete.

In Western society taboos have generally evolved historically through three basic topics: matters of religion, sex, and race. However, the relationship with censorship is complex and often reveals a double standard. In the nature of things, censorship deals with public forms of expression, such as printing, broadcasting, theater, or film. But the unfettered language of the street goes on. Thus in the Middle Ages, although religious swearing and blasphemy were greatly disapproved of by the Church, they clearly flourished, as can be copiously seen in the works of Chaucer and Langland, as well as in medieval drama. Furthermore, the medieval genre of the fabliau (see chapter 7) was essentially a subversion of the values of an age of faith. In the same period both obscenity and xenophobia flourished. During the Renaissance religious oaths, out of deference to authority, were generally "minced" or euphemized. Yet Queen Elizabeth reportedly "swore like a man," the main dispute being whether "God's wounds!" or "God's death!" was her favorite oath. Bawdy humor and ethnic slurs thrived, as the studies of Eric Partridge (1947) and Gordon Williams (1997) have demonstrated. The same dynamic continued in the Restoration.

From the eighteenth century, the dictionary became increasingly regarded as the arbiter of usage, rather than the reflector of currency, essentially promoting and endorsing the double tier notion of language. Sexual language clearly became taboo in public, since it was suppressed in print. Only in the past century have all the "four letter" words even been included in dictionaries, although their general currency has never been disputed. During the same period religious oaths have not been censored lexicographically, but in recent decades racial epithets have increasingly been eschewed or become the subject of warnings in the form of usage notes. They remain the principal area of taboo.

Whereas the religious establishment previously safeguarded the use of Christian symbols and references, and the Master of the Revels and the Lord Chamberlain censored plays prior to performance up to 1968, there has never been a similar agency to control other forms of insulting language. The proposals for an English Academy similar to the Académie Française foundered, the last trenchant word coming from Dr Johnson, who in his Preface to his Dictionary (1755) commented that it was a project which he hoped "the spirit of English liberty will hinder or destroy." Consequently, vague notions of "public decency" have instead prevailed. Many anecdotes attest to the resulting double standards. When two ladies "very much commended the omission of all naughty words" from his dictionary, Dr Johnson replied archly, "What! My dears! Then you have been looking for them?" (Hughes, 1991, pp. 157–8). In 1914 George Bernard Shaw denounced the hypocrisy of the English press for discussing but not printing the word *bloody* (which he had sensationalized in *Pygmalion*), since, he claimed, the word "is in common use as an expletive by four-fifths of the English nation, including many highly educated persons" (statement to the *Daily News*, April 18, 1914). By contrast, the *OED*'s entry emphasized class difference, marking *bloody* as "now constantly in the mouths of the lowest classes." In 1969 the editors of *Oz* magazine wrote to Oxford University Press complaining that the *Shorter Oxford Dictionary* did not include the word *fuck*, adding disingenuously, "We would be interested to know the reason for this curious omission." (The correspondence is to be found in the *Times Literary Supplement*, October 13, 1972, p. 1233.) The original *OED* had not included *fuck* and *cunt*, possibly from fear of prosecution for "obscene libel," omissions which the *Supplement* (1972–86) made good. However, it had included *nigger, coolie, frog, kaffir, coon, yid*, and a host of such demeaning ethnic terms. The only lawsuit brought against the dictionary's publisher concerned offensive uses of the word *Jew* (*Schloimovitz v. Clarendon Press*). The case was rejected with costs on July 5, 1973.

In modern times the different areas of sensitivity and disapproval conscientized by feminism and by political correctness have created new areas of taboo, such as demeaning terms for women, homosexuals, foreigners, minorities, as well as mentally and physically handicapped people. R. W. Holder observed in his *Dictionary of Euphemisms*: ". . . we have created fresh taboos, relating to skin pigmentation, charity, education, and commercial practice" (1995, p. ix). To take a simple crude instance, the insulting dismissal of a woman as, say, a "stupid fat cow" has become completely unacceptable in recent decades, but for different reasons. Feminists would previously have objected to "cow" but more recently political correctionists would also object to "fat" as being "fattist." There seems to be more sensitivity and less clarity, as Lynne Truss observes:

> Thus our good intentions are often thwarted in today's politically sensitive world. Offence is so easily given. And where the "minority" issue is involved, the rules seem to shift about: most of the time a person who is female/ black/disabled/gay wants this *not* to be their defining characteristic; you are supposed to be blind to it. But then, on other occasions, you are supposed to observe special sensitivity, or show special respect. . . . I mention all this because "political correctness" is sometimes confused with respect, but it operates quite differently . . . it's mainly about covering oneself and avoiding prosecution in a world of hair-trigger sensitivity. (2005, pp. 163–4)

As we have seen, *taboo* is used in an increasingly loose fashion for topics which are considered "inappropriate" or "unacceptable" to mention in public. Given the *anomie* or "normlessness" of modern cosmopolitan societies, there remain few taboo areas. Truly taboo subjects provoke shock, anger, even hysteria. Herrnstein and Murray's *The Bell Curve* (1994), claiming innate ethnic differences in IQ, produced exactly such reactions in the United States, not because the proposition was untrue, but because it violated the fundamental tenet of the Declaration of Independence, the "self-evident truth" that "All men are created equal." The issue is discussed further in chapter 2. Murray argued in a subsequent article, "The Inequality Taboo," that "The assumption of no innate differences among groups suffuses American social policy. That assumption is wrong" (2005, p. 14). Looking at "difference" from another point of view, Murray wrote his article "Jewish Genius," being careful to point out that he is "a Scots-Irish Gentile from Iowa" (*Commentary*, April 2007, p. 29). He concluded by boldly taking refuge in the hypothesis that "The Jews are God's chosen people." The subsections on "Dictionary omissions" and "Assessments of currency" in chapter 3 deal with other aspects of taboo and censorship.

Censorship

Censorship takes various overt forms, principally "prior restraint" – that is, prevention of publication by the state or some official agency – or punitive prosecution subsequently. It has a dismayingly long history, lying outside the scope of this study, but despite increasing liberation in many social areas, the practice is far from over. Many other agencies come into play, such as church councils, political parties, and publishing houses, as well as more insidious factors leading to self-censorship, such as sensitivity to what is socially and politically acceptable. Earlier comments on censorship such as those of Milton included in the epigraphs to this work emphasized the superiority, if not the invincibility of truth. John Stuart Mill similarly argued from a moral perspective:

> The peculiar evil of silencing the expression of an opinion is that it is robbing the human race; . . . If the opinion is right, they are deprived of the opportunity of exchanging error for truth: if wrong, they lose what is almost as great a benefit, the clearer perception and livelier impression of truth, produced by its collision with error. (from "On Liberty," 1859)

A prime instance was the pressure put on Galileo to deny the Copernican system in favor of the traditional Ptolemaic version. As *The Independent* wrote when an Austrian court sentenced David Irving to three years' imprisonment for Holocaust denial, "The principle of free speech cannot apply only to those who hold views with which we agree" (February 21, 2006).

Today moral absolutes are less in evidence, and the notion of the truth is more politicized. "Direct and unambiguous censorship, as part of state control, is easier to combat than the indirect results of it," observes Doris

Lessing in her penetrating essay "Censorship" (2004, p. 73). She included some frank comments on the prevalence of what she called "the tyranny of Political Correctness," which she interprets as having moved into the vacuum left by "the certainties of communism." Lessing recounts various contemporary episodes: "In a certain prestigious university in the United States two male faculty members told me they hated PC but did not dare say so if they wanted to keep their jobs. They took me into the park to say it, where we could not be overheard, as used to happen in communist countries" (2004, p. 77).

A similar pattern is detected in a completely different realm by Ronald Harwood in his history of the British theater, *All the World's a Stage*. An actor and playwright, Harwood describes a critical change of régime: "The Lord Chamberlain's long theatrical censorship came to an end in 1968. . . . Nudity, uninhibited language and political satire broke out. Yet, in the 'serious' theatre, censorship quite as severe as any imposed by the Lord Chamberlain now came into force. Plays had to be 'committed' (so did actors, directors, and scene designers) or else they were nothing" (1984, p. 306). But is this truly censorship or merely an entrenched fashion?

Endorsing Harwood's observation are the contemporary emergence of the vogue words *committed* and *engagé*. Although both were neologisms in English usage attracting a fair amount of comment, they were always used to denote or imply a left-wing concern or focus, even though logic-ally they could be used of any political view. *Committed*, the translation of French *engagé*, is first recorded in the translation of Sartre's *What is Literature* (1950) in this scathing quotation from the Foreword: "The worst artists are the most committed. Look at the Soviet painters." *Engagé* emerges contemporaneously in Herbert Read's *Art Now* (1948, p. 139): "L'art engagé, art in the service of the revolution." A quotation from the *Listener* in 1966 echoes Harwood's sentiments: "We hear a lot about the duty of the artist to be 'committed' and 'engagé' " (March 17). A related term was *relevant*, logically general in meaning, but widely used to sug-gest a vague social concern or application.

The terms *committed, engagé,* and *relevant* are not as *en vogue* as they were 20 years ago. But political correctness is still a major force in cul-tural matters. Wagner remains posthumously tainted as anti-Semitic, not intrinsically, but contaminated by the admiration of Hitler and the Nazis. What if Hitler had admired his fellow-Austrian Mozart? Productions at Bayreuth now eschew the heroic world of the Germanic gods and its Aryan associations, presenting the ancient deities as alienated and absurd figures in modern dress. An Austrian production of *Die Fledermaus* in 2006 was preceded by a long statement that the production was a protest against the current rise of neo-Nazism in that country. The production was consequently an anachronistic travesty, the aristocracy being presented as decadent drug addicts giving Heil Hitler salutes.

Media censorship is regarded as being a typical feature of totalitarian regimes and tyrannies, but occurs even in relatively free societies. Censorship of the more familiar kind, that is, the publicized banning of books, films, and television coverage, tends to be counterproductive, giving the banned item unwarranted publicity and even a false value. A classic instance was *Lady Chatterley's Lover*, the banning of which in 1928 provoked five pirated editions and an expurgated version within a year. The controversy that this one novel attracted fundamentally skewed Lawrence's literary reputation. At the watershed trial (*Regina vs. Penguin Books*, 1960) the consensus of literary experts called as witnesses was that the book was not one of Lawrence's best. Nevertheless, the victory of Penguin Books guaranteed enormous sales through the publicity of the trial, to the point that this is now the work most associated with Lawrence's name.

Consequently, the most effective censorship is surreptitiously pre-emptive, either institutionally or as a result of self-censorship. The prime case of pre-emptive institutional censorship was the newspaper *Pravda* (meaning "Truth"), which from 1918 became "the official organ" of the Soviet Communist Party. Subscription was mandatory for state-run organizations such as the armed forces. (Ironically it had been originally founded in 1908 by Trotsky in exile, published in Vienna to avoid censorship, and was smuggled into Russia, where it was very popular.) Unlike most newspapers in the West, *Pravda* was "put to bed" twice. It was first set up ready to print and a few copies submitted to the Politburo. There was then half an hour delay before the duty editor certified that the paper was "ready for printing." Angus Roxburgh's study *Pravda: Inside the Soviet News Machine* (1987) noted: "Like all printed matter in the Soviet Union, *Pravda* was censored by a member of the *Glavlit* (the Chief Administration for the Protection of State Secrets in the Press) – twice, once before printing and once before distribution" (p. 66). Roxburgh enumerates many enlightening revisions, including even doctored photographs, wherein *personae non grata* disappeared and new favorites suddenly materialized. *Pravda* was closed down by President Yeltsin in 1991.

This is a typical extreme instance of news management of a kind generally unknown in the free world. However, the notorious affair between Edward VIII and Mrs Simpson leading to the Abdication crisis produced curious double standards. Although Mrs Simpson's name appeared in the Court Circular, the major British press proprietors colluded with the Prime Minister, Stanley Baldwin, to suppress reports of the scandalous liaison.

The American press, on the other hand, sensationalized every development, so that by 1936 the distributors of *Time* magazine in London even scissored out potentially libelous stories. Today, of course, "the royals" are a free-for-all. Occasionally, the "national interest" overrides other considerations. Paul Hoch cites a prime political example of a story for *Time* magazine being suppressed: it was filed under the ideologically devastating title of THE WAR IN VIETNAM IS BEING LOST (1974, p. 102). Political correctness has recently extended to the public doctoring of photographs. On posters in the Paris underground the trademark pipe of the famous comedian Jacques Tati has been replaced by a toy windmill and Jean-Paul Sartre's omnipresent cigarettes have been extinguished.

The publishing history of George Orwell's *Animal Farm* (1945) is highly illuminating of political attitudes and publishing pressures in postwar Britain. The book was initially rejected by a number of distinguished British publishing houses. These included Gollancz (with whom Orwell actually had a contract), André Deutsch, Faber & Faber, and Jonathan Cape, the last "on the advice of the Ministry of Information" (Holderness, 1988, p. 18). In his report for Faber, T. S. Eliot (who knew Orwell personally) wrote: "We can all see what you're against. But what are you for?" The deductions and implications were obvious: Russia had been an ally of Britain in the war and it was thus "politically incorrect" to criticize Communism, or at least Bolshevism, at that time. Some more "positive" message or standpoint was required, even though the Stalinist purges were well known to any informed person in the West. Eventually published by Secker & Warburg, *Animal Farm* became an instant best seller and has remained so, showing that the public was far more accepting and tolerant than the would-be moral guardians of what was suitable to read.

Orwell subtitled his book "A Fairy Story," an absurd designation, since the work obviously invited interpretation as a *roman à clef* of the ideological and personal power struggle between Stalin, Lenin, and Trotsky. As time has passed, the details of Stalinist tyranny have receded from the public memory and the forms of semantic engineering which Orwell illuminated as Newspeak and Doublethink have become routine political programs, so that *Animal Farm* is now read more as a political allegory showing the emptiness of "revolution" and that régime change is all too frequently a case of *plus ça change. . . .*

Self-censorship is obviously more difficult to trace. Thus no one will know except me what I have left out of this book for fear of repercussions. Sometimes these things are acknowledged at the time, as Virginia Woolf admitted in her novel *The Pargiters* (written in 1932 but published only in 1977): "There is, as the three dots used after the sentence 'He unbuttoned his clothes . . .' testify, a convention, supported by law, which forbids, whether rightly or wrongly, any plain description of the sight that Rose, in common with many other little girls, saw" (cited in Smith, 1993, p. 119). Other cases only surfaced much later. Thus E. M. Forster wrote his homosexual novel *Maurice* between 1910 and 1913, but did not feel able to publish it even after the laws governing homosexuality were revised in 1967. It eventually appeared in 1971, the year after his death.

There are also the unmeasurable factors of intimidation and fear of retaliation, both of which inhibit free expression of criticism. In recent years there has been, quite rightly, an eagerness to criticize Mr Blair and President Bush for their conduct over the war in Iraq. But simultaneously there has been in Britain an unwillingness to criticize certain alien practices of immigrants such as Islamic Fundamentalists, especially Jihadist terrorists and suicide bombers, or parents who commit the crime of "honor killing," even though these activities are regarded as morally repugnant and contrary to "the British way of life." This double standard underscores the irony that in a modern democracy you can criticize the head of state, but not people of a minority religion. Contrariwise, in Reformation times you could vilify the Pope or other sects, but not criticize the head of state.

In terms of the recent and current debate, the strongest outcry has occurred in the United States, where the issue of free speech is fiercely contested, with many arguing that politically correct speech codes are a violation of the freedom of speech underwritten by the First Amendment, and their opponents claiming that this freedom is being abused to promote hate speech or fighting words. Indeed, the practice was seen as paradoxically a kind of conformity without the expected enforcement of a politburo or Big Brother. This aspect of the debate will be taken up in more detail in Part III.

A notable case concerned Lawrence Summers, the President of Harvard, who on January 14, 2005 addressed a small private conference on "Diversifying the Science and Engineering Workforce." Addressing the issue that women are underrepresented in tenured positions in science and engineering at top American universities, he concluded: "So my best guess, to provoke you . . . [is] that in the special case of science and engineering there are issues of intrinsic aptitude . . ." (quoted in *Commentary* April, 2005, p. 32). Once publicized, these remarks provoked an uproar and pressure mounted on Summers to resign, which he did on June 30, 2006.

Self-censorship inhibits the publication of truths regarded as ideologically unacceptable or politically incorrect. In some cases, such as those inhibiting hate speech, this restraint is a good thing. However, in others it serves to perpetuate error or myth. In his article "The Inequality Taboo" Charles Murray, coauthor of *The Bell Curve* (1994), admitted that "the furor over its discussion of ethnic differences in IQ was so intense" that "I have deliberately not published anything on the topic." But he observed, chidingly: "The Orwellian disinformation about innate group differences is not wholly the media's fault. Many academics who are familiar with the state of knowledge are afraid to go on the record. Talking publicly can dry up research funding for senior professors and can cost assistant professors their jobs" (Murray, 2005, p. 13). He was provoked, he said, into writing the article by the case of Summers, who had "offered a few mild, speculative, off-the-record remarks about innate differences between men and women in their aptitude for high-level science and mathematics" (p. 13).

In this context we may consider what has become in many ways the acid test of political correctness: what can freely be said or written in public by a reasonable person without a political agenda on matters of public importance. The reader may care to consider the following three statements and assess them as either common, tenable generalizations, or prejudiced and politically incorrect:

A   Men are generally promiscuous.
B   Black men are generally promiscuous.
C   Gay men are generally promiscuous.

Whatever the answers, the real questions are these: are these statements all equally utterable in public, or has the notion of what is "offensive" or "unacceptable" or "racist" now taken on such broad dimensions that open debate on such contentious issues is an impossibility?

Textbooks and library books

Much of the debate on the censorship aspect of political correctness has been bound up with current exchanges rather than on causes, as is usual with debates. However, Diane Ravitch's study *The Language Police: How Pressure Groups Restrict What Students Learn* (2003) focuses on the roots of censorship in the production of school textbooks in America. Ravitch shows very convincingly that censorship starts with publishers' guidelines and intensifies in pressure, from both Left and Right, in the areas of textbook adoption and library purchase. The practice covers every aspect of production of fiction and history, investigating roles, stereotypes, and of course language, all policed by "bias and sensitivity panels," some of which were in office as far back as 1981.

Ravitch observes: "No one speaks of 'censoring' or 'banning' words or topics; they 'avoid' them. The effect is the same" (2003, p. 158). She continues: "The censorship that has spread throughout American education has pernicious and pervasive effects. . . . Censorship distorts the literature curriculum, substituting political judgments for aesthetic ones. . . . Censorship distorts the history curriculum by introducing political considerations into interpretations of the past, based on deference to religious, ethnic, and gender sensitivities" (2003, pp. 159–60).

One of many instances cited by Ravitch is a true story about a blind mountain climber which was perversely regarded by such a panel as being "biased *against* people who are blind" (2003, p. 11). More predictably, the panel objected to Aesop's fable of "The Fox and the Crow" on the grounds that the vain and foolish crow is female, while the clever fox is male. The panel revealed its own bias by proposing a reversal of the genders. From her experience in the US Department of Education and other research, Ravitch reveals that the New York State Education Department excised references to Jews and Gentiles in Isaac Bashevis Singer's memoir *In My Father's Court*, about growing up in prewar Poland. She gives other examples of senselessly obliterated cultural contexts in biography, and the general suppression of invidious cultural comparisons. Thus from John Holt's study on the success of the Suzuki method of learning the violin, *Learning All the Time*, "the state deleted his comment that Japanese women spend more time at home with their children than American women" (2003, p. 116). This is a sociological fact: according to research quoted by the London *Times*, "about 70% of women quit their jobs when they become pregnant and most do not return to work for at least 15 years" (November 5, 2007).

"Everything written before 1970 was either gender biased or racially biased" was the summary judgment offered by the president of a major publishing house (Ravitch, 2003, p. 20). In the context of testing, "bias" was defined as "anything in a test item that might cause any student to be distracted or upset." Control of stereotyping extends to occupations, activities, roles, community settings, and physical attributes: thus "African Americans should not be portrayed as athletes; Caucasians should not be portrayed as businesspeople; men should not be portrayed as breadwinners; women should not be portrayed as wives and mothers" and so on (2003, p. 27).

Ravitch further reveals that "because of industry mergers, educational publishing was dominated in the 1990s by four large corporations: Pearson, Vivendi, Reed Elsevier and McGraw-Hill." (Incidentally, the last-named company issued its "Guidelines for the equal treatment of the sexes" in 1974.) She demonstrates a remarkable consistency in these companies' notion of bias. Her analysis of the Scott Foresman–Addison Wesley guidelines (which run to 161 pages) contains the following comments: "Combining a tone of idealism and authoritarianism, they impose a strict code of political and social correctness"; "The document is an extended celebration of multiculturalism"; "The company's products must contain 'a fair and balanced representation' of the population." In the depiction of the aged, "aprons, canes, rockers, orthopedic shoes, walkers, and wheelchairs" should be avoided, while the ageist vocabulary of *codger, geezer, old maid, senile*, and *spinster* are banned, together with hundreds of others. Inevitably, the new politically correct terminology of *physically challenged* and *differently abled* is recommended (2003, pp. 35–8). Her study concludes with a Glossary of Banned Words, Usages, Stereotypes, and Topics. She lists over 400 banned words.

Furthermore, Ravitch shows that Houghton Mifflin had guidelines called *Eliminating Prejudice* as far back as 1981, the details of which are stupefying in their comprehensiveness. An (unpublished) update of 2001 recommends that stories about African Americans "must avoid or limit those that are about slavery . . . that depict [them] as athletes, musicians, or entertainers, that are about controversial people like Malcolm X, and that are about civil rights" (2003, pp. 46–8). Not all of these guidelines were even easily available. Further, the head of the testing program in the Connecticut Department of Education responded to her request for passages rejected for bias and sensitivity reasons by writing that "it wouldn't be appropriate to share that material with you" (2003, p. 167).

The battle of the books, that is, the contest over the acceptance of textbooks and library books, has been carried on nationwide by various groups, both left- and right-wing. The American Library Association publishes regular lists of the most frequently challenged books, together with the grounds. The list contains many surprises:

100 Most Frequently Challenged Books 1990–2000
3   *I Know Why the Caged Bird Sings* by Maya Angelou
5   *The Adventures of Huckleberry Finn* by Mark Twain
6   *Of Mice and Men* by John Steinbeck
7   *Harry Potter* (series) by J. K. Rowling
#13   *The Catcher in the Rye* by J. D. Salinger
#18   *The Color Purple* by Alice Walker
#25   *In the Night Kitchen* by Maurice Sendak
#31   *Kaffir Boy* by Mark Mathabane
#37   *The Handmaid's Tale* by Margaret Atwood
#41   *To Kill a Mockingbird* by Harper Lee
#42   *Beloved* by Toni Morrison
#52   *Brave New World* by Aldous Huxley

Of these, *Catcher in the Rye* was listed among the 10 Most Frequently Challenged Books in 2005, for "sexual content, offensive language, and being unsuited to age group." Both *The Adventures of Huckleberry Finn* and *Of Mice and Men* have been "regulars" for years.

Ravitch rightly stresses the unrealistic disjunction which consequently exists in the life of the high school student today. This is between the mediated home experience consisting variously of news actuality of terrorism, hijackings, massacres, and famines; the movies of fantasy, passion, romance, and violence; the music of hip-hop and rap; contrasted with the school experience, which is sanitized, bowdlerized, and equalized from gender and racial perspectives, becoming in essence boring, banal, and unchallenging. "By avoiding controversy, we teach them to avoid dealing with reality. By expurgating literature, we teach them that words are meaningless and fungible" (2003, p. 165).

We may conclude with some observations on the melancholy topic of the burning of books. "Wherever books will be burned," wrote Heinrich Heine, "men also, in the end, are burned" (*Almansor*, 1823). George Steiner, in his essay "Humane Literacy," endorsed both the power of books and their destroyers: "Men who burn books know what they are doing. The artist is the uncontrollable force" (Steiner, 1969, p. 29). Ray Bradbury's "fireman" in *Fahrenheit 451* is an untroubled functionary, enthusing: "It's fine work. Monday burn Millay, Wednesday Whitman, Friday Faulkner, burn 'em to ashes, then burn the ashes. That's our official slogan" (Bradbury, 1979, chapter 1).

The ethics of publication

The great satirist John Dryden wrote in 1693: "We have no moral right on the reputation of other men. It is taking from them what we cannot restore to them" (from *The Original and Progress of Satire*). These fine sentiments are of course not always observed, nor were they by Dryden himself. Taboo topics of all sorts continue to be published, for a variety of motives, pornographic, scandalous, for character assassination, and to inflict political damage. It is therefore vitally important to clarify the sources of evidence and to use discriminating criteria in assessing the validity of statements, not simply taking them at face value. This includes examining the degrees of deliberation of an utterance, from spontaneous to measured, and the mode and degree of publicity, whether oral (anecdotal or first hand), spoken, or written (letters, memoirs, diaries, biography, fiction) and when published, whether they are unofficial, authorized or official.

In this context, the reader may care to assess the following cases:

In 1972, two weeks prior to the primary election in Maine, a letter appeared in the New Hampshire *Union Leader* saying, *inter alia*, "we don't have blacks, but we have Cannocks [sic]." The form intended was *Canuck*, a derogatory nickname for a Canadian. The letter was attributed to an aide of the Democratic senator for Maine, Edmund Muskie, whose campaign suffered from the subsequent fallout.

In 1997 in a telephone conversation the Springbok rugby coach André Markgraaf repeatedly referred to the rugby management board as "fokken [fucking] kaffirs." The conversation, which had been taped, was leaked to the South African press. As a consequence, Markgraaf resigned immediately.

In 2006 a Republican candidate George Allen referred to "a young political activist of Indian descent" as a "Macaca." Most of the audience were ignorant of the meaning, but a headline announced "Republican golden boy trips up on a single taboo word" (*Sunday Times*, August 20, 2006). It turned out that *macaque* means "monkey" in French, also an ugly person, and is an ethnic slur against North Africans.

In all these cases the language used was "inappropriate," in the Clintonian sense, in the Blair sense, and more importantly, in the real sense. It was racist or demeaning. But the motive for publication was basically to manipulate public opinion or some power group against the speaker.

Conclusion

We have seen that political correctness is a highly complex topic with many aspects, sources, influences, and manifestations, most of which will be taken up in greater detail later. A simple definition is not really possible, since the phrase now encompasses a whole range of attitudes which have undoubtedly affected both behavior and language. Among the primary sites of struggle for semantic redefinition which we shall consider are race and ethnicity, disability, AIDS, disease, the canon, culture, curricula, gender and sexual orientation, xenophobia, the environment, animal rights, addiction, criminal behavior, and mental disorders. These and other topics are treated in detail in Part III. In all some 200 established terms and new lexical formations will be discussed and analyzed.

In broad terms, political correctness seeks, by focusing on these categories, to stress human communality and correspondingly to downplay engrained differences and exclusivity, discouraging judgmental attitudes and outlawing demeaning language. In this process a new framework of values and morality has arisen, one which has to some extent supplanted traditional orthodox categories. These are admirable initiatives. But they raise a methodological problem concerning semantic engineering, in that in the history of linguistic study, the modern era is supposed to be that of descriptive linguistics, that school which respects actual usage, regarding itself as a period of modern enlightenment succeeding the earlier dominance of prescription (laying down rules of usage) and proscription (outlawing certain forms and practices). The extent to which the invented forms of political correctness have achieved a viable and effective currency can be more meaningfully assessed after an interval of time, when the heat of the initial debate has cooled. Ferdinand de Saussure, the founding father of linguistics, observed that "Of all social institutions, language is least amenable to initiative," because of what he identified as a "collective inertia towards innovation" (1966, pp. 73–4). But Saussure's *Cours* was first published nearly a century ago, prior to many mediated and Orwellian changes. The enterprise of political correctness was and continues to be an attempt to change or suppress, not the whole *langue* or linguistic system, but the meanings of particular *paroles*. More especially it forms an attempt to establish a new polite public discourse to replace various forms of personal or demotic usage of a prejudicial and demeaning kind. Has the initiative succeeded, and if so, to what extent? Or has "collective inertia" prevailed?

How current is the language of political correctness, really? And how seriously is it taken? It seems hard to believe that anyone could say or listen to "significant other" with a straight face, or write "differently abled" without a grimace or a sigh, or worst of all, speak of "inappropriately directed laughter." Yet despite its anomalous breeding ground and its essential oddity, this strange "new world or words" has developed a certain currency. While the currency of politically correct language is indisputable, its meanings, applications, and acceptance are still controversial. This semantic aspect is the primary focus of the first three parts of this work and supplies the rationale of its contribution to the debate. We shall now turn our attention to the debate which threw up these terms, and the evolution of the phrase *political correctness* itself.

Chapter 2

The Origins and the Debate

Introduction

This chapter deals with some of the ideas and the rhetorical strategies that mobilized and articulated political correctness and the origins of the formula. The basic question: "Who started political correctness?" has both a historical and a moral dimension, somewhat like controversies over the origins of a war. (As we shall see, analogies with wars and battles came to be used quite frequently.) A less contentious form of the question, "Where did it start?" would limit one to a source in history. The historical dimension derives from political theory and practice, while the moral dimension is bound up in what is perceived to be fair and right in contemporary educational reform and in cultural politics. This chapter is accordingly concerned mainly with the debate in America, especially over what was regarded as fundamental in tertiary education, namely the traditional "canon" or a multicultural approach, and the verbal weapons employed. The counterclaims of the canon and multiculturalism became the broad seminal issue out of which grew many other matters, discussed in Part III under "Zones of Controversy." In addition to the ideas and the rhetoric employed in the debate, it is important to consider the whole issue of the definition of words by various authorities, traditional and alternative. These topics are covered in Part II, "The Semantic Aspect."

As the subsequent discussion of the "Origins of the Phrase" shows, political correctness started as a policy concept denoting the orthodox party line of Chinese Communism as enunciated by Mao Tse-Tung in the 1930s. It was then borrowed by the American New Left in the 1960s, but with a more rhetorical than strictly programmatic sense, since Communism has never gained a significant foothold in the United States. Paradoxically, political correctness increased in vogue in America precisely when hard-line Communism was waning. Under Communism it referred simply to the correct party line as enunciated by the hierarchy in a dynamic of "consensus by command." It had no specific content. The modern American manifestation emerges in quotations dating from 1970, in the contexts of left-wing politics and feminism. In fact the first "site of struggle," in terms of rights, status, and semantics, was that engaged in from the late 1960s by feminism, which has few affiliations with Communism. The later applications of political correctness were bound up, as Dinesh D'Souza has observed, with "the assorted ideologies of the late 1960s and early 1970s: black consciousness and black power, feminism, homosexual rights, and to a lesser extent, pacifism, environmentalism, and so on" (1991, p. xiv). Today, still other "assorted ideologies" have come into play, as we shall see.

The moral dimension of political correctness is tied up with a major feature of the modern American debate, the attribution of blame by both "Left" and "Right" (or "liberal" and "neoconservative," to use the more current labels) to the "other side" for what each regarded as illegitimate political interference in academic and cultural matters. (It is obviously naïve to assume that matters of culture and the curriculum can ever be entirely free of politics.) There even developed a side debate as to whether political correctness really existed or was the invention of its opponents. (Almost annually a similar debate surfaces over "The War on Christmas.") There are those who claim that political correctness was a chimera or imaginary monster created by some on the Right of the political spectrum to discredit those who wished to change the *status quo*. In Britain, Richard Gott, the literary editor of the *Guardian*, made this claim: "[PC] is a notional construct put together by the Right to create a non-existent monster on the Left that it can then attack" (June 1, 1993). (We have encountered the same view expressed by the British Labour politician Clare Short in chapter 1.) In the US Robin Tolmach Lakoff, among others, is very direct about the appropriation of the formula: "There are more than a few ironies in the history of political correctness. The New Right virtually copyrighted the term as its own, yet they did not originate it, but borrowed it from the enemy, the Old Left" (2000, p. 92). We shall encounter similar views from Stanley Fish. But before discussing the debate, it seems wise to consider the semantic evolution of the concept.

Origins of the Phrase

Although the phrase "politically correct" can be traced back to a remote early instance by Justice James Wilson in a Supreme Court case in 1793, it was then used in a literal rather than an ideological sense: ". . . 'The United

States,' instead of 'The people of The United States,' is the toast given. This is not politically correct." Clearly the intended meaning in this context was "politically accurate."

The modern origins of the phrase are inextricably bound up with Communist doctrine, although it evolves through various forms and tones. It was concerned not just with "doing the right thing" but "thinking the right thoughts." One of Mao Tse-Tung's edicts, "On Correcting Mistaken Ideas in the Party" (December 1929), begins with characteristic dogmatism: "There are various non-proletarian ideas in the Communist Party organization in the Fourth Red Army which greatly hinder the application of the Party's correct line." Having identified the problem with "peasants and other elements of petty-bourgeois origin," Mao berates "the failure of the Party's leading bodies to wage a concerted and determined struggle against these incorrect ideas and to educate the members in the Party's correct line." Mao insisted that "The correct line is formed in the struggle with the incorrect line" (1965, p. 105). The related phrase "a correct political perspective" derives from Trotsky's study, *Problems of the Chinese Revolution* (1932, p. 198). From the continuing orthodoxy of the Chinese Communist Party came the later ruling by Liu Shao Chi: "Our Party's correct political line cannot be separated from its correct organisational line" (1951, p. 52).

All of these are clearly serious ideological statements emanating from within the Party hierarchy. Even at this stage *correctness* was being used to mean "adherence to Maoist doctrine," as is evident in this quotation: "When professors and scholars praise the 'correctness' of Marxism-Leninism, the communists hope that the common people will be more inclined to accept the new ideology" (Yu, 1955, cited in *OED*). Russian Communism naturally adopted the same vocabulary: a report in *Izvestia* in 1933 quoted an investigation into 65,000 Soviet pupils criticizing "Bad grammar, abundance of mistakes in spelling . . . superficial and often politically incorrect information in civics and social sciences" (*Christian Science Monitor*, November 28, 1933). Obviously, the semantic premises of the Communist uses are that *correct* applies to politics, not grammar, and that *educate* means not "to open the mind to various possibilities," but "to persuade the people to adopt the right, that is, the party's way of thinking."

Two illuminating instances of semantic transition from the doctrinaire to a deprecating sense occur in examples from the Communist era in Europe. John Strachey commented in 1934 that "We are sometimes a little apt to pretend, to wish, to suggest that such writers [Marxists] are necessarily better writers because they are more politically correct than are our fellow travelers" (*Literature and Dialectical Materialism*, p. 47). On the issue of a writer having the "right" perspective is this revealing comment:

"A politically correct theme would not have saved him from the critics' attack . . . because he described the concentration camp as he personally had seen it, not as one was *supposed to see it*" (original italics). This comes from *The Captive Mind*, the devastating memoir of the moral and psychological effects of Communism in Poland by Czeslaw Milosz (1955, p. 120). Here an ironic disjunction is clearly being set up between individual views that are honest or frank reflections of reality, and those which were acceptable to some authority.

From its origin in the *Quotations of Mao Tse-Tung*, better known as Mao's *Little Red Book* (1964), the phrase became familiar in the West. The modern revival has been traced back to the American New Left, which in the late 1960s adopted the phrase as part of the rhetoric of the Chinese Communist Party. This is the argument of Ruth Perry's article, "A Short History of the Term *Politically Correct*" (1992) while Barbara Epstein (1992) argues in her article "Political Correctness and Identity Politics" that the link with Chinese Communism lay in an extension of the formula "correct lineism."

Subsequent quotations (set out below) show two trends: politically correct attitudes and academic acceptance start to go hand in hand, and the phrase "politically correct" starts to be used ironically. Although, as has been shown, the Maoist sense was "conforming to the party line or expectations," the formula came to be used in an ironic or self-deprecating sense by insiders even in the early years of its currency. The quotations are as follows:

1970 – Toni Cade, *The Black Woman*: "A man cannot be politically correct and a chauvinist too."
1975 – Philip Gerber, *Willa Cather*: "If a literary thesis was unmistakable and politically correct, a favourable reception for the work was assured."
1975 – *Facts on File*: "On the lesbian issue she said that NOW [the National Organization of Women] was moving in the 'intellectually and politically correct direction'."
1975 – Peter Fuller, Journal, March 29, in *Marches Past*: "The jostling for rarefied, nuanced, over-tuned theoretical [Marxist] 'positions' heats up. As one might expect of 7, Carlisle Street [office of the *New Left Review*] . . . everyone vies with each other for the most perverse and punishing 'correctness'." (This appears to be the first instance in the UK.)
1979 – *Washington Post*, September 16: "No matter what criticisms are hurled at this feminist fiction, no doubt the author will be cushioned by her political correctness."

1984 – *Women's Student International Forum*: "The deformed sexuality of patriarchal culture must be moved into an arena for struggle, where a 'politically correct' sexuality of respect will contend with an 'incorrect' sexuality of domination and submission."

1991 – *Village Voice*, December 3: "I've been chided by a reader for using the word *gringos* and informed that *European American* is politically correct."

As has already been noted, there is a common equation of political correctness and feminism. This is apparent in four of the seven quotations above. To some extent this association is to be expected, since the quotations reach back to the 1970s.

Paul Berman outlined the shift in voice and tone in the American debate: " 'Politically correct' was originally an approving phrase on the Leninist left to denote someone who steadfastly toed the party line. Then it evolved into 'P.C.,' an ironic phrase among wised-up leftists to denote someone whose line-toeing fervor was too much to bear" (1992, p. 5). The evidence shows that the uses of the abbreviation PC, which come later, are critical from the beginning:

1986 – *New York Times*, May 11: "There's too much emphasis on being P.C."

1992 – *The Economist*, January 11: ". . . subjects like science and engineering, where the ravages of P.C. are unknown (or at least rare)."

2003 – *This Magazine*, February: "Common expressions with racist roots are used by even the proudest of the P.C., while every day, thousands of average joes are slapped on the wrist for using words that sound racist."

The fundamental shift from seriousness to irony is simply explained. In the totalitarian context of its Communist and Maoist origins, *political correctness* had a serious doctrinaire sense. Once it was borrowed into a democratic and liberal political milieu, it became an anomaly, an empty formula of conformity open to subversion.

As has been mentioned, the debate over political correctness in the United Kingdom developed later than in the United States, in the mid-1990s. Among the more politically alert, however, the French phrase *bien pensant* ("right thinking") was borrowed earlier, for example by Roger Scruton in his essay on "Sense and Censorship" in *The Times* (March 25, 1986), but it did not develop a common currency. (The French phrase is recorded as far back as 1934, according to an article, "Les Nouveaux Bien-Pensants", in *Le Point*, January 3, 2003.) In his collection of essays published between 1983 and 1987, *Untimely Tracts*, Scruton (1987) does not actually use the phrase *political correctness* in his provocative discourses on controversial topics such as rape, the death penalty, standards in schools, class and politics, the new racism, and the use of *fascist*.

Politically incorrect

Although the phrase *politically incorrect* had been part of Communist rhetoric, and became generally current in the US in the early 1990s, there is a remarkable anticipation in Vladimir Nabokov's *Bend Sinister* (first published in 1947), a satirical allegory on a totalitarian dystopia in which all individuality is discouraged. Amongst the propagandist journalism which the protagonist Professor Krug regularly receives is this commentary about obligatory socializing: "A person who has never belonged to a Masonic Lodge or to a fraternity, club, union, or the like, is an abnormal and dangerous person. . . . It is better for a man to have belonged to a politically incorrect organization than not to have belonged to any organization at all" (1960, p. 155).

This curious prescription obviously derives from Nabokov's acute understanding of warped totalitarian thinking, which regards the free, unassociated individual as some kind of threat to the state. It also has some resemblances, incidentally, to his view of himself as given in an interview on June 5, 1962: "I have never worked in an office or in a coal mine. I have never belonged to any club or group. No creed or school has had any influence on me whatsoever. Nothing bores me more than political novels and the literature of social intent" (Nabokov, 1973, p. 3).

Nabokov's ironic comment on "a politically incorrect organization" is essentially the formal designation one associates with a politically conformist society. Although the constraints associated with such a situation should no longer apply in the free world, in fact they do. One often encounters comments on unfashionable politicians such as: "X dares to say in public what many people will say only in private." This sums up in essence both the context and the content of the politically incorrect in modern times. In the course of this study we shall come across similar expressions of constraint in a nominally free society, ranging from the observations of Doris Lessing in a university context to the section on jokes in chapter 8.

The Debate: Redefining Territories and Establishing Boundaries

The political correctness debate was more intense, wide-ranging, and more of a major public issue in the United States than in Britain. It started in the universities, and since nearly half of all Americans go to college, both the major issues and the new words became widely debated. Furthermore, the major American universities are independent institutions, whereas the majority of British universities are subsidized by the government. As has been mentioned, the participants included President Bush (briefly), administrators, public intellectuals, major academics, and journalists of all hues and persuasions.

The course of the debate was outlined by Paul Berman from its public origins in the fall of 1990 through to the publication of the casebook *Debating PC* (1992), which he edited. The opening section of the volume (containing 21 contributions in all) included essays on the general topic of the title and different perspectives on the Modern Language Association conference in Chicago in 1990. These were followed by sections on Politics and the Canon, Free Speech and Speech Codes, Multiculturalism, the Public Schools, and the Future. Contributions varied greatly in tone and style, including jeremiads, polemics, and satires. They ranged from relatively neutral offerings such as "The Value of the Canon" and "The Politics of Knowledge" to more combative pieces such as "Whose Canon is it, Anyway?", "Freedom of Hate Speech," and "Public Image Limited: Political Correctness and the Media's Big Lie," to irate complaint-titles such as "Critics of Attempts to Democratize the Curriculum Are Waging a Campaign to Misrepresent the Work of Responsible Professors." Although most of the contributors were academics, some noted journalists and social critics were included.

How important is the debate now? The question can be properly answered only after some assessment, but in essence it remains significant for various reasons. Firstly, the broader public gained an insight into the political agendas and values which lay behind issues not normally thought of as "political," such as education, the curriculum, and culture. They also saw intellectual heavyweights entering the fray. Furthermore, in the wide range of issues raised there were two contrary tendencies: the prime academic issue involved a questioning of the traditional canon and an expansion of the boundaries of the curriculum in the direction of multiculturalism. But there were accusations and suspicions of constraints being placed on the limits of expression and of contentious topics being avoided. There were reports of newly arrived students being given, not just reading lists, but lists of proscribed words. Were the new initiatives "Preparing Americans for a wider world . . . or narrowing academic freedom?" was the question posed by Berman's collection. In her Introduction to the similar British publication, *The War of the Words* (1994), Sarah Dunant observed that political correctness had succeeded in "offending both the right and a good deal of the left at the same time . . . For many liberals a movement which claimed to be about opening up the culture to allow more voices in has, instead only succeeded in alienating voices that were already there" (1994, p. xi). This antithesis or contradiction at the core of political correctness was encapsulated by two notable titles: D'Souza's *Illiberal Education* in America and Melanie Phillips's "Illiberal Liberalism" (1994) in Britain. We shall be returning to these issues, especially that of the canon, later in this chapter.

Furthermore, in the wider world political correctness had already started to assume a moral dimension and a public agenda. The case of Robert Bork, nominated for the US Supreme Court in 1987 yielded the verb *bork*, recorded from the same year, meaning "to vilify or defame someone systematically, especially in the mass media, on the grounds of their allegedly illiberal or extreme views, in order to prevent them from gaining public office" (*OED*). The *New York Times* referred in 1993 to "This powerful political force that now goes around 'Borking' politically incorrect nominees" (May 23). In Lakoff's interpretation it was a Republican coinage meaning "to subvert a political appointment by stealth" (2000, p. 122). The campaign against Bork was successful. Both *bork* and *borking* were resuscitated in the subsequent (but unsuccessful) challenge to the appointment of Judge Clarence Thomas in 1991.

It is possible to see two illuminating verbal parallels with *bork*. The first is with *boycott*, deriving from the victimization of Captain Boycott by the Irish Land League in 1880. The second and more common was with *McCarthyism*, especially in its sense of "persecuting individuals for holding 'inappropriate' political views." This latter comparison was superficial, since McCarthy's methods were far more sinister, but his name was frequently invoked in the debate. Although *bork* has not achieved the global semantic currency of *boycott* or *McCarthyism*, the cases of both Bork and Thomas aroused passionate interest in the United States. David Mamet's controversial play *Oleanna* (1992), discussed in chapter 8, was clearly a comment on political correctness on the American campus, but was also interpreted as an allusion to the Thomas case.

The beginnings

The controversy had been prefaced, or rather initiated, by a number of significant publications, such as William Bennett's *To Reclaim a Legacy* (1984), Allan Bloom's *The Closing of the American Mind* (1987), Lynne V. Cheney's *Humanities in America* (1987), the American Council of Learned Societies' *Speaking for the Humanities* (1989), Roger Kimball's *Tenured Radicals: How Politics has Corrupted Our Higher Education* (1990), and Dinesh D'Souza's *Illiberal Education: The Politics of Race and Sex on*

Campus (1991). Those of Bloom, Kimball, and D'Souza represented a surprising new publishing phenomenon, the academic best seller. In addition, "There was a national debate in 1988 about the curriculum at Stanford University and the merits of substituting 'multiculturalism' for the traditional study of Western Civ." (Berman, 1992, p. 4). Considerable coverage appeared in conservative journals such as *Commentary*, the *New Republic*, and *The New Criterion*, as well as in the national weeklies: the cover story for *Newsweek* on January 14, 1991 was "Thought Police," an evocation of Orwell's *1984*. To this mixture of serious polemic and sensationalist investigative journalism were to be added various ironic and parodic contributions.

As can be seen from the titles, many participants entered the fray announcing their positions and intentions in advance. This trend was to continue: Arthur M. Schlesinger, Jr. produced his reflections on a multicultural society, *The Disuniting of America* in 1992; Robert Hughes added his *Culture of Complaint: the Fraying of America* in 1993; Stanley Fish announced his programmatic title *There's No Such Thing as Free Speech, and It's a Good Thing, Too* (1994); while Robin Tolmach Lakoff introduced her study *The Language War* (2000) with a section "What I am Doing Here, and How I am Doing It," explaining: "This book is written with what some will allude to (with a sneer) as 'a liberal slant'." After considering "whether there is such a thing as true objectivity," Lakoff concluded: "So get it: I'm a liberal" (2000, p. 14).

Through popularity or unpopularity the phrase *political correctness* rapidly acquired a great vogue. In her essay " 'Political Correctness' and Hate Speech," Lakoff uses various databases to demonstrate the tremendous rise in the number of citations of the formula (from about 30 in 1985 to about 450 in 1990), followed by a rapid decline from the early 1990s onwards (2000, pp. 94–5). This rise and fall no doubt reflects the increasing heat of controversy, followed by a cooling-off period and an avoidance of the formula, especially by those on the left of the political spectrum. Lakoff also concedes that "My dictionary, published in 1992, does not contain any definition of 'p.c.' or its equivalents" (2000, p. 290). She does not explain the omission, but it is possibly because the issue had become too problematic and contentious.

In the space of a few years political correctness had become sufficiently unpopular that few would admit to being "politically correct" and most commentators simply avoided the formula. It seems significant that Stanley Fish preferred to call his 1995 study *Professional Correctness*. As we have seen, the abbreviation *PC*, an indication of the acceptance and familiarity of political correctness, can be traced back to a critical quotation from the

New York Times (May 11, 1986): "There's too much emphasis on being PC." In the same period *The Independent* noted (November 11, 1989): "We thought we'd be accused of not being PC." The quotations are revealing, the first showing hostility, the second a sense of anxiety at not conforming. These negative reactions continued. "PC is a dirty word in nineties Britain," wrote Sarah Dunant in her Introduction to *The War of the Words* (1994). She continued: "To call someone PC is less a description than an insult, carrying with it accusations of everything from Stalinism/McCarthyism to (even worse?) having no sense of humour" (p. vii). Deborah Cameron concurred in *Verbal Hygiene*: " 'PC' now has such negative connotations that the mere invocation of the phrase can move those so labelled to elaborate disclaimers, or reduce them to silence . . ." (1995, p. 123).

In Britain the debate was less of an exclusively academic affair, for there was some powerful journalistic input. Much of the initial commentary was ironic, focusing on the curious verbal innovations rather than the ideologies behind them. It also developed later, the main collection of essays, *The War of the Words*, appearing in 1994. It was a comparatively slim volume of 188 pages containing 11 essays, two of which focused on America and a third on France. In the Introduction Sarah Dunant commented on "the great liberal divide" namely "passionate disagreement as to whether PC is a political and liberal aberration, betraying all that liberalism stands for (Melanie Phillips), or a long overdue force for change which has exposed a hypocrisy at the heart of liberalism . . . (Yasmin Alibhai-Brown)" (1994, p. xiii).

As the reader will have noticed, one central term which became a major source of confusion was *liberal*. After a long and distinguished career, *liberal* can today mean variously "generous," "broad-minded," "supporting individual liberty and democracy," "progressive," or "supporting free market policies to a reprehensible degree," depending on context and user. In British usage it is generally a favorable word, while in American it is more critical, strongly connoting "left-wing." How could these meanings relate to the worthy notions of a "liberal education" and the "liberal arts," which were the founding senses of the word in the Middle Ages?

But political correctness did not become a national issue in Britain. There were no controversial academic best sellers equivalent to those of Bloom, Kimball, and D'Souza. The university syllabus has never been the source of passionate public debate in Britain. Even the controversy over the racism in Philip Larkin's posthumously published letters in 1992 was engaged in only by a few academics and literati. This difference in emphasis reflects the importance attached to civil liberties and to public issues by academics and intellectuals in the United States, and their status as opinion makers, as against the comparatively reserved approach of their British counterparts. The difference has continued to be apparent in the US in the widespread academic engagement in protest against the Iraq War, seen even in editorials in the premier journal of the humanities *PMLA* (*Proceedings of the Modern Language Association*), compared with relative acquiescence in the UK. Among contemporary scholars Noam Chomsky is a major participant in the controversies over American military involvement, notably in his studies *Acts of Aggression: Policing "Rogue" States* (1999) and *9/11* (2001).

The category of the public intellectual was introduced into the debate in America as if it were a new species. In itself it is a problematic concept, since "public" implies a journalistic superficiality or a syndicated readership, while "intellectual" suggests "reclusive," "recherché," "recondite," and probably "radical." As Christopher Hitchens observed in his obituary for Susan Sontag: "Between the word 'public' and the word 'intellectual' there falls, or ought to fall, a shadow. The life of the cultivated mind should be private, reticent, discreet . . ." (Hitchens, 2004).

In historical fact, of course, the tradition of the public intellectual reaches back to that composite figure which has come to be known as "the Victorian Sage," including Matthew Arnold, John Stuart Mill, Cardinal Newman, John Ruskin, Harriet Martineau, and Thomas Carlyle. (This is obviously leaving aside Socrates, Plato, Cato, Cicero, and other major figures of classical antiquity.) All these Victorians wrote on major political and cultural issues. The idea of the canon was first clearly articulated by Arnold, while Mill traversed many contemporary issues in his essay "On Liberty" and Newman's *Idea of a University* is still a seminal formulation. Further, several of the major Victorian novelists, notably George Eliot, were serious intellectuals. In France the tradition of the public intellectual, incarnated in writers like Emile Zola and Victor Hugo, continued much longer in the figures of Jean-Paul Sartre, Simone De Beauvoir, and Albert Camus.

By contrast, few public figures, writers, or academics in Britain have made significant or resonant comments on controversial public issues since the debate over nuclear disarmament. Indeed, Bertrand Russell was probably the last public intellectual, although Roger Scruton has written a series of provocative essays (alluded to elsewhere) on the main issues of political correctness. Another signal example is Doris Lessing, whose trenchant writings, especially on censorship, are quoted in this study.

Various commentators referred to the American exchanges as "the Culture Wars," since early in the controversies multiculturalism was regarded as an essential aspect of political correctness and often equated with it. In his outline of the debate in *Professional Correctness*, Stanley Fish indulged in this piece of rhetorical exaggeration:

> As everyone knows, the debates about "political correctness" and multiculturalism have focused on the humanities, and one bizarre side-effect has been the demonizing of a few professors of English, philosophy and French who have been declared responsible for disasters of a kind usually attributed to nuclear war or the bubonic plague: the collapse of Western civilization and the triumph of force over reason. (1995, p. 61)

More seriously, Fish suggested a conspiracy: ". . . the strategy by which a consortium of right-wing think-tanks, foundations and well-placed individuals (the Secretary of Education, the Chair of the National Endowment of the Humanities . . .) with the help of journalists . . . saturated the media . . ." (1995, pp. 62–3). In other words, the debate was not fought on points, like a boxing match, but by big battalions against small academics. In his other contribution, *There's No Such Thing as Free Speech* (1994), Fish commented ironically on the brilliance of the tactics of ". . . the neoconservative participants in the recent culture wars. Perhaps their most stunning success has been the production (in fact a reproduction), packaging and distribution of the term 'political correctness' " (1994, p. 8). This view was echoed by Deborah Cameron (1995, p. 123). However, this attribution does not appear to be supported by the considerable evidence adduced under "Origins of the Phrase" above. Furthermore, many of the more absurd and extreme prohibitions of political correctness actually derived from university administrations: thus *laughism* was the unfortunate coinage of the University of Connecticut back in 1988.

As it developed, the debate became increasingly word-centered, as had happened in the earlier exchanges on feminism. Thus Beard and Cerf's *Official Politically Correct Dictionary and Handbook* (1992) resembled earlier works, such as Kramarae and Treichler's *A Feminist Dictionary* (1985). Both were "dictionaries" of a new genre, emanating from different sides of the argument, either advocating and advancing the new forms and meanings or criticizing, satirizing, and caricaturing them. Both works contain many examples of what C. S. Lewis described as "tactical definitions," that is, prescribing what words "should" mean, although his prime examples were conservative, not innovative (Lewis, 1960, pp. 17–18). Other surveys of political correctness emphasizing the semantic aspect included Walter Nash's *Jargon* (1993), Robin Tolmach Lakoff's *The Language War* (2000), and Diane Ravitch's *The Language Police* (2003).

Not all the participants adopted the same serious tone or strategy to unearth the origins of political correctness. Thus *The Official Politically Correct*

Dictionary and Handbook (1992) was the collaboration of Henry Beard, one of the original editors of the *National Lampoon*, and Christopher Cerf, a successful television scriptwriter. The mock-serious title was clearly designed to attract a readership of those who had anxieties about their conformity to the new orthodoxy. (Articles were appearing in the national press asking the question "Are You Politically Correct?") Cerf described himself parodically in the terms of the newly fashionable categorizations as "a melanin-impoverished, temporarily abled, straight, half-Anglo-, half-Jewish-American male, a graduate of Harvard (a college described by former Dartmouth dean Gregory Ricks as 'one of the slickest forms of genocide going') . . . He has spent most of his life trying, and failing, to atone for these shortcomings" (1992, p. 175).

The ironic tone of the work was deceptive, since it was thoroughly sourced, exposing the origins of many of the formulas of political correctness as originating, not from the neoconservative right, but the American colleges themselves. Thus the first entry, for *ableism*, runs: "The Smith College Office of Student Affairs defines this as 'oppression of the differently abled, by the temporary able'." Similarly, *acquaintance rape* is "A term defined by Swarthmore College training manual as spanning 'a spectrum of incidents and behaviors ranging from crimes legally defined as rape to verbal harassment and inappropriate innuendo'." And so on, through *genetically oppressive* for "White" (Department of Rhetoric, Berkeley handout) and *lookism*, "the belief that appearance is an indicator of a person's value" (Smith College Office of Student Affairs). The work artfully juxtaposed text and image: the opposing categorization of "sun people" and "ice people" claimed by Leonard Jeffries Jr, defines "sun people" as "humanistic, communal, and caring," illustrated in the text by Idi Amin. More overtly satirical was James Finn Garner's *Politically Correct Bedtime Stories* (1994), subjecting the fairy tales of Hans Christian Andersen and the brothers Grimm to the strictures of politically correct behavior and vocabulary. It is discussed further in chapter 8.

As the temperature rose the debate became concerned with class and race, and often *ad hominem* rather than *ad rem*:

William Bennett and Allan Bloom, the dynamic duo of the new cultural right . . . symbolize the nostalgic return to what I think of as the 'antebellum esthetic position,' when men were men and men were white, when scholar-critics were white men and when women and people of color were voiceless, faceless servants and laborers, pouring tea and filling brandy snifters in the boardrooms of old boys' clubs. (Gates, 1992b, pp. 190–1)

Focus often devolved on how the debate was being conducted, with accusations against certain participants for illegitimately exploiting the First Amendment to justify prejudicial language, fighting talk, even hate speech. A great deal of "placing" of participants (discussed further below) labeled them as right-wing syndicated columnists, left-wing apologists, establishment figures, outsiders, and so on. If a participant appeared in an unexpected quarter, this became in itself an object of discussion. Paul Berman observed that the public had "the amusing experience of watching people on the right argue for the First Amendment and people on the left against it" (1992, p. 5).

In Britain Kenneth Minogue of the London School of Economics asked the disquieting question "But what were universities actually *for?*" in the Introduction to his revised edition of *The Concept of a University*. In his sardonic scenario "the idea of 'scholarship' disappeared altogether from the public rationale for having universities," being replaced by " 'research', whose point would be to solve the practical problems of the world." Minogue argued that the student rebellion of the 1960s was "the first barbarian assault upon the universities in the Western World," and more dismayingly, that the "second barbarian assault" came from governments: "That assault took the familiar form of seduction: first subsidize, then control by demanding accountability over the use of the taxpayers' money" (2005, p. x). "As the new morality of 'political correctness' took hold," Minogue continued, "governments began to remove from universities their autonomy in being able to select those candidates they judged suitable. Soon governments were legislating the social composition of universities" (2005, p. xvi).

Minogue's attack was directed in essence at the Thatcherite strategy of imposing utilitarianism, and his provocative resuscitation of the terms *barbarian* and *barbarism* was a form of homage to Matthew Arnold's *Culture and Anarchy* (1869). While his argument might be overstated, Minogue reminds us that British universities are now for the most part dependent on state subsidy, as opposed to the major American universities, which are essentially independent institutions. He also observed that ". . . for all the talk of 'diversity', most undergraduates emerge from universities as homogenized creatures tending to share fixed tastes and opinions" (2005, pp. xvi–xvii).

A different aspect of political correctness was emphasized by Alan Kors and Harvey Silverglate, whose *The Shadow University: The Betrayal of Liberty on America's Campuses* (1998) traversed and analyzed some of the notable campus events discussed in earlier studies. In one notorious episode in 1993 at the University of Pennsylvania, where Kors is a professor of history, an exasperated student attempting to study was repeatedly frustrated by loud singing from above. When his remonstrations were unsuccessful, he shouted out of the window "Shut up, you water buffalo!" The other students turned out to be black women. A disciplinary enquiry followed, on the grounds that the student might have violated the university's racial harassment policy. Eventually, in the face of negative publicity from the press, the charges were dropped.

As with most adversarial contests, the debate generated more heat than light, and few participants emerged with their reputations enhanced. Indeed, there seemed to be a concession that an open and fair debate was almost impossible, since certain parties had an unfair advantage through their entrenched positions in the media. Stanley Fish's *Professional Correctness* (1995) acutely diagnosed the impotence of academics and intellectuals in open public debate, concluding ironically that, in common with other interest groups, perhaps they should hire lobbyists.

Rhetorical strategies

One common strategy was to claim that "the other side" started it, giving "your" side the right to retaliate. Another familiar tactic was to dispute the validity of key terms and concepts. As we have seen, both Fish and Lakoff in their different ways claim that the formula *political correctness* was the invention of neoconservatives who cynically attributed it to the Left, a claim which the "Origins of the Phrase" above does not support. In his book *There's No Such Thing as Free Speech*, Fish outlined the tactics used in the debate whereby one side "seizes the high ground by laying claims to a certain charged vocabulary and uses it not to further argument but to shut it down in a fit of moral posturing" (1994, p. 11).

Merit was obviously a key term. Fish had already claimed that "There is no such thing as intrinsic merit" (quoted in Kramer and Kimball, 1995, p. xi) and that merit is "a political viewpoint claiming for itself the mantle of objectivity" (quoted in D'Souza, 1992, p. 176). He proceeded in a section provocatively called "Meritscam" to announce his intention to "deprive the backlashers of a vocabulary to which no one has an exclusive claim" (1994, p. 11). This raises the issue of whether it is really possible for one debater to "deprive opponents of a vocabulary." Furthermore, how can this be done *after* they have already laid claim to particular keywords? In a number of sophisticated essays, such as "You Can Only Fight Discrimination with Discrimination," Fish dissected the political realities behind most of the key cultural terms.

Issues of race and racism hovered round tactical definitions and tactical accusations, often employing code words, discussed in chapter 3. A stark example from earlier times was James Baldwin's observation that "Education is indoctrination if you're white and subjugation if you're black." Double standards were also evident: "The text explains that a non-white 'may discriminate against white people or even hate them' but cannot be called 'racist' " (Will, 1992, p. 259). There are similar claims quoted in this study by Spike Lee and in episodes concerning Dinesh D'Souza. Diane Ravitch commented that the consultants assessing a 1989 report "A Curriculum for Inclusion":

> vigorously denounced bias without identifying a single instance. . . . Instead the consultants employed harsh, sometimes inflammatory rhetoric to treat every difference of opinion as an example of racial bias. The African-American consultant excoriates the curriculum for its "White Anglo-Saxon (Wasp) value system and norms," its "deep-seated pathologies of racial hatred" and its "white nationalism." . . . The report is consistently Europhobic . . . All people with a white skin are referred to as "Anglo-Saxons" and "WASPs." (Ravitch, 1992, pp. 291–2)

Accusations of racism were both overt and covert. An extreme instance came from Leonard Jeffries Jr, who referred to Diane Ravitch as "the ultimate, supreme, sophisticated debonair racist . . . a sophisticated Texas Jew" (Teachout, 1995, p. 106). Jeffries, head of the Black Studies department at City College, New York was fired – whether for incompetence or for public anti-Semitism is a matter of dispute – then sued his employers and won. He was the originator of the terms "sun people" for blacks and "ice people" for whites.

Placing

This strategy consists of presenting arguments, not in a neutral fashion, but first "placing" authors or participants within the political spectrum, so that their contributions will be read in a certain way. It is a major feature of the political correctness debate, as of many others. Thus Deborah Cameron labels Robert Hughes as a "liberal" and Roger Scruton as "the English right-wing philosopher," as against plain "Stanley Fish" and, rather absurdly, "St George Orwell" (1995, pp. 155, 151, 142, 145). While it goes without saying that no one is a completely neutral observer or participant, it seems unfair to "place" some people and not others. Stanley Fish is, of course, a major participant in the debate. In *There's No Such*

Thing as Free Speech, he used a variation, the anonymous shotgun placing approach, claiming that "the antimulticulturalist, anti-affirmative action, antifeminist, antigay, antiethnic studies backlash has proceeded in just the manner I have described . . ." (1994, p. 11). In a more personal fashion, Edward Said, in his Afterword to *Orientalism*, dismissed Paul Johnson simply as "once a Left intellectual, now a retrograde social and political polemicist" (1995, p. 349).

Furthermore, placing often does more than simply contextualize a reading, as is evident in the following two extracts, both dealing with the emergence of the phrase *politically correct*: "The earliest instance of the formula *politically correct* is the comment (dating from 1970) by Tony [sic] Cade that 'a man cannot be politically correct and a chauvinist too'" (quoted by Perry, 1992). Here is the same comment contextualized differently: "The earliest print citation Perry reports for 'politically correct' occurs in a 1970 article by the African-American feminist Toni Cade (later Toni Cade Bambara), which included the statement 'a man cannot be politically correct and a chauvinist too' . . . here the term is used straightforwardly to argue that sexism has no place in radical black politics" (Cameron, 1995, p. 126). Cameron's narrower and more detailed political contextualization places demographic limits and a particular agenda on what is by all accounts a general observation.

A classic piece of placing is found in this journalistic account of an article by Charles Murray:

> Jews are an exceptionally accomplished group with an IQ of between seven and fifteen points above average and a startling record of achievement in the arts and sciences, according to Charles Murray, the social theorist.
> "Jewish genius", Murray admits, is a sensitive topic that Jews rarely address. Writing in *Commentary*, a neo-conservative journal, he argues that anti-Semitism makes it easy to understand that reluctance. . . . Critics complain that Murray is once again "racialising" intelligence by claiming that some groups are more genetically intelligent than others, the charge levelled at him when *The Bell Curve* was published in 1994.
> As a "Scots-Irish gentleman from Iowa", Murray feels no inhibition about tackling such a politically incorrect subject as high Jewish IQs. (Sarah Baxter, *Sunday Times*, April 8, 2007)

Here placing consists of putting forward Murray and Herrnstein's contentious claims for innate differences in IQ advanced in *The Bell Curve* (discussed below) and then discrediting them by stigmatizing the author (and the journal) by means of anonymous "critics" rather than refuting the argument.

Accordingly, in Part III of this study, where the major topics of political correctness are discussed, placing is deliberately avoided. Quotations are given without attribution, leaving readers to make their own assessment of the author's position in the political spectrum. This methodology reveals some surprising alignments, showing that authors do not always fit into their allotted or assumed "place."

Emotive and neutral vocabulary

The use of emotive or loaded vocabulary is a regrettable feature of most controversy. A notable instance concerned Herrnstein and Murray's study *The Bell Curve: Intelligence and Class Structure in American Life* (1994), which put forward its disturbing thesis of race differences in intelligence scores in simple value-free vocabulary: "Despite the forbidding air that envelops the topic, ethnic differences are neither surprising nor in doubt. . . . East Asians . . . , whether in America or in Asia, typically earn higher scores on intelligence and achievement tests than white Americans." "The average white person tests higher than about 84 per cent of black." "The average black and white differ in IQ at every level of socio-economic status (SES), but they differ more at high levels of SES than at low levels" (p. 269). "In the world of college admissions, Asians are a conspicuously unprotected minority" (p. 447).

Two notable responses to *The Bell Curve* in the ensuing controversy were bluntly titled *Measured Lies* (1996) and *Inequality by Design* (1996). Emeritus Professor Arthur Jensen, who had received death threats for his earlier article "How Much Can We Boost IQ and Scholastic Achievement?" (1969), stressed these excesses in responses to *The Bell Curve*: "Consideration of the book's actual content is being displaced by the rhetoric of denial: name-calling ("neo-nazi," "pseudo-scientific," "racism"), red herrings ("Hitler misused genetics"), falsehoods ("all the tests are biased"), hyperbole ("throwing gasoline on the fire"), and insults ("creepy," "indecent," "ugly") (*National Review*, December 5, 1994).

Dinesh D'Souza gave his controversial commentary on American higher education the ironic title *Illiberal Education* (1992), naming his chapters contentiously "The Victim's Revolution on Campus," "More Equal than Others," "The Last Shall be First," "In Search of Black Pharaohs," "The New Censorship," and "The Tyranny of the Minority." This provoked an extreme case of "placing," accompanied by *ad hominem* denigration: "D'Souza arrived in this country from India in 1978, and he has spent the past thirteen years moving steadily up the national conservative food chain" (Berubé, 1992, p. 139). The implication is clearly that D'Souza is an outsider, a predator, and therefore somehow illegitimate. One imagines that if his views were left of center he would be acceptable to his critics. Most attacks did not assess the quality of D'Souza's arguments, nor even engage with them, but emphasized his high earnings, his red Jaguar, his up-market address, and so on.

When some scholars attempted to institute a chapter of the conservative National Association of Scholars at Duke, Professor Stanley Fish characterized the NAS as "widely known to be racist, sexist, and homophobic." This description comes from Jerry Adler's article in *Newsweek*, which continues: "That, notes one of the proponents, is like calling someone a Communist in the McCarthy era" (Adler et al., 1990).

The obverse tactic, the avoidance of emotive or loaded vocabulary, is typical of politically correct language. Perhaps the most effective mode is the use of apparently neutral terms, such as *proactive, constructive, engagement,* and *equity.* (This is one of several points illustrated further in chapter 4, "The Evolution of the Word Field.") In this semantic area the currency of one common element, *non-* , originally dating from the fourteenth century, has expanded extraordinarily. The religious and political movements of the seventeenth and eighteenth centuries generated many forms, such as *nonconformist* (1619) and *non-juror* (1691). These were followed by such political categories as *non-combatant* (1811), *non-aggression* (1903), *non-racial* (1909), *non-violence* (1920), *non-white* (US, 1921), *non-black* (1926), *non-U* (1954), *non-aligned* (1960) and *non-proliferation* (1965). Thurber coined the ironic term *non-ism* in 1961 to refer to the practice of prefacing words with *non-*. It is increasingly used in an opaque fashion in the US in matters of race or religion: thus *WASP* is defined in Chapman (1986) as "A person of nonminority or nonethnic background, ancestry etc, as conceived in the United States." The *British Medical Journal* quoted *non-heart beating donor* as a euphemism for *corpse* (cited in Holder, 1995). The whole debate over abortion in the US has avoided the central inflammatory term, using the alternatives *choice* and *life.* The exchanges were, nevertheless, fulsome: "What hypocrisy to call such anti-humanitarian people 'pro-life.' Call them what they are – antichoice." (*Ms*, October 8, 1978). "The legal battles . . . have virtually all been decided in favor of pro-choice" (*Ms*, September 3, 1975). From the same period came *pro-lifer* (1976).

The Canon and Multiculturalism

Paul Berman, in the Introduction to *Debating PC*, compared the debate to the Battle of Waterloo as described by Stendhal in *The Charterhouse of*

Parma: a murky fog and the din of battle obscured the maneuvers and even the identity of the participants, making the conflict difficult to analyze. A similar metaphor borrowed from Tennyson's "The Charge of the Light Brigade" provided the witty title of Lisa Jardine's (1994) essay, "Canon to Left of them, Canon to Right of them," and *Loose Canons* by Henry Louis Gates, Jr (1992a). Jonathan Swift's mock-heroic title, *The Battle of the Books* (1704) was resuscitated by James Atlas in 1992. (Swift's original envisaged a struggle between the ancient and the modern authors for supremacy, then conceived as pride of place on Mount Olympus.)

In chapter 1 we considered the "battle of the books" from the point of view of censorship and what, according to some, should *not* be read. Now we turn to the issue of what a person *should* read to be "well read." *Canon* became and continues to be the key term in the debate. This ancient word deriving from Latin originally meant "a rule," and for centuries its meaning and application were not open to dispute. It was an early borrowing into Anglo-Saxon in various ecclesiastical senses. From "the canon," meaning the body of canon (i.e., ecclesiastical) law, it acquired the extended sense of the accredited books of the Bible, a meaning that was subsequently applied to the Shakespeare canon from 1922. (Interestingly, the term *apocrypha* was applied both to his plays and to biblical texts not considered genuine.)

The idea of the literary canon was essentially élitist, a concretization of Matthew Arnold's definition of "Culture, the acquainting ourselves with the best that has been known and said in the world" (from the Preface to the 1873 edition of *Literature and Dogma*). In Britain F. R. Leavis, very much a disciple of Arnold, stressed the relationship between the sensibility nourished by a literary culture and the quality of a society as a whole. His major work, *The Great Tradition* (1948), embodied such exclusivity. This notion was subsequently to take the transatlantic forms of the Great Books Program at Columbia and the University of Chicago, also being assumed in the contents of the Modern Library. Vladimir Nabokov famously gave a series of lectures at Cornell under the title of "Masterpieces of Western Literature." These became established, somewhat like the Seven Wonders of the World, by tradition and assumption.

However, what really brought the term into general focus was the public controversy generated by Stanford's decision to drop its required canonical course in Western culture called Western Civ., essentially a "great books" curriculum, and replace it with a multiculturalist course termed CIV (Culture, Ideas, and Values). The new requirement stipulated the inclusion of courses that would "confront issues relating to class, ethnicity, race, religion, gender, and sexual orientation" (Atlas 1992, p. 35). After a long and acrimonious series of debates, during which the campus had been transformed into a virtual war zone, a sparsely attended meeting of the Stanford Faculty Senate voted by 39 to 4 for the change on March 31, 1988. The Secretary for Education, William Bennett, condemned this as "a political, not an educational decision," a problematic assertion, given his own political status. However, more disturbing was his judgment that "a great university was brought low by the very forces which modern universities came into being to oppose: ignorance, irrationality, and intimidation" (Atlas 1992, p. 34). From then on "canon" was seen as antithetical to "multicultural."

Significantly, no similar debate or public engagement occurred in Britain. There the issues were the demographics of who should go to university (more especially what school system they should be from), who should pay, and the utility of research. Rightly or wrongly, what is taught at universities is left to the institutions themselves. Thus *canon* is not a familiar term, except among Shakespearean and biblical scholars. Revealingly, the first *OED* citation of *canon* being used of a body of literary works is dated 1929 in relation to American literature, but generally the word had little currency prior to the contentious uses starting from the late 1980s in the debate over issues of race, gender, authorship, readership, and the politics of literature.

The essentially élitist and hierarchical notion of the canon was questioned and set in opposition to the concept and the terms *multicultural, multiculturalism*, and the familiarizing abbreviation *multiculti*, advocating the widening of the canon by the equalization of texts. This last aspect was satirized by the *Wall Street Journal* as "From Western lit to Westerns as lit" (quoted in Atlas 1992, p. 48). Henry Louis Gates, Jr. asked the pertinent question "Whose Canon is it, Anyway?" in his broadside in the *New York Times Book Review* (February 26, 1989). John Searle referred more broadly to "the canon of traditional western culture," defined as existing "from say, Socrates to Wittgenstein in philosophy and from Homer to James Joyce in literature" (1990, p. 34). Some might argue that this combination of ancient Greek foundations, modern Anglo-Saxon philosophy, and modernist Irish fiction had some claims to be "multicultural," a point to be taken up by Harold Bloom, discussed below. In her Presidential Address to the MLA in 1990 Catharine R. Stimpson confessed: "I am baffled why we cannot be students of Western culture and multiculturalism at the same time" (Stimpson, 1992, p. 45).

Not everybody was so accommodating. "Who is the Tolstoy of the Zulus?" asked Saul Bellow provocatively, adding "[and] The Proust of the Papuans?" (Atlas, 1992, p. 111). This fundamental question was never adequately answered, but was often resurrected as being quintessentially politically incorrect. The opening chapter of Roger Kimball's *Tenured Radicals* (1990) took as its combative theme "The Assault on the Canon," while Dinesh D'Souza's *Illiberal Education* (1992) had an extensive chapter on "Multiculturalism at Stanford," opening with students chanting "Western Culture's got to go." The *New York Review of Books* commented subsequently that "The canon was under attack from feminists and social historians who saw it as the preserve of male and bourgeois dominance" (November 4, 1999). Roger Scruton observed wryly in a lecture at Boston University in December 1992: "The radical curriculum is not so much a *reformed* curriculum as an anti-curriculum" (quoted in Kimball, 1990, p. xiv). Surveying some academic offerings at the MLA in Chicago in 1990, Kimball saw, not an opening up of perspectives, but limitation: "The effect is not to make one more politically 'sensitive', but to transform a concern with literature into an obsession with one's race, one's sex, one's sexual preferences, one's ethnic origin" (Kimball, 1992, p. 74). "Deculturation prefigures disintegration" was the dire prediction of James Atlas (1992, p. 117).

It was not long before agendas of race, class, and gender surfaced. Tactical definitions also abounded: "Multiculturalism is not a tourist's eye view of 'ethnicity,' nor is it a paean to the American mythology defining this nation as a collection of diverse and plural groups living happily together and united by their knowledge of and proper respect for something called 'Western culture'" (Gordon and Lubiano, 1992, p. 249). A variation was the tactical accusation: "The traditional curriculum teaches all of us to see the world through the eyes of privileged, white, European males and to adopt their perspectives as our own. It calls books by middle-class, white, male writers 'literature' and honors them as timeless and universal, while treating the literature produced by everyone else as idiosyncratic and transitory" (Rothenberg, 1992, p. 265).

A more inflammatory semantic intervention in the debate was the unfamiliar coded acronym *DWEM* (a derogatory categorization for "Dead White European Males") to stigmatize culture deriving from such an exclusive racial and gender base. Used from about 1990, the term showed precisely the kind of abusive racist and sexist bias supposedly taboo in politically correct language. Although the form is now largely passé, it reveals the double standard which characterized the debate.

In *The Western Canon* (1994) Harold Bloom threw down the gauntlet, attacking the foundations and the arguments of those who sought to announce the demise of the Canon, a term he consistently and defiantly capitalized:

> The death of the author, proclaimed by Foucault, Barthes, and many clones after them, is another anticanonical myth, similar to the battle cry of resentment that would dismiss all of the dead, white European males – that is to say, for a baker's dozen, Homer, Virgil, Dante, Chaucer, Shakespeare, Cervantes, Montaigne, Milton, Goethe, Tolstoy, Ibsen, Kafka, and Proust. (Bloom, 1994, p. 37)

Dismissing the anonymous coiners and perpetuators of the racist acronym DWEM, Bloom continued: "Livelier than you are, whoever you are, these authors were indubitably male, and I suppose 'white.' But they are not dead, compared to any living author whomsoever" (1994, p. 37). Some would see a certain irony surrounding Virginia Woolf, the one woman (albeit white) included in Bloom's complete Canon. When Woolf died her status as an author was problematic. However, having been championed by feminists, especially for *A Room of One's Own* and *Orlando*, she became posthumously a classic author. Bloom reached his "Elegiac Conclusion": "Finding myself surrounded by professors of hip-hop; by clones of Gallic-Germanic theory; by ideologues of gender and of various sexual persuasions; by multiculturists unlimited, I realize that the Balkanization of literary studies is irreversible" (1994, p. 483).

In his *Orientalism*, originally published 1978, and especially in the Afterword of 1995, Edward Said argued strongly against essentialism (Frenchness, Englishness etc.) claiming that "cultures are hybrid and heterogeneous," continuing:

> How can one speak today of "Western civilization" except in large measure as an ideological fiction, implying a sort of detached superiority for a handful of values and ideas, none of which has much meaning outside the history of conquest, immigration, travel and the mingling of peoples that gave the western nations their present mixed identities? This is especially true of the United States, which today can only be described as an enormous palimpsest of different races and cultures . . . (Said, 1995, pp. 348–9)

On that persuasive argument, a multiculturalist approach seems the natural option.

With proposals for broadening the curriculum, *multicultural* and especially *multiculturalism* became major terms of debate. The earliest uses of the first term are difficult to trace, but seem to lie in an *OED* quotation dated 1941 referring to "a 'multicultural' way of life." *Multiculturalism* surfaces in 1957, first used in a descriptive fashion, but a quotation from 1988 indicates controversy: "Professor Blainey's claim that multiculturalism is another name for ethnic discrimination . . ." (*Brisbane Courier Mail*,

June 14). Similarly: "It's time to get serious about protecting the culture of our nation from liberal socialists and multiculturalists" (*Denver Post*, 1995, cited in *OED*). The abbreviation *multiculti* became part of US slang from 1989, being memorably used by Robert Hughes in his lecture "Multi-Culti and Its Discontents." Hughes set out by commenting that "*multiculturalism* has become a buzzword with almost as many meanings as there are mouths to utter it" (*Culture of Complaint*, 1993, p. 83). Barbara Ehrenreich commented on the currency given to the term by *Newsweek* and others: "I believe most readers had never heard of it until they read it in the magazines" (Ehrenreich, 1992, p. 334).

In the context of the multiculturalism debate the term *particularism* had a brief innings. Diane Ravitch made the distinction between "pluralistic multiculturalism" (which is inclusive) and "particularistic multiculturalism" (which is exclusive). Explaining that "Particularists reject any accommodation among groups," she commented acerbically: "Particularism is a bad idea whose time has come" (Ravitch, 1992, p. 280).

Diversity, another key term in the vocabulary of pluralism, previously had a traditional descriptive sense, meaning simply "difference" or "variety." However, during the multiculturalism debate *diversity* came to be used as a goal or a "good" to be aspired to, or even assumed as a norm. The comments by Dinesh D'Souza are significant here:

> The monolithic ideological focus of the so-called "studies" programs seems to have produced a relentless, even fanatical, conformity of thought in which "diversity" loses its procedural meaning and assumes substantive content. In other words "diversity" does not refer to a range of views on a disputed question, but rather entails enlisting a regiment of ideological causes which are identified as being "for diversity." (D'Souza 1991, p. 214)

The new sense is shown in this quotation from the *Guardian*: "Government is failing to create a diverse judiciary" (January 18, 2008).

Diversity has largely supplanted the older term *pluralism* which, somewhat like *canon*, has a rich semantic history, including ecclesiastical, philosophical, political, and scientific senses, prior to the prime current meaning of toleration of diversity of ethnic or cultural groups. "Cultural Pluralism is a controversial expression," observed Horace Kallen in *Cultural Pluralism and the American Idea* in 1956 (p. 46). *Alternative* has traditionally denoted "one of two," but from 1967 started to be used in the categories of the *alternative society* and the *alternative press*. *Alternative* (as a freestanding form) is recorded from 1970 as "applied to lifestyle, culture etc., regarded by its adherents as preferable because it is less conventional, materialistic and institutionalized." *Alternative medicine*, although actually older in practice, is recorded from 1983 in the *British Medical Journal*.

Eurocentric was originally (from c. 1963) a descriptive term used in the field of global political strategy, but was co-opted into the multicultural-ism debate as a value-laden term to stigmatize traditional emphases on European culture at the expense of others. Thus Molefi Kete Asante used the phrase "Eurocentric hegemony" four times in his 12-page reply to Diane Ravitch in "Multiculturalism: An Exchange" (Asante, 1992). The counter-coinage was *Afrocentric*, also dated earlier, from about 1967, but this term has always been used to imply a legitimate cultural focus. Asante, the author of three books on the subject, insisted in this exchange that "Afrocentricity is not an ethnocentric view" but commented that "Even Ravitch might be taught the Afrocentric method!" (1992, p. 308).

The Other has steadily lost clarity as it has become an intellectual vogue word. Simone de Beauvoir's seminal use half a century ago was a little mys-tical, but comprehensible: "she [woman] is the incidental, the inessential as opposed to the essential. He [man] is the Subject, he is the Absolute – she is the Other." She continued illuminatingly: "The category of the Other is as primordial as consciousness itself" (1972, p. 16). The *OED* (in an additional entry in March 2005) was even more abstract: "chiefly philo-sophical, frequently with capital initial, that which is the counterpart or converse; in structural or post-structural, critical and psychological thought, . . . that which is not the self or subject, that which lies outside or is excluded from the group with which one identifies oneself. In Lacanian thought the unconscious, the symbolic order." Even Edward Said, whose discussions of the concept were usually illuminating, commented: "The word has acquired a sheen of modishness that has become extremely objectionable" (1992, 175). Nevertheless, as we shall see, the variants *othered* and *othering* developed a currency during the debate.

What was the upshot of the debate? Those who were expecting a meas-ured Platonic dialog were manifestly disappointed. In essence it could be described by the neologism *dissensus*, the absence of unanimous or collec-tive opinion. This in itself is not surprising in academic matters. As Paul Berman claimed: "No three people agree about the meaning of central terms like 'deconstruction,' 'difference,' 'multiculturalism,' or 'poststructuralism' " (1992, p. 6). What was perhaps more disturbing was that the Culture Wars were fought along the lines of the Civil War, with departments often lin-ing up on one side or the other. Over a decade later the vocabulary is little clearer, but *multiculturalism* and *diversity* have certainly established them-selves, whereas *the canon* has become something of an archaism.

Part II
The Semantic Aspect

Chapter 3

Words and Authorities: Dictionaries and Lexicographers

Political correctness can be seen as the establishment of new agendas by the introduction of new terms and the redefinition of established words. We will discuss the evolution of the word field of political correctness in the next chapter, but it is important first to consider briefly the whole issue of words and their definition, whether by dictionaries, authorities, or pressure groups. Reflecting what Jacques Derrida called the "logocentric" emphasis in Western epistemology, the glossary and the dictionary have understandably always had a revered status in definition. This despite the problematic facts that words do not have stable meanings over time, nor do they always have agreed meanings, even in a given speech community at a given time. Despite these vagaries, it is common to encounter the mode of argument which starts with a dictionary definition as if it were an undisputed fact.

There is the basic problem over whether historical definitions should take precedence over current meanings. From Johnson's *Dictionary* (1755) onwards the historical method has been dominant in major dictionaries. By this method meanings are separated chronologically from the earliest to the latest. In the nature of things, the earliest will be closer to the etymological root of the word. By the "argument from etymology" this is often fallaciously assumed to be the "real" meaning. Thus *democracy* is routinely defined etymologically as "government by the people," even though this political notion is greatly watered down into "representative democracy," with additional compromises accommodating corporate power via lobbying and so on. Only in Switzerland are major political and social decisions actually made by the people voting in referenda. The rival claims of historical and current meanings are often juxtaposed in discussions of controversial terms like ethnic slurs, such as *nigger* and *Jew*, aspects covered in Lakoff (2000, p. 89) and Burchfield (1989, pp. 83–108).

Dictionaries tend to be regarded as impersonal authorities, even though earlier works by Dr Johnson and others clearly bore the stamp of their authors' personalities and prejudices. Furthermore, older dictionaries tended to reflect established written usage, preferring what Johnson called "the wells of English undefiled," eschewing words which were "new-fangled" or "low." Today, of course, dictionaries cast their nets wider and deeper, trawling words to vie with each other in being all things, namely "authoritative," "up to date," and "comprehensive," with selling points such as *Collins English Dictionary*'s "Find out what the very latest buzz words mean."

However, there was a vibrant tradition of underground dictionaries which actually preceded what is regarded as the "proper" dictionary. These "canting" dictionaries dated back to Elizabethan times and explicated the thriving underworld slang of gambling, brothels, card-sharping, and confidence tricksters. A surprisingly fruitful source of politically incorrect attitudes is Captain Francis Grose's splendid *Classical Dictionary of the Vulgar Tongue* (1785, 1794). Among various ironic absurdities Grose has *snowball*: "a jeering appellation for a negro"; the euphemism *blue skin*: "a person begotten on a black woman by a white man"; *negroes' heads*: "brown loaves delivered to the ships"; *frosty face*: "one pitted with the small pox," and *porker* for a Jew. More surprising are *horse godmother*: "a large masculine woman" and *riding St George*: "the woman uppermost in the amorous congress, that is, the dragon upon St George." Among national nicknames tinged with xenophobia Grose included *Itchland* for Scotland and *Bogtrotter* for Irishman. Numerous terms referring to the gruesome ritual of public hanging, often with a good measure of schadenfreude, are covered in the section on "Crime and Punishment" in chapter 6. Yet in some ways the prejudices of Johnson and the frank humor of Grose are preferable to the appearance of impartiality given by major works.

The monumental *Oxford English Dictionary* (*OED*; 1884–1928) was the collaboration of James Murray (pre-eminently), Henry Bradley, William Craigie, and C. T. Onions "with the assistance of many scholars and men of science." For decades it was regarded as above serious criticism, although there were omissions and deficiencies. However, in his *Keywords* (1976), Raymond Williams expressed these reservations: ". . . the air of massive impersonality which the *Oxford Dictionary* communicates is not so impersonal, so purely scholarly, or so free of active social and political values as might be supposed from occasional use. Indeed, to work closely in it is at times to get a fascinating insight into what can be called the ideology of its editors" (1976, p. 16). Ania Loomba points out, for example, that the *OED* definition of *colony* is framed from the point of view of the colonizer, not the colonized (2005, p. 1). *Suffragette* is defined as "A female supporter of the cause of women's political enfranchisement, *esp.* one of a violent or 'militant' type."

Aspects of gender and class in lexicography, not much canvassed previously, have surfaced in the discussions of Willinsky (1994) and Mugglestone (2000). In *The Empire of Words*, Willinsky criticized the OED in the words of Jonathon Green, for being overly middle-class, masculinist, chauvinist, imperialist, and insulting to minority groups (1996, p. 373). From their earliest appearance in the sixteenth century up until the latter part of the twentieth century, dictionaries on both sides of the Atlantic were written exclusively by men, mainly bourgeois men. Mugglestone (2005) shows that behind the phalanxes of imperturbable type considerable differences of editorial opinion played themselves out, with very few female voices being consulted. This practice extended up to the *OED Supplement* (1972–86), edited by R. W. Burchfield and an editorial team, half of which were women.

Words and Women

As far back as 1949 the seminal feminist thinker Simone de Beauvoir made this programmatic recommendation: "Language is inherited from a masculine society and contains many male prejudices . . . Women simply have to steal the instrument; they don't have to break it or try *a priori* to make it something totally different. Steal it and use it for their own good" (1972, p. 123). The response came much later in the form of various examples of feminist redefinitions in publications mainly or exclusively written by women. These have expanded from *Oz* (launched in February 1967) and *Spare Rib* (launched in June 1972) to become a new genre, concerned with the redefinition of experience from a woman's and a feminist perspective. Some, such as Jane Mills's *Womanwords: A Vocabulary of Culture and Patriarchal Society* (1989), a recasting of entries in the OED, show rigorous scholarship. Others are more obviously propagandist. Thus Casey Miller and Kate Swift in their *Handbook of Non-Sexist Writing* (1981) claimed some new currencies and meanings. On *fellow* they asserted: "All forms of the word – with the exception of *fellow-man* – can be used sex-inclusively" (p. 98). Similarly, they claim, "*Fathering* has acquired the meaning of 'caring for or looking after someone,' previously ascribed only to *mothering*" (p. 79).

More radically, *A Feminist Dictionary* (1985) by Cheris Kramarae and Paula A. Treichler preferred "a flexible format [that] is a conscious effort to honor the words and arguments of women, to liberate our thinking about what can be said about language, and to guard against lexicographical ownership of words and definitions" (1985, p. 17). But "lexicographical ownership of words," advocated by de Beauvoir, is precisely what the semantic aspect of the debate is all about. Furthermore, they justified their title by saying "we are particularly interested in the words of writers and speakers who have taken a self-conscious stand in opposition to male definition, defamation, and ignorance of women and their lives" (1985, p. 12). Their work carried the following definitions of *brother*: "A male who has a close relationship with another. A term which is not a symbol of universal human kinship, when it ignores generations of sisters." By contrast *sister* is defined as "A term of affiliation used among girls and women." On *Love Potions*: "The celebrated love potions of ancient texts may actually have been poisons: women's last defense against patriarchal power." On *Love Story*: "The story of the pre-marital struggle." *Labia* is defined as "Four lips protecting the inner sanctum of the female genitals."

As Jonathon Green observed in his historical survey of lexicographers: "Headwords are very much drawn from an alternative lexicon; definitions are consciously oppositional to what is dismissed as the 'male' norm . . . They want quite specifically to produce something that is not the traditional 'dick-tionary'" (1996, p. 377). More to the point, their tactical definitions clearly did not and still do not reflect current general usage, being more in the realm of semantic engineering based on ideological wish fulfillment than fact, designed as consciousness-raising strategies rather than descriptions. By this semantic strategy it is claimed that *fellow* and *fathering* are not male-specific. This is not so. However, in American usage at any rate, and without any obvious manipulation, two other established male terms have come into play: *guy* has come to be used sex-inclusively, as has *parenting*, coined about 1959.

Miller and Swift went further in their programmatic suggestions, quoting with approval the neologisms proposed by the US Department of Labor, such as *charworker* for *charwoman*, *fisher* for *fisherman*, *sewer* for *seamstress*, and so on. *The New Fowler's Modern English* quoted Brigid Brophy's review of "M & S (as she called them)," castigating their "leaden literalness of mind . . . their tin ear and insensibility to the metaphorical contents of language" (Burchfield 1996, p. 705).

Nonstandard coinages like *wimmin*, *herstory*, and *physically challenged* were intended to draw attention to a particular issue, but have tended to provoke derisive hostility. However, in the case of *wimmin* it is important to place this seemingly modern coinage in historical context, since it is preceded by many folk etymologies playing on the supposed semantic link between *woman* and *woe*. The *OED* notes that usages "in the 16th and 17th centuries frequently play on a pseudo-etymological association with *woe*." Even the noted humanist Sir Thomas More could pun rather ponderously in 1534: "Man himselfe borne of a woman, is in deede a wo man, that is ful of wo and miserie." John Ruskin preferred another pseudo-etymology, since he "found pleasure in reminding the married women in his audience, that since *wife* means 'she who weaves', their place was in the home" (Potter, 1961, p. 106). (Skeat's 1882 *Etymological Dictionary* was emphatic in its contradiction: "certainly not allied to weave"). Jane Mills's *Womanwords* (1991) quotes a number of similar prejudicial instances.

Citations for *wimmin* in the *OED* are as follows:

1979: "We have spelt it this way because we are not wo*men* neither are we fe*male* . . . ," quoted in Kramarae and Treichler (1985).

1981: Used in association with the Greenham Wimmin who protested at the American Air Force base at Greenham Common in Berkshire, England.

1982: "The War Against Wimmin," *Literary Review* April 1992, parodying Marilyn French's *The War Against Women*, reviewed in that issue.

The *OED* entry reveals both the successes and the dangers of publicity in four quotations from a few weeks in the year 1983: *Observer* March 13 on the Greenham Common women: "We want to spell women in a way that does not spell men"; *Sunday Times* April 10: "the eccentric re-spelling of words like 'wimmin'"; *Listener* April 14: "Meanwhile, what of the Peace Women ('wimmin' in feminist placards)?"; *Private Eye* April 22: start of a satirical column headed *Wimmin*.

These feminist interventions showed two features which were to become common in the political correctness debate. The first was the assumption that meanings could be commandeered by pressure groups, and that verbal substitutions could be prescribed. Since historically the general trend of lexicography has been away from prescription (ruling what words are acceptable and what they should mean) in the direction of description (reflecting actual usage) this initiative is anachronistic and regressive. We shall see the process at work in the section on "Gender and Sexual Orientation" in chapter 6. The second feature was the generally dogmatic attitude and acrimonious tone of the debate, in many ways a reflection of the hostility aroused by attempts at linguistic manipulation. "Reviewing the *Random House Webster's College Dictionary* (1991), *Time* magazine (June 24, 1991) assailed its editors for their inclusion of such words as *chairperson, herstory, humankind,* and *womyn,* suggesting "that such catholicity failed to 'protect English from the mindless assaults of the trendy'" (Green, 1996, p. 371). *Collins English Dictionary* (2003) includes *chairperson, herstory,* and *humankind.* Dinesh D'Souza has some comments on feminist manipulation of vocabulary in university courses (1991, p. 212).

Usage Markers

Although English dictionaries have been compiled for some four hundred years, it was only from the eighteenth century that they started to discriminate between levels of usage. Dr Johnson, in the magisterial Preface to his great work (1755) clearly saw himself as a linguistic Newton come to impose order on unruly philology: "Every language has its improprieties and absurdities, which it is the duty of the lexicographer to correct or proscribe." His notion of "improprieties" was twofold: the perpetually flourishing but generally unstable slang of the criminal underworld (such as *fence* and *beak*, which he simply excluded) and in-group fashionable exaggeration, such as *frightful, horrid,* and *monstrous.* These usages (which are still with us) he marked as "ludicrous," "cant," or "low."

The original *Oxford English Dictionary* (1884–1928) attempted to be genuinely comprehensive, but drew the line at *fuck* and *cunt.* It objected strenuously to *bloody,* commenting: ". . . now constantly in the mouths of the lowest classes, but by respectable people considered 'a horrid word' on a par with obscene or profane language. . . ." But it had no markers for *hottentot, coon, wog,* and *Jew* used in various insulting ways, although *nigger* was marked "colloquial and usually contemptuous." When the four-volume *Supplement* edited by R. W. Burchfield was issued (1972–86), all these words were given historical notes explaining their prejudicial uses.

The publication of *Webster III* (*Webster's New International Dictionary*) in 1961 generated a lexicographical controversy of unique ferocity, mainly deriving from the perception that the dictionary had kowtowed to the current "permissive school" of descriptive linguistics, thereby abandoning its assumed role of arbiter and authority in usage. The burning issues were not political or sexual, but grammatical, the entry on *ain't* provoking some notably vehement and revealing tirades. Some four years later usage markers concerning religious and ethnic entries were criticized by Philip Perlmutter in an article, "Prejudice Memorialized" (*Frontier* Magazine, 1965). He noted that entries for *dago, kike, nigger, sheeny, spick,* and *coon* had the bland usage note "usually taken to be offensive." He argued, rightly, that this "strange explanation" suggested that the words themselves were essentially neutral and "free of any offending characteristics."

Despite its significant content, Perlmutter's article did not generate much controversy, but 30 years later Lakoff noted that the entry for *nigger* in the 10th edition of *Merriam-Webster's Collegiate* dictionary (1997) "has roused the ire of the African-American community because it does not state immediately that the word is offensive" (2000, p. 39). Lakoff's discussion of the point is valuable and illuminating, starting with "public disagreement . . . for instance, over who determines what constitutes a 'slur'," and quoting a director of the NAACP objecting to the definition of *nigger*. Lakoff comments, somewhat surprisingly: "the idea that *anyone* – let alone members of historically unempowered groups – can take issue with a dictionary, its makers or definitions, is shocking. But Mr Bryant's argument is reactionary rather than revolutionary. . . ." The point, she concludes, is that "True revolutionaries would reject the authority of the dictionary to define them altogether" (2000, p. 40).

The *Dictionary of South African English on Historical Principles* (ed. P. Silva et al., 1996) felt obliged to distance itself from the more contentious semantic evidence of apartheid, notably the use of *Bantu*, discussed in chapter 5. By contrast, *The Australian National Dictionary* (ed. W. S. Ramson, 1988) is a curious anomaly, dispensing with the modern practice of usage markers. Arguing that "Australian English allows easy movement between formal and informal usage" the Introduction continues: "Labels like *coarse, colloq., derog., slang, and vulgar*, which tend unnecessarily to categorize, have therefore been omitted." This ruling is followed by a slightly nervous disclaimer: "Inclusion of words that many will find offensive does not mean that the editors endorse the sentiments they frequently express" (p. vii). This policy makes the dictionary unique in modern times, when usage "warnings" are now *de rigueur* in areas of sex, obscenity, blasphemy, and especially racist slurs. Furthermore, the work simply omits racist epithets like *slant, slit-eyes, opium-smoker,* and *paddy*.

Taking a universally insulting word like *nigger* as a test case in terms of dictionary policy, the first authority to stress its offensiveness, noting that it was "hated, abhorred, bitterly resented" was H. L. Mencken in 1945, well after the original *OED* termed it "colloquial" and *Webster II* (1934) commented that it "was often used familiarly; now chiefly contemptuously." Slightly bromidic formulas like "usually taken to be offensive," used by *Webster III* (1961) then followed, and are still found. However, the *Webster Collegiate* mentioned above did add at the end of the definition: "It now ranks as perhaps the most offensive and inflammatory slur in English." The word is basically taboo, except in special situations of irony and reclamation.

Dictionary Omissions and Assessments of Currency

Omissions can be unintentional, covert, deliberate, or advertised. Dr Johnson was generally hostile to the currently fashionable influxes of French words and to English slang, said so in his Preface, and either omitted or curtailed their entries. The *OED* included a huge range of slang, profanity, and ethnic slurs, but famously though silently omitted *fuck*, *cunt*, and *condom*, although they had appeared in other dictionaries. The files at the *OED* give a clear sense of the pressure on Murray to omit *condom*, but surprising support for *cunt*. Less commented on was the surprising omission of *African*, a sixteenth-century word, which was included in the first *Supplement* (1933), when it was joined by *Africanism* (1641), *Africanize* (1841), *Africanoid* (1899), and *Afro-* (1890). Some would argue that these omissions reveal a Eurocentric emphasis; others might claim that such an oversight is understandable at the beginning of the huge enterprise, when the progress through what Dr Johnson called "the treadmill of the alphabet" was painfully slow.

The policy of advertised omission was termed *Guralnikism*, the coinage of R. W. Burchfield in 1973, alluding to Dr David B. Guralnik, Editor in Chief of *Webster's New World Dictionary*, Second College Edition (1970). He justified in the Preface the exclusion of such words as *dago*, *kike*, *wog*, and *wop* on the following grounds: "It was decided in the selection process that this dictionary could easily dispense with those true obscenities, the terms for racial and ethnic opprobrium, that are, in any case encountered with diminishing frequency these days." This was another harbinger of political correctness. Burchfield commented: "I want to stress the importance of rejecting Guralnikism, the racial equivalent of Bowdlerism, as a solution as far as historical and 'unabridged' dictionaries are concerned" (1989, p. 100). (Dr Thomas Bowdler famously announced in the Preface to the 1806 *Family Shakespeare* that "those words and expressions are omitted which cannot with propriety be read aloud in a family.") This policy of verbal sanitization is continued in the *Oxford American Dictionary* (1999) and even the *Chambers Dictionary of Etymology* (1988), previously the *Barnhart Dictionary of Etymology*. These are revealing instances of the influence of social change upon the lexical status of particular words and of the changing notion of "obscenity" from sexual to racial matters.

Dictionaries have generally commented only on the rarity of words, not their popularity, except when there is editorial disapproval, as in the *OED*'s comment on *bloody*, quoted above. In recent years it has become common for dictionaries to comment on offensive or taboo words, such as *cripple* or *spastic*. With the advent of computerized data it has become possible to devise a *corpus* or *corpora*, showing the relative frequency of words based on actual usage. Dictionaries initiated and started to incorporate the findings of corpora over the last three decades. The British National

Corpus (BNC) contains 100 million words. American usage can be derived from a subset of 140 million words of the American English Cambridge International Corpus (CCAE) including various kinds of written English and transcriptions of spoken discourse. The Oxford Corpus of 2006, a third generation corpus, contains more than two billion words. The Collins dictionary series is based on COBUILD, a collaboration between Harper Collins and the University of Birmingham initiated in 1980, while the *Longmans Dictionary of Contemporary English* (1995) reflects data from the British National Corpus. This work establishes the relative frequency of the 3,000 most common words in both spoken and written English, rating them on a scale of 1 to 3. Thus *bloody* is rated S3 and W3, meaning that it is in the top 3,000 words, both written and spoken. In the same field, *fuck* is rated S3, that is, in the top 3,000 spoken words, while *ass*, *bugger*, and *shit* are rated S2. The use of corpora is valuable in assessing whether notional taboos against obscenities, ethnic slurs, and terms for disability are sustained in actual usage. In constructing a corpus there is always a problem of using the range of evidence in a discriminating and balanced way. Thus a search for *nigger* in the British National Corpus yielded 50 cases, 17 of which are from a novel in which Nigger is the name of a character and two from schoolgirl essays on *To Kill a Mockingbird*.

Political Correctness and Traditional Registers

Register is typically conceived on a hierarchical scale, ranging from high to low, or from formal to slang. In his magisterial Preface to the original *OED* in 1884, Sir James Murray set out in a single illuminating diagram a configuration representing the diversity of registers. It took the form of a circle with the "common" words in the center and a vertical axis depicting the traditional hierarchical arrangement of registers with the categories of "Literary," "Common," "Colloquial," and "Slang" arranged in descending order:

LITERARY
COMMON
COLLOQUIAL
SLANG

Today, of course, "Literary" is no longer a discrete category confined to the upper register, and lexicographers are not so concerned with distinguishing between "Common," "Colloquial," and "Slang." A more viable modern arrangement would be:

FORMAL
COMMON
SLANG
TABOO

("Taboo" was not a category included by Murray; nor was "obscene," since in his times obscenities were literally unprintable, even in dictionaries.) If we apply these registers to particular human categories prior to the coming of political correctness, we find the following configuration:

	"prostitute"	"cripple"	"deaf"	"spastic"
Formal:	prostitute	cripple	deaf	palsied
Common:	whore	cripple	deaf	spastic
Slang:	hooker	basket case	Mutt and Jeff	spaz
Taboo:	- - - - -	- - - - -	- - - - -	- - - - -

This was the traditional situation which obtained broadly up to the 1980s. In other words, there were no taboo words for these categories, although obviously *whore* was so emotionally charged as to be avoided in polite company. Thus George Bernard Shaw's controversial play *Mrs Warren's Profession* (1892) was centered on the issue of prostitution, but avoided the embarrassing vocabulary.

Slang is often resorted to, and perhaps even generated, when particular lexical areas become "impolite" or taboo. In this category, *basket case* is in origin a military term, and is described further under "Disability" in chapter 6, as is *spastic*. Rhyming slang is a useful disguise mechanism, here generating *Mutt and Jeff* for "deaf." Similarly, *raspberry* (= *raspberry ripple*) is rhyming slang for "cripple." The older use of *raspberry* in rhyming slang was *raspberry tart* (= *fart*). Jonathon Green's *Slang Thesaurus* (1999) includes *spastic* in the sense of "convulsed with laughter," while Tony Thorne's *Dictionary of Contemporary Slang* (3rd edn, 2007) lists various juvenile uses.

As we saw in Part I, the introduction of new terms into a semantic field has the effect of disturbing the existing configuration. The arrival of political correctness has had the dual effect of introducing a double standard in the category of "Formal" and redesignating common words as the new taboo terms:

	"prostitute"	"cripple"	"deaf"	"spastic"
Formal PC:	sex worker	differently abled	hearing impaired	cerebral palsy
Common:	whore	cripple	deaf	spastic
Slang:	hooker	basket case	Mutt and Jeff	spaz
Taboo:	whore	cripple	deaf	spastic

Official and Unofficial Language

Official language takes many forms, legal, administrative, and scientific. Political language is more problematic, being partly natural, containing terms like *government, power,* and *franchise* with accepted traditional denotations, and partly contrived, as in the labels *socialist, conservative, liberal,* and *democratic.* It also contains catch phrases such as "the will of the people," "the public interest," and "public opinion," all of which fall under the category well described by W. B. Gallie as "essentially contested concepts" (1964, p. 157).

Ideological vocabulary can similarly be made up of natural, ordinary words, like *rights, power,* and *society,* or less familiar terms like *alienation* and *exploitation.* Their acceptance generally depends on the register employed. Thus plain Anglo-Saxon *workers* has a strong emotive appeal, exploited in slogans like "Workers of the world, Unite!" More abstract and artificial vocabulary produces a response closer to indifference. Thus the Communist uses of *proletariate* and *bourgeoisie* as class terms have never become generally accepted in English. This could, of course, reflect the general lack of impact and appeal of Communism in Britain. The use of the satirical abbreviation *prole* is largely owing to George Orwell, who wrote of "The dumb masses whom we habitually refer to as 'the proles', numbering perhaps 85 per cent of the population" (Orwell, 1972, p. 167). Among the more philologically aware, *proletariate* is recognized as an unfortunate word, since its basic sense, deriving from Latin *proles,* is "having a lot of children."

Unofficial language is often ironic, derisive, parodic, and even subversive. Thus just one year after the Year of the Revolutions (1848), Ebenezer Elliott produced his wry little rhyme: "What is a communist? One that has yearnings / For equal division of unequal earnings." The early nickname *red* rapidly caught on, subsequently generating the McCarthyite "red scare," "reds under the bed," and the nuclear disarmament slogan "Better Red than Dead." Elsewhere in the spectrum, *pink, green,* and *lavender* have taken on various code senses. These suggest an affiliation or an agenda, sexual or environmental, but are not specific.

Furthermore, official formulas can be extended in a subversive fashion. Thus the earliest reference to *affirmative action* in the *OED* is dated 1935, but the key usage is in a US Govt Executive Order of 1961: "The contractor will take affirmative action to ensure that applicants are employed, and that employees are treated, during employment, without regard to their race, creed, color, or national origin." The modern currency of *affirmative action* has led to *affirmative shopping* as an ironic euphemism for looting, from references to Zaire (now Democratic Republic of the Congo) in the 1990s. Similarly, in South Africa *affirmative* is used as a code word among some whites for a Black person. Perhaps for this reason the original formulas have been superseded by *positive discrimination* and (in the UK) by *positive action*. Incidentally, the formula *equal opportunity employer* arose almost contemporaneously with *affirmative action* in the US in 1963. As with any policy of social engineering in a genuine meritocracy, this has caused great controversy. One semantic marker of opposition was the new sense of *token*: "a nominal or 'token' representative of an underrepresented group" (US, 1968). This was followed a few years later by *tokenism*.

The South African taboo against *Kaffir* has similarly led to the use of the abbreviated *k*, as in *k-sheeting* (coarse striped mattress material) and *k-factor*, referring to built-in precautions against anticipated abuse, as in "This machine has a high k-factor." In her study on insults, Sarah Britten observed: "Once, not so long ago, the K-word was everywhere and the F-word was forbidden. Now the F-word is everywhere and the K-word is forbidden" (2006, p. 42). In certain reactionary circles the code acronym *Viking* is reportedly current for "very important kaffir in government." An older code use is *African time*, recorded from 1963, according to the *Dictionary of South African English* (*DSAE*) and explained simply as "Two-fifteen African time means four o'clock" (schoolgirl informant, Grahamstown). Professor Guy Butler wrote in his biography: "It was the first time I found myself on the receiving end of what is affectionately known as African time" (*Bursting World*, 1983, p. 103). The authority cites one black usage (in the magazine *Tribute*, 1987). This politically incorrect characterization is seldom heard outside private conversation. In the new South Africa *pale* means "white," especially in the rhyming form *pale male*, suggesting an unrepresentative number of white males in an organization. A totally white management is termed *lily white*. These uses are all fairly recent, having emerged in the new political régime which has disposed of the old official population categories of *White* and *Non-White*.

Openly subversive are such ironic slogans as "Save the gerund and screw the whale!" (Tom Stoppard) or cynical definitions, such as this for *African democracy*: "One man, one vote, once." Among its political enemies the

ANC (standing for African National Congress) has been cynically inter-preted as an acronym for Arrogance Nepotism Corruption. In similar circles, the official interpretation of NEPAD is "New Extended Pathway for African Democracy," but the parodic version is "New Extended Permission for African Dictators." These subversive forms are dismissed by the powers that be as merely cynical; for others they sometimes con-tain a grain of disturbing truth.

Buzzwords and Code Words

Buzzwords are essentially a form of jargon, often deriving from specialist or in-group use, then becoming fashionable in general discourse, despite not being entirely understood, since they no longer have a clearly defined meaning. They were first commented on in the 1970s, and seemingly derive from *buzz* in the sense of "excitement." Having been useful terms in a particular context, usually to do with politics or sociology, they become mere vogue words. Typical examples are *community, diversity, alter-native*, and *parameter*. They commonly "have a short life, but a busy one" giving "a spurious sophistication" to an utterance (Green, 1992, p. 41).

Code *words* naturally take some time to develop, often arising in under-ground language, before becoming fashionable as in-group words. Some can be subtle. Thus the bland question "Is Smith sound?" appears to ask if Smith is honest, principled, and reliable. In a British political context this really means "Is Smith reliable, loyal to the party, and does he have the same views and class values as us?" This is a genuine code word, since insiders would understand its real intent, while outsiders would not. A less subtle example runs: "When you see the word 'qualifications' used, remember that this is the new code word for whites" (Michael Harris, Professor of Religious Studies at the University of Tennessee, quoted by D'Souza, 1991, p. 4). Clearly, this is a false code word, since it needs to be translated, and the "translation" is a travesty of an essential term in academic currency.

More obvious in its symbolism is *Oreo*, in origin an American brand name for a chocolate cookie with a white vanilla filling. The *OED* definition runs: "*US Slang (depreciative)*: "In African-American use: an African-American who adopts or identifies with middle-class white culture as opposed to urban African-American culture." However, the earliest quotation is an unexpected reference in 1961 to *Oreo queen*: "a black homo-sexual man who prefers white men as sexual partners." In the late 1960s *Oreo* suddenly emerged in general Black English meaning "a black person who inappropriately adopts white attitudes, fashions, or the like – used derisively" (*Random House Dictionary of American Slang*). This source has an initial quotation from 1968 and four from 1969, all of which explain the symbolism in the text. The first free-standing quotations are from 1972, leading up to the comment in *Village Voice* (1991): "Clarence Thomas . . . is the very model of an Oreo." *Random House* records a similar code use in the US Hispanic speech community of *coconut*: "A Hispanic person who has adopted the values of white American society," with quotations from 1980: "Blacks have their 'oreos'; Hispanos their 'coconuts' and so on."

Interestingly, *coconut* has developed a similar but expanding currency in South Africa, first as a term of derision meaning a "sellout," originally in Coloured politics, where assimilation to whites and difference from them are vigorously contested. In official parlance the term is sufficiently insulting to be categorized as unparliamentary. The political sense has recently been extended to black critics of the government, implying that they are disloyal. But socially it has been widely reclaimed by young urban blacks to satirize those who are materialistic "mall rats" and adopt "correct" English accents.

Both *coconut* and *oreo* are significant, firstly for their ironic code references to color, but also for their underlying political assumption of racial solidarity, more especially that blacks should not break ranks and adopt the mores of middle-class white society. This should be a politically incorrect assumption in a free society, but as is mentioned in chapter 5, it became a factor in initial political reactions to Barack Obama. The whole dynamic which has generated the *oreo/coconut* syndrome works only one way: a black person can be criticized for having white middle-class aspirations and mores, but not the other way around.

Inner city originally described urban development of US cities like Detroit or Los Angeles where the bourgeois moved away from decaying downtown areas to the suburbs. Recorded from 1968 in the *Saturday Review* in a reference to "failure of schools in inner cities," it has increasingly become a code term for "slum" or "ghetto." It is seldom used literally to mean simply "central." Thus to say "They have expensive inner city flats in London, Paris, and New York" would be completely confusing: one would have to substitute "downtown" or "central." Green notes that it is also used to refer to "those who tend to live in these areas, usually coloured immigrant groups" (1992, p. 135). Similar code terms are English *tower block* and French *banlieu*.

Fundamentalism was originally "A religious movement originating in certain Protestant bodies in the US after WWI based on strict adherence to certain tenets (e.g. the literal truth of Scripture) held to be fundamental to the Christian faith" (*OED*). It arose in the contexts of the Northern Baptist Convention (1920), and was much associated with William Jennings Bryan. In 1926 one H. F. Osborn commented: "The fundamentalist movement sought to re-establish the Biblical literalism of the time of Cromwell, Milton, and the Puritans." But *Webster III* (1961) carried the definition of "an extreme conservative," the basic present sense. Applications to other religions such as Islam date from 1957, and the abbreviation *fundie* from 1988.

Hegemony derives from ancient Greek *hegemon*, "leader," especially "leadership or predominant authority of one state in a confederacy of others" (*OED*). It was subsequently used in the Marxist sense denoting the predominance of one social class over another, for example, *bourgeois hegemony*. These senses were basically factual, referring to military dominance or majoritarian politics without moral implication. However, in the political correctness debate in the US it was often used with implication or denotation of racism. Thus Molefi Kete Asante (1992) used the term 14 times in a 12-page article on multiculturalism, referring to what he regards as an illegitimate racist monopoly over educational policy in the US: "white hegemony" (twice), "white hegemonic thinkers," "white hegemonic ideas," "white hegemonic education," "white contextual hegemony," and "white hegemonic studies." In addition "Eurocentric hegemony" is used four times.

Acronyms

Normally acronyms are neutral and useful abbreviations, like NATO or AIDS. However, they can form another category of code term in derogatory acronyms such as WASP and DWEM, both of which use *white* in a stigmatizing way, and leave the potential user with a quandary: either to ignore them or be drawn into a complicit relationship of acceptance of their agenda by using them. WASP ("White Anglo-Saxon Protestant") appears to have been the coinage of E. B. Palmore in the *American Journal of Sociology* in 1962. He was open about the rationale for using the form: "For the sake of brevity we will use the nickname 'Wasp' for this group." It was a shorthand neutral description of what the *OED* defined as "the American white Protestant middle or upper class," even though America technically does not have a class system of the more ingrained English type. In 1965 W. H. Auden archly described the unusual appearance of girls at his Oxford college in the 1930s: "there were three or four who . . . like token Jews in a Wasp community, were accepted by us" ("As It Seemed to Us," *New Yorker*, April 3, 1965).

In a classic instance of the categorizations of political correctness, *WASP* itself was opaquely defined in Chapman (1986) as "A person of non-minority or nonethnic background, ancestry etc, as conceived in the United States." Most recent uses, however, endorse the use of WASP to mean one of an élite: "The Republican Party is run largely by 'wasps'" (Stewart Alsop, cited in Chapman 1986). In tandem, *Anglo-Saxon*, originally a historical term referring to England and its language after the Germanic invasions, was used in the nineteenth century to denote the communality of England and America, but is increasingly used in America to mean simply "white."

DWEM by contrast, does not have a literal or referential meaning, since "Dead White European Male" is obviously too large and generalized a category to be useful. (The term was discussed in chapter 2 concerning "the canon.") The attempt by the *OED* to supply a meaning is amusing in its woodenness and opacity: "A notable male figure in Western cultural history . . . etc." The tautology of *white* and *European* obviously comes about since DWM would be unpronounceable. DWEM is essentially a derogatory code form which by its inflammatory racist and sexist component terms seeks to signal a protest against the traditional emphases of Western culture in university curricula. Like many of the terms in PC vocabulary, DWEM seems to have no coiner. The first print instance (in *Forbes* magazine in October 1990) is clearly from an outsider's point of view: "That [i.e., PC] and DWEM (dead white European male) are, I gather, two of the most common acronyms on campus" (October 1).

All these coded terms, namely *coconut* and *oreo*, *WASP* and *DWEM*, show covert racism. The first two have grown up spontaneously, while the second two are more subtle, being contrived propagandist coinages in a cultural debate that is supposed to avoid racist terms. All thus reveal double standards in differing degrees.

Disguise systems

Whereas code words are comparatively recent, there are older, more developed disguise systems which have grown up in particular communities. The most notable in English is Cockney rhyming slang, recorded back in the eighteenth century and continuing to expand and thrive globally. By this system an offensive term is avoided, being alluded to by means of a rhyming word. The topics cover "bodily functions" and the genitalia, as well as allusions to race and alternative sexual preferences. Thus *four by two* and *kangaroo* are rhyming slang for *Jew*, *Brighton Pier* and *ginger beer* are covert references to *queer* (i.e. homosexual), while *razor blade* and *Lucozade* similarly refer to *spade*, in itself a coded reference to *black as the ace of spades*. Its origins are unexpected: according to the *OED*, *spade* was originally a slang usage "formerly among U.S. Blacks [for] a very dark-skinned Negro." The sense is recorded in the *OED* from 1928, exemplified in C. McKay's *Home to Harlem*: "She was of the complexion known among Negroes as spade or chocolate-to-the-bone." The dictionary's entry includes a number of politically incorrect quotations, such as this from Colin MacInnes's *City of Spades* (1957): "A British lady with a wild love of Spades, and a horrid habit of touching you on the shoulder because, she says, 'to stroke a darkie brings you luck'." An American quotation from 1966 runs "I find a disturbing minority of my English contemporaries . . . pointedly tossing off inconsequential remarks about spades and spooks in my company." More recently, Rosalie Maggio, in *The Bias-Free Word-Finder* (1992) ruled that the phrase "to call a spade a spade" is "associated with a racial slur and is to be avoided."

Various American speech communities use coded references: the terms for blacks include *schwartze* (Yiddish), *blaue* (German), *melanze* (Italian for "aubergine" or "eggplant"), and, among some blacks, the abbreviation *HN* for "house nigger." Not all code abbreviations are to do with race: *phat* is variously interpreted as "pussy, hips, arse, and tits" or "pretty hole at all times." Reflecting an overlap of sexual, racial and political taboos, certain words show double alphabetism. Among them are c-word (*cunt/cancer/colored*), f-word (*fuck/fail*), l-word (*lesbian/liberal*) and n-word (*nigger/nuclear*).

Newspeak

In half a century *Newspeak* has acquired an astonishing currency. Together with *Big Brother*, it is the most enduring of Orwell's coinages from his dystopia *Nineteen Eighty-Four* (1949). In the novel "Newspeak was the official language of Oceania, devised to meet the ideological needs of Insoc or English Socialism." It is an artificial language made up entirely of coinages, including unnatural compounds like *goodfeel* and unidiomatic collocations like *double plus ungood*, such as a computer or a robot might devise. In addition to its ideological function, the purpose of Newspeak was "to make all other modes of thought impossible" (1972, p. 241). Uniquely, the vocabulary diminished annually, narrowing the range of thought, to make "thoughtcrime" an impossibility.

However, as it gained currency, *Newspeak* was used to refer to any contrived political discourse, essentially euphemistic and polysyllabic, official and obfuscatory, classically apparent in the Orwellian formation *pacification.*

It now incorporates coded forms such as *friendly fire* and *collateral damage*. Deborah Cameron asks the question: "If *collateral damage* is a euphemism, what exactly is it a euphemism for?" (1995, pp. 73–4). The question is naïve, since it cannot be answered, precisely because the cynical effectiveness of the euphemism obscures the facts: it is not a standard euphemism like *pass away* for *die*. Being artificial and contaminated, Newspeak has no natural currency in the wider speech community, existing only in ironic and parodic forms such as "The car ran out of control and caused quite a lot of collateral damage." Imagine the scenario continuing in this manner: "Sadly, the injuries sustained by the driver were so severe that she was physically challenged for life, resorting to substance abuse, so that her significant other finally abandoned her." It becomes clear that it is only a short step from Newspeak to the artificial forms of what might be called "PC-speak."

Many of the fashionable buzzwords of political correctness were almost immediately regarded as a form of Newspeak. In Britain Walter Nash preferred an older word for his *Jargon* (1993), including a 100-page Glossary of the new terms with extensive, incisive, witty, and generally ironic commentary, evident in his entry for *political correctness*:

> It means using words and expressions which will (a) display your own social credentials as one who has a sensitive respect for women, or homosexuals, or people of non-European race, or the disabled, or the mentally retarded, or the chronically sick, or the elderly and aged, or the undersized, or the oversized, or vandals or drunks or ram raiders or drug addicts – among others, and (b) not give offence to anyone belonging to any of these groups. (Nash, 1993, p. 178)

Nash had a field day, introducing terms for the current jargons such as *educationese, rockspeak, techspeak, militarese,* and *ecotalk.* Ruthlessly translating the various uses of *challenged,* such as "*aesthetically challenged* (ugly)," he rightly observed that they were "difficult to take in sober earnest." Commenting on the evasiveness of many new euphemisms, he pertinently noted that "*child abuse* too easily and queasily accounts for so many unspeakably abominable acts" (1993, p. 112). Kenneth Minogue observed sardonically that "the written word, treated with reverence in civilized circles, is a mere object of use to the barbarian. For this reason, quite a lot of what is called 'modernization' resembles barbarism" (2005, p. x).

In America Diane Ravitch's penetrating study, *The Language Police* (2003), discussed in chapter 1, applies Orwellian forms of thought control to publishing and teaching practices in the US today. It includes a "Glossary of

Banned Words, Usages, Stereotypes, and Topics." Others regard the newer manifestations with irony. Satirizing the obsessive mind set of extreme "political correctionists" is this comment: "We cannot all be 'career' discrimination experts, of course. But . . . we can all make sure that the subject of discrimination – whether racist, sexist, heightist, weightist, ageist, brainist, beautyist or tokenist – is never absent from our waking thoughts." The source (the *Daily Telegraph*) is not as surprising as the date: November 19, 1975. It shows that satire can anticipate extremism, a point taken up in the sections dealing with humor and satire in chapter 8.

Chapter 4

The Evolution of the Word Field

Introduction

This chapter serves as a bridge between the topics covered in Chapter 3 and those in Part III, "Zones of Controversy." The word field, which consists of some two hundred items arranged chronologically, includes a variety of words and formulas, some used in the debate (*ableism, canon, multiculti*), some associated with it (*animal rights, nimby, shock jock*) and some showing the characteristics of politically correct language (*inappropriately directed laughter, compassion fatigue, significant other*), as well as ironic or intemperate reactions (*feminazi, wigger, waitron, meritscam*). Politically incorrect forms such as *affirmative shopping* appear in italics.

As with many social changes, there is often a question of which came first, the idea or the word, or was the development symbiotic. In the case of political correctness a surprising number of words and formulas anticipated the debate, but were co-opted into it. Certain terms, such as *African-American, homophobia*, and *chauvinist*, do not have continuous histories, having been coined in previous decades or even centuries before resurfacing or being exploited in the modern debate. In such cases the modern date is chosen rather than the original (which is placed in parentheses).

Dates cannot always be absolutely accurate, in the nature of things, especially in the case of words like *gay* and *diversity* which had general meanings for long periods before being politicized. Even the recently publicized senses of *gay* to mean "rubbish" or "lame" can be traced back to the 1980s. While some coinages, such as *ageism* and *heterosexism* can be pinpointed, it usually takes some years for currency to become established. Many of these dates come from dictionaries, which even with the most thorough searches cannot always be up to date.

2007 pink plateau

2004 anti-Hamitism

2003 freedom fries

1999 carbon footprint

1998 ASBO (UK, Anti-Social Behaviour Order)

1995 genetically modified, tree house, othered, othering

1994 dumb down, meritscam, pink (1950), rendition (1649)

1993 *wigger*, GLBT

1992 demographics, ecological footprint, item, trophy wife

1991 crusty (UK, dirty and unkempt young beggar or traveler), ethnic cleansing, jungle fever, queercore (hardcore homosexual), zero emissions

1990 *affirmative shopping*, anorexia (1598), canon (medieval), clause 28, *cockocracy*, disorder (eating), DWEM, Europhobic, *feminazi, happy-clappy*, harassment, -impaired (1946), *nigga* (1925), pale (SA), out (vb.), Queer Nation, S & F, single parent

1989 disadvantaged, eco-friendly, gay bashing, multiculti, ungreen, *wrinklie*

1988 fundie, hate speech, himbo, inappropriately directed laughter, neo-conservative (1883)

1987 Bork (vb), *Brixton briefcase*, fattism, positive discrimination

1986 bioethics, carbon tax, disablist, HIV, passive smoking (1971), personkind, posse, PWA, shock jock, yardie

1985 animalist, -challenged, compassion fatigue, necklace (vb SA, to set a person on fire by means of a petrol-filled tyre), safe sex, *towelhead*

1984 cottage (vb), eco-, glass ceiling, hate crime, move goal posts, unfriendly

1983 AIDS, womanist

1982 -friendly, *ghetto-blaster*, -impaired, sex worker

1981 abled, ableism, ableist, level playing field, sizeist, toy boy

1980 animal companion, *coconut*, gender bender, informal sector (SA), Inuit, nimby, pink, waitron

1979 environmental footprint, heterosexism, neocon, wimmin

1978 animal rights, bulimia (14th c.), choice, feminization, lookism, masculist

1977 boat people, chicken run (first used of whites fleeing the new Zimbabwe, now for whites emigrating from the new South Africa), dissensus, global warming, loony left, phallocratic, significant other (1940), white supremacist (1959)

1976 CFC, *crumblie* (UK, old person), friendly fire, prolifer, psychobabble

1975 collateral damage, phallogocentric, speciesism, substance abuse

1972 blaxploitation, tokenism, cottaging

1971   chairperson (salesperson 1920), Greenpeace, logocentric, Paki-
bashing, heightist
1970   abuse/abused, Green, herstory, marginalized, multicultural, politically correct, *pussy power*, queer bashing, alternative
1969   African-American (1863), ageism, eco-, homophobia (1920), immigrant (1792), MCP, senior citizen (1938)
1968   Black Studies, chauvinism, chauvinist, cellulite, compassion fatigue,
gas guzzling, ghetto, inner city, *oreo*, sisterhood
1967   Afrocentric, alternative, *basket case* (1919), environmental pollution
1966   Black Power, centerfold
1965   Black Panther, cultural revolution, Red Guard
1964   developing
1963   *African time*, Eurocentric, gender, Third World
1962   Black Nationalism, disadvantaged, greenhouse (1937), WASP
1961   affirmative action
1960   Black Muslim, bunny girl, Caucasian (1795)
1959   *jungle bunny*
1958   supremacist, *diesel dyke*
1957   consenting adult, multiculturalism, transsexual
1955   Amerindian
1954   activism
1953   élitist, ethnicity
1951   ethnocentric (1900), minorities (1837)
1949   doublespeak, underdeveloped
1948   apartheid
1947   hegemony

Analysis

Origins

There are very few native (i.e., Anglo-Saxon) terms, in fact less than
10 percent. At first sight this seems astonishing, but on reflection it is to
be expected, since the prime semantic tactic of political correctness is that
of unfamiliarity. (In this respect, see "Degrees of opacity" below.) Some
40 terms in the word field are highlighted by the computer spell-check program. Even standard native terms like *green, greenhouse,* and *tree house*
have developed political meanings, as has the artificial form *ungreen*.
Other original formations made out of ancient words are *dumb down, hate
speech,* and *Third World*. Whereas *man* has been replaced by *person* in

many forms, *woman* appears in the unfamiliar formations *womanist* and *wimmin*. The little word *out* has, of course, recently gained a new and significant force as a verb in sexual politics. But overall, a very high proportion of the field is made up of classical elements, modified in various ways, such as *heterosexism, masculist,* and *supremacist.*

Word formation

The great number of compounds is the most obvious feature. These make up over 40 percent of the field, ranging from *ethnic cleansing, hate crime, towelhead, significant other,* and *single parent* to numerous forms using *eco-, non-, neo-* and *un-* as first elements and *-impaired, -challenged* and *-friendly* as second elements. Less obvious compounds are those made up of classical elements like *bioethical, homophobia,* and *phallocratic.* A comparison with the semantic field of traditional political terms in my study *Words in Time* (1988, p. 190) is revealing. Out of some 75 terms, there was only one compound formula (*civil disobedience,* a coinage attributed to Thoreau). The new forms show a significant shift in idiom.

The use of the suffixes *–ism* and *–ist* now has the effect of politicizing neutral words or introducing agendas: thus *fat > fattist, look > lookism, species > speciesist.* The broad practice is one of long standing, of course, as is shown in the epigraph quotation at the beginning of the book, dated 1680, which contains the forms *Jesuitism, Puritanism* and *Quaqerism* (Quakerism). However, there is a significant difference: these old *–ism* words were essentially stigmatizing labels for splinter groups, sects, and their adherents. In modern usage there has been a notable change from "follower" or "adherent" of particular philosophies or ideologies (as in *Communist* and *imperialist*) to new agendas, criticizing *racism* (1936) and *sexism* (1968). The most recent forms, such as *ageism* (1969), *lookism* (1978), *ableism* (1981), and *fattism* (1987), criticize prejudicial attitudes, but on less obvious moral grounds. Perhaps the last word should be given to a "Professor Leftist . . . but tired of clichés, sloppy thinking, and PC holier-than thou-ism" in an advertisement in *New York Review of Books,* March 27, 1995.

Neologisms

These naturally constitute a high proportion of the word field, some of them no longer very obviously original because they have become familiar. They include most of the words not in common use previously, such as *demographic, disadvantaged,* and *disabled.*

Coinages and respellings

Many of these are covered elsewhere in the text. They include *wimmin*, *herstory*, *Eurocentric*, *Afrocentric*, *Americentric*, and *Europhobic*. Ironic or humorous formations include *blaxploitation*, *blacklash*, *whitelash*, and *wigger*.

Nonce words

These are obviously less numerous and often have an inflammatory quality. The most notable example is *feminazi* coined by Rush Limbaugh in 1990 (*Atlanta Journal and Constitution*). Stanley Fish coined the term *meritscam* to expose what he regarded as a dishonest use of *merit* (1994, p. 11). Others include *Europhobic*, coined by Diane Ravitch, and *neo-Aryan*, coined by Martin Bernal in *Black Athena*, quoted by Asante (1992, p. 301), and *anti-Hamitism*, coined by Christopher Heywood. (It means prejudice against black people.) There is always a problem of whether to include nonce words: thus the opposing categorizations of *sun people* and *ice people* were the coinages of Leonard Jeffries, Jr, but should they be regarded as genuine or spurious formations?

New negative formations

Neo, "denoting some new or modern form of some doctrine, belief or practice," has proved highly productive. The *OED* lists some 100 forms, many of them philosophical and religious. The political terms are generally negative, for example, *neocapitalism* (1968, but no *neocommunism*), *neoconservative* (surprisingly old, dated 1883, but increasingly common from 1960), *neofascist* (1946), *neonazi* (1950), *neocolonialism* (1961), *neoimperialism* (1962), *neo-Marxist* (1974), and *neocon* (1988). *New*, by contrast, has managed to preserve positive overtones, in *New Deal* (1932), *New Age* (1971), *New Man* (1982), *New Negro* (1922) and to some extent, *New Labour* (1992). All of these were preceded by the *New Woman* (1894).

Degrees of opacity

Much politically correct language is in coded form, depending on tacit understandings. We may distinguish four categories, although not all readers will agree with the examples chosen:

1   Meaning relatively transparent: these would include *chairperson*, *disorder*, *-impaired*;

2   Meaning dependent on agenda: *diversity, challenged, developing, tree house, substance abuse*;
3   Meaning dependent on context: *friendly fire, collateral damage, boat people*;
4   Meaning needs to be decoded: *significant other, consenting adult, anti-Hamitism, glass ceiling, cottaging, jungle bunny*.

Creative and humorous elements

Much of the language of political correctness is ponderous and dour, as this study and the word field show. These qualities have rendered it susceptible to satire and parody. However, such early feminist coinages as *male chauvinist pig* and *pussy power* demonstrate the effectiveness of lively rhetoric and of humor, as well as the effective juxtaposition of formal and rude words. This technique is also evident in *cockocracy*, parodying the artificial classical coinage *phallocratic*.

Metaphors with impact included *gas guzzler, carbon footprint*, and *ghetto blaster*, while *crusty, crumblie*, and *towel head* use a lighter tone. *Nigga* and *wigger* are fairly obvious ironic code forms. Alliteration is exploited in *diesel dyke, dumb down*, and *pink plateau*, while rhyme and reduplication appear variously in *gender bender, happy clappy, multiculti* and *shock jock*.

Conclusion

Before we lose sight of the wood for the trees, we should ask the broad question: how do these words fit in to the tripartite scheme of semantic changes (symbiotic, mediated, and Orwellian) set out in chapter 1? At that point of the argument we observed: "Virtually all of them are mediated: words like *abled, waitron*, and *wimmin* had no semantic history prior to their induction into the vocabulary of political correctness; others like *multicultural, homophobic*, and *challenged* were recycled in new senses." This generalization holds true, and the great number of words shows the effectiveness of pressure groups in creating, not just new formulations, but terms carrying new agendas, which we discuss in Part III.

Part III
Zones of Controversy

Chapter 5

Issues of Race, Nationality, and Difference

Introduction

In Parts I and II we outlined the origins of political correctness and the opening salvos of the debate, focusing on the more academic aspects, namely the competing claims of the traditional literary canon and multiculturalism as essential to a university syllabus. Many of the relevant terms are placed in the word field in chapter 4. However, as is well known, there is a wide and expanding variety of other agendas and concerns which fall under the broad umbrella of political correctness. These include various aspects that are categorized under "difference," some of them traditional, such as race and ethnicity, xenophobia, disability, disease, and mental disorders. Other areas of difference, ranging from the natural, such as gender and sexual orientation, to the more extreme socialized forms, namely criminal behavior and addiction, have also been recognized for centuries.

In the past these matters were spoken and written about openly. The significant emphasis in recent decades has been on suppressing judgmental or stigmatizing language either by discouragement or by the institution of speech codes. In America these practices have in some instances been legally challenged and withdrawn on the grounds that they infringe the First Amendment. These issues are covered in the section on "Hate Speech and Speech Codes."

Out of this wide range of topics there is a problem of what organizing principle to use. In a study of this kind it seems logical to start with the historically embedded areas of difference, namely race and ethnicity, colonialism, and xenophobia, which are discussed in this chapter. In chapter 6 we shall look at matters of gender and sexual orientation, followed by disability, disease, and mental disorders, then criminal behavior and addiction, and also consider some completely new emphases and concerns, with the environment and with animal rights.

Race, Ethnicity, and Identity

These concepts, which have deep, complex and ancient roots, surfacing increasingly in modern discussions, bear on the broad question "Where did political correctness start?" As we observed in the Introduction, one impulse behind political correctness derives from a recognition of multiculturalism and the attempted accommodation of those who have traditionally been considered "outsiders." But one must explore the process whereby they came to be so considered. Were these differences inherent or the consequences of colonialism, slavery, and segregation?

There are fundamental difficulties in discussing these topics. Both the standard vocabulary and the key concepts are problematic, since the popular notions do not cohere with the scientific and historical facts. Race is obviously a central feature and an inflammatory issue in much discussion in modern societies: we have seen, even in the curriculum debate in America, how frequent are accusations of racism, some of them admittedly opportunistic. Yet scientists claim that "race" is not a simple matter and that "characteristics such as skin colour and physiognomy, which are popularly taken as indicators of race, are genetically very superficial" (Scruton, 1982, p. 390). Genome research traces geographically defined lines of reproducing ancestral populations in which race and color are not relevant. Be that as it may, individuals commonly have a strong sense of belonging to or identifying with one racial group, often regarding others with hostility, for reasons which may be personal, historical, social, economic, and political, but which are also certainly bound up with appearance. In his major study *The Ethnic Phenomenon*, Pierre L. Van den Berghe claimed that one source of the academic problem is that "the social sciences are riddled with ideology" (1981, p. 1), arguing rather that "Ethnicity and 'race' are extensions of kinship" (p. xi).

The basic vocabulary has revealing and confusing origins. In its major entry for *race* the *OED* makes this significant concession: "The term is often used imprecisely; even among anthropologists there is no generally accepted classification or terminology." Hence one can speak variously of "the human race," "the Germanic race," and in earlier times, even "the race of women." The word itself is of Romance origin, but uncertain etymology: the earliest recorded use (in 1520) referred, curiously, to a particular class of wine. Van den Berghe consistently uses the word in quotation marks, arguing that it is "a *social* label attributed to groups of people in particular societies at particular times" (1981, p. 29). The practice has continued. But significantly, both *racism* and *racist* surfaced only in the political turmoils of the 1930s. Ruth Benedict claimed in *Race: Science and Politics* (1940) that "Racism is an *ism* to which everybody in the world today has been exposed" (cited in *OED*). Certainly the semantic history of *race* is full of compounds reflecting emotive and violent division, some of them of surprising duration, such as *race discrimination* (1875), *race hatred* (1882), *race prejudice* (1890), *race riot* (1875), and *race war* (1897).

The concept of "identity" is also complex and variable, being individual, familial, social, and public. The modern bureaucratic state assigns each person an official identity categorized according to race, gender, nationality, and so on, but that so-called "individual" may be divided into several identities according to what he or she identifies with, and what roles he or she prefers to play. The root of the word in Latin *idem*, "the same" gives us the clue to the verbal sense: you identify with someone you wish to copy or emulate. But the ultimate source in Latin *idem et idem*, "the same over and over again," yields the public or bureaucratic sense.

One may conveniently start with the counterclaims of identity and ethnicity. In his study *Ethnic Chauvinism*, Orlando Patterson analyzes two primal drives, one which "pulls us towards the bosom of the group; and the other which pushes us towards the creation of ourselves as separate and distinct individuals" (1977, p. 13). He derives this antagonistic model from Kant's paradox, articulated in 1784, of "the asocial sociability of men," since "man has an inclination to associate himself," but a contrary "propensity to isolate himself" (from his "Idea for a Universal History with Cosmopolitan Intent," cited in Patterson, 1977, p. 13).

This insight can be fruitfully allied to that of Edward Said in his *Orientalism*, especially in the 1995 Afterword, in which, arguing against essentialism, Said claimed that "the development and maintenance of every culture requires the existence of another and competing *alter ego*. The construction of identity . . . while obviously a repository of distinct collective experiences, *is* finally a construction, which involves establishing opposites and 'others' . . . Each age and society creates its 'Others' " (1995, p. 333).

Patterson shows in his wide-ranging historical study that ethnicity has been a fundamental but inconsistent factor in social identity from ancient times. He points out that the Greeks, "within the confines of their homelands, whatever their incomparable intellectual achievements, were at heart ethnic chauvinists and often downright racists" (1977, p. 51). "The Romans, on the other hand, were essentially inclusive and anti-ethnic in their bestowal of Roman citizenship" (1977, p. 51).

Although *ethnic* derives ultimately from Greek εθνος, meaning a nation, the more direct form εθνικ-ος meant "heathen" or "pagan"; indeed, in the words of the *OED*, referring to less sophisticated etymological times, *ethnic* was "formerly imagined to be the source of English *heathen*." The exclusive sense referring to "nations not Christian or Jewish" was dominant from the fifteenth to the nineteenth centuries, when the modern generalized sense "peculiar to a given race or nation" took over. Since then it has come to define smaller groups, as in the *OED Supplement* definition: "having common racial, cultural, religious or linguistic characteristics, esp. designating a group within a nation." *Ethnic minority* is an American coinage dating from the 1940s, and has steadily spread in British usage. The modern colloquial sense of *ethnic* as "foreign or exotic" dates from the 1960s. It is increasingly used in a euphemistic way, as in *ethnic slur* and in this quotation: "The former 'ethnics', a polite term for Jews, Italians and other lesser breeds just inside the law" (*TLS*, November 17, 1961). *Ethnicity* is also a relatively recent coinage, deriving from an article by the sociologist David Riesman in *The American Scholar* in 1953.

A key term in the cultural studies debate has been *ethnocentric*, that is, "regarding one's own race or ethnic group as of supreme importance" (*OED*). The phenomenon was originally observed by ethnologists and anthropologists as a feature of other cultures. In 1900 W. J. McGee commented in the journal *American Ethnology*: "In primitive culture the ethnocentric views . . . are ever-present . . ." (cited in *OED*). But the term is also applied by anthropologists to themselves. "This ethnocentric attitude has to be abandoned," wrote Evans-Pritchard in 1951 in his major study *Social Anthropology* (cited in *OED*). In America it was applied generally to scholarship, as in the article by John Stanfield of Yale, "The Ethnocentric Basis for Social Science Knowledge Production" in *Review of Research in Education* (quoted by Ravitch, 2003, p. 283). The argument is increasingly put forward that both social science and science in general are "Euro-American" knowledge systems which reproduce "hegemonic racial domination." *Ethnocentrism* was coined by W. G. Sumner in *Folkways* back in 1906 and is nearly always used pejoratively. Other important terms associated with extremes of ethnocentricity are *chauvinism* and *triumphalism*.

In discussions of ethnicity and demographics, *community* is a central term with increasingly problematic definition. The word no longer has a clear meaning of referring to a coherent group, as in "the Jewish community of Warsaw," since it is basically used in three ways: in a specific sense, as in "the black community of New Orleans" or "the gay community of San Francisco"; in a generalized sense, as in "the community is up in arms over the crime wave"; and in a broad sense, as in "the international community." The broad sense is virtually meaningless, since the so-called "international community" is divided by various alliances, political, commercial, geographical, and strategic. Even the specific sense can be problematic, since it assumes that, say, "the black community of Los Angeles" denotes a coherent group with the same interests. There is also often a degree of euphemism at play, as Simon Hoggart has pointed out: "Thus 'Jews' is thought too harsh and even anti-Semitic. Politicians [in Britain] prefer to say 'members of the Jewish community' . . . and prefer to say 'our Asian community' [for] the diverse collection of Indians, Bengalis, Sikhs and Pakistanis who live in Britain" (Hoggart, 1986, p. 176). Writing later, Mike Bygrave was more outspoken: " 'Community' is a rallying cry among PCs. They tend to use it as an all-purpose buzz word" ("Mind your Language," *Guardian Weekly*, May 26, 1991).

Another key term, *minority*, obviously has two meanings: a literal statistical sense and an acquired political code sense to refer to people of different ethnic background from the white majority, usually with the implications that their rights need to be protected or are being ignored. The term originated in the US, the first *OED* quotation (1837) referring to "strong sympathy with minorities." A later quotation (1951) shows the modern code sense, the *Journal of Negro Education* referring to the "hiring of minorities." R. W. Holder's *Dictionary of Euphemisms* (1995) is very direct in decoding the demographic: *minority group* is defined as "non-whites in a country where the majority is white," adding the euphemistic comment: "The usage avoids a direct reference to skin pigmentation."

Majority, unlike *minority*, is normally a term without ethnic connotations, acquiring assumptions from national or local politics. The formulation *moral majority* dates from 1936, but became the name of a political group of evangelical Christians founded in 1979 (disbanded in 1989) advocating an ultraconservative political and social agenda. The *silent majority*, originally a Victorian euphemism for the dead, started during the 1970s to take on the sense of the mass of moderate people who tend to be overlooked in adversarial politics. They have since been identified (not very precisely) as "Middle America" or "Middle Britain."

"Why are ethnic minorities still absent from most books?" asked the *Guardian* (June 20, 2006). The simple answer to this begged question would be "because they are minorities." Clearly the question is loaded by the uses of "ethnic" and "still," implying that the time has come for a change. *Minority* has never really become current in the UK, even though historically the population has been made up of many minorities. Instead, *immigrant*, originally literal, has become the preferred code word. It is discussed elsewhere. In South Africa *minority* has a quite different sense, referring to those different from the black majority. Consequently, *previously disadvantaged* has become current as a code term for what were previously called "nonwhites."

The Melting Pot

The dynamics of racial identities and their names have evolved differently in the USA and in Britain. "America is God's Crucible, the Great Melting-Pot where all the races of Europe are melting and re-forming!" was the powerful and resonant image Israel Zangwill evoked a century ago (in his 1908 play, *The Melting-Pot*). The ideology and symbolism of the melting pot emphasized the dilution of the immigrant nationalities and their merging into a national identity, but with the important exceptions of American Indians and blacks, most of whom had been born and bred in America before the Declaration of Independence and certainly before European immigrants started to arrive at Ellis Island. This point was made caustically by Malcolm X in the Spike Lee movie: "We didn't land on Plymouth Rock. It landed on us!" Also unincluded in "the melting pot" were the Japanese and Chinese immigrants, the latter being subjected to the Chinese Exclusion Act of 1882.

Historically, and up to the early twentieth century, the emphasis was on the primacy of American identity. Theodore Roosevelt's dismissal of "Hyphenated Americans" (*Metropolitan Magazine*, October 1915, p. 7) was preceded by his declaration that "There can be no fifty-fifty Americanism in this country" (Republican Convention, April 14, 1906). This notion of nationality, seeking to avoid the dilution of American identity by too great a recognition of its composite quality, has since been ignored or bypassed.

The following discussion traces the development of principal terms, such as *Negro*, *African American*, and *black*, preferred by radicals, as in *Black Power* and *Black Panther*. The terms for Indians were successively *Redskin*, *Red Indian*, and *Native American*. The first reference in the OED is to "Indian tobacco" in 1618. *Red Indian* followed much later, the first references being by Thomas Carlyle (1831) and Andrew Lang (1887). Political correctness has generated or emphasized many new labels for minorities, usually avoiding or downplaying the aspect of color.

In what may be called "The Return of the Native," *Native American* is described by the OED as "Now the preferred term in the US." It has a complex history, the first reference being from 1737: "As to his Birth and Parentage, I cannot say whether he is a Native American or a Creole." One of the most recent is 1977 in the *Detroit Free Press*: "It's a hidden attack by commercial interest on Native Americans." Between these dates it was adopted in the 1840s as the name of a nationalist political party characterized by hostility to immigrants and Catholics. A quotation from 1844 runs: "The riot was caused by a branch of the Native Americans, 'the very dregs of society, bent upon the annihilation of the Roman Catholics.' " The point which emerges is that *native*, which in most colonial discourse of the time denoted the aboriginal inhabitants, was here being claimed by whites born in America to distinguish themselves from immigrants.

The ideal of the melting pot has not entirely been borne out by subsequent political and semantic developments, which have stressed division rather than unity. A prominent feature of American English is the variety of slang terms used for the various populations that make up the United States. These are not simply descriptive, as is shown in Irving Lewis Allen's study *The Language of Ethnic Conflict* (1983), in which, "Over a thousand usually derogatory terms for more than fifty American groups have been accumulated in scholarly records of slang and dialectal English" (1983, p. 7). This is a huge number in comparison with, say, Britain.

In the United Kingdom, by contrast, origins have traditionally been emphasized, so that people regard themselves as English, Scots, Welsh, or Irish first and British second, if at all. "Britain" has always been more of a political and administrative entity than an emotional identity, except abroad. Likewise, with those sometimes called "new Britons," the emphasis tends to be on origins, such as Caribbean, Pakistani, Indian, or Ghanaian. But there are no hyphenated categories, such as "Pakistani British" in the manner of African American or Pennsylvania Dutch. The matter was put quite crisply two decades ago: "Can you explain why black Englishmen and women who win Olympic medals are described as 'English', while those who riot and throw petrol bombs are almost invariably 'West Indian'?" (letter to *Daily Telegraph*, September 13, 1985).

The "melting pot" has never been a powerful notion in Britain. Indeed once immigration from the Commonwealth increased, steps were taken to halt it. "It is time someone spoke out for the white man in this country," said Sir Cyril Osborne in the House of Commons as early as October 1958. In this context, the political career of Enoch Powell was highly significant. As Tory Minister of Health, Powell "welcomed West Indian nurses to Britain" (Fryer, 1984, p. 373). But his notorious speech at Birmingham on April 20, 1968 proved to be a major event in race relations. Widely and persistently reported as the "rivers of blood" speech, Powell was actually more circumspect: "As I look ahead I am filled with foreboding. Like the Roman, I seem to see 'the river Tiber foaming with much blood'." Powell was a classical scholar, the "Roman" alluded to was Virgil, and the quotation is from the Sybil's prophecy in *Aeneid* VI. But *Powellism* had already emerged as a derivative term for the policy of restricting or terminating the right of immigration of nonwhite people from Commonwealth countries. The *Economist* commented on this "new term" on July 17, 1965.

It was soon joined by the contemporary *Powellite*. According to Peter Fryer, "The Commonwealth Immigrants Act (1968) was steamrollered through Parliament in three days emergency debate with the sole purpose of restricting the entry into Britain of Kenyan Asians holding British passports" (1984, p. 373). Although many agreed tacitly with Powell, he was publicly regarded as an irresponsible alarmist, immediately dismissed from the shadow cabinet, and denigrated in the press. His treatment provoked protests and demonstrations of support all over the country. The sense of rejection felt by Caribbean immigrants was bitterly articulated from within the community by Delano Abdul Malik de Couteau in his poem, "Motto Vision 1971":

> An I hear Powell
> talking
> SEND DEM BACK
> In de land
> Of HOPE AND
> G-L-O-O-O-R-Y!

Colonialism

Colonialism has obviously been fundamental in creating new forms of identity and role models through power relations based on race, between citizen and native, master and slave, and so on. From the English perspective the process is usually thought of as beginning in the late sixteenth century with the founding of England's first colonies in America. However, a longer view of the national history reminds us that Britain was colonized and recolonized long before it became a colonial power, first by the Romans, then by the Anglo-Saxons, then in the North by the Scandinavians, and finally by the Normans. But of these invaders, only the Romans were true colonials in that, under pressure, they retreated to their original "home." The others stayed.

Colonists are not necessarily homogeneous. According to Bede's account in his *Ecclesiastical History of the English Peoples*, the "Anglo-Saxons" comprised three separate peoples, the Angles, the Saxons, and the Jutes, who settled in different parts of the country. Roman citizenship was granted to a range of people within the Empire, as Orlando Patterson pointed out. This explains the arresting opening statement that "There were Africans in Britain before the English came here" in Peter Fryer's *Staying Power: The History of Black People in Britain*. Fryer is referring, of course, not to immigrants, but to Roman soldiers garrisoned in Celtic Britain. He recounts an amusing anecdote with racial overtones concerning the emperor Septimius Severus while visiting Hadrian's Wall in about 210. The emperor, who had been born in Libya, "was far from pleased to encounter a black soldier flourishing a garland of cypress boughs. . . . Severus was troubled not only by the ominous nature of the garland, but by the soldier's 'ominous' colour. 'Get out of my sight!' he shouted" (1984, p. 1).

The colonial perception of foreign and especially "primitive" cultures is dominated by three models. The first is the exclusive categorization whereby they are regarded as "other" or inhuman, as beasts, brutes, savages, barbarians, cannibals, amazons, and so on. In his excellent explication of the colonial mentality, Van den Berghe quotes the saying of the Andean Mestizos: "The Indian is the animal which most closely resembles man" (1981, p. 86). As Jeremy Black points out, this perception provided a rationalization for slavery: "African slavery was widely regarded by European thinkers as justified by natural law" (2006, p. 25). The conquering Anglo-Saxons indulged in this typical colonial mode of naming, calling the Celtic inhabitants *wealas* (the origin of *Welsh*, but meaning "foreigners"), an impressively arrogant projection by the invaders. Also revealing of the "barbarian syndrome" was their related verb *wealian* meaning "to behave corruptly." The whole stereotype of the *cannibal* derives from a false perception and a false etymology, from Columbus's use of the term *Canibales*, rather than the root *carib-*. Likewise, *amazon*, commonly derived from Greek to mean "breastless," endorsed the myth that Amazons mutilated themselves to be more proficient with the bow and arrow. See, in this respect, W. B. Tyrrell's study *Amazons: A Study in Athenian Mythmaking* (1984). It should also be remembered that the American Declaration of Independence referred to the "merciless Indian Savages whose known rule of warfare is an undistinguished destruction of all ages, sexes, and conditions."

The contrary view, far less influential in earlier times, is of an inclusive humanity, exemplified in Bartolomé de las Casas' view that the Indians are "men like us" in his devastating *Short Account of the Destruction of the Indes* (1552), covered in more detail under "The Conquest of the Americas" below. Similar in approach was Michel de Montaigne, especially in his skeptical essay "On the Cannibals" (1580), and the French explorer François Le Vaillant, who in his *Travels into the Interior Parts of Africa* (1790) rejected the stereotypes of the Hottentots and Caffres (Kaffirs) as savage and untrustworthy. Le Vaillant developed very personal relationships with the natives, and came to regard "my dear Klaas," "my worthy Klaas" (his Hottentot companion) as "my equal, my brother, and the confidant of all my pleasures, misfortunes and secrets" (1790, p. 230).

The third model is that of the idealized "noble savage," traditionally attributed to the ideas of Rousseau. In fact Rousseau never used the phrase, which is first recorded two centuries earlier in 1672 in Dryden's *The Conquest of Granada* (I, l. 7). The formula was quite well established in English before the Romantic movement. The basic idea of "primitive man" seen as or idealized as superior to "modern man" can be traced right back to Tacitus's representation of the Germanic tribes in his *Germania* (AD 97–98). Nevertheless, the phrase became established in the discourse of colonialism.

Colonialism typically emphasized the differential aspect of skin color. The Anglo-Saxons referred to the Celts as dark, and in a famous anecdote, St Gregory, upon seeing some Angles in the slave market in Rome, made the pun that they were "angels, not Angles." As is well known, the indigenous population of North America were called "Redskins" and "Red Indians." In the Caribbean and in South Africa gradations of skin color became significant factors in racial categorization.

However, in the sensitive area of color and sex, Van den Berghe has confounded traditional colonial thinking with his formulation of "The Snow White Syndrome":

> Although virtually all cultures express a marked preference for fair female skin, even those with little exposure to European imperialism, even those whose members are heavily pigmented, many are indifferent to male pigmentation or even prefer men to be darker. Only highly stratified societies extend their "leukophilia" to both sexes. . . . Leukophilia is not confined to societies dominated historically by Europe and North America. Nor is it limited to the after-effects of colonialism and African slavery. It may be found in Moorish Spain . . . and in many societies that were never or only briefly colonized, such as Japan and Ethiopia. (Foreword to Frost, 2005)

The overall historical semantic development of the word field has been that racial stereotypes and differences were previously referred to openly, as were ethnic nicknames and slurs, but these have become increasingly taboo in recent decades, in public or official discourse at any rate. Consequently, a double standard has evolved: many euphemisms and code terms have arisen in order to allude to the offensive terms indirectly. In some cases the terms themselves have been reclaimed by the target communities. The major catalyst in the evolution of ethnic slurs is their use by a dominant or colonial group. Thus even *nigger* was originally only a descriptive term: a proclamation by Queen Elizabeth I in 1601 refers plainly to "negars and Blackamoores." It became an insult when whites started to use it demeaningly of negroes (as they were then called) from about 1800. The same is true of *Kaffir*. Both terms are discussed in detail later in the argument.

Colonial Perspectives

There are a number of phases and perspectives in the perception of race: those of explorers, missionaries, colonists, historians, and anthropologists. Naming is an essential part of the dynamic of colonialism, whereby the colonized are labeled and represented as inferior, savage, other, different. After this initial phase anthropologists and ethnologists seek to correct these errors and stereotypes, with partial success. Thereafter, usually at the period of independence, political pressures lead to the renaming of the given peoples and territories in accordance with their origins, identity, and aspirations.

It seems instructive to set out quotations revealing various attitudes, without identifying the author in advance:

1   "In general they are the most ugly, ill-proportioned people I ever saw, and in every respect different from any we had ever met with in this sea. They are a very dark-coloured and rather diminutive race, with long heads, flat faces and monkey countenances."

2   "Civilization did not begin in Australia until the last quarter of the eighteenth century. Early on the golden morning of 13 May 1787, a fleet of eight ships. . . ."

3   *Canoe*: "used generally for any rude craft in which uncivilized people go upon the water . . . most savages use paddles instead of oars."

4(a)   "When I first walked about the streets I found myself the victim of Barbarian insolence. My dress attracted rude notice, and I soon adopted the common garb."

4(b)   "London, therefore, not wanting in a certain air of greatness in some parts, really expresses very clearly the traits of the English Barbarians. It is gloomy, morose, huckstering, repulsive. Huge it is, like the English barbaric power; but incoherent, uninformed, unlovely, without the beauty of refinement."

5   "No matter what the difference in the colour of their skin had been, it was impossible to say that the kafir's bones were less white than Hans Welman's."

6   "Nearly all blacks believe the whites to be cannibals."

7   "I used to be coloured, right? Then I was a Negro. Then I turned into an African-American. After that I was just a member of a Minority Group. Now I'm black."

8 " 'I ought to have known there was ideology behind this. *That's* the nigger in the woodpile.' 'The negro in the woodpile,' murmured Domna and was instantly ashamed of the joke. The President [of the university] threw back his head and roared. *'Touché!'* he cried and grew thoughtful. 'It's an ugly thing how our language is defaced with expressions of prejudice.' "

The sources of the quotes are as follows:

1 Captain Cook, describing the inhabitants of the Sandwich Islands, July 23, 1774 (*Voyages Round the World*);
2 Manning Clark, *A History of Australia* (1962);
3 *Oxford English Dictionary*;
4 (a) and (b) Ah-Chin-Le, *Some Observations Upon the Civilization of the Western Barbarians*, 1876, (quoted in H. and P. Massingham, *The London Anthology*, 1978);
5 Herman Charles Bosman, *Unto Dust* (1947);
6 David Livingstone, *Narrative of an Expedition to the Zambesi* (1865);
7 Paul Theroux, *The London Embassy* (1982) (quoted in Holder, 1995);
8 Mary McCarthy, *The Groves of Academe* (1953). ("Nigger in the woodpile" originated in a blackface minstrel song dated 1843, "Nigger on de woodpile." The modern sense is recorded from the 1850s.)

Explorers generally describe what they see, but from their own cultural perspective. Captain Cook's description of the natives of the Sandwich Islands is an obvious instance. Today, no writer would dare use the term "monkey" of a person, however appropriate the metaphor might seem. Yet etymologies like Malay *orang utang*, meaning literally "man of the woods" are revealing. John Aubrey also reminds us that the scientist Sir William Harvey (1578–1657) "was wont to say that man was but a great, mischievous baboon" (*Brief Lives*). Incidentally *baboon* is recorded as a term of abuse from about 1500: "He then began to storm, Cries 'Fool, fanatick baboon!' " (*Robin Hood*, cited in *OED*). And a famous speech in *Measure for Measure* condemns "Man, proud man, . . . / like an angry ape / Plays such fantastic tricks before high heaven / As make the angels weep" (Act II, scene ii). The quoted comments of Manning Clark and the definition of the *Oxford English Dictionary* both express attitudes of colonial superiority, while those of Mary McCarthy and Paul Theroux are typical reflections of the political correctness and semantic shifts of the modern era.

Principal Terms Used in Colonial Discourse

Barbarian and savage

In the discourse of colonialism *barbarian* is an obvious key term. The epithet is grounded in language, deriving from Latin *balbus*, meaning "stammering," and epitomizes demeaning attitudes towards foreign languages, seeking to belittle them as sounding like infantile babbling. This is notably apparent in the early descriptions of the Hottentot language below. The semantic history of *barbarian* is also revealing of chauvinist relativity, since the term has been successively applied to outsiders by Greeks, Romans, and Christians to denote savagery. Montaigne, as one might expect, supplies one of the earliest rational dissections of the prejudiced use of *barbarian* at the outset of his essay "On the Cannibals" (1580): "When King Pyrrhus crossed into Italy, after noting the excellent formation of the army which the Romans had sent ahead towards him, said, 'I do not know what kind of barbarians these are' (for the Greeks called all foreigners barbarians), but there is nothing barbarous about the ordering of the army which I can see!' "

Savage is etymologically rooted in Latin *silva*, "a wood," and thus originally refers to one living in a state of nature, out in the wild like an animal or without the benefits of civilization, a term rooted in Latin *civis*, a city. This somewhat simplistic contrast is hardly sustained in modern lifestyles. *Savage* was a basic term in colonial discourse, instanced in the *OED* definition of *canoe* cited earlier.

The attribution of savagery is not an entirely one–way process. For their part the Chinese applied the term *barbarian* (via the character 'I') to the English. In this context the scathing comments quoted above by the visiting Chinese, Ah-Chin-Le in his *Observations Upon the Civilization of the Western Barbarians* in 1876 are especially piquant. So, of course, are those of Dr Livingstone about cannibals. The name *Eskimo* derives from Proto Algonquin, meaning "eater of raw meat." The people called themselves *Inuit* (the name they have since reclaimed) meaning "the men," and according to Benjamin La Trobe, English secretary to the Moravian missions (writing in 1774), "looked upon the Europeans as upon dogs, giving them the appellation of Kablunets, that is, Barbarians." The indigenous Canadian Indians are now called *First people*, the name being introduced in the 1980s in response to the claims by the English and the French to be the "two founding nations."

In 1688 the natives of New Holland, on the North-West coast of Australia, were thus described by William Dampier, the buccaneer and explorer:

> The Inhabitants of this Country are the miserablest [poorest] People in the World. The Hodmadods [Hottentots] of Monomatapa [Southern Africa], though a nasty People, yet for Wealth are Gentlemen to these . . . And setting aside their Humane Shape, they differ but little from Brutes. They are tall, strait-bodied and thin, with small long Limbs. They have great Heads, round Foreheads, and great Brows. Their Eye-lids are always half closed, to keep the Flies out of their Eyes . . . therefore they cannot see far. . . . They have great Bottle Noses, pretty [fairly] full Lips, and wide Mouths. . . . They are long-visaged, and of a very unpleasing Aspect; having no one graceful Feature in their Faces. (Dampier, 1906, vol. I, p. 453)

Robert Hughes, citing this passage of "the Ignoble Savage, orphan of nature," called Dampier's description "a minor classic of racism" (R. Hughes, 1988, p. 48). But Coleridge, perhaps less inclined to be judgmental in matters of race, wrote of "Old Dampier, a rough sailor but a man of exquisite mind" (from *Table Talk*, March 17, 1832). Nevertheless, nearly a century after Dampier, in 1770, Captain Cook took issue with his judgment:

> They may be some of the most wretched people on earth, but in reality they are far happier than we Europeans; being wholly unacquainted not only with the superfluous but the necessary conveniences so much sought after in Europe, they are happy in not knowing the use of them. They live in Tranquillity which is not disturbed by the Inequality of Conditions. (*Journals*, vol. 1)

Historically the indigenous populations of South Africa were named in the typical dynamic of colonialism variously as *Hottentots, Bushmen, Kaffirs, Natives, Non-Whites, Bantu*, and so on. The first three names were originally specific terms which have since become insults, especially *Kaffir*, now the most demeaning word which can be used of a black person, and thus completely taboo. The first European colonists at the Cape of Good Hope named the hunter-gatherers *Boesjemens* (Bushmen), the pastoralists *Hottentoos* or *Ottentots* (Hottentots), and the mixed farmers *Caffres* (*Kaffirs*). An early Dutch explorer noted in 1670 that "*Hottentot* is a word meaning 'stutterer' or 'stammerer', applied to the people on account of their stuttering speech." Two later explorers took a similarly disparaging view of the Bushmen languages, with their complex systems of phonetic clicks, comparing them to the clucking of turkeys.

Dampier's description of the Cape Hottentots in 1691 is less critical, but undeterred by fancy: "The Natural Inhabitants of the Cape are the Hodmodods, as they are commonly called, which is a corruption of the Word Hottantot; for this is the Name by which they call to one another, either in their Dances, or on any Occasion; as if every one of them had this for his Name." From this hilariously implausible explanation, Dampier proceeds to describe the people in considerable detail, showing a genuine interest in their rituals, but concluding that "they are a very lazy sort of People . . . which choose rather to live as their Fore-fathers, poor and miserable, than be at pains for plenty" (1906, vol. I, pp. 517–22). Dampier typifies the importation of Eurocentric norms and values in his descriptions. So in part does Le Vaillant, whose attitudes are more humanistic: he observes that "The Hottentots, naturally careless and inconstant, often run away when they expect severe labour, and leave their masters in great embarrassment" (1790, vol. I, p. 100).

Hottentot was borrowed into English and by the eighteenth century had become a fairly common insult meaning "a person of inferior intellectual or culture" (*OED*). Condemning the state of Oxford in 1726, Nicholas Amherst commented that "he was surprized to find a place so much renown'd for learning, fill'd with grey-headed novices and reverend Hottentots." The term died out in the late nineteenth century, but still survives in South African English as *hotnot*, basically meaning "oaf," but "an offensive mode of address or reference to a coloured person" (*Dictionary of South African English*). The word has been partly reclaimed by the community. Adhikari notes that the magazine *South* (which had a predominantly Coloured readership) stigmatized the earliest Coloured recruits to the ruling white National Party as "Hotnats" – a play on the racial slur *hotnot* (2005, p. 159). Although *bushman* has generally been a descriptive term, it is also used disparagingly in the Coloured community as *boesman* to stigmatize one who is regarded as "wild" or "primitive." Both these latter instances show the internalization or assimilation of the outsider's insult. Athol Fugard used the term in his notable play *Boesman and Lena* (1969) about two Coloured vagrants surviving on the margins of Port Elizabeth.

The Hottentots' name for themselves was *Khoi Khoi*, meaning "men of men," first recorded by Le Vaillant in 1791. Their name for the bushmen was *San*. Modern ethnological scholarship has coined the compound *Khoisan* for these early peoples: "The term [*Khoisan*] is compounded of the names Khoikhoin, by which the Hottentots called themselves, and San, applied by the Hottentots to the Bushmen. The latter have no collective name of their own" (L. S. Schultze in Shapera, 1930, vol. I, p. 5).

Kaffir

Kaffir comes from a quite different source, namely Arabic *kafir*, meaning "heathen," "infidel," or "unbeliever" (from the Muslim point of view). It is the oldest of the terms for the indigenous population, the legacy of the Arab traders who, as they moved down the East African coast, converted many of the coastal people to Islam, applying the word *kafir* to the peoples of the interior. The term was subsequently adopted by the Portuguese navigators and the Dutch and British colonists, so that by 1599 the whole area of the Eastern part of the Cape Colony came to be termed *Cafir-land* or *Cafraria. Kaffir* became a common regional term applied to the Xhosa-speaking peoples of the Eastern Cape Colony and then to dozens of place-names (*Kaffirstad*) as well as hundreds of items of flora (*kaffirboom*) and fauna (*kaffir finch*). Although *Kaffir* had this wide sense approximating to "natives," those named regarded it as derogatory. As the Rev. William Shaw observed in his *Diary* in 1847: " 'Kaffir' is not a term used by the native to designate either themselves or any other tribe. . . . The Border Kaffirs know that the white nations apply the term to them and many regard it as a term of contempt" (December 28).

In the New South Africa there were increasing cases of *crimen injuria,* the specialized legal term for the offense of impugning a person's dignity, by action, gesture, or using a racist epithet or ethnic slur, especially by the use of *kaffir.* The different grounds and conditions are covered in Burchell and Milton's *Principles of Criminal Law* (1997, pp. 753–7). President Mbeki saw it as part of his function to raise the issue of racism in some of his public utterances. One such occurred in his "Letter from the President" (in *ANC Today,* vol. 7, no. 10, pp. 16–22, March 2007), under the heading: "Freedom from Racism – a fundamental human right." After referring to two leaders of opposition parties who had stressed the need for debate, the presidential letter continued as follows:

KAFFIRS AT THE WORK PLACE

Recently I was privileged to receive a report prepared by a group of independent investigators who had been asked to assess the cause of a labour dispute. . . . The report says that one of the white managers, Mr X "admitted that he and other white managers used the term 'kaffir' generally in everyday conversation . . ." [but did not use it when other Africans were present, nor to their face].

The President proceeded to retail the racist language and views of Mr X in some detail and then concluded: "This account tells the story that racism is alive and well at the workplace. . . . It has a direct negative material impact on the lives of our people, communicating the message that apartheid is not dead."

After a section on crime in the USA, President Mbeki's newsletter continued: "THE KAFFIRS ARE COMING!" In this case the given headline was not a quotation, but a putative reaction: "... every reported incident of crime communicates the frightening and expected message that – the kaffirs are coming!"

Non-White and *Bantu* were later inventions of the semantic engineering of the system of apartheid. (*Bantu* had in fact been coined in 1862 by W. H. I. Bleek, the pioneer researcher into African languages.) As the Preface to the *Dictionary of South African English on Historical Principles* (1996) noted, the political contamination proved to be a problem for serious scholarship:

> The deeply resented adoption by the National Party government of the word *Bantu* as a racial designation (from 1953 to 1978) has resulted in widespread rejection of this word among black South Africans, and avoidance of it by whites. .... The question has generated lengthy discussion and some dissension among the [editorial] staff.

European, native, and settler

In colonial contexts *European* has a recorded usage from about 1696 as a code term for what the *OED* calls "a white person, especially living in a country with a predominantly non-white [sic] population." This usage initially reflected the fact that all the colonial powers were European. It became used broadly in colonial contexts for "British." Thus a report on the Indian Mutiny in the *Manchester Guardian* (August 25, 1857) referred to "the growing estrangement between the European officers and their men" (*Guardian* August 25, 2006). In South Africa, as elsewhere, *European* was commonly used of whites without regard for any actual ties with Europe. Thus the Immorality Act of 1927 referred to "illicit carnal intercourse between Europeans and natives." Ezekiel Mphahlele recalled the terminology of apartheid South Africa in his autobiographical novel *Down Second Avenue* (1959). In it *European* and *White* are equated, although *Afrikaner* and *Boer* are not subsumed under this broader category. *Black* is virtually unused, *African* being preferred throughout. When he and a schoolboy friend are threatened by some Afrikaner youths and under provocation swear at them "Voetsek, you Boers!" ("Bugger off, you Boers!") their Headmaster remonstrates: " 'Do you want us thrown by the European people out from this place?' the stocky Yorkshire Headmaster said" (1959, p. 127). Today, of course, this reads anomalously. Although *European* now has the general literal sense of "relating to Europe," the assumption that whites have European colonist roots still lingers and surfaces from time to time.

Remarkably, the basic early sense of *native* was "one born in bondage," recorded from about 1460. In the course of the sixteenth century the general sense developed of "a person born in a place, as opposed to visitors and foreigners." The term was always used by the colonists to distinguish the indigenous population from themselves, the *Europeans*. It continued to be used in this racially exclusive sense even after several generations of colonists had been born, despite the pre-emptive implication of *native vis à vis* the colonial term *settler*. In South Africa it became a basic term of racial classification even as "the Native Question" became an increasingly ominous issue. In the transition to the New South Africa there were various changes in the dynamics of naming, as J. M. Coetzee observed in his essay "Taking Offense":

> In the early 1990s, an instructive shift took place in public discourse in South Africa. Whites, who for centuries had been genially impervious to what blacks thought about them or called them, began to react touchily and even with outrage to the appellation *settler*. One of the war-chants of the Pan-Africanist Congress struck a particularly sensitive nerve: "ONE SETTLER ONE BULLET". (1996, p. 1)

"Part of their outrage," Coetzee continued, "was at tasting an impotence of which being-named is the sign" (1996, p. 2). While there is undoubtedly truth in this argument, the more dramatic point was that the PAC slogan obviously carried a violent message deeply at variance with the prevailing spirit of reconciliation and "rainbowism." Furthermore, *settler*, which in the South African context has traditionally meant a farmer who took up a land grant offered by the British government in 1820, was now extended to mean any white landowner or white person who could claim nationality overseas and who was therefore regarded as not entirely committed to South Africa. This ambiguity obviously created further insecurity.

Coloured and Colored

Coloured is defined by the *OED* as "having a skin other than 'white'; wholly or partly of Black or 'coloured' descent." It was introduced by John Speed in his curiously titled book, *Theatre of the Empire of Great Britain* (1611): "Their coloured countenances and curled hair" (cited in *OED*). There are basically two distinct regional uses, in the US and in South Africa. In the US it was first used as an alternative term for *Negro*, then as a euphemism, the object of much irony and comment by outsiders, who regarded it as a hypocritical misnomer. Thus in Dickens's *Martin Chuzzlewit* (1843), when an acquaintance uses the phrase "a man of colour," Martin responds tartly:

"Do you take me for a blind man ... when his face is the blackest that ever was seen?" (chapter 17).

It was retained as a deliberate anachronism in NAACP (National Association for the Advancement of Colored People, founded in 1909) as a continuing reminder of the reduced status of black people. Although borrowed into British English, it is less common than in the US. Thus a politician's reference to "colored people" and an objection by the opposing party generated this comment in the *TLS* (November 17, 2006) on what it called "the c-word": "It is okay to use the expression 'people of colour', and to say he was rejected 'because of his colour', but not, for some reason, to describe someone as 'coloured' " (p. 16). In the same article the *TLS*'s "Harlem correspondent" comments wryly that " 'people of colour' is almost chic, but 'coloured people' is anachronistic. We've gone from 'coloured' to 'Negro' to 'black' to 'Afro-American' to 'African American'."

In South African usage, *Coloured* has never been a euphemism, but a specific term for people of mixed race living in the Cape Province. The first reference occurs in the Rev. William Shaw's *Diary* in 1829, commenting on "the poor black and coloured children" (September 20). Another is to "The hunters and wagon-drivers ... generally half-breeds, who are known by the distinctive title of *coloured people*" (in Schulz and Hammar, *New Africa*, 1897). The *Milner Papers* (1897), concerned with the future political dispensation, referred to the *Cape Coloured* community. François Le Vaillant, who visited the Cape earlier, in the 1780s, commented on the population in quite different Gallic terms:

> On arriving at the Cape one is astonished to see a multitude of slaves as white as Europeans; but this astonishment ceases when it is known that the negresses, if they are in the least handsome, have each a soldier of the garrison, with whom they may go and spend every Sunday in whatever manner they choose. Self-interest makes the masters wink at the irregularity of their slaves, because they expect to reap considerable profit from this licentious cohabitation. (1790, vol. I, p. 102)

Although *Coloured* had become established by the 1930s to refer to people of mixed race, the term carried increasingly stigmatic overtones in the racial categorization of the apartheid system, formalized in the Population Registration Act of 1950. The simplistic division of the population into "White" and "Non-White" inflicted particular injustice on many Coloureds, who were virtually indistinguishable from many Whites, but who were nevertheless designated as "Non-White." Aspiration for the prestige category led to frequent attempts to "try for white", that is, to cross the color line.

Despite increasing ideological emphasis on African identity, many South African Blacks prefer to imitate white models. The Coloured poet James Matthews is scathingly critical about the removal of indigenous features:

> white syphilization
> taints blacks
> makes them
> carbon copies . . .
> the women
> faces smeared
> skin bleached
> hair straightened
> (quoted in Adhikari 2005, p. 20)

With the coming of the new democratic and egalitarian dispensation after the watershed election in 1994, various pressure groups started to campaign for the substitution of "mixed race." However, a survey of the people themselves carried out by the Johannesburg *Star* newspaper in 1994 found that 75 per cent of those polled "did not mind being referred to as Coloured" (October 15–16, p. 9). In the new South Africa the term is now standard in political and general parlance.

Shortly after the 1994 election, IDASA (the Institute for Democracy in South Africa), held a symposium under the title of *Now That We are Free: Coloured Communities in a Democratic South Africa* (James et al., 1996). In the opening chapter of the proceedings President Mandela commented that "Non-racialism is one of those ideals that unites us. It recognises South Africans as citizens of a single rainbow nation, acknowledging and appreciating difference and diversity" (1996, p. 7). This was the generally prevalent idealistic view of the times, when the political transition to democratic majority rule had gone smoothly. However, one article skeptically took "A politically incorrect view of non-racialism and majority rule." In it Hermann Giliomee, Professor of Political Studies at the University of Cape Town, argued that "non-racialism" was a problematic term because of its diversity of meanings, and that "Imperialistic non-racialism fosters and conceals the African demand for power and control of the widest range of political and social institutions." Giliomee pointed out several ironies, firstly that "The ANC, as the party most strongly espousing non-racialism, is in fact a racial party, depending on Africans for 94% of its support"; secondly that the "non-Africans in the ANC cannot be said to represent in any significant way their respective communities," and finally that "affirmative action as a policy pursued by the ANC will continue to

racialise our society" (James et al., 1996, p. 93). He concluded: "Comparative analyses show that in deeply divided societies such as South Africa,
electoral alliances will be built on race or ethnicity and they will be stable"
(p. 98). Discussions elsewhere in this study, especially that on the term *transformation* in chapter 1 (p. 34), endorse Giliomee's point about affirmative
action continuing to racialize South African society and undermine the
original vision of rainbowism.

A significant contribution to the debate has come from within the community in the form of Mohamed Adhikari's study, *Not White Enough, Not
Black Enough: Racial Identity in the South African Coloured Community*
(2005). Adhikari's title is derived from the commonly articulated complaint
(entirely justified) of the marginalized status of the Coloured community,
first under apartheid and subsequently in the New South Africa. Unlike
others who have preferred "mixed-race" or "person of color," Adhikari has
no problems with the use of the term, only with the punctuation: "During
the apartheid period and after, some scholars, myself included, refused
to capitalize the first letter of the term Coloured in order to indicate both
opposition to the enforced classification of people into racial and ethnic
categories and distaste for ethnocentric values" (2005, p. xv).

Brown has been used of skin color from Anglo-Saxon times, but not
commonly. John of Trevisa commented in the fourteenth century that "Hot
countries produce both black and brown people." Only in South Africa
has the term *brown people* been accepted demographically, largely as a loan
translation from Afrikaans *bruinmens*. Thus in one of the IDASA conference papers on the Coloured communities, Julian Sonn commented: "As
brown people, we have internalized the white racist message that 'white is
right' and 'West is best'" (James et al., 1996, p. 62).

Caste was much used in earlier colonial discourse. Deriving from
Latin *casta*, "pure," the term's original dominant sense in Spanish and
Portuguese was thus "pure bred," first used of the hereditary caste system
in India from the early seventeenth century. This older sense survives in
half-caste (recorded from c. 1789) and is the root of the phrase "to lose
caste," borrowed into English society from the mid-nineteenth century.
However, when applied to the South American colonial situation, *caste* took
on an opposite sense of "a mixed breed." This meaning was also borrowed
into English, as evidenced in the translation of Juan y Santacilia and
Ulloa's *A Voyage to South America* (1760): "The inhabitants may be divided
into different casts or tribes who derive their origin from a coalition
of Whites, Negroes and Indians" (cited in *OED*). As we shall see, the
hierarchy of the caste system came to apply to different gradations of
"colored" people, but not in an entirely standardized way.

Stereotypes of the Colonial Mindset

Stereotypes of the child and the servant

As we have seen, an essential part of the bifocal mindset of colonialism was to view the natives as both savages and as children, in Kipling's words, "half-devil and half–child," in need of civilizing. Further, the root of *barbarian* emphasizes the lack of a proper language. More obvious is the persistence, through to postcolonial times, of demeaning terms like *boy*, *girl*, *child*, *maid*, and so on. *Piccanin*, a pidgin term deriving from Portuguese *pequeno ninos* meaning "small child," spread all over the world in the sense of a black child, recorded from about 1653 in the Caribbean and the United States, from about 1817 in Australia and New Zealand, and from about 1855 in South Africa. Although still used globally, its racial connotation has made it politically incorrect. One cannot imagine a modern white leader reminiscing, as Sir Roy Welensky did on the BBC television program *Face to Face* in 1960, that as a youngster he used to swim "bare-arsed . . . with many piccaninnies."

Another feature of colonial discourse is that of reification, referring to people impersonally in terms of their work role. Hence "the maid" or "the domestic," standard euphemisms for a (black) household servant, an extension of the practice found closer to home in "the char," "the help," "the nanny," or just plain "cook." Colonial titles of high status borrowed from indigenous languages include *bwana*, *memsahib*, *nkosi*, and *baas*.

Stereotypes of savagery, virility, and sexuality

These are typically part of the mindset of colonialism and the creation of "the Other," discussed previously under "Race, Ethnicity, and Identity." Yet colonial expressions of contempt for the natives often show the colonial in the worst possible light. A powerful and revealing instance occurs in Lieutenant-General Cradock describing punitive measures taken against some natives in the Eastern Cape of South Africa, which, it was hoped, "induced in these savages a proper degree of terror and respect" (letter to Lord Liverpool, March 7, 1812). Some unflattering comments by Richard II on the Irish (in Shakespeare's *Richard II*, Act II, scene i) elicit an interesting observation on stereotypes by Ania Loomba: "Various English administrators, such as Edmund Spenser, John Davies and Fynes Morison describe the Irish as wild, thieving, lawless, blood-drinking, savage, barbarous, naked; these are also the terms routinely used to describe New World Indians" (2002, p. 41).

President Mbeki of South Africa raised in Parliament on October 18, 2004 the stereotypes imposed on black people: "Others whose minds have been corrupted by the disease of racism, accuse us, the black people of South Africa, Africa and the world, as being, by virtue of our Africanness and skin colour, lazy, liars, foul-smelling, diseased, corrupt, violent, amoral, sexually depraved, animalist, savage and rapist." The last epithets possibly allude to an acceptance speech by Professor Jerry Coovadia, a world expert on AIDS, on June 24, 2003 upon the award of an honorary doctorate by the University of the Witwatersrand, Johannesburg. Seeking to explain the denialism of the Mbeki government in the face of "HIV/AIDS ripping through millions of our people," Coovadia's analysis was that "unbridled sexuality, especially the promiscuity of men, was too uncomfortably part of the remembrances of racism to be accepted by newly independent people as the prime cause of HIV."

Accusations of racism and resorting to negative stereotyping in matters of controversy have become regrettably common in recent years, precisely when the Constitution has banned racism and the legal sanction of *crimen injuria* is more frequently invoked. One such episode arose from an unexpected catalyst, namely claims of a political blacklist in the South African Broadcasting Corporation, made by a Johannesburg newspaper (*The Sowetan*, June 20, 2006). An official internal enquiry in October 2006 found that interventions by the SABC Head of News, Mr Zikalala, indicated that certain political commentators had been blacklisted. The SABC refused to publish the report, which was then leaked over the internet, increasing the level of controversy. The Chief Executive, Advocate Dali Mpofu, responded in a press article in the following terms:

> They want to attack us for not feeding into their gluttonous, greedy smell of black blood which must be sacrificed at their every whim. This ambitious goal they will achieve over my dead body. . . . This battle is not about one or other commentator or a "blacklist" or Zikalala. It is about wresting control of the SABC, of the hearts and minds of the SABC and ultimately of the country, from us barbarians. Well folks, it is over for good. The savage natives are in charge, and democratically so. (*City Press*, Johannesburg, October 22, 2006, p. 27)

This would appear to be a form of reclamation with irony.

The attribution of superior sexual powers to outsiders is also a major characteristic of perceptions of the Other. "Blacks, the sons of Ham, are thus traditionally represented as emblems of hypersexuality . . . as megaphallic figures," argues Sander Gilman in his *Sexuality: An Illustrated*

History (1989, p. 29). A Roman mosaic in Algeria shows a black bath attendant with an improbably large penis (Loomba 2002, p. 50). Shakespeare includes a number of allusions, notably the amused question, "Have we some strange Indian with the great tool, come to court, [since] the women so besiege us?" *Henry VIII* (Act V, scene iii). (*Tool* is recorded in the sense of "penis" from 1553.) *Othello* is full of similar allusions, such as "An old black ram is tupping your white ewe" (Act I, scene i). In a different mode, a famous front cover of *Private Eye* used a photograph of Enoch Powell, the noted opponent to Commonwealth immigration, with a speech bubble saying "Some of them have them this long!," using the gesture favored by fishermen for "the one that got away." Perhaps the last word must go to Spike Lee, who emphasized "fear of the big black dick" as an essential aspect of his film *Jungle Fever*, discussed in chapter 8.

"It is indeed in the physical appearance of the Hottentot that the central icon for sexual difference between the European and the black was found," writes Gilman (1989, p. 291). The "Hottentot Venus" was the name under which Sarah Baartman, also called Saartjie or Saat-Jee Baartman, was exhibited in Europe as an object of prurient interest for five years prior to her death in 1815. Gilman points out that "Eighteenth-century travelers to southern Africa, such as Le Vaillant and Barrow had "described the so-called 'Hottentot apron', a hypertrophy of the labia and nymphae caused by the manipulation of the genitalia and serving as a sign of beauty among certain tribes" (1989, p. 292). In his *Travels into the Interior Parts of Africa* (1790), Le Vaillant describes how one evening his curiosity was greatly roused by peals of laughter coming from his camp-followers and that on investigation "I learnt from Klaas [his faithful guide] that he had discovered . . . a Hottentot woman who had that peculiar conformation which I always considered as a fable" (vol. II, pp. 347–8). After delicate but persistent negotiations, the woman ("confused, abashed and trembling") was persuaded to reveal herself. The plate displaying this feature (see Figure 5.1) was subsequently suppressed or bowdlerized.

However, as Gilman correctly adds, Sarah Baartman was exhibited more to present another anomaly, her steatopygia or protruding buttocks. The contemporary images of Baartman emphasize this feature, as does an engraving of another "Hottentot Venus" at the Ball of the Duchess du Barry in 1829. George Cruikshank's satirical cartoon of George IV in his Brighton Pavilion (1826) shows a Hottentot woman in profile immediately above the King's mistress, the amply endowed Lady Hertford: between the two figures is a tart comment "Regency Taste!!!!" However, the autopsies of Hottentot females centered on the sexual parts: those of Sarah

HOTTENTOTE A TABLIER. *Tom. 2. Pag. 349.*

Figure 5.1   The Hottentot "Apron". From François le Vaillant, *Voyage dans l'interieur de l'Afrique* (Paris, Chez Leroy, 1790), vol. 2, p. 349.

Baartman, who died in France in 1815 aged 26, remained on display at the Musée de l'Homme in Paris until her remains were eventually returned to South Africa for proper burial in May, 2002.

The depiction of Baartman's body in posters and prints has naturally raised issues about "difference" and colonialist perceptions of the colonized. Clearly she was different from the European norm. Was the use of the soubriquet "Venus" a compliment or a cruel irony? Rachel Holmes concludes her excellent biography *The Hottentot Venus* with some damning judgments: "European racism made Saartjie a Frankenstein's monster of its own invention" (2007, p. 184). A review claimed that "Visual representations of her body are fraught with the negative consequences of reproducing offensive iconography." This raises the broad question: What is "offensive iconography"? Is it only cross-cultural, or does it include the work of Diane Arbus, Joel-Peter Witkin, and Annie Liebovitz's grim images of the last days of Susan Sontag? An interesting development in the past few years has been the "reclamation" of steatopygia by some South African black women via a forum called BUM, an acronym for "Booties United in Movement." For a fuller discussion, the reader should consult Strother (1999).

The Conquest of the Americas

Accounts of the "discovery" or conquest of the "New World" have been divided into those that see the initiative as an act of divine providence in the conversion of the heathen, and those that see it as an act of genocidal pillage. Stephen Greenblatt opens his Introduction to *New World Encounters* (1993) with the epiphany described by Samuel Eliot Morison:

> The main conception and aim of Columbus, to carry the Word of God and knowledge of His Son to the far corners of the globe, became a fact: Christ had been made manifest to a new race of Gentiles. . . . To the people of this New World, pagans expecting short and brutish lives, void of any future, had come the Christian vision of a merciful God and a glorious Heaven. (Morison, 1974, p. 737)

Greenblatt describes this account as "the articulation of a traditional position – let us call it 'the vision of the victors' – against which all of these essays in this volume . . . are written" (1993, p. vii).

However, long before revisionist histories of colonialism were being written, the enterprise was being condemned. *A Short Account of the Destruction of the Indes* (1552) is the self-descriptive title of Bartolomé de las Casas' devastating account of the genocide inflicted by the Spanish conquistadors on the natives of the Caribbean and the Americas. This is one of three works written by Las Casas, who was originally a missionary monk prior to his conversion to become the Apostle of the Indians. Las Casas consistently stressed that the Indians are "men like us" and that he wrote as an eyewitness. His work was addressed to "the most high and the most mighty" Philip II of Spain. The Prologue is an ingenious combination of diplomatic political correctness and radical exposé. Beginning with a shrewd variation of the conventional doctrine of Divine Right, Las Casas emphasizes regal responsibility:

> As Divine Providence has ordained that the world shall, for the benefit and proper government of the human race, be divided into kingdoms and peoples and that these shall be ruled by kings, who are . . . fathers and shepherds to their people and are accordingly the noblest and most virtuous of beings. . . . It follows that if the commonwealth suffers from some defect,

or shortcoming or evil, the reason can only be that the ruler is unaware
of it; once the matter is brought to his notice he will work with utmost
diligence to set matters right and will not rest content until the evil has been
eradicated. (Las Casas, 1992, p. 5)

Arguing that his Highness was evidently unaware of the atrocities which
went under the name of "conquests," and which "are contrary to natural,
canon and civil law," Las Casas continues: "I therefore concluded that
it would constitute a criminal neglect of my duty to remain silent about
the enormous loss of life as well as the infinite number of human souls
dispatched to Hell in the course of such 'conquests', and so resolved to
publish an account of such outrages" (1992, p. 6).

In his Prologue Las Casas leaves open the question of whose souls will
be "dispatched to Hell," but in the main text he is unambiguous, asserting that the Spanish fell upon the innocent and peaceful Indians "like
ravening wolves upon the fold." The catalog of destruction is endless:
the population of Hispaniola (now Haiti and Dominican Republic) was
reduced, he claims, from some three million to 200. Las Casas is bold in
warning his king against "conniving at the gravest of mortal sins, worthy
of the most terrible and everlasting punishment" (1992, p. 7).

Between Las Casas and Morison lies the sardonic account of colonialism satirized by Swift at the end of *Gulliver's Travels* (1727). "I doubt,"
comments Gulliver, "whether our conquests in the countries I treat of, would
be as easy as those of Ferdinando Cortez over the naked Americans":

> For instance, a Crew of Pyrates are driven by a Storm they know not
> whither; at length a Boy discovers Land from the Top-mast; they go ashore
> to mob and Plunder; they see an harmless People, are entertained with
> kindness, they give the Country a new Name; they take formal Possession
> for their King; they set up a rotten plank or a stone for a memorial, they
> murder two or three dozens of the natives, bringing home a Couple more by
> force for a Sample, return home and get their pardon. Here commences a
> new Dominion with a title by *Divine Right*. (Book IV, chapter 12)

Slavery and its consequences

Slavery is such an ancient and widespread practice of empire that this
discussion can focus only on its main features and their consequences in
British and American history. Despite their common ideologies of liberty,
it took a dismayingly long time for this terrible commodification of human
beings to be regarded as a moral problem in both nations. The tardiness
in seeking proper political solutions and redress has generated many of the

race issues which plague both societies and now fall under the agendas of political correctness.

Although there was slavery from Ireland in Anglo-Saxon times, the word *slave* is recorded from 1290, derived from *Slav*, but the early uses are curiously metaphorical. The first instance in the *OED* of the literal state of slavery is, remarkably, the famous quotation where Othello refers to having been "sold into slavery" (Act I, scene iii). Both Britain and the American colonies profited greatly from the slave trade. The first Negro slaves arrived in Virginia in 1619, about a century after the first recorded English slaveholders, so that by the time of the Declaration of Independence (1776) there were some 500,000 slaves in the United States. But the word *slave* is not mentioned in the Declaration or the Constitution. Subsequent actions by slave owners ranged from complete abolition to complete retention. The most prominent example of ambivalence is Thomas Jefferson, who owned many slaves, including Sally Hemings, lampooned by Jefferson's enemies as "Black Sal," who bore him children, but was not freed upon his death. By 1860 the number of slaves in the Union had risen to four million.

In England King Charles II, the Duke of York, the Earl of Sandwich and many upper-class people were investors in the slave trade via the Royal Africa Company and owned slaves directly. It was quite common for slaves to be given as presents. The practice was countenanced under English law by a ruling in 1677 in which the court held that "the negroes usually bought and sold among merchants, as merchandise, and also being infidels, there might be a property in them." But in two crucial judgments Sir John Holt, the Lord Chief Justice, ruled in 1701 that "as soon as a negro comes to England he is free," and in 1707 "by the common law no man can have a property in another" (Black, 2006, p. 14). The first opposition to slavery had come from the Quakers in 1671, but the key term *abolition* was first recorded over a century later in 1788, and actual abolition was finally achieved in the British Empire only in 1833. By this time several of the northern American states had freed their slaves and there had been several slave revolts in the South. Slavery became, of course, a major but not the exclusive cause of the Civil War (1861–65) and Lincoln's Emancipation Proclamation freeing the slaves in the rebel states from January 1, 1863 was essentially a war measure.

The bitterness engendered by the war profoundly exacerbated race relations and damaged the political future of the Union. Sherman's brutal policy of total war inflicted on the whole of the South destroyed its economy. Furthermore, his field order issued in January 1865 promising the freed slaves that "Every family shall have a plot of not more than forty acres" was an undertaking which the federal government did not fulfill. The Southern states instituted "Black Codes" in 1865–66 regulating the status of former slaves. More severe were the "Jim Crow" laws of the 1890s depriving black people of the right to vote and establishing segregation in schools, public transport, restaurants, public places, and employment. Most sinister was the founding of the Ku Klux Klan in 1866 by veterans of the Confederate Army with the intention of restoring white supremacy.

Alienated by such discriminatory legislation and resistance, the more moderate blacks joined organizations such as the NAACP (National Association for the Advancement of Colored People), which achieved the landmark legal victory of *Brown vs Board of Education*, but only in 1954. The more radical rejected their "slave names" and identified with or joined racist movements opposed to integration like the Black Muslims and the Black Panthers. In Martin Luther King's famous "I have a dream" speech delivered on the anniversary of the Emancipation Proclamation, he observed with poignant imagery "One hundred years later, the life of the Negro is still sadly crippled by the manacles of segregation and the chains of discrimination." Barack Obama coined the resonant phrase of "the original sin of slavery" in a key speech on March 18, 2008.

The legacy of slavery did not generate simple loyalties or consequences, even among the oppressed, issues taken up in the section below on "Color and Loyalty." Indeed, Van den Berghe detected a whole spectrum of social consequences. At one end he placed Mexico,

> ... where the descendants of slaves are almost totally assimilated to, and undistinguishable from, the rest of the population. ... At the other end of the continuum, the United States stands out as a rigid racial-caste society ... Whites who, for over two centuries, had lived and interbred with blacks in situations of intimate and continuous contact suddenly shuddered at the thought of living with them as equals. They discovered a concern for the purity of their blood [and] created a system of racial segregation that confined all those tainted with the stigma of African blood to pariah status, including in many cases their own relatives. (Van den Berghe, 1981, p. 135)

Elsewhere, the results of interbreeding generated a whole new range of racial categories. "The Inhabitants of Jamaica," a writer of 1707 informs us, "are for the most part Europeans, who are the Masters, and Indians, Negroes, Mulatos, Alcatrazes, Metises, Quarteroons & Co, who are the Slaves" (cited in *OED*). Clearly *European*, that is, white, is the standard, against which *mulatto* is half white, *quadroon* is one quarter white and *octoroon* is one eighth white. According to Dr Kelly Miller, before 1890 the US Census Bureau sought to use these categories, "but found it impossible to make such sharp distinctions . . . on the advice of Booker T. Washington it began calling all persons of African blood *Negroes*" (cited in Mencken, 1963, p. 630). There are still other categories, such as *mestizo* and *zambo*, covered in the discussion of the topic in Ania Loomba's study *Colonialism/Postcolonialism*. She includes the extraordinary anecdote in which Papa Doc Duvalier told a surprised American journalist that 98 percent of the Haitians were white, on the grounds that they had some white blood in them (2005, pp. 103–4).

The modern debate about slavery has tended to focus principally on the Atlantic slave trade, ignoring the Arab, Ottoman, and Indian Ocean aspects, even though they have also been well researched. Some scholars have seen elements of bias and political correctness in this difference of emphasis. Jeremy Black has argued that "This trade does not fit with the narrative of Western exploitation, and is therefore widely neglected in public history, as well as in the demand for apology and public compensation" (2006, p. 9). On these latter issues the UK Government issued in September 2006 a "statement of regret," while Tony Blair made a public "statement of sorrow" on November 27, 2006. Some regard such statements as necessary recognitions of guilt, others as tokens avoiding serious forms of reparation.

Terms for Foreigners and Others

Out of a large field, many of the older words, such as *blackamoor*, *macaroni*, *nigger*, and *frog* started out as specific terms and then became insults, as did the later terms *wog*, *honky*, and *gook*. For a more detailed study of these developments see Hughes (1988, pp. 126–38). With the advent of political correctness, such uses became unacceptable, and various euphemisms or code words sprang up. Thus *boat people*, first used literally of those Chinese who lived in boats (from 1839), came to refer to Vietnamese political refugees from 1977, but subsequently generalized. This section is concerned with these euphemistic and generalized terms.

In this context the semantic change of *immigrant* is significant. From a long historical perspective, most of the populations of the UK and the USA consist of immigrants. Hence such passé claims as "Our family came over with the Conqueror/the Mayflower." However, these were either conquerors, colonists, or refugees. *Immigrant* is originally an American term dating from 1792, when it was remarked on as a neologism. The first British instance is nearly two hundred years later in 1969, in a report in the *Times*: "Wolverhampton Grove School was described as the '90 per cent immigrant school'. There was some criticism of this high proportion of immigrant children" (July 18). Holder (1995) is much more direct in his definition: "a black person living in Britain." He also notes that "any white person" born outside Britain would not be so categorized.

Both *discriminate* and *discrimination* entered the language in the seventeenth century. Originally used in intellectual and artistic contexts, they were positive terms. The familiar modern senses of "to make distinctions prejudicial to people of a different race or color" and "the making of such prejudicial distinctions" are first recorded in American English in 1866 in a key speech by Andrew Johnson: "Congress can repeal all State laws discriminating between whites and blacks" (March 27). (This was in the immediate aftermath of the Civil War.) About a century later Winston Churchill argued, with reference to the case of *Constantine v. the Imperial Hotel* (1944 – won by Learie Constantine, the great West Indian cricket player) that "Anti-discrimination legislation would draw attention to race and colour and thus foster discrimination rather than erase it" (in Mullard, 1973, p. 53).

Demographic has likewise become a code word for ethnic change in population, usually as a consequence of black immigration, as in "There has been rapid demographic change in Brixton." In American usage it alludes to an increasing number of blacks in a given social context. Thus "We have demographics on our side. We have history on our side" (William King, President, Black Student Union, Stanford University, quoted in D'Souza, 1991, p. 59). Hence *demographic strain*, defined by Holder (1995) as "too many people." He continues: "It is taboo to suggest that poor countries face starvation because ignorant people breed too fast and medical science allows too many to survive." An earlier code term is *developing*, recorded from 1964, with this commentary by John Ayto (1999), together with its original italics: "The latest of the litany of 20th-century euphemisms which *English has come up with* to avoid sounding patronizing to poor countries: in this case *the previous offender* which needed replacing was *underdeveloped* (1949)." By contrast, Holder (1995) is blunter: "poor and relatively uncivilized." Robin Blackburn commented in 1969: "Bourgeois economists once talked about economically 'backward' countries; then 'underdeveloped' was felt to be a kinder adjective. They now prefer to refer to poor capitalist nations as 'developing nations'" (cited in *OED*).

Third World dates from 1956, being a translation of French *Tiers Monde*, the title of a book by Georges Balandier relating to the Bandung conference of 1955. Originally the term was ideological, referring to countries, especially those of Africa and Asia, which during the Cold War were aligned neither to the Communist or non-Communist bloc; hence underdeveloped or poorer. In 1964 the *Economist* referred to "The ingredients common to most 'third world' countries (poverty, ignorance, love-hate of the former colonial powers)" (October 26). Shiva Naipaul wrote a penetrating essay on the topic in the *Spectator* (May 18, 1985). Holder (1995) defined it as a euphemism for "poor and uncivilized," while Matthew Parris was openly sarcastic about the Prime Minister's lack of credibility: "Thanks, Mr Blair, for bringing a Third World flavour to our politics . . ." (*Times*, July 15, 2006). *Banana republic*, an older formulation dating from 1935, was originally South American in reference.

Ethnic, discussed under "Race, Ethnicity, and Identity" above has become a general euphemism for "racially distinct." The horrific Orwellian formula *ethnic cleansing* (for *genocide*) derives from Serbo-Croat *etniko cisjene*, dating from 1991, referring to the massacres in Bosnia.

Terms for Whites

The semantics of *white* are rooted in favorable associations, and have hardened into ideological formulas. Semantically and etymologically *white* is beautiful. As the *Chambers* (previously *Barnhart*) *Dictionary of Etymology Dictionary* points out under *fair*: "The sense 'of a light complexion' is an early development . . . the notions of lightness and beauty being closely connected in Germanic." Anglo-Saxon *fæger*, glossed as Latin *pulchritudo*, is used of a beautiful person or work of art, a joyous sound, pleasing words, attractive bearing and so on. Commenting on Anglo-Saxon *hwit*, the *OED* quotes Cynewulf's *Elene* (c. 900): "Wlitescyne . . . hwit & hiwbeorht" ("With shining countenance, white and bright of hue"), adding "often as a poetic term of commendation." Sense 4 of the adjective is defined as: "Applied to those races of men (chiefly European . . .) characterised by light complexion," quoting E. Grimstone's translation of D'Acosta's *History of the Indies* (1604): "[in] a part of Peru . . . the inhabitants are white" (possibly expressing surprise). This is followed by C. Nesse, whose *Compleat and Compendious Church History* (1680) divides the sheep from the goats in this fashion: "the White Line (the Posterity of Seth) [and] the black Line the Cursed brood of Cain" (original capitals). While the etymological argument is indisputable, the glosses of the Old Testament are not, as David Goldenberg shows in his valuable study, *The Curse of Ham* (2003).

Of the other terms, *Aryan* in Sanskrit meant "of noble or good family," but the word has never had a general currency in English. The *OED* explains: "The idea current in the 19th cent. of an Aryan race was taken up by nationalistic historical and romantic writers . . . given special currency by de Gobineau, who linked it with the theory of the essential inferiority of certain races [*Essai sur l'inégalité des races humaines*, 1855]. The category of the 'Aryan race' was revived for the purposes of political propaganda in Nazi Germany." Thus in April 1933 the so-called Aryan decrees were introduced. According to Hitler's *Mein Kampf*, as translated by the *Times*: "The exact opposite of the Aryan is the Jew" (July 25, 1933). *Aryan* is defined by Holder (1995) as "without Jewish ancestry." Although the word was used by some linguistic scholars like Max Müller in the nineteenth century, its contamination by the Nazis ensured its demise.

Caucasian was coined by the German anatomist and anthropologist Johann Freidrich Blumenbach, who in 1795 distinguished five principal races, deriving the origins of the "white race" from the region of the Caucasus. Blumenbach's theories, based mainly on skull measurements and positing degeneration rather than evolution, are now generally discredited. This makes the survival of *Caucasian* in official American terminology somewhat ironic.

The idiomatic use of *white man*, applied to someone who is "honorable, square-dealing" is noted by the *OED* as "originally US," dating from 1877: "A good fellow is Rayner; as white a man as I know" (Besant and Rice, *The Golden Butterfly*). More openly ideological was Kipling's now notorious phrase "the White Man's Burden," the title of his poem of 1899. Kipling's imperialist vision was remarkably crude in its references to "Your new-caught sullen peoples / Half-devil and half-child" and its pessimistic anticipation: "Watch sloth and heathen Folly / Bring all your hopes to naught." Twenty years later C. E. M. Joad wrote caustically of "Little nationalised Jingoes who are ready enough to adopt any parrot cry such as 'The White Man's Burden' or the 'Kultur of the Fatherland' " (*Common Sense Theology*, 1922, cited in *OED*).

Other relevant semantic forms are *white supremacy*, dating from 1902, and *supremacist*, originally US, first recorded in the *Times Literary Supplement* (*TLS*) in 1958. *White supremacist*, coined at the same time, has made a notorious resurgence in British politics: a *Times* report of 1977 alluded to "Mr John Tyndall, the NF [National Front's] founder and chairman [who] describes himself as 'an unashamed white supremacist' and regards whites as intellectually superior to blacks" (August 30).

The strongest critical terms for whites have come, significantly, from America. They are found in the poem *TCB* by Sonia Sanchez, which has three-line "verses" made up of the repetition: "wite/motha/fucka / wite/ motha/fucka / wite/motha/fucka." Each verse is followed by a standard black term of insult: *whitey, ofay, devil, pig, cracker,* and *honky*, concluding "now. That it's all sed / let's get to work." Although *whitey* is a predominantly

American term, the earliest recorded usage (dated 1828) is Australian. *Time* commented (July 31, 1964) that "Harlem is where the white man is no longer the 'ofay' but 'Mr. Charlie' or 'the man', and mostly 'whitey', derived from the Black Nationalist talk of 'the blue-eyed white devil'." In a rare early borrowing Chris Mullard fulminated in his Preface to *Black Britain* (1973): "Whitey! One day you'll have to pay!" *Ofay*, the subject of much inconclusive etymological speculation, dates from the 1920s, and took several decades to be known by American whites. *Honky*, deriving from *hunky* and *hun*, surfaced in the 1950s and has remained exclusively American. So has *cracker*, dating from the eighteenth century and originally referring to a Southerner. But none of these terms has truly been borrowed into British English. Tony Thorne's *Dictionary of Contemporary Slang* (2007) lists all of them as "American." The lack of seriously wounding terms for whites in British English is noteworthy.

A coinage from the 1990s is the portmanteau or blend form *wigger* (white nigger), described as "African American slang for white people who mimic stereotypical black mannerisms" (Nirpal Dhaliwal, *Independent on Sunday*, June 3, 2007). He quotes Eminem's criticism of "cocky Caucasians who think I'm some wigger who just tries to be black 'cause I talk with an accent and grab on my balls." It is largely confined to the rap and hip-hop cultures. Coined in 1990 was *DWEM* for "dead white European male," politically correct in agenda, but racist in content, discussed further in chapter 3 under "Acronyms." In contemporary South African usage *pale* has become a euphemism for "white," especially in the compound "pale male".

Terms for Blacks

In its early semantic history *black* was a color term rather than a demographic description. The reasons varied: when Charles II made his escape after the Battle of Worcester in 1651, he was described in "wanted" posters as "a tall black man" – a reference to his hair color. This was one of the standard early uses, often found in phrases like "a pretty black woman" in the *Diary* of the incorrigible flirt Samuel Pepys. The earliest instance of *black* to refer to a people dates from about 1380: "Among the black Saracens." The principal early terms were *Moor* and *Ethiop*, both dating from the fourteenth century. John Wycliffe used *ethiop* (derived from Greek *aethiopos*, meaning "burnt face") in his Bible of 1382. Indeed, *Aethiopia* became a common name for Africa on maps from the early seventeenth century. It has returned in the form of *Ethiopianism*, referring to the movement of American blacks to return to their ancestral home in Africa. While *Moor* retained its geographical association with North Africa, *blackamoor* became more generally used to mean a person of African descent. Andrew Boorde introduced an interesting complication in his *Introduction to Knowledge* (1547), noting that "there be whyte mores and black moors."

In his *History of Black People in Britain since 1504*, Peter Fryer shows that their problems of discrimination and identity are by no means new. On July 11, 1596 Queen Elizabeth sent an open letter to the Lord Mayor of London and other mayors and sheriffs: "Her Majestie, understanding that there are of late divers blackmoores brought into this realme, of which kinde of people there are allready here to[o] manie . . . Her Majesty's pleasure therefore ys that those kinde of people should be sent forth [out] of the lande" (1984, p. 10). In 1601 Elizabeth found it necessary to issue a similar royal proclamation stating that she was "highly discontented to understand that great numbers of negars and Blackamoores (as she is informed) are crept into this realm . . . who are fostered and relieved [fed] here to the great annoyance [harm] of her liege people . . . as also for that the most of them are infidels, having no understanding of Christ and his Gospel" (1984, p. 12). Clearly the characterization in terms of the Other was under way.

Continuing with the history of *black*, it should be noted that all the word's modern negative connotations of evil, wicked, portentous, malign, and so on are recorded relatively late, from the sixteenth century. In the past 50 years two kinds of semantic engineering have occurred, both in America. The first was militant and exclusive, seen in *Black Muslim* (1960), *Black Nationalism* (1962), *Black Panther* (1965), *Black Power* (1966), and *Black Studies* (1968). The second was amelioration by slogan, as in *Black is Beautiful*, described by the *OED* as "a slogan asserting pride in Blackness and Black self-awareness." The capitalization is significant. The publication *Liberation* noted in September 1965: "Radical blacks turn inward . . . to 'black is beautiful' as an ideological principle." *Black Panther* commented: "The hangup is that they have tried to sweep 'Black' under the rug and can't stand us digging 'Black is Beautiful' " (July 20, 1967). In Britain Chris Mullard articulated a very different view in his book *Black Britain*: "Merely because of the colour of their skin, black children become second-class citizens, doomed to a life of ostracism, exploitation, difference" (1973, p. 146). In South Africa *Black Beauty* (Anna Sewell's 1877 best-seller about a horse) was banned under apartheid.

In the intervening decades *black* has become less fashionable in the United States, with various compounded forms becoming current. The curious history of *African-American* is germane here. First formulated in the 1850s in the United States by black social leaders who wished to avoid the stigmatic overtones of *black* and *Negro*, it then diminished in currency before being revived from the 1960s as the politically correct designation. In the interim, in a speech on October 12, 1915, Theodore Roosevelt made the declaration that "There is no room in this country for hyphenated Americans." The later riposte came from Toni Morrison: "In this country American means white. Everybody else has to hyphenate" (*Guardian*, January 29, 1992). Deborah Cameron asks the reasonable question: "is that not precisely the point of the linguistic intervention – to challenge the kind of discourse that defines people by skin colour?" (1995, p. 145). While this sounds perfectly plausible, the attitudes of those actually affected by prejudice, when they are consulted, turn out to be quite different. David Crystal points out: "In one 1991 survey of black Americans, carried out in the USA by the black-oriented Joint Center for Political and Economic Studies, over 70 per cent of blacks said that they preferred to be called *black*, notwithstanding the supposed contemporary vogue for the politically correct *African-American*" (1995, p. 177).

   Afro-American had a similar early currency, dating from 1853, mainly confined to political contexts, before a decline and a revival. There was also a variant form *Aframerican*, recorded from 1910. H. L. Mencken observed ironically: "When the *New York Times* announced in an editorial on March 7, 1930, that it would capitalize the word *Negro* thereafter, there were loud hosannahs from the Aframerican intelligentsia" (*American Speech*, 1944). *Afro-American* has since become preferred, although there are earlier variant forms such as *Afrocentric*, recorded from 1967, with an interesting quotation from *Ebony* in 1992: "I've always thought of myself as an enlightened Afrocentric person who considered *all* black people beautiful." *Afrocentricity* gained currency from the title of Molefi Kete Asante's book in 1980. But Orlando Patterson had some strong criticisms of such cultural and symbolic assertions: ". . . by publishing a spate of third-rate books on the greatness of the African tradition, by the glorification of black roots, and most cruel of all, by introducing into the curriculum of the nation's colleges that strange package of organized self-delusion which goes by the name of Afro-American Studies" (1977, p. 155).

Nigger

Notoriously the most complex and emotive term, *nigger* has in its predominantly American semantic history been through the phases of description, insult, reclamation, and generalization. Early descriptive uses, dating from the 1570s, as in "one niggor Boy" are associated with slavery, which was to mark the race and ruinously divide American society. As was shown earlier, Queen Elizabeth used the form *negar* descriptively in 1601. So did Captain John Smith, the founder of Virginia, in 1624, noting a transaction in which "a dutch mann of warre sold us twenty Negars" (*Description of Virginia*). The root association between *Negro* and "slave" is clearly alluded to in Francis Grose's slang dictionary (1785): "figuratively used for a slave," quoted in uses like "I'll be no man's negro." Insulting uses, invariably by whites, date from about 1800, becoming more offensive with the passage of time, while reclamation dates from around 1925. The dynamic was well described by Carl Van Vechten in *Nigger Heaven*: "While this informal epithet is freely used by Negroes amongst themselves, not only as a term of opprobrium but also actually as a term of endearment, its employment by a white person is always fiercely resented" (1925, cited in *OED*). Generalization, the most recent phase, is the use of the term to refer to any exploited or underclass group.

It is difficult in a study of this scope to give due weight to the range and offensiveness of *nigger* over a long period of time. The entry in H. L. Mencken's *The American Language (Supplement One)* covers many of the issues (1963, pp. 618–31). The *Random House Dictionary of American Slang* (1997) records hundreds of compounds, such as *niggerhead* (dark tobacco), *nigger heaven* (topmost balcony in a theater), *nigger-lover* and *nigger luck* (undeserved good fortune), most dating from the 1850s. In *Martin Chuzzlewit* (1843) Dickens satirized pompous rhetoric masking overt racism. A conversation with Colonel Driver and Jefferson Brick takes an unexpected turn when the colonel speaks of "one of the ennobling institutions of our happy country as – ," and Mr Brick suggests, "As nigger slavery itself" (chapter 16). Later General Choke reads out a letter written "In Freedom's name" which has the audience cheering at every mention of the word, up to the shocking revelation that the writer is an advocate "of Nigger emancipation!" (chapter 21). Even in 1937 John Dollard commented in *Caste and Class in a Southern Town*: "Evidently Southern white men say 'nigger' as standard practice, 'nigruh,' a slightly more respectful form, when speaking to a northerner (from whom they expect criticism on the score of the treatment of Negroes), but never Negro; that is a hall-mark of a northerner and caste-enemy" (1937, p. 47).

One continuing issue is the survival of the term in the literature of the period. As was noted in chapter 1, there have been consistent objections to *Huckleberry Finn* (1884) because of Mark Twain's frequent, but mainly juvenile, use of the word. Protests have increased rather than declined, despite the validity of arguments such as those of Lionel Trilling:

This is the only word for a Negro that a boy like Huck would know in his place and time – that is, an ignorant boy in the South before the Civil War. . . . The fact that offensive words were once freely used ought not to be suppressed. For it is a fact that forms part of our national history, and a national history is not made up of pleasant and creditable things only . . . it is something to be confronted and dealt with, not evaded or forgotten. (cited in Ravitch, 2003, p. 81)

The original *OED* entry (1907) marked *nigger* as "colloquial; usually contemptuous"; the *Supplement* (1976) was more analytical: "Except in Black English vernacular, where it remains common, now virtually restricted to contexts of deliberate and contemptuous ethnic abuse." Amongst its sedate columns one reads of a protest by CARD (the Co-Ordinating Committee Against Racial Discrimination) against a performance of Agatha Christie's *Ten Little Niggers* in Birmingham, UK. More surprising was the comment in the *Church Times* of November 21, 1958: "You can call a man a *Kaffir-Boetie* in Johannesburg and a *nigger-lover* in the Southern States; but both mean precisely the same thing and have the same accent." Today the term would provoke prosecution in South Africa, regardless of accent.

Nigger remains one of the few genuinely taboo words for the majority of people. In the O. J. Simpson trial the two opposing black lawyers showed its potency: it was exploited by Johnny Cochrane for the defense, but Christopher Darden for the prosecution refused to utter it, saying "It's the filthiest, dirtiest, nastiest word in the English language" (*New York Times*, January 14, 1998). Frank Rich commented in 1995 on "Dropping the N-Bomb."

Nigger became a basic term to demean black people in the colonial era, especially in Australia, where it was initially common, but its currency has since declined. (Curiously, it has never become current in South African English, although it was used by the British.) From the mid-nineteenth century there were American references to "nigger hunts" (for escaped slaves). The phrase appears in Australia in 1901 and has been resuscitated in modern Britain. Following a spate of antiblack operations by the Brixton police, who called what they were doing "nigger hunting," Joseph A. Hunte's report was published in 1966 as *Nigger Hunting in England?* (Fryer, 1984, p. 391). In *Society and the Policeman's Role* (1973), Maureen Cain, a sociologist, found that policemen generally believed that "niggers" or "nigs" "were in the main . . . pimps and layabouts living off what we pay in taxes" (Fryer, 1984, p. 392).

Other insulting American variants include *house nigger*, originally one who worked in a slave-owner's house. As Clarence Major explains, "during slavery blacks working in the big house tended to be looked on by fellow slaves working in the field as traitors because they often seemed more loyal to the slaveholders than to their own people" (1994, p. 244). Although Major claims that "the term was made popular in the fifties and sixties by Malcolm X," the first recorded instance in the *OED* is J. C. Harris's *Uncle Remus* (1880). The modern sense is a black person who is subservient to a white, an Uncle Tom, recorded in the *Random House Dictionary of American Slang* from 1970.

For over 30 years *nigger* has also come to be used of people who are victims of prejudice, exploited, or disenfranchised. This is the principal non-American or generalized sense: "The Jewish, the Italian and Irish people are the niggers of the white world" (*Atlantic* magazine, December, 1972). In *The Commitments* (1987) Roddy Doyle concurred: "The Irish are the niggers of Europe, lads" (1987, p. 13). Curiously, this sense turns out to be a resuscitation of *white nigger*, recorded from 1835 for a person who does manual labor. The *OED* notes under the lower-case sense, "used by blacks as a neutral or favourable term" from 1831. More curious are Karl Marx's savage remarks about "The Jewish NIGGER Lassalle," discussed under "Xenophobia and Anti-Semitism" below.

In the last few years the term has appeared in various provocative book titles, such as *Capitalist Nigger* by the Nigerian author Chika Onyeani (2003) and *Nigger: The Strange Career of a Troublesome Word* (2002) by Randall Kennedy, commented on in the *TLS* (December 8, 2006). In an interestingly ironic footnote, Clarence Major noted that "after the mid-seventies a 'Negro' was a black person accused of cultural or racial disloyalty" (1994, p. 318). Finally, *nignog*, generally regarded as a euphemism for *nigger* and first recorded in 1953, was, according to the *Times*, "used on the railways and elsewhere long before coloured immigrants appeared. . . . It is a mildly contemptuous but good-humoured name for an unskilled man or novice" (November 30, 1967).

So inflammatory is *nigger* that problems have arisen with phonetic approximations. Thus *niggardly* became a flashpoint in Washington mayoral politics in January 1999. In a highly publicized incident the Mayor of Washington, Anthony A. Williams, pressed for the resignation of his staff member, David Howard, because he had used the word *niggardly* in a private staff meeting on January 15. Howard resigned on January 25, but on the 28th Julian Bond, Chairman of the NAACP, said that Williams had overreacted by accepting Howard's resignation and Howard was reinstated. Mayor Williams is black. Mr Howard is white (*Washington Post*, February 4, 1999). A number of American guides to English usage now actually recommend avoiding the use of *niggardly*. A similar problem is developing around *denigrate*. With the independence of the Republic of Montenegro, the formal question has arisen of what to call a person from Montenegro. The logical answer would be a *Montenegron*. However, because of the unfortunate but accidental associations with *negro*, the preferred alternatives are *Montenegran* and *Montenegrin*.

Ebony and Ebonics

The symbolic term *ebony* has become associated with black pride, notably in the prestige magazine of the same name. This has given rise to the journalistic category of the *ebony élite*. Yet the term has a complex history, originally being an American pseudo-euphemism for a black person, recorded in Melville's *Moby Dick* (1852, cited in *OED*). J. S. Farmer commented in *Americanisms* (1889): "An ebony is a negro in common parlance." An unexpected extension was *Ebonics*: "The linguist Robert L. Williams coined the term in his 1975 book *Ebonics: The True Language of Black Folks* by combining the words *ebony* and *phonics*" (Lakoff, 2000, p. 245). The school board in Oakland, California, recognized Ebonics as a distinct second language in 1996, since to reject it would be discriminatory, thus provoking a national debate. In an extended discussion, Lakoff shows how various agendas – linguistic, ethnic, political, and cultural – came into play, confusing the essential educational issue (2000, pp. 227–51). On this point the reader might consult Louis Menand's essay "Johnny Be Good" (*New Yorker*, January 13, 1997).

In discussing a basic feature of Black English, William Labov persistently avoided the traditional critical term "double negative," substituting the more positive neologism "negative concord" (1972, pp. 145–52). By contrast, J. L. Dillard's *Black English* used "double negative" (1973, p. 102), while in his study *Class*, Paul Fussell regarded the double negative as an absolute class marker: "Probably the most important usage dividing the prole classes from the middles and highers is the double negative, as in 'I can't get no satisfaction'" (1984, p. 153).

Ghetto, gollywog, and others

Just as *nigger* has become generalized to apply to an exploited underclass, so *ghetto* has been extended to refer to inner city slums inhabited by American blacks. First appearing in Thomas Coryate's *Crudities* (1611), it referred to the area of the Foundry (*il getto*) in Venice where the Jewish community had to live. Similar ghettos such as that described in Israel Zangwill's *Children of the Ghetto* (1892) grew up in European cities, notably

Warsaw. The first social reference to "Negro city ghettos" seems to occur in the *TLS* (November 29, 1957). The compound *ghetto-blaster* dates from the early 1980s. In his *New Dictionary of American Slang* (1986), Robert L. Chapman avoids referring to blacks, but includes the synonym *coon box*. *Ghetto-blaster* was also common in the UK, as well as the more recent *Brixton briefcase*, recorded from 1986.

While *ghetto-blaster* is "considered by some to be racially offensive" (*Oxford Dictionary of New Words*, 1992), there is no doubt that *golly-wog* has become politically incorrect, because of its cartoon appearance and fortuitous similarity to *wog*. Originally a heroic character, Golliwogg was invented by Bertha Upton in a series of children's books. Her sister Florence illustrated the first "Golliwogg" book using an old, rather tattered "nigger doll" (as they were then called). *The Adventures of two Dutch dolls – and a 'Golliwogg'* came out in 1895, followed by 10 books, from *The Golliwogg's Bicycle Club* (1895) to *The Golliwogg in the African Jungle* (1908). Two stereotypical images of the past are resuscitated in the follow-ing fictional description from 1969: "A short, slightly built negro whose appearance reminded me of one of those golliwogs that decorate the labels of Robertson's marmalade jars" (J. Kemp, cited in *OED*). The word became the center of a minor scandal in Britain in February 2009 when Carol Thatcher (Lady Thatcher's journalist daughter) was sacked from a BBC TV show for comparing a black tennis player to a golliwog in an off-air conversation. The resulting controversy prompted many news-paper discussions of the word and its history (e.g., "From bedtime story to ugly insult: How a Victorian caricature became a racist slur," *Guardian*, February 6, 2009).

In American usage *jungle bunny*, dating from 1959, has become a highly offensive term for "a colored person." The sense seems to derive from "a US Marine from a jungle area of operations" (*Random House Historical Dictionary of American Slang*). People unfamiliar with these semantic areas tend to use the word as if it was an amusing metaphor. The *OED* adds that it is a "derogatory term for Blacks in Australia." Also American, and as yet unrecorded in the *OED*, is the modern sense of *jungle fever*. This clearly derives from the title of the Spike Lee film (1991), discussed in chapter 8 and coyly defined in the *Random House Dictionary of American Slang* as "romantic interest between a black person and a white person." Also associated with film is the portmanteau *blaxploitation* dating from 1972, meaning "exploitation of Blacks, especially as actors in films of historical or other interest to Blacks" (*OED*).

A more scholarly term is *Hamite*, that is, "a descendant of Ham . . . (cf. Gen. ix. 18, 19), viz. the Egyptians and the other African races," recorded from 1645, and "a term of obloquy" (*OED*). This has given rise to *anti-Hamitism*, a new politically correct term for prejudice against blacks. It is used by Christopher Heywood (2004) in his discussion of South African literature. The term draws on the biblical authority for the "curse of Ham," an apparent misinterpretation of Scripture ably treated by David Goldenberg (2003).

Cablinasian is the ingenious coinage of Tiger Woods, resisting the pressure to be labeled black or African-American, to describe his complex roots by using elements of *Caucasian*, *black*, *Indian*, and *Asian*. "In so doing he unleashed highly vocal positive and negative responses in editorials, letters to the editor and conversations among individuals. His claim to multi-ethnic identity was welcomed by those who saw this statement as legitimizing his own sense of self. Others decried his statement as a blow for Black racial solidarity" (Oyserman and Harrison, 1998, p. 288).

Among terms which allude indirectly to blacks is *minstrel*, recorded in 1843 in this odd series of euphemisms: "The Ethiopian Serenaders or Boston Minstrels," thus avoiding *nigger minstrel*. It is more trenchantly defined by Holder (1995, p. 241) as "a black person in a predominantly white-occupied country. Especially in derogatory use by British whites of immigrants from the West Indies." *Private Eye* noted in 1981 that Enoch Powell "was responsible for admitting the Minstrels in such numbers in the first place." However, in South Africa *minstrel* has become used to denote Cape Coloured bands of musical entertainers in the New Year carnival. It has largely replaced *coon* as an acceptable alternative. *Yardie* is defined by the *OED* as "a member of any of a number of West Indian (esp. Jamaican) gangs engaged in usually drug-related organized crime." A similar sense is carried by *posse*, recorded in the same period.

Uncle Tom

The long-suffering eponymous slave hero of Harriet Beecher Stowe's classic *Uncle Tom's Cabin* (1851–2) was the object of critical discord from the start. One school praised his stoic piety, another regarded him as having "too much piety" and a third was overtly racist, making savage puns on "Uncle Tom-Foolery" and "Sambo's woes," declaring "We hate this niggerism," this "woolly-headed literature" (George Graham in *Graham's Magazine Review*, Philadelphia, 1853). His name has since become a label of opprobrium among American blacks for "a Black man who is submissively loyal or servile to White men" (*OED*). In essence this change has come about through stereotyping, racial identification, and the supplanting of religious values by political loyalties.

Hugh Rawson notes that among whites "Tom's name was being used within a year of [the novel's] publication in such forms as *Uncle Tomitude, Uncle Tomitized* and *Uncle Tomific*" (1991, p. 400). It is difficult to trace the first use of the name as a pejorative label among blacks, but the first instances seem to be in speeches by Marcus Garvey in 1921, 70 years later. Since then *Uncle Tom* has taken on a strong sense of racial disloyalty, shown in Clarence Major's definition: "a black person who is culturally disloyal; a black person who does not practice racial or cultural loyalty; a pejorative term for any African-American perceived by any other African-American to be 'middle class', to own property and to have money in the bank" (1994, p. 492). The assassination of Malcolm X provoked in Eldrige Cleaver the searing question: "Why'n't they kill some of those Uncle-Tomming m.f.s?" (1968, p. 51).

The novel now appears less in Black Studies courses, despite its obvious importance in American literature. (There have been some 600 editions of what was called "The Greatest Book of the Age". Twenty-five years later Anna Sewell's popular novel *Black Beauty* sometimes carried the improbable parasitic subtitle of *The Uncle Tom's Cabin of the Horse*.) Henry Louis Gates Jr, coeditor of the new Annotated Norton edition, interprets the hostility of black militants of the 1960s to the novel in this way: "They meant Uncle Tom to be a metaphor for Martin Luther King. King, they thought, was the long suffering, too Christian person leading the movement astray" (*TLS*, March 30, 2007, p. 4). Gates tells an ironic story, partly against himself, of a lecture he once gave to some black students on the complexities of American Black Studies. Although the lecture was balanced and nuanced, he got a single response: "Yeah brother, but what we want to know is: was Booker T. Washington an Uncle Tom?" Although the sobriquet is generally limited to American usage, it is occasionally used in other contexts for a politician regarded as insufficiently militant: "Arafat was always attacked by Marxist-oriented militants as being a Palestinian 'Uncle Tom', neither sufficiently radical or violent" (*Guardian*, July 15, 1971).

African

It has taken *African* a long time to come into its own as a positive political term, largely as a consequence of developments in the new South Africa. As has been shown, the range of stigmatizing names given to the indigenous population by the settlers and colonists ranged through *Hottentots, Bushmen, Kaffirs, Natives, Non-Whites,* and *Bantu.* Curiously, *Black* was generally avoided by both the government and the governed. The major exception was the development of the radical Black Consciousness Movement (from 1969), especially associated with Steve Biko. But *African* became the general preference of the liberation movements, namely the African National Congress (ANC, founded 1912), and the Pan Africanist Congress (1959). The latter movement, which insisted on an exclusively black membership, also promoted the alternative spelling *Afrika* (pronounced "Afreeka"), used in its founding statement rejecting the Dutch establishment of the colony of the Cape of Good Hope as "The Act of Aggression against the Sons and Daughters of Afrika, by which the African people were dispossessed of their land and subjected to white domination." After the banning of most Black Consciousness organizations, the socialist Azanian People's Organisation (AZAPO, founded 1978) preferred this ancient and exotic name, which occurs in the *Periplus of the Aegean Sea* (c. AD 60) and is found on some old maps, but not covering the southern portion of Africa. Although *Afrika* is occasionally encountered in political rhetoric, *Azania* is becoming a complete rarity.

The term *African* is general since, like *European* or *Asian*, it carries with it a complex range of qualifications – geographical, historical, social, and political. It was given a significant defining moment on May 8, 1996 when Thabo Mbeki, second President of the New South Africa, delivered a keynote speech in the House of Assembly in Cape Town. Widely termed the "I am an African" speech, it received a great deal of media attention, comment, and praise. Mbeki's conception of an African was accommodating and pluralistic rather than exclusive, as well as poetic, romantic, and in many ways mystical, starting with symbiotic natural notions: "I am an African. I owe my being to the hills and the valleys, the mountains and the glades, the rivers, the deserts, the trees, the flowers, the seas and the ever-changing seasons that define the face of our native land."

Mbeki claimed as his ancestors a whole diversity of victims and conquerors, seeing his Africanness as a microcosm of the violent and suffering past of the nation and the continent:

In my veins courses the blood of the Malay slaves who came from the East. Their proud dignity informs my bearing, their culture a part of my essence. The stripes they bore on their bodies from the lash of the slave master are a reminder embossed on my consciousness of what should not be done.

I am the grandchild of the warrior men and women that Hintsa and Sekhukhune led, the patriots that Cetshwayo and Mphephu took to battle, the soldiers Moshoeshoe and Ngungunyane taught never to dishonour the cause of freedom.

> My mind and my knowledge of myself is formed by the victories that are the jewels of our African crown, the victories we earned from Isandlwana to Khartoum, as Ethiopians, and as the Ashanti of Ghana, as the Berbers of the desert.

Perhaps Mbeki's most surprising self-identification came in the following passage, alluding to the horrors inflicted by the British in the Anglo-Boer war: "I am the grandchild who lays fresh flowers on the Boer graves at St Helena and the Bahamas, who sees in the mind's eye and suffers the suffering of a simple peasant folk, death, concentration camps, destroyed homesteads, a dream in ruins." Mbeki's speech was given at the session of Parliament which adopted the new constitution, a point to which he returned at intervals:

> The constitution whose adoption we celebrate constitutes an unequivocal state-ment that we refuse to accept that our Africanness shall be defined by our race, colour, gender or historical origins.
> It is a firm assertion made by ourselves that South Africa belongs to all who live in it, black and white.
> It gives concrete expression to the sentiment we share as Africans, and will defend to the death, that the people shall govern.

However, the peroration of this inspiring speech showed a distinctly mili-tarist and even triumphalist tone:

> Today it feels good to be an African.
> It feels good that I can stand here as a South African and as a foot soldier of a titanic African army, the African National Congress, to say to all the parties represented here, to the millions who made the input into the pro-cesses we are concluding, to our outstanding compatriots who have presided over the birth of our founding document . . . congratulations and well done!

Mbeki's idealistic vision of an inclusive African identity reflected the pre-vious example of Nelson Mandela. At the opening of the first democratic parliament in 1994, Mandela made an extraordinary presidential gesture, quoting a long-forgotten poem from the apartheid era, "The child who was shot dead by soldiers at Nyanga," by Ingrid Jonker, adding: "She was both an Afrikaner and an African." But this idealism was to be challenged by the practical problems of implementing affirmative action by means of a racial quota system, as required in the Employment Equity Bill. The pre-vious discussion on *transformation* in chapter 1 opened the discussion, show-ing how various traditional terms and categories have come under semantic stress as a consequence of political and economic agendas, more especially that for some *African* has become a pre-eminent category, superior to, or more potent than, *Black*.

On a broader front, shortly after his celebrated "I am an African" speech with its optimistic sentiments, Mbeki made a statement in Parliament on October 29, 1997: "It is a priority with the government to address the matter of an African Renaissance." Since then – on the ideological plane – "the African Renaissance" has become a virtual cliché, and has raised hopes and expectations, despite awareness of the actual misery, poverty, genocide, and civil war afflicting many African states. Even within South Africa there are social problems of service delivery to the poor and the devastating effects of the AIDS pandemic.

"Black African"

As a consequence of the problems of definition surrounding "African," more especially the claims and qualifications of Coloureds, Indians, and Afrikaners to be called "African," the more exclusive designation "black African" was brought into play, notably in the Transformation Charter. This new nomenclature has obviously been a source of concern.

Simultaneously, and somewhat ironically, South Africa has suffered major problems arising from illegal immigration of Africans from dysfunctional states, especially Zimbabwe and further North, from "black Africa" and as far afield as Somalia. Consequently, xenophobia, which was virtually unheard of up to liberation, has become an increasing social problem, since these foreigners compete with locals in the job market in a situation of high unemployment. Unlike the Coloureds who are "not Black enough," these immigrants are identified, harassed, and persecuted because they are "too Black." The Provincial Government of the Western Cape commissioned a study on "Foreign African Migrants" as far back as 2001. By 2008 there were an estimated 3,000,000 illegal immigrants nationally, and dozens of articles appeared in the local press and in research pamphlets.

In May 2008 there were sudden outbreaks of deadly xenophobic violence directed at Zimbabweans, Shangaans, Mozambicans, and Somalis by their black township neighbors. Although there had been similar attacks on foreign migrants for several years, the first reactions were of shock and outrage that black South Africans could turn on their "African brothers and sisters." President Mbeki gave a national television broadcast denouncing the attacks as "an absolute disgrace," reminding his audience of the important contributions to the liberation struggle made by Africans outside South Africa. This response was politically correct in the sense of being an ideologically orthodox expression of pan-Africanism. But it did not solve the actual social problems on the ground. The migrants were either repatriated or housed in refugee camps. The government, obviously not wishing to reintroduce an apartheid solution, set out proposals for "reintegration." These were met with general hostility from most quarters. The outbreaks of violence caused a national psychic shock, since they violated all the tenets of the rainbow nation.

The victims became identifiable outsiders known as the *kwere kwere* or *amakwerekwere*, foreigners so called because they pronounce the "l" sound as "r." (Traditional Zulu, for example, has no "r" sound.) *Kwere kwere* is a comparatively recent term, perhaps 10 or 15 years old. Contemporary cartoons exploited the linguistic aspect with savage captions, such as "I knew he was a *kwere kwere* because he didn't know the meaning of *ubuntu* [humanity]" (*Sunday Times*, May 25, 2008). Among many comments, the article by Fred Khumalo in *The Sunday Times* (June 15, 2008) underscored the problems of being "too black" and speaking the "wrong" variety of a local language. The foreigners were recognized and targeted by their speech, on the same basis as the original *shibboleth*, discussed in chapter 1, and in the same way as the Flemings were identified in the Peasants' Revolt of 1381, as is mentioned in the discussion of Chaucer in chapter 7.

Color and Loyalty: Issues of Nativism

As we have seen, issues of color and loyalty have a complex history epitomized in the American histories of *Oreo* and *Uncle Tom*. These issues form an ironic "Return of the Native," a theme covered in "The New Black Nativism," an article by Orlando Patterson, the Harvard sociologist, carrying the subtitle: "Obama's not black enough? Sad times for a community once proud of its diversity" (*Time*, February 19, 2007, p. 51). "The sad truth," wrote Patterson early in the Democratic primary campaign, "is that Obama is being rejected because many Black Americans don't consider him one of their own and may even feel threatened by what he embodies." Patterson noted that the defining characteristic of black American identity has been any person born in America of African ancestry, however remote. Blacks exploited "the infamous one-drop rule" imposed by white racists to claim a diverse heritage. Many of the black civil rights icons were actually descendants of Caribbean immigrants: they include W. E. B. DuBois, Marcus Garvey, Stokely Carmichael, Malcolm X, Louis Farrakhan, Harry Belafonte, and Sidney Poitier. Patterson continued:

In recent years, however, this tradition has been eroded by a thickened form of black identity that, sadly, mirrors some of the worst aspects of American white identity and racism. A streak of nativism rears its ugly head. To be a black American in this view, one's ancestors must have been not simply slaves, but American slaves. Furthermore, there is the growing tendency to define blackness in negative terms – it is to be not white in upbringing, kinship or manner, not to be too at ease in the intimate ways of white Americans.

Patterson argued that Obama's credentials as a black American are sufficient in terms of lineage, marriage, and community service in the ghettos, but they are compromised by "the fact that he is the son of an immigrant and that he was brought up mainly by middle-class whites whose culture is second nature to him." Patterson also wrote of "a growing pattern of self-segregation among the black middle class." Richard Rodriguez observed similarly that "the era that began with the dream of integration ended up with scorn for assimilation" (quoted in Schlesinger, 1992, p. 112). The subsequent election victory of Obama has, of course, changed the whole dynamic of race and politics in the US.

Patterson's analysis of current "self-segregation" reminds us that segregation is partly a naturally process. In 1552 Bishop Latimer noted that "the Anabaptists segregated themselves from other men," in the manner of the Amish in America. The Latin root of both *congregation* and *segregation*, namely *grex, gregis,* meaning "a flock," translates into the proverb "birds of a feather flock together." *Segregation* was a neutral term for centuries: the negative denotation arose principally from the administered forms of apartheid in South Africa and segregation in America.

Segregation can take more subtle forms than legalized separation. The *Times Literary Supplement* (January 19, 2007) carried an illuminating item under the title of "Racial Segregation in the Literary World: An Update." "For years," the article explained, "we have been objecting to awards, workshops and prizes that are open to one ethnic group" (principally on the grounds that a prize established exclusively for whites would be against the law). The *TLS* protested against the Decibel Penguin Prize for Short Stories, sponsored by Arts Council England, which claimed to "raise the voice of culturally diverse arts in Britain." The article continued:

> The cant term "culturally diverse" disguises a practice that in practice is narrow: "black" and Asian writers were eligible for the prize; white writers – whatever that means – were not. Asked about the prize last year, the Culture Minister David Lammy played the race card and accused critics of putting down ethnic minorities. Now the Arts Council has been informed by the Commission for Racial Equality that banning particular racial groups from entering the competition is illegal. (p. 14)

Racist Utterances

The reader may care to consider the following quotations drawn from the past century and a half. The first group concerns blacks, seen from within and outside the group.

"The rest of the world – Niggers and what not" (letter from Lord Byron to Francis Hodgson, 1811); "A similar error has turned Othello into a rank, woolly-pated, thick-lipped nigger" (Hartley Coleridge, *Essays*, 1848). A century later a noted theater critic wrote of Paul Robeson's famous Othello: "This was nigger Shakespeare" (James Agate, *Brief Chronicles*, 1943). "All Coons Look Alike to Me" was the title of a minstrel song written in 1896 by Ernest Hogan, a black. According to H. L. Mencken, the somewhat naïve Hogan was "amazed and crushed by the resentment it aroused among his people" (1963, p. 386). Kenneth Tynan punningly referred to Orson Welles in the role of Othello in 1951 as "Citizen Coon" (*Evening Standard*, October 19). More poignantly amusing was the comment that "It is a great shock at the age of five or six to discover that in a world of Gary Coopers you are the Indian" (James Baldwin, in a speech at the Cambridge Union, February 17, 1965).

Two more recent effusions are of a different tone: "Fuckin' jungle bunny goes out there, slits some old woman's throat for twenty-five cents. Fuckin' nigger gets Doris Day as a parole officer. But a good fella like you gets a ball-busting prick." "Now ain't that a sad sight, daddy, walks into jail a white man, walks out talkin' like a nigger. It's all that black semen been shooting up his butt. It's backed up into his brain and comes out of his mouth" (Quentin Tarantino, *Reservoir Dogs*, 1994, p. 51). The views of Byron and Hartley Coleridge, while surprising, can be explained as being part of the routine racism of their times. But it is anomalous that the most virulent comments should come from the work of Tarantino, a supposed cultural icon, in the 1990s.

The second group of quotations is a more complex mixture of views on race and racism. We may start with the episode at Tufts University where an African-American Studies professor accused Dinesh D'Souza (who is of Indian origin) of "advancing racist views," but explained paradoxically that D'Souza could not be a racist: "No way. You are a person of color. *You cannot be a racist.* You don't have power in this society. Only whites can be racist" (D'Souza, 1991, p. xii).

1   "The white race *is* the cancer of human history" (Susan Sontag, "What's Happening in America," in *Partisan Review*, Winter 1967, p. 57). Sontag later "retracted" the statement by saying that it slandered cancer patients (Hitchens, 2004).

2   "Coleman had taken attendance at the beginning of the first several
         lectures so as to learn their [the students'] names. As there were still
         two names that failed to elicit a response by the fifth week into the
         semester, Coleman, in the sixth week, opened the session by asking,
         'Does anyone know these people? Do they exist or are they
         spooks?'" (Philip Roth, *The Human Stain*, 2000, p. 6). This ironic,
         innocent throwaway question contains what Roth calls "the single
         self-incriminating word out of the many millions spoken aloud in
         his years of teaching and administrating." It leads to the destruction
         of Coleman Silk's brilliant career, and potentially to his wife's
         death. The word *spooks*, obviously used by Silk in its general sense,
         is opportunistically interpreted as a racist insult by the two absent-
         ing students, who turn out to be black and bring a charge of racism.
         Although fictional, the episode and its consequences are clearly a
         protest by Roth against the witch-hunts all too current in the atmo-
         sphere of political correctness.

3   "I think that most Indians, like most English people, are shits"
         (E. M. Forster, letter of September 27, 1922, cited in *OED*).

4   "He might be described as an underprivileged, colonial, working-
         class victim of religious and political persecution" (The Duke of
         Edinburgh on Jesus (*A Question of Balance*, 1982).

5(a)   "It was the week before Christmas, Monday midday, mild and
         muggy, and the muezzins of West London were yodelling about there
         being no God but Allah: '*La ilaha illa'lah. La ilaha illa'lah*'"

5(b)   "King Charles III, a rather podgy bat-eared man in his late thirties,
         spoke of this happy and sacred time and God bless you all"
         (Anthony Burgess, *1985*, 1978, pp. 105, 127).

6   "Not only did we play the race card, we played it from the bottom
         of the deck" (Robert Shapiro, originally leader of the defense team
         in the O. J. Simpson trial, *The Times*, October 5, 1995).

Xenophobia and Anti-Semitism

Xenophobia, meaning literally "fear of strangers," is only about a hundred
years old as a term, but the attitudes it describes are obviously ancient, if
not primordial. They originate historically in martial and religious rivalry,
continue in economic competition and war, and are apparent in racist
hostility in many modern societies, often as a consequence of immigration.
Thus at different stages of British history Catholic nations like Italy and
Spain have been regarded as enemies, as has Ireland to a lesser extent, while

Holland, Germany, and Japan have been regarded as martial threats. The French have for centuries qualified on both counts. However, as we have seen, Commonwealth immigration introduced a new source of difference, namely color. The modern sense of xenophobia is closer to "hatred of foreigners."

Xenophobia tends to be strongest in societies dominated by a nationalist ideology and driven by religious, martial, or commercial motives. Commenting on the emotions sustaining national identity, Edward Said admitted that "no-one finds it easy to live with the sense that a stable essence is under threat," continuing "Patriotism, extreme xenophobic nationalism and downright unpleasant chauvinism are common responses to this fear" (1995, p. 333). When national identity is perceived to be under threat, it often becomes constricted to forms of extreme nationalism, providing a seedbed for tyranny, fascism or totalitarianism. Rampant inflation in Germany undoubtedly contributed to anti-Semitism, and the threat of Communism in America generated McCarthyism.

Whereas the targets of xenophobia have changed with social developments, anti-Semitism has a long and persistent history. It can be rationalized as deriving from doctrinal roots (the Jews' rejection of Christ as the Messiah and the assumption of their responsibility for his death), from a general unwillingness to assimilate religiously, and from commercial practices (notably the practice of usury, which was contrary to medieval Canon Law). Accusations of ritual murder by Jews stem from 1144 and were particularly focused on the death of St Hugh of Lincoln in 1255. A common qualifying adjective for *Jew* in medieval times was *corsed* (*cursed*), much used by Chaucer's Prioress in her savage and melodramatic tale based on the legend of the murder of St Hugh. A thirteenth-century manuscript shows Jews being attacked in London: they are identifiable by the two strips of yellow cloth they were legally required to wear (British Library, MS Cotton Nero D. ii. fol. 183v.).

The great anomaly in the development of these vicious stereotypes is that many of them grew up between 1290, when Jews were expelled by Edward I and 1655, when they were readmitted by Oliver Cromwell. This strongly suggests that they were based on legend, fabrication, and propaganda. Furthermore, the use of the noun *Jew* in what the *OED* records as "a name of opprobrium or reprobation" dates from about 1600 and multiplied greatly thereafter in compounds such as *Jew-boy* and the provocative name *Christ-killer*. The chronology of the main nicknames is *sheeny* (c. 1810), *ikey* (1864), *yid* (1874), *kike* (1880s), and *hymie* (1973). The last four are listed in Thorne's *Dictionary of Contemporary Slang* (2007). Irving Lewis Allen (1983) shows that in the United States there are 64 nicknames for Jews, more than for any other immigrant group.

A crucial development was the seminal anti-Semitic document, *The Protocols of the Elders of Zion*, privately printed in 1897 and published in various European languages from 1905 with savage propagandist caricatures. It was ostensibly a record of a secret Zionist Congress at Basel to plan world domination. However, after an exposé by the London *Times* in 1921, a judicial inquiry in 1934 revealed that the document was a forgery generated by the Russian Political Police (the Okhrana). Sections had been copied from a novel, *Biarritz* (1868), by Hermann Goedsche. But since this agenda perfectly fitted the stereotype of a Jewish conspiracy, it was highly effective as propaganda and was widely disseminated, notably by Adolf Hitler and the Nazis, and by Henry Ford in the United States. Its influence still lingers.

It is generally assumed that anti-Semitism and racism are typical features of the political Right, which traditionally puts great emphasis on the purity of the national culture and bloodline, and thus has a greater propensity for xenophobic attitudes. Contrariwise, it is assumed that the political philosophy of the Left is more universalist and accepting of diversity and therefore of foreigners. Anti-Semitism seems to be a feature of all classes, not confined simply to what used to be called "the lower orders." It is thus instructive and revealing to match some significant authors and their quotations in the following passages:

1   The capitalists would rake in the shekels, and make fortunes by buying up wreckage. Capital, he said, had no conscience and no fatherland. Besides, the Jew was behind it and the Jew hated Russia worse than hell. "The Jew is everywhere, but you have to go far down the backstairs to find him . . . if you're on the biggest kind of job and are bound to get to the real boss, ten to one you are brought up against a little white-faced Jew in a bath-chair with an eye like a rattlesnake."

2   The Jewish NIGGER Lassalle who, I'm glad to say, is leaving at the end of this week, has happily lost another 5,000 talers in an ill-judged speculation . . . It is now quite plain to me – as the shape of his head and the way his hair grows also testify – that he is descended from the negroes who accompanied Moses' flight from Egypt (unless his mother or his paternal grandmother interbred with a NIGGER). Now, this blend of Jewishness and Germanness, on the one hand, and basic negroid stock, on the other, must inevitably give rise to a peculiar product. The fellow's importunity is also niggerlike.

3   "I do not like the Jewish voice, I do not like the Jewish laugh."

4   Referring to Benjamin Disraeli, anglicized, baptized, and twice Prime Minister: "a superlative Hebrew conjuror" "a cursed old Jew not worth his weight in cold bacon."

5 "The rats are underneath the piles. / The Jew is underneath the lot."
"My house is a decayed house, / And the jew squats on the window
sill, the owner, / Spawned in some estaminet of Antwerp."

6 The population should be homogeneous; where two or more cultures
exist in the same place they are likely either to be fiercely self-conscious
or both to become adulterate. What is still more important is unity of
religious background; and reasons of race and religion combine to make
any large number of free-thinking Jews undesirable.

Authors are as follows:

1 Lord Tweedsmuir, Governor General of Canada, better known as John
Buchan, author of the highly popular political thriller, *The Thirty-Nine
Steps* (1915). The somewhat crass conspiracy theory explicated here by
Scudder to Richard Hannay in the opening chapter corresponds eerily
to the propaganda embodied in *The Protocols of the Elders of Zion*.

2 Karl Marx, himself a Jew, in a letter (July 30, 1862) to Friedrich Engels,
the coauthor of the *Communist Manifesto* (1848), referring to the German
politician and sociologist Ferdinand Lassalle. Marx, who had been the
beneficiary of Lassalle's considerable generosity over the years, was incidentally dark-skinned and nicknamed *der Mohr* ("The Moor") even by
his friend Engels. The passage was suppressed in several editions.

3 Virginia Woolf, *Diaries*. Her husband, Leonard Woolf, was Jewish.

4 Thomas Carlyle (1795–1881), perhaps the greatest Victorian intellectual (Sutherland, 1975, p. 224).

5 T. S. Eliot, "Burbank with a Baedeker: Bleistein with a Cigar," and
"Gerontion," from *Poems, 1920*.

6 T. S. Eliot, *After Strange Gods*, lectures given at the University of Virginia
(1934, pp. 30–1). Eliot's anti-Semitism, generally ignored in early
reviews, took several decades to be raised in public debate. George
Steiner's major attack half a century later in *Bluebeard's Castle*, originally published in the *Listener* in 1971, provoked in the main only
summary and contemptuous rejections in the correspondence columns
(15 April to 13 May). In a reply Steiner quoted the offensive lines from
"Gerontion" and from "Burbank," noting that "Eliot's uglier touches
tend to occur at the heart of very good poetry" (Steiner, 1971, p. 34,
also quoted in Ricks, 1988, p. 28). Indeed, Eliot himself wrote to his
brother in 1920 that he regarded "Burbank" as being "among the best
things I have ever done" (Sharpe, 1991, pp. 60, 170–1). Since then the
topic has been canvassed more broadly, notably by Christopher Ricks
(1988). Perhaps the crispest comment came from Edward Pearce: "To

hell with political correctness: Eliot's politics affront common decency" (*Literary Review*, December 1992, p. 11).

The Holocaust

The Holocaust has rightly been seen as the absolute nadir in civilization, a genocide more terrible, more bureaucratic, and more industrial than its many predecessors. It took time to find words to frame the horrors: *genocide* was coined in 1944 at the Nazi war crimes tribunal and *holocaust* took on its specialized sense among historians only in the 1950s. George Steiner saw it more drastically as a failure of civilization. In the Preface to *Language and Silence* he wrote: "We know that a man can read Goethe or Rilke in the evening, that he can play Bach and Schubert, and go to do his day's work at Auschwitz in the morning" (1969, p. 15). In the same collection, in "Silence and the Poet" he quoted Adorno's famous dictum "No poetry after Auschwitz" (1969, p. 75).

To deny the Holocaust is now a crime in some countries, with varying degrees of punishment. The offense led to the historian David Irving being imprisoned in Austria and a French university lecturer being denied tenure. Paradoxically, to deny the existence of God, previously blasphemy, is now acceptable. The difference, presumably, is that denying the Holocaust is offensive to its victims and their memory, whereas offending believers is no longer considered serious. However, even on Holocaust denial there is a global double standard. It is a criminal offence in Austria, but acceptable propaganda in Iran, even fostered by the Iranian Prime Minister, Mahmoud Ahmadinejad. He organized a Conference in December 2006 in which "An international cast of established Holocaust deniers and implacable foes of Israel were given an open forum by Iran to support Ahmadinejad's contention that the murder of six million Jews by the Nazis was a 'myth'" (*Guardian*, December 12, 2006). He repeated the slander at Princeton University in 2007.

Islam

Historically Islam was regarded as the militant enemy of Christianity, usually designated by the chauvinist religious terms *heathen* and *infidel*. In typical xenophobic fashion, in medieval times the name Muhammad came to mean "an idol" and was corrupted to two forms: to *mawmet*, meaning "a false god," and to *Mahounde*, also meaning "a devil," "false prophet," or "a monster," often invoked in oaths by evil characters. Mahound was also transformed into a stage character, defined by the *OED* as "a violent and overbearing personage representing a deity supposedly worshipped by Muslims." Since Islam posed no threat to Britain or its religion after the medieval period, these hostile attitudes cooled and the insulting terms became obsolete. Indeed, in his controversial novel *The Satanic Verses* (1988), Salman Rushdie commented on the process of reclamation: "To turn insults into strengths, Whigs, Tories, Blacks all chose to wear with pride the names they were given in scorn." He then alluded to "our mountain-climbing, prophet-motivated solitary . . . the Devil's synonym: Mahound" (p. 93).

The vexed publishing history of *The Satanic Verses* shows the radical difference between the generally blasé secularism of the West and the fundamentalism of Islam. The novel was banned in India and burnt on the streets of London and Bradford. In 1989 the Ayatollah Khomeini of Iran imposed a death sentence or *fatwa* on Rushdie, his publishers, and translators, concluding: "Whoever is killed in this path will be regarded as a martyr." In *God is Not Great*, Christopher Hitchens explains that "Rushdie had been brought up as a Muslim and had an understanding of the Koran, which meant in effect he was an apostate. And 'apostasy', according to the Koran, is punishable only by death. There is no right to change religion" (2007, p. 29). The Iranian government formally withdrew their support for the *fatwa* in 1998, but it was reaffirmed in 2005. Malise Ruthven's study *A Satanic Affair* (1990) originally carried the subtitle *Salman Rushdie and the Rage of Islam*, but in the paperback edition (1991) this was modified, significantly, to *Salman Rushdie and the Wrath of Islam*. Julie Burchill claims in her acerbic account of the affair that Rushdie was not entirely consistent in his dealings with the Iranian regime, neither were his literary colleagues in their support (1992, pp. 16–19).

In June 2007 the news that the Queen was to give Rushdie a knighthood generated violent reactions in the Muslim world. According to the *Guardian*, "The committee . . . did not discuss any possible political ramifications and never imagined that the award would provoke the furious response that it has done in parts of the Muslim world." The British ambassador in Teheran denounced "remarks supposedly made by the Iranian Minister for Religious Affairs, Mohammed Ejaz ul-Haq, which appeared to justify suicide bombings as a response to the award" (*Guardian*, June 20, 2007). In a letter to the *Guardian*, leaders of 12 million British Muslims decried the knighthood as "a deliberate provocation and insult to the 1.5 billion Muslims around the world."

The suicide bombing of the World Trade Center on September 11, 2001 naturally provoked widespread anger and hostility in the West, just as the bombs in London on July 7, 2005 hardened attitudes in Britain. The term *Islamophobia*, recorded from 1976, has consequently become increasingly current. Despite these outrages, there has been a general reluctance to enter into open debate, partly out of respect for multiculturalism and for fear of being labeled as racist. Thus very few feminists have criticized the status and rights of women under Islam. One exceptional critic was Martin Amis, who condemned Jihadism as "racist, homophobic, totalitarian, genocidal, inquisitorial and imperialistic." "Surely there should be no difficulty in announcing one's hostility to that," he observed, "but there is" (*New York Times*, March 9, 2008).

In an ironic return to medieval idiom, extremist Muslim leaders such as Osama bin Laden have resuscitated inflammatory and archaic religious terminology by referring to America as "the Antichrist," to Christians as "Crusaders," and Jews as "Zionists," although the last term is late nineteenth century and is not in itself offensive or inflammatory. In this martial context the root of *assassin* in "hashish-eater" is a memorial, as the *OED* points out, of "certain Moslem fanatics in the time of the Crusades, who were sent forth by their sheikh, the 'Old Man of the Mountains' to murder Christian leaders."

Targets of xenophobia

Historically, the prime targets of English xenophobia have been the French, the Germans, the Irish, the Dutch, the Italians, the Spanish, and the Japanese. Being hostile to the French has a long tradition, becoming fashionable, even a natural patriotic reaction, during the Napoleonic wars. Previously they were the nation most associated with "dubious" sexual practices: hence *French letter*, *French prints* (pornographic pictures), and *French disease* for syphilis, discussed in greater detail in chapter 6. Many of these attitudes still persist, but more in the form of rudeness.

The English have a complex historical relationship with the Germans, being originally descended from the Germanic tribes known as the *Anglo-Saxons*. After the Norman Conquest the Germans were generally not hostile to the English, and from 1714 the German House of Hanover assumed the English throne for two centuries. However, the increasing belligerence of Prussia became encapsulated in the word *Hun*, which was applied, uniquely and ironically, by Kaiser Wilhelm II himself to the Germans. In an inflammatory speech given to German troops about to sail to China in 1900, the Kaiser appealed to an atavistic and barbarian mythology: "No quarter will be given. . . . Just as the Huns a thousand years ago, under the leadership of Etzel [Atilla], gained a reputation in virtue [strength] . . . so may the name of Germany become known in such a manner that no Chinaman will ever again even dare to look askance at a German." Although the original Huns were in fact an Asiatic race, this alarming invocation was the seed of the stereotype of the modern Hun, brutal, militaristic, and robotic. Wartime antipathy towards the Germans generated the nicknames *bosch* (1914), *fritz* (1915), and *jerry* (1918). These have passed away, but *Hun* remains common in English upper-class slang.

In medieval times "the wild Irish" were those who lived literally "beyond the pale," the palisade built by the English colonists. Stereotypes of backwardness and incompetence appear in many idiomatic uses. *Irish* itself is used ironically in numerous combinations, such as *Irish dividend* for a fictitious profit. Francis Grose (1785) included early insulting epithets such as *bogtrotter* and *Tory* ("an Irish vagabond and robber") and *Irish beauty* for "a woman with two black eyes." A more recent arrival, *Irish wheelbarrow* for an ambulance, is marked as "now usually considered offensive" by the *Random House Dictionary of American Slang* (1997). The Irish capacity for self-irony is second only to that of the Jews and unique in the British Isles. In this tone Paddy Doyle wrote in *The Commitments* (1987, p. 13): "The Irish are the niggers of Europe, lads. An' Dubliners are the niggers of Ireland . . . An' northside Dubliners are the niggers of Dubliners – Say it loud. I'm black an' I'm proud" (quoting the James Brown song of 1968).

The numerous ironic uses of *Dutch* in compounds such as *Dutch courage* and *Dutch auction* are explained by the *OED* as survivals "largely due to rivalry and enmity between the English and the Dutch in the 17th century." In 1667 the Dutch navy sailed up the river Medway, creating panic over the possibility of an invasion. The authority includes *Dutch widow* for a prostitute (1608), *Dutch feast*, where the host gets drunk before his guests (1700), and *Dutch reckoning* (1700), an account which is a lump sum without details. Eric Partridge includes many similar examples in his edition of Grose's slang dictionary. Although the Dutch are now regarded as allies rather than enemies, other lexical additions are *Dutch treat* and *Dutch cap*.

Italy has been by turns venerated through medieval and Renaissance times as the cultural repository of Roman civilization and detested after the Reformation as the decadent, corrupt, and devious center of Papism. The continuing misinterpretation of Machiavelli's *The Prince* (1513) generated the stereotype of the Machiavel on the English stage and the continued negative use of *Machiavellian*. Italy was equally notorious for its courtesans and its perversion: "Buggery is now almost grown as common among our gallants as in Italy," wrote Samuel Pepys on July 1, 1663. Opera, introduced from Italy, was seen as the preserve of homosexuals and eunuchs, a reputation which was not enhanced by the subsequent Italian war record. The stereotypical association with the Mafia, founded in historical fact, has continued in fiction. But most of the politically incorrect nicknames originated more recently in the United States. These include *dago*, *eytie*, *greaseball*, *guinea*, *spic*, and *wop*, the more familiar of over 50 nicknames, according to Irving Lewis Allen (1983).

The religious enmity of Spain culminating in the Armada (1588) obviously left its prejudices, somewhat similar to those against Italy. The Spanish Civil War (1936–9) divided Europe as it did the nation. But the key word, prior to the fascination with bullfighting, was *mañana*, recorded from 1845 in a quotation about Andalucia: "those talismanic words which mark the national character, the Manana [sic]," followed by "Their *mañana* never came, never was intended to come" (1889, cited in *OED*). The Moorish invasion of Spain left some unexpected survivals, namely *Moors and Christians*, a dish of rice and black beans, and German *Mohrenkopf*, an oval chocolate-coated cream cake.

For centuries, the Japanese remained an unknown and alien race to most of the West. However, the importation of indentured labor into California from the 1840s made them rivals with the American workforce, and the unprovoked attack on Pearl Harbor on December 7, 1941 established them as stereotypical traitors who were consequently interned and remained segregated. *Jap* rapidly acquired many insulting senses. Since the British experience was different until World War II, the Japanese were seen more as comic aliens attracting various puns on *nip*. The postwar Japanese recovery generated by a potent mixture of corporate fascism and feudalism, provoked criticisms, especially this virulent comment: "Ants . . . little yellow men who sit up all night thinking how to screw us," made by Edith Cresson, the French Prime Minister, in 1991 (L'Estrange, 2002, p. 313). In the ensuing furor Cresson was forced to resign.

The extensive criticism of England and the English derives expectedly from their traditional enemies such as the French and the Germans. Some well-worn criticisms have been assimilated, such as "Perfidious Albion" ("L'Angleterre, ah la perfide Angleterre"), deriving from Jacques-Benigne Bousset, Metz, 1652. A more analytical modern voice, reprising Napoleon, comments: "You never hear debates here about ethics or morals, just about saving money. . . . Britain really is a nation of shopkeepers" (Patrice Claude, London correspondent of *Le Monde*, March 10, 2001).

Resident or insider views of England were previously in the main rather favorable and tinged with patriotism until the sharper Victorian observations of Dickens, Mayhew, Gissing, Booth, and others. The more recent are decidedly pessimistic or critical, with increasing emphasis on race. "England's not a bad country. It's just a mean, cold, ugly, divided, tired, clapped-out, post-imperial, post-industrial slag-heap covered in polystyrene hamburger cartons" (Margaret Drabble, *A Natural Curiosity*, 1989, p. 308). "England has become a squalid, uncomfortable, ugly place . . . an intolerant, racist, homophobic, narrow-minded, authoritarian rat-hole run by vicious suburban-minded, materialistic philistines" (Hanif Kureishi, in the *Guardian*, January 15, 1988).

Hate Speech

As can be seen in the previous section, what is now called "hate speech" has deep and ancient roots. The section on the Reformation in chapter 7 similarly shows that the sectarian controversies of that period were conducted in language of astounding, indeed un-Christian ferocity.

In parts of the New World, where many religious refugees sought sanctuary, there were strenuous attempts to outlaw such language. In Maryland, for instance, the Act of Toleration (1649) established legal restraints against "persons reproaching any other by the name or denomination of Heretic, Schismatic, Idolatour, Puritan, Round-Head, Separatist, or by any other name of term, in a reproachful manner relating to the subject of religion." It ordered fining, whipping, or imprisonment for offenders who did not publicly supplicate for forgiveness (Myers, 1943, p. 46). This determination, both idealistic in its aims and drastic in its methods, shows some of the characteristics of political correctness.

The actual formulation *hate speech* originated in America centuries later, in a *Newsweek* report quoting a law professor's view that "continuing tensions can only fuel wider interest in banning hate speech" (June 6, 1988). Samuel Walker's study *Hate Speech* makes this familiar observation: "Almost every country prohibits hate speech directed at racial, religious, or ethnic groups. The United States, by contrast, has developed a strong tradition of free speech that protects even the most offensive forms of expression" (1994, p. 1). The opinion of Justice Holmes on the principle of free thought, even "freedom for the thought that we hate" (1929, among the epigraphs at the beginning of the book), is often quoted as an endorsement of this principle. However, what is at issue here is not "the thought" but the words.

The key notion is the category of "fighting words," deriving from the watershed case of *Chaplinsky v. New Hampshire* (1942), arising from an altercation in which Chaplinsky called the local town marshal a "Goddamned racketeer" and a "damned fascist," both highly provocative in 1942. In a unanimous ruling for the State, the Supreme Court established "fighting words" as language unprotected by the First Amendment, defining them as "The lewd and obscene, the profane, the libelous, and the insulting or 'fighting' words – those which by their very utterance inflict injury or tend to incite an immediate breach of the peace." Chaplinsky's words clearly corresponded with these criteria, thus falling outside the category of protected speech, that is, words expressing ideas of "social value" or concerned with the search for the truth.

Hate speech became a major issue in the political correctness debate because of its ambiguous constitutional status. Research into its sources has focused on whether it is a symptomatic "result of cultures clashing and merging," or should be admitted "as part of a culture rather than extraneous to it" (Whillock and Slayden, 1995, pp. ix, xiii). At one extreme it was argued that "Hate speech promotes an open society where both sides of a conflict are examined" (Whillock and Slayden, 1995, p. 227). More commonly it provoked institutions to frame speech codes, with controversial and legal consequences, all involving the interpretation of the First Amendment.

Speech codes and the First Amendment

As is well known, the First Amendment, like Habeas Corpus, establishes a fundamental freedom for all as a matter of right. It is not the intellectual property or monopoly of any group. Nor does it give publishers *carte blanche*. In 1907 Justice Holmes ruled that "the purpose of the guarantee of the freedom of the press was only to prevent all restraints previous to publication, but not to prevent subsequent punishment" (Boorstin, 1966, p. 158).

In his essay "'Speech Codes' on the Campus and Problems of Free Speech" (1991), based on visits to more than 20 colleges and universities, Nat Hentoff noted "reverse expectations – with liberals fiercely advocating censorship of 'offensive' speech and conservatives merrily taking the moral high ground as champions of free expression" (Hentoff, 1992, p. 215). He found few faculty members who were against speech codes and even they spoke only on condition of anonymity, not wishing to be categorized as racists. Dinesh D'Souza's *Illiberal Education* (1991) included a chapter on "The New Censorship" dealing with the problems of university administrators faced with a rising tide of racist behavior and sexist insults. One, the University of Michigan, instituted a policy making punishable "any behavior, verbal or physical, that stigmatizes or victimizes an individual on the basis of race, ethnicity, religion, sex, sexual orientation, creed, national origin, ancestry, age, marital status, handicap, or Vietnam-era veteran status" (1991, p. 142).

Jonathan Rauch's study *Kindly Inquisitors: The New Attacks on Free Thought* (1993) was one contribution to the debate. But perhaps the most provocative sally into the topic was Stanley Fish's *There's No Such Thing as Free Speech, And it's a Good Thing Too* (1992). Somewhat opportunistically, Fish took as his epigraph Dr Johnson's famous dictum "Patriotism is the last refuge of a scoundrel" (in Boswell's *Life*, April 7, 1775). He simply appropriated and parodied it as "Nowadays the First Amendment is the first refuge of scoundrels (Samuel Johnson and Stanley Fish)" (1994, p. 102). While some would pass this off as a sly academic in-joke, it is also an effective but illegitimate form of point-scoring. Using the tactics we have seen under the subheading of "Rhetorical strategies" in chapter 2, Fish claimed that " 'Free Speech' is just the name we give to verbal behavior that serves the substantive agendas we wish to advance" (1994, p. 102).

The major riposte came in the form of Stephen A. Smith's article, "There's Such a Thing as Free Speech: And it's a Good Thing Too" (1995). Rather than redefine "free speech," Smith surveyed the legal outcomes of cases of hate speech, especially those in which the recently imposed speech codes had been challenged. These involved a variety of episodes at the universities of Michigan (1989), Wisconsin (1991), George Mason (1991), and Central Michigan (1993). His conclusion was clear: "In every case in which a campus hate speech code at a public institution has been tested against the commands of the First Amendment, the courts have rejected virtually every defense and found them to be unconstitutional" (Smith, 1995, p. 227). The consequence was that numerous other universities repealed similar speech codes. Robin Tolmach Lakoff's stimulating chapter on "Political Correctness and Hate Speech" in *The Language War* also discusses the concept from its origins through to the problems of outlawing it (2000, pp. 86–117). A more recent study is that of Anthony Lewis, *Freedom for the Thought That We Hate* (2008).

Almost simultaneously with the emergence of *hate speech* as a formula, *hate crime* was first recorded in the US from 1984, being defined in the *Washington Post* (July 14) as "violence against racial or religious minorities." The *Chicago Tribune* (June 19, 1993) gave a wider definition: "victims [targeted] because of race, religion, ethnicity, sexual orientation or disability." The *Independent* (August 17, 2001) commented on an ugly new refinement: "Scotland Yard is creating a category of hate crime, 'transphobic crime', to cover offences against transgender people." This expanding range of targets encapsulates a history of prejudice against outsiders.

Exploitation of Fascist icons

As was noticed in the seminal case of *Chaplinsky v. New Hampshire*, Chaplinsky called the local town marshal, amongst other things, a "damned fascist," a highly provocative term in 1942. This episode recalls the justification of a defendant in an assault case in the Middlesex Police Court in 1915: "He called me a German and other filthy names" (Partridge, 1933, p. 7).

Fifty years after the formal end of Fascism and Nazism, instances continue to be surprisingly common. An early recorded emotive use comes from the *Times* in 1963: "As the main body of demonstrators began to move away . . . screams of 'Fascist pigs' and 'Gestapoism' continued" (March 27). In April, 2004 during a political confrontation, Mr Alex Jones of the Merseyside Coalition Against Racism and Fascism referred to the British National Party (BNP) as "Nazi scum!" and "Fascist!," to which a BNP member retorted "Communist!" (*Guardian*, April 26, 2004). "Who are these politically correct gauleiters?" was the question raised by Paul Johnson in his opinion piece "Time for St George to Start Slaying Dragons Again" (*Spectator*, December 17/24, 2005). Christopher Hitchens noted that "In 2004 a soap-opera film about the death of Jesus was produced by an Australian fascist and ham actor named Mel Gibson" (2007, p. 110). However, *fascist* has also come to be used in a comparatively trivial sense to mean someone who advocates a particular viewpoint in a manner regarded as intolerant or authoritarian. The *OED* carries references to "body fascists" from 1978, "green fascists" from 1987, "tobacco fascists" from 1997 and "gender fascists" from 1999.

Contexts can be unexpected. In 2006 a cricket test match between England and Pakistan ended prematurely in sensational and bitter circumstances when the umpires awarded the match to England, a correct decision, but a unique occurrence. Two days later the *International Herald Tribune* carried a front-page photograph of teenage cricketing fans in Pakistan protesting against the decision. One of their placards compared the umpire at the center of the controversy, the Australian Darrell Hair, to Hitler.

A South African Cabinet Minister, Mr Ronnie Kasrils, made some downright criticisms of the Israeli invasion of Lebanon in 2006, provoking a global frenzy of retaliation. He too was compared with Hitler, denounced variously as "a Jew-hating ignoramus" and as a "Nazi/Islamic pig" and his newspaper column described as "neo-Nazi propaganda worthy of Goebbels." When the German Chancellor Angela Merkel criticized the Mugabe regime in Zimbabwe at the Europe-Africa summit in December 2007, the Zimbabwean Information Minister was reported as calling her "a racist, fascist and Nazi" (*Cape Times*, December 12, 2007).

Given the strong tenor of political correctness in our times, when the slightest implication, innuendo, or minor slur can be used as a sign of prejudice, racism, or homophobia, these virulent outbursts are astonishing. They show, not only extraordinary intolerance, but various double standards in the use of insults.

Chapter 6

Agendas Old and New

This chapter continues with the theme of "difference." It considers the different agendas which have over time come to surround matters of gender and sexual orientation, disability, disease and mental disorders, criminal behavior, and addiction. It also focuses on some completely new emphases and concerns, with eating disorders, appearance, with the environment, and with animal rights.

Gender and Sexual Orientation

Gender traditionally referred to an abstract grammatical notion, but has in recent decades been used in expanded areas of reference. As the *OED* puts it, somewhat awkwardly: "in modern (esp. feminist) use, a euphemism for the sex of a human being, often intended to emphasise the social and cultural, as opposed to the biological distinctions between the sexes." The dictionary's earliest key quotation is from Alex Comfort's *Sex in Society* (1963): "The gender role learned by the child of two years is for most individuals almost irreversible, even if it runs counter to the physical sex of the subject." Other formulations are "gender identity," "gender models," and "gender gap." Not everybody was persuaded that this important semantic change had come about symbiotically. Roger Scruton, in an editorial in the *Literary Review*, insisted that the change was engineered:

> During the 1970s American feminists seized on the idea of gender as a social construct, and used it to hide the truth about sex as a biological destiny. By replacing the word "sex" with the word "gender" they imagined that they could achieve at a stroke what their ideology required of them – to rescue sex from biology and to recast it as a complex social choice. (December 2002/January 2003, p. 1)

This may be true of gender as a social construct, but does not alter the complexities that lie in the relationship between sex and gender.

The roots of the gender debate, already touched on in "Words and Women" in chapter 3, lie in the feminist focus on reconceiving the role of women in society in political, economic, and sexual spheres by the advocacy of their equality and rights. Traditional roles of male dominance and female subservience were criticized, as was the perception and the industrialization of women as sexual objects. This involved various forms of semantic engineering, outlined and exemplified in the earlier discussions of *wimmin*, *herstory*, *male chauvinist*, *sex worker*, and so on. The militant slogan *Women's Liberation* was coined in 1966, leading to the abbreviation *women's lib* from 1969 and *libber* from 1972, but as John Ayto has observed, "this became the target of trivializers and within a decade or so supporters had largely abandoned it in favour of *feminism* (a late-nineteenth-century coinage)" (1999, p. 453). The blander formula *the women's movement* also became preferred. In many ways these feminist interventions, marked by both political agendas and semantic programs, can be seen as the first wave of political correctness. The interventions have been marked by many successes, but also by criticisms.

A revealing example of semantic recycling lies in the key word *chauvinism*, a homonym commemorating the extreme patriotism of the nineteenth-century French veteran Nicolas Chauvin. The sexist extension of the meaning was a significant triumph for the women's movement in the US, starting with the quotation from *Ramparts* (1968): "Paternalism, male ego and all the rest of the chauvinist bag are out of place today." *Male chauvinist* rapidly became a virtual cliché in the formula *male chauvinist pig* as early as 1970. This curious amalgam provoked ironic responses in the same year in the *New Yorker* – "Hello, you male-chauvinist racist pig" – and in *Punch* in 1972: "I know, me male-chauvinist pig, you Jane." The abbreviation *MCP* is found in *Playboy*, May 1970. Yet in the same year Kate Millett observed: "At times there is a curious note of female chauvinism" (*Sexual Politics*, cited in *OED*). After a few decades of considerable publicity the phrase has become passé, and *chauvinist* has started to re-establish itself in its earlier patriotic sense. This rise to prominence and subsequent decline is a common pattern, showing that the conscientizing effect of original forms and formulas can be of limited duration. A curious footnote is found in a story in the *New Yorker* about "a feminist from Greenwich Village" who dressed up as a man and went to a bar. "She bought an ale, drank it, removed her cap, and shook her long hair down on her shoulders. Then she called Bill a male chauvinist, yelled something about the equality of the sexes, and ran out." What is unusual is that the story, "Old House at Home" by Joseph Mitchell, was published in 1940.

The modern debate became more concerned with broader issues of gender identity, rights concerning sexual orientation, and discrimination against homosexuals. This involved similar techniques of borrowing, semantic extension, and publicity. Thus when *homophobia* was first coined in the 1920s it referred generally to "fear or hatred of men, i.e. people," but in the 1970s it started to be popularized by the Gay Liberation Movement in the modern sense of "fear or hatred of homosexuals." The American writer George Weinberg is often cited as being influential in the change.

Semantic shock tactics are often exploited as a form of protest, as in these feminist comments on advertising in a London tube station: "All these ads with huge images of giant rubber peach-tone breasts, wet lips, denim bums are like his gang, – telling him I am a cunt-thing, a leg-thing, a breast-thing and that I am ready for him" (Rowe, 1982, p. 65). Not all feminists took the same line. Germaine Greer commented archly in one vein, referring to some protesters: "the Tufnell Park ladies clung quietly to their banners (saying 'We are not sexual objects' – a statement no one appeared inclined to dispute). . . ." But in another mode: "Revolutionary women may join Women's Liberation Groups and curse and scream and fight the cops, but did you ever hear of one of them marching the public street with her skirt high crying 'Can you dig it? Cunt is beautiful!' The walled garden of Eden was CUNT" (1986, pp. 27, 37).

Here we see two extremes of lexical exploitation, the obscene (*cunt*) and the contrived formula made up of classical elements (*sexual object*). *Cunt* was quite commonly used in medieval times, first appearing in a street name, but having been taboo for centuries, its political and programmatic use is arresting. Greer (in some ways an honorable descendant of Chaucer's Wife of Bath) gave the title of *Cunt Power Oz* to an edition of the underground magazine she edited, and included a section in *The Female Eunuch* (1970) on *pussy power*.

In the formal register *sex object* can be traced back to 1916, but became an essential form in the feminist debate from the 1980s. Similar formulations are *significant other* (from c. 1977), and the more rarified polysyllabic and artificial battery of *phallocentric, phallocratic,* and *phallocracy* (c. 1977) and the most ponderous, *phallogocentric,* naughtily translated by Terry Eagleton as "cocksure" (2008, p. 164). Also showing that not everybody took these forms seriously, Gary Taylor referred to "a phallocentric cockocracy, a phallogocentric cocktalkocracy" in *Reinventing Shakespeare* (1990, p. 343). Other innovations in the semantics of sexuality are the forms *bisexual* from 1914 and *transsexual* from 1957 (in the *US Journal of Psychotherapy*), set against humorous reduplications like *gender bender*, in a reference to "Mr David Bowie" in the *Economist* in 1980, and the contemporary *toy boy* from 1981. There are also contrived blends of provocative and serious elements, found in *feminazi*, the coinage of Rush Limbaugh in 1990: "Let commie-liberals, femi-nazis and other bleeding hearts quibble over that" (*Atlanta Journal and Constitution*). A similar satirical mixture can be seen in the *Private Eye* column "Loony Feminist Nonsense." Kingsley Amis, in his archaically titled guidebook *The King's English* (1998), was summarily dismissive about *feminism*: "This is so notorious already, and such a joke, that I will offer only one comment" (p. 67).

This impatience seems to have been provoked by many interventions in word formations designed to remove gender-specific terms like *salesman* or *waitress*, as well as coinages like *herstory* and *wimmin*. In the first category there was a great proliferation of new forms using *person*, although in American usage *salesperson* is recorded from 1920 in *Harpers Magazine* as "a name intended to apply to an employee of either sex." However, it would seem that there was not a consistent in-house policy in some publishing houses. Thus *The Oxford Dictionary of New Words* (1997) contained this curious entry:

> Consciousness of Political Correctness in the eighties and nineties has encouraged the development of such forms, and tended to result in a less self-conscious use of many of the resulting compounds. A visitor to a restaurant may expect to served by a **waitperson** (and even refer to the activity as **waitpersoning**); watching a local news report he or she might see an **alderperson** or a **clergyperson** being questioned by a **pressperson**.

This passage seems far-fetched to the point of parody. None of the hypothetical forms in bold has achieved any currency. The 1992 edition of the same work had included *personkind*. Displacing the mythical *waitperson*, the odder form *waitron* has emerged, possibly regarding waiting at tables as a mindless robotic activity. In 1980 the *Washington Post* quoted the chorus of a satirical song titled "I used to work as a waitron . . . Now I work for my senatron, and I live in Arlingtron. I'm just a Washingtron." Pam Peters (2004) comments: "Waitron was concocted in the US in the 1980s, but it has never caught on, by the dearth of evidence in the Consolidated Corpus of American English."

Robert Burchfield's edition of *The New Fowler's Modern English* (1996) was much less concessive: "At first to the puzzlement, and then to the amusement, and now often to the despair, of many people (both men and women), feminists began to use, and then to insist that others use *person* or *-person* instead of *man* or *-man*" (p. 588). The second edition of the *OED* commented on *person*: "used as a substitute for MAN . . . In practice usually employed to avoid alleged sexual discrimination and widely regarded as having amusing combinations. . . . Frequently in self-conscious and mocking nonce-uses from 1970s onwards." It included *chairperson* (1971), *congressperson* (1972), *henchpersons* (1973), *yardperson* (advertisement, 1976), and "a *pair of homosexual network anchorpersons*" (*TLS*, 1977). Two useful discussions of the issue are to be found in Dennis Baron's *Grammar and Gender* (1986) and Deborah Cameron's account of the "feminist verbal hygiene campaign" for gender-free language at the University of Strathclyde (1995, pp. 130–9).

A classic instance of neutralized or "decriminalized" language was the substitution of *sex worker* for *prostitute*, recorded in the *OED* from 1971 in a *New York Times* quotation and defined as "a person who works in the sex industry, especially as a prostitute (usually used with the intention of reducing negative connotations and of aligning the sex industry with conventional service industries)." A splendid letter by Tracy Quan of PONY (Prostitutes of New York) in the *New York Review of Books* (November 5, 1992) explained: "In the '80s *sex work* was coined by activists to describe a range of commercial sex. Porn stars, erotic dancers, peep show performers, sex writers and others in the trade made it obvious that the prostitutes' movement should broaden its language." Describing herself as an "an activist hooker," Quan conceded that *sex worker* is gender free and that "*sex work* connotes that prostitutes are engaged in labor rather than business," but finally objected that "we who purvey erotic pleasure are increasingly desexualized by politically correct language." Some publications prefer the term: The 2001 *Rough Guide to Travel Health* warns that "Syphilis prevalence has increased globally over recent years, especially in inner cities, where it is associated with sex workers and drug use" (cited in *OED*).

Reflecting modern fixations, the *OED* has in the semantic field of sex approximately 40 combinations, exemplified in: *sex maniac*, 1895; *sex offence*, 1911; *sex object*, 1916 and 1963 (Betty Friedan); *sex discrimination*, 1916 (US); *sex drive*, 1911; *sex appeal*, 1924; *sex crime*, 1925; *sex offender*, 1939 (US); *sexpot*, 1957; *sex kitten*, 1958; *sex bomb*, 1963; *sex shop*, 1970; *sex killer*, 1972. *Sex and shopping* (for *shopping* and *fucking*) dates from the 1980s, as does *sex toy*, a euphemism for vibrators and other mechanical purveyors of erotic pleasure. With the spread of AIDS came *safe sex* and *safer sex*, in a presentation for PWA (People with Aids) in 1983.

The Women's Movement co-opted *sister*, defined by Kramarae and Treichler (1985) as "a term of affiliation used among girls and women," and established in the noted feminist collection *Sisterhood is Powerful* (Morgan, 1970). Previously, *sister* and *sisterhood* were euphemisms for pro-stitution, in the Sisters of the Bank (1550) and the sisterhood of Billingsgate (1793). Commenting on euphemisms for prostitutes, Thomas Dekker explained in *Westward Ho* (1607): "The serving man has his punk, the student his nun . . . the Puritan his sister."

Wimmin, previously discussed in chapter 3, attracted a lot of publicity in 1982–3 before going through the phases of satire and obsolescence prior to fading away. A similar feminist coinage was *herstory*, briefly institu-tionalized in the acronym "WITCH – Women Inspired to Commit Herstory," in Robin Morgan's *Sisterhood is Powerful* (1970, p. 551). Jane Mills made this telling observation in her compendium *Womanwords*: "The rewriting or respeaking of *history* as *herstory* – coined by some feminists in the 1970s – is guaranteed to annoy most men, many women and almost all linguists" (1989, p. 118). Although the currency of *herstory* has declined, Elaine Showalter showed further creativity in her study *Hystories: Hysterical Epidemics and the Modern Media* (1997).

WITCH took its role and its protests seriously, groups making dramatic appearances as covens which hexed various institutions, such as Chase Manhattan Bank, Morgan Guaranty Trust, the Chicago Transit Authority, and *Playboy* magazine, where they demanded that a representative take off *his* clothes (Morgan, 1968, pp. 282–3). The publication for February, 1969 carried a manifesto starting "Marriage is a dehumanizing institution – legal whoredom for women" (Morgan, 1968, p. 543). Although these extreme protests are a thing of the past, there are still semantic signs of hostility to the commerce of marriage, for example *trophy wife*, recorded from 1992. Another effective metaphor concerning the role of women is *glass ceiling*, recorded from 1984. Whereas slogans can both motivate and alienate, unusual metaphors such as these, dramatizing the morality of marriage and the advancement of women, are often more thought-provoking.

Demeaning or belittling terms such as *babe*, *bimbo*, and *dolly bird* con-tinued to be highlighted. In the spectacular climax of David Mamet's play *Oleanna* (1992), the trivial injunction by the student, "Don't call your wife baby," is the last straw, leading to an explosion of rage by the exasper-ated and ruined professor, who shouts "You think that you can come in here with your political correctness and destroy my life?" (p. 79). Strictly speaking, this is not political correctness, but the comment reveals how feminist agendas came to be equated with it.

More disturbing to the feminist cause has been the establishment and extended currency of *Playboy* terms like *bunny girl*, *centerfold*, *sexpot*, *sex bomb*, and *sex kitten*, coinages of the 1960s (the related terms *Lolita* and

nymphet were the earlier creations of Vladimir Nabokov in *Lolita*, 1955),
as well as the continuing use of *ho* in American Black English, defined by
Clarence Major (1994) as "whore; a promiscuous female; prostitute." A
newish term in the British field is *slapper*, recorded from 1988 and defined
by the *OED* as UK slang for "a promiscuous woman" and by John Ayto
as a "promiscuous or tarty woman." The *Bloomsbury Guide to Word Origins*
explains: "A working class term from East London and Essex, possibly from
Yiddish *schlepper/shlepper* "a slovenly or immoral woman." Also British
is *stunner*, or *stunnah* for the readers of the *Sun* tabloid. Its modern
currency dates from 1985, but it was first recorded in 1848.

Yet curiously, the older established and frank terms describing sexual
relationships, such as *lover* and *mistress* have been phased out under political correctness in favor of coy euphemisms like *boyfriend* or less judgmental,
even anodyne terms like *companion*, *partner*, *significant other*, and the
abstract *item*. There was a reluctance by the British press to use any judgmental term of Mrs Parker-Bowles during her long extramarital affair with
Prince Charles. Similarly, a *TLS* article on Ségolène Royal, the Socialist candidate for the Presidency of France in 2007, referred to "her companion,
François Hollande." The Civil Partnership Act, which came into force in
Britain in 2005, has of course, given *partner* an official status.

As *male chauvinism* has become less current, so *macho* has been co-opted,
although it truly describes a different cultural notion in Spanish, "a
notably or ostentatiously masculine or virile man." It is used emotively in
this report: "Our macho political system excludes half the population.
Rampant male chauvinism thwarts the Westminster ambitions of many
women" (Dr Katherine Rake of the Fawcett Society, *Guardian*, October
5, 2006). More formal and ideological were recycled terms like *paternalism*, originally neutral and political, dating from 1881. Likewise, *paternalistic*
and *patriarchy*, which was in origin ecclesiastical, dating from 1561. In
the same register was the coinage *masculist*, recorded from 1978, and its
variant *masculinist*, used strikingly in the comment "Geography is masculinist" by Gillian Rose (1993, p. 4). Alice Walker, the coiner of *womanist*, commented that "Womanist is to feminist as purple is to lavender"
(1983, p. xi). The *OED* explained: "Adopted by . . . Alice Walker as more
relevant to Black people than *feminist*."

Also recycled is *heterosexual*, dating from Krafft-Ebing's *Psychopathia
Sexualis* (1892) referring to "normal" sexual relations therapy, used to remove
"the impulse to masturbation and homo-sexual feelings" (cited in *OED*).
Nearly a century later *heterosexism* emerged, but with emphasis on the
-sexism rather than the *hetero-* in the press report that "The students' union
at Warwick University . . . has invented a new term: heterosexism" (*Daily*

Telegraph, February 16, 1982). An *OED* quotation from 1985 stressed that "We should be struggling against racism and heterosexism."

In 1909 one Elizabeth Robins, in a play called *Votes For Women*, issued the dire warning: "This ferment of feminism . . . [is] likely to bring a very terrible thing in its train . . . sex antagonism." A century later the renegade feminist Camille Paglia was to comment "Feminism has not brought sexual happiness." But this was in Bill Maher's provocative television series *Politically Incorrect* in 1995.

Terms concerning homosexuals

Historically, the word field for homosexuals (which extends from the Middle Ages) has reflected public attitudes by being predominantly male and entirely hostile. The words accordingly range from traditional critical and criminal terms like *sodomite*, *bugger*, and *pederast*, through contemptuous forms like *he-whore*, *miss nancy*, and *molly*, to pseudo-euphemisms like *fairy*, *queen*, and *pansy*, dating from the 1930s. The unflattering *rent boy* dates from about 1975. *Bugger*, a semantically rich word in British English, now including the tones of contempt, familiarity, and humor, is something of a rarity in American English. *Pederast*, together with other classical terms like *catamite*, has always been formal. John Aubrey unceremoniously wrote of Francis Bacon in *Brief Lives*: "He was παιδερασιής [a pederast]. His Ganimeds [lovers] and Favourites tooke Bribes."

The Kinsey Report on *Sexual Behavior in the Human Male* (1948) proved to be a watershed document. Demonstrating an unexpected variety of sexual behavior, it also clarified the legal issues: "Perversions are defined as unnatural acts contrary to nature, bestial, abominable and detestable. Such laws are interpretable only in accordance with the ancient tradition of English common law . . . which is committed to the doctrine that no sexual activity is justifiable unless its objective is procreation" (Kinsey et al., 1998, p. 264). The key term here is the code word *unnatural*: "The severe penalties imposed upon unnatural practices in our own country by an Act of 1886 have merely had the effect of advertising them," sagely observed Frank Richards in his war memoir *Old Soldier Sahib* (1936). Although the euphemism could cover a polymorphous variety of sexual activity, Holder (1995) bluntly equates it with "homosexual." Anthony Storr gave his 1964 study the title of *Sexual Deviation*, but conceded that "the term deviation implies the existence of a standard of normality . . . but no absolute standard can be found" (p. 11).

Queer has had a long, unstable underground history with criminal associations, making its explicit homosexual connotations difficult to detect, while a similar ambiguity has surrounded the more positive word *gay*. More to the point, there is no neutral term in the word field, although *homosexual* (coined only in 1869) now has the best claim. In 1957 the landmark Wolfenden Report on Homosexuality had the effect of enlightening the public and of giving currency to the key phrase *consenting adult*.

Lesbianism, recognized more openly in previous ages, was grudgingly acknowledged in polite English society only about a century ago. A source of confusion derived from the ambiguity of the root *homo* in *homosexual*, intended to be from Greek *homos*, "the same," but misinterpreted to derive from *homo*, the Latin term for "man." This misinterpretation partly explains the late arrival of *lesbian* in about 1890. (Ben Jonson introduced in 1601 the word *tribade*, from a Greek root meaning "to rub.") Underground usage and a conspiracy of silence long served to suppress clarity on the answer to the question posed by Jeanette Winterson: "What Do Lesbians Do in Bed?" (1998, p. 34). Although this was one area unexplored by D. H. Lawrence, most readers are surely shocked at the vehemence of Mellors's outburst: "When I'm with a woman who's really Lesbian, I fairly howl in my soul, wanting to kill her" (*Lady Chatterley's Lover*, 1960, p. 212). *Sapphic*, surprisingly omitted from the *OED* (only the metrical usages being given), was an early pseudo-euphemism for *lesbian* which subsequently became politically correct. Thus Evelyn Waugh asked archly in a letter of May 1951: "I think Swedish Countess was a Sapphist?" while "Sapphic Crises" was an allusion to Victoria Sackville-West's scandalous lesbian affair with Violet Trefusis (*Literary Review*, June 1992, p. 43).

Much discussion of the semantic history of *gay* suggests or asserts that it was a positive and sexually innocent term for most of its life up to the 1970s, when it was co-opted by the homosexual lobby as a major instance of semantic engineering to counter the negative denotations and connotations of *homosexual*, *queer*, *bent*, and so on. Philip Howard commented dryly: "It is a paradox that it has been expropriated by one of the sadder groups in society" (1977, p. 34). Paul Johnson denounced the process in much stronger language: "I can see why these people want to designate themselves by some non-pejorative term. But it was a monstrous piece of verbal larceny to appropriate one of the most delightful and useful words in the language" (*Spectator*, July 5, 1986, p. 22).

There is some truth in the historical generalization, since the dominant traditional meaning defined by the *OED* as "light-hearted, exuberantly merry, sportive, cheerful" is not only the earliest sense, recorded from about 1310, but the most enduring, existing up to modern times, albeit with diminishing currency. Obviously the cliché "gay bachelor" carries different assumptions nowadays from those of 30 years ago. However, this overview is an oversimplification, since for much of its life *gay* was also a slang or underground term suggesting vigorous but clandestine sexual activity, especially in the phrase "gay girl" or "gay lady," recorded from the mid-fourteenth century. In Chaucer's *Miller's Tale* a blacksmith working at his foundry early in the morning jokingly asks Absolon, one of the suitors of the adulterous Alyson, whether he has been kept up by "som gay gerle." It then generalized to mean "addicted to social pleasures," consolidating into the phrases "gay dog" and "gay Lothario." However, it was also used from about 1825 as a slang euphemism for a prostitute, as in "two sisters, both gay."

The emergence of the homosexual sense has been the object of much discussion. Even the semantic and lexicographical authorities are not in agreement, mainly because the term is used in a suggestive sexual way (like modern *romp* or *hanky-panky*), making definitive instances difficult to pinpoint. The *OED* quotes a glossary of prison slang dated 1935 which defines *geycat* as "a homosexual boy," but the authoritative *Random House Historical Dictionary of American Slang* (1994) gives the first written instance as 1922 (in a quotation by Gertrude Stein). The *OED Supplement* (1972) revealed a much earlier instance from the Cleveland Street Scandal in 1889, which centered on a homosexual brothel in London frequented by many respectable society gentlemen. In the proceedings a male prostitute, John Saul, referred to his associates as "gay" (Pearsall, 1969, p. 574). But whichever date is chosen, *gay* has had an underground homosexual sense for nearly a century. Similarly, *cottage* (originally a slang term for a urinal) is usually regarded as having acquired its homosexual usage fairly recently, exemplified in "Chateau Charles, a cottaging queen with a penchant for young boys" (*TLS*, February 24, 1984). But W. H. Auden referred to "An underground cottage frequented by the queer" in 1932 (*Review of English Studies*, August 1978, p. 294). This is also one of the earliest recorded instances of *queer*.

In trying to keep up with the more recent extensions of *gay*, the *OED* Additional Series includes records for *gay liberation* (1969), *gay lib* (1970), *gay pride* (1970), *gay marriage* (1971), *gay plague* (1982), *gaydar* (1982), *gay bashing* (1984), *gay gene* (1986), and *gay-friendly* (1989). (The first three of these come from advertisements or announcements, rather than from common usage.) This new field contains a revealing series of witness words for the complexities of the relationship between homosexuals and the wider society.

The *OED* also records the US slang senses of *gay* as "foolish, stupid, socially inappropriate or 'lame'" from as far back as 1978. However, considerable controversy arose in the UK in June 2006 over the contemptuous use of *gay* to mean "rubbish" or "useless" by the talk-show host Chris Moyles on BBC Radio 1 in a program with an audience of 6.3 million. *The Times* reported: "The word 'gay' now means 'rubbish' in modern playground-speak and need not be offensive to homosexuals, the BBC Board of Governors has ruled" and added a note saying "Children and students use gay as shorthand for 'rubbish'" (June 6, 2006). In its response, "Straight Talk?" the *Guardian* disagreed (June 7, 2006). Here we can see an interesting double standard, since the more establishment newspaper accepts the semantic change, while the more radical is unhappy that the word's established negative sense should be countenanced by the national broadcaster.

Other modern terms for homosexuals with surprisingly long histories include *dyke*, recorded in Peter Tamony's *Americanisms* (1931): "Benches in the more obscure parts are used continually by couples, pansies and dykes." The etymology is given by the *Random House Historical Dictionary of American Slang* as *morphadike*, a dialect variant of *hermaphrodite*. The link with another variant, *mophrodite*, is established, amazingly, in Fielding's *Joseph Andrews* (1742), when a society lady is warned that if she continues to dismiss all her servants, "You must ... get a set of mophrodites to wait upon you" (Book I, chapter ix). A variant form, probably from the same source, is South African slang *moffie*. *Diesel dyke* dates from 1958.

Similar in tone, contemporary, but more American in provenance is *lavender*, dating from the 1930s, although the line between "effeminate" and "homosexual" is not always clear. A Cole Porter song of 1929 runs: "I'm a famous gigolo, and of lavender, my nature's got just a dash of it." However the *Random House Dictionary of American Slang* has an allusion to 1874. Although many terms for homosexuals first surface in American English, fear of exposure has always been acute, as David Johnson shows in his study, *The Lavender Scare: The Cold War Persecution of Gays and Lesbians in the Federal Government* (2006).

Pink is recorded in the *Dictionary of the American Underworld* in the phrase *pink pants*, meaning "a young passive pederast" (1950). The homosexual association was also underscored by the use of the pink triangle in Nazi concentration camps, but recorded semantically only from 1950. As homosexuals started to "come out" in the business establishment, so *pink pound* appeared, first in the *Guardian* in 1984, while the *pink plateau* surfaced suddenly in April 2007 in the wake of the revelations and resignation of Lord Browne. The *Independent on Sunday* publishes an annual Pink List, its "annual celebration of the great and the gay," who in 2008 were ranked from 1 to 101.

As has been mentioned, *queer* is recorded from the 1920s, mainly in American contexts, generally in hostile quotations, such as: "There was even a little room . . . where the 'fairies', 'pansies' and 'queers' conducted their lewd practices" (Lee Duncan, 1936, cited in *OED*). (*Fairy* is recorded in American usage from 1895.) From the 1960s the process of reclamation started, as homosexual pressure groups started to use *queer* openly in public discourse and to give it respectability in academic contexts. Queer Nation was founded in North America in 1990, while *queercore*, for aggressively open young homosexuals, surfaced in 1993. University programs and articles started to appear under titles like "Queer Theory," "Queer Studies," and "Queer Culture." A recent addition is *The Queer God*, by Marcella Althaus-Reid (2003).

Faggot, largely American in provenance in spite of its complex semantic history, has always been provocative, and shows few signs of being reclaimed. The word is a flashpoint in some Spike Lee movies, notably *Get on the Bus* (1996). There is also an astonishing quotation from Hemingway's *The Sun Also Rises* 70 years earlier: "That was what the Civil War was about. Abraham Lincoln was a faggot. He was in love with General Grant" (1926, chapter 12). This outrageous view is, admittedly, part of a rather absurd conversation between Jake and Bill.

Around 1990 there emerged new code uses such as *to out*, meaning "to expose as an undeclared homosexual (especially a prominent or public figure)" (*OED*). This controversial practice, really an invasion of privacy, was a tactic of gay rights activists, deriving from the American idiom "to come out of the closet," dating from about 1975. In Britain the bureaucratic curiosity *clause 28* acquired the sense of "promoting homosexuality," although it was in fact part of the UK Local Government Bill of 1988 forbidding public spending by local authorities on any activity promoting homosexuality. The abbreviation *GLBT* (for gay, lesbian, bisexual, and transgendered) is recorded in the *OED* from 1993 in *Bisexual Community & Identity* (a Usenet group): "I think that the identity and the community should be closely examined in order to give the movement and all bisexuals a strong and mature place in the GLBT community." Stranger was *OTPOTSS*, the bureaucratic coinage of the British Department of Trade and Industry in 2002 signifying "orientation towards people of the same sex."

This is certainly a long way from Henry James's fulmination that "'Hosscar' Wilde is a fatuous fool, tenth-rate cad, 'an unclean beast'" after their first meeting (in New York, 1882). Wilde's biographer Richard Ellmann explains pointedly, "James's homosexuality was latent, Wilde's was patent" (1987, p. 171). But beneath the urbane public façade of tolerance, prejudice used to thrive in unexpected places: "Everything is controlled by the sods. The country is riddled with homosexuals who are teaching the world how to behave – a spectacle of revolting hypocrisy," commented Sir Thomas Beecham (in Charles Reed, *An Independent Biography*, quoted in Pepper, 1987). Less judgmental was the comment "Truman Capote was the sort who gives sodomy a bad name" (*Guardian Weekly*, September 11, 1988, p. 29). Beecham's intemperate remarks suggest that there was no "pink plateau" in his time.

An interesting footnote underlining this cultural shift is the case of W. H. Auden's poem "Funeral Blues." This was first written in 1936 as an ironic lament for a politician in *The Ascent of F6*, then rewritten as a song in 1937, retaining only the first four stanzas. After being virtually unknown for decades, the poem became enormously popular after its dramatic use as a funeral eulogy for a homosexual in the film *Four Weddings and a Funeral* (1994).

Class

English society has notoriously been concerned with class, more especially with the minutiae of class differences. Although modern democratic societies are ideologically egalitarian and technically classless, several vestiges remain, more in England than elsewhere. In Anglo-Saxon society there were, of course, gradations of rank, but moral assumptions were not made on the basis of class. Revealingly, among the numerous ancient words for "man" were *eorl*, *ceorl*, and *cniht*, which now have completely separate class rankings as "earl," "churl," and "knight." Largely as a consequence of the Norman Conquest, class notions are clearly apparent in the roots of such words as *gentle* and *noble* (both originally French and meaning "well-born"), contrasted with *knave* and *villain* (both meaning "low-born").

The judgmental use of these terms, well defined by C. S. Lewis as "the moralisation of status words" (1960, p. 7) started to become entrenched in the Middle English period. There are dozens of examples, including *wretch*, *lewd*, *uncouth*, *blackguard*, and *rascal*, originally referring to people of low status. In *The Canterbury Tales* (1386–1400), the coarse, loud, obscene Miller is designated "a cherle" who tells a "cherles tale," that is, crude, bawdy, and mean. By contrast the "parfit, gentil, noble knight" tells an elevated and idealistic romance. But, in the relevant epigraph, Chaucer pointedly notes that the Knight never made any disrespectful comment to any person. Snobbery, which may be defined as excessive concern with class, is vividly embodied in Chaucer's Franklin or land baron, who is obsessed with "gentillesse" or nobility, to the point of provoking the Host's contemptuous riposte "Straw for your gentillesse!" The Franklin's tale is anxious to show that every man in his station can be "gentil." Today, of course, *gentle*, *noble*, *churlish*, and *peasant* are no longer class-bound terms.

During the postmedieval period the upper class tended to become freer in their expression of contempt for the lower orders, an attitude today regarded as politically incorrect. Chapter 7 contains some virulent expressions of class difference in Shakespeare. These come mainly from the nobility in the English plays and especially the patricians in the Roman plays. Expressions include "the mutable rank-scented meiny" and "the green and soggy multitude." The contempt of the great warrior Coriolanus for the plebs is transparent. Although the Duke of Wellington famously commented that "The Battle of Waterloo was won on the playing fields of Eton," less well known is his dismissal of his rank and file as "the mere scum of the earth" (*Stanhope's Conversations*, November 4, 1831).

In recent years *classism* has been recycled, having been first recorded in 1844 during the impact of Marxist terminology as "the curse of England and Englishmen" (Samuel Bamford, *Passages in the Life of a Radical*, cited in *OED*). However, in general the word *class* is much less used than say 50 years ago: *lower class* is now virtually taboo, while *working class* is largely the preserve of sociologists. *Middle class* has expanded greatly, paradoxically also in American usage, where it is increasingly becoming a code term for *conservative*. Two other code class terms which have lost currency in British English are *common* and *vulgar*. Originally both meanings overlapped with those of *base*, shown in the *OED* entries for *vulgar* (II 9) and *common* (IB8 and II) as "of ordinary occurrence and quality; hence mean, cheap." Parental injunctions such as "You shouldn't play with Johnny any more. His parents are common" or condemnations like "What a vulgar little man!" both difficult for outsiders to decipher, have spontaneously passed away in the past few decades, in public discourse at any rate, as the egalitarian ethos has gained ground. In their place less obvious excluding designations like "not quite one of us" have emerged.

Furthermore, new but vaguer class terms, mainly based on financial status, have come into play. Even among the wealthy there is the class distinction between "old money" and "new money," just as the distinction between being "in trade" as opposed to being in a profession lingered in the nineteenth century. Occupation has naturally maintained a role in perceived status, even in America. Although *trash* was first used of a person by Shakespeare in *Othello* (Act V, scene i), *poor white trash* is first recorded, surprisingly, in the actress Fanny Kemble's *Journal* of her visit to the American South (June 1, 1833) in a most revealing sociological observation: "The slaves themselves entertain the very highest contempt for white servants, whom they designate as 'poor white trash'." It has since been joined by *trailer park trash* (from about 1943). Frances Trollope noted in her contemporary *Domestic Manners of the Americans* (1832) the stigma associated with service: "Young women . . . believe that the most abject poverty is preferable to domestic service."

In the past decade the Romani word *chav* (meaning a boy) has sprung into prominence, defined by the OED as "a young person of a type characterized by brash and loutish behaviour and the wearing of designer-style clothes (esp. sportswear); usually with connotations of a low social status." Controversy has arisen over whether this is a class term masking snobbery or a type term criticizing feckless materialism.

Within the English system the upper class are generally less bound by taboos in general and political correctness in particular. Thus entries in *The Official Sloane Ranger Handbook* (1982) included *Jew's canoe* for a Jaguar, *wog* used generally for a foreigner (notably in "the wogs begin at Calais"), *spastic* and *thick* commonly used for "stupid," *poncy* for "effeminate," and *bin* or *loony bin* for "lunatic asylum." Some members of the Royal Family have a penchant for the politically incorrect. The Duke of Edinburgh acknowledged his abilities in coining the term *dentopedalogy* which, he explained, "is the art of opening your mouth and putting your foot in it. I've been practising it for years" (*Times*, November 21, 1960). One of his notorious gaffes was warning some British students in China: "You'll end up with slitty eyes if you stay too long." A palace spokesman later explained lamely that Prince Philip was concerned that strong light might be affecting them (L'Estrange, 2002, p. 311). In milder tone Prince Charles described the handover of Hong Kong as "The Great Chinese Takeaway" and a typically impassive Chinese delegation as "waxworks," admittedly in private emails. In 2005 Prince Harry caused a furor by going to a party wearing a Nazi shirt with a swastika armband.

Crime and Punishment

Until a few decades ago the justice system had an Old Testament ferocity and inflexibility. Criminals were categorized as such, although often condemned on the basis of questionable process, and suffered cruel consequences. Some offenses seem arbitrary from a modern perspective: thus the legal phrase *a common scold* denoted a woman who was a public nuisance who could be punished with a muzzle called the *scold's bridle*. Punishments were commonly savage and public. The pillory, an institution recorded from about 1275, was the humiliating and sometimes lethal punishment endured by thousands of offenders, notably Titus Oates for perjury in 1687 and by James Egan and James Salmon, two gangsters-*cum*-informers, in about 1756. Egan did not survive the hail of missiles, and Salmon died later of his injuries. Not only was the death penalty *de rigueur*, public executions became highly popular social events. People of all classes flocked to Tyburn outside London to enjoy the spectacle. John Hamilton noted in his sketch of October 14, 1767 that "It was the custom of Lamplighters . . . to erect their ladders for persons to mount them at 2d & 3d to see the Execution" (Fox, 1987 p. 204). Jokes about hanging abounded, appearing in the most unexpected places, such as Feste the Jester's observation that "Many a good hanging prevents a bad marriage" (*Twelfth Night*, Act I, scene v). Francis Grose's *Classical Dictionary of the Vulgar Tongue* (1785) has dozens of entries, such as *twisted*: executed, hanged; *sheriff's picture frame*: the gallows; *neck weed*: hemp; *morning drop*: the gallows; *new drop*: the scaffold used at Newgate; *die hard*: to show no signs of fear or contrition at the gallows, and *Jack Ketch*: a hangman, "from a famous practitioner of that name, of whom his wife said that any bungler might put a man to death, but only her husband knew how to make a gentleman die sweetly."

Some criminals acquired a dubious status, part comic part mock-heroic. The novels of Henry Fielding (a magistrate) and Dickens (a court reporter) abound in examples. Fielding's satire *The Life of Jonathan Wild the Great* (1743) tells the story of a notorious criminal as if he were a great man. The tradition of the criminal as hero continued in the Far West with the exploits of Butch Cassidy, the Sundance Kid, the Wild Bunch, Billy the Kid, Bonnie and Clyde, and in Australia with Ned Kelly.

The modern regime is obviously milder and more civilized. But among the current euphemisms, *delinquent* has a long complex history from Caxton onwards. *Juvenile delinquent* is also surprisingly well established, being first recorded in 1816 in the *Report Investigating the Causes for Increase in Juvenile Delinquency*. In a perennial observation, the report found that "Juvenile Delinquency existed in the metropolis to a very alarming degree" (cited in *OED*). Dickens's concern with social problems surfaces in a reference to the "Juvenile Delinquent Society" in *Oliver Twist* (1837, chapter 19). *Borstal* (1902) is a toponym derived from the juvenile reformatory at Borstal, a village in Kent near Rochester.

Although the renaming of *prisons* as *correctional services* in government nomenclature is comparatively recent, the formula *House of Correction* is four centuries old, being coined in 1575 in Act 18 of Queen Elizabeth, making provision "in every county" for "Houses of Correction" for putting rogues to work and punishing them.

Disability and Illness

Mental disorders

Mental abnormality has a complex semantic field, since the condition was held in greater respect in earlier times, when a relationship between lunatics and seers was accepted and when fools held privileged positions in courts. It was recognized, in Dryden's concise phrase that "Great wits are sure to madness near allied." Furthermore, the insane provided a spectacle which was exploited in various ways. Nearly all of Shakespeare's major tragedies explore madness in a disturbing fashion, including the terrifying lunacy of Lear, Timon of Athens, and Titus Andronicus, the ravings of Othello, the paranoia of Macbeth, the enigmatic frenzy of Hamlet's "antic disposition," and the simulated nonsense of Edgar in *King Lear*. This last role of Poor Tom, a "bedlam-beggar," half-cured and licensed to beg, is a spectacle generally embarrassing to modern audiences, but was evidently a drawcard in earlier times, since it featured on the title page of the 1608 Quarto text: "With the unfortunate life of Edgar, sonne and heire to the Earle of Glocester, and his sullen and assumed humor of Tom of Bedlam." *Bedlam* derives from the Hospital of St Mary of Bethlehem, an ancient institution which had become an asylum by 1400. The final scene of Hogarth's famous series *The Rake's Progress* (1735) is set in Bedlam, where "two young women have come as was the fashion, to view the entertainment" (Fox, 1987, p. 239). The modern sense of *bedlam* meaning an uproar or scene of confusion dates from about 1700.

Attempts to mollify the unsympathetic vocabulary, a general feature of political correctness, have not been successful. In the word field there appears to be a perpetual semantic cycle whereby broad traditional terms (*mad, crazy, idiot*) and dismissive slang terms (*loony, barmy, nuts*) are replaced by precise technical terms (*maniac, psychotic, neurotic, schizophrenic*), which in turn become generalized and judgmental. The list of such terms can be expanded to include *hysterical, obsession, psychopath, schizoid*, all of which have complex and interesting histories, but are now generally unsympathetic or condemning. This development has necessitated a new wave of technical terms such as *bipolar disorder* taking over from *manic-depressive*. The whole field is discussed in greater detail in Hughes (2000, pp. 382–6). It is worth noting that even experts disagree over *schizophrenia*: "It was found that hospital psychiatrists in New York included under 'schizophrenia' part of what British hospital psychiatrists diagnosed as mania, psychotic depression and personality disorder" (*International Rehabilitatory Medicine*, 1979, cited in *OED*).

Disability

"Historically, linguistic usage reflects widespread social insensitivity in referring to those now termed 'physically disabled' or 'handicapped'. Words like *cripple* and *spastic* not only had wide currencies, but until recently were also terms of insult, black humour and belittlement" (Hughes, 2006, p. 129). As Auden observed, "About suffering they were never wrong, / the Old Masters" ("Musée des Beaux Arts"), since they, Breughel and Velasquez especially, included it unflinchingly but without special emphasis in their works as part of life. By contrast, some modern works, such as the sculpture "Alison Lapper Pregnant," make a statement by monumentalizing deformity.

Cripple, related to the verb "to creep," is an Anglo-Saxon term found notably in the ancient place-name Cripplegate in London, recorded from about 1000 to the present. Lack of sympathy and even superstition are evident in an old saying recorded by Angel Day in 1586: "Of ancient time it hath often been said that it is ill halting before a Creple" (*The English Secretary*, cited in *OED*). Several older terms are recorded in Francis Grose's *Classical Dictionary of the Vulgar Tongue* (1811): in addition to *cripple* as a slang term for a sixpence, "that piece being commonly much bent and distorted," he includes the slang use of *lord*, defined as "A crooked or hump-backed man," adding "These unhappy people afford great scope for vulgar raillery." In the same vein is *hopping Giles*, "a jeering appellation given to any person who limps or is lame," since, as Grose explains: "St. Giles was the patron of cripples, lepers &c." He also has *timber toe* for "a man with a wooden leg" and a *one finned fellow* for a seaman who has lost an arm. Later uses (from the 1880s) in the *OED* are *cripple gap* for "a small hole in a wall for sheep to get through" and, more gruesomely, *cripple stopper* for a small gun.

The semantic field has changed radically over time and is full of surprises. *Handicap*, for example, has a curious origin as the name of a medieval game referred to in *Piers Plowman* in the late fourteenth century; the modern sense emerges only about a hundred years ago in "The Handicapped Child," the title of a section of a book published in 1915. Although *disabled* is first recorded in a religious poem by George Herbert in 1633 ("I am in all a weak disabled thing"), the current sense is recorded from about 1695. *Invalid* as both noun and adjective surfaces in the early eighteenth century as a military borrowing from French.

Quite rapidly in the course of the 1980s new politically correct forms such as *differently abled*, *physically challenged*, and *hearing impaired* developed wide currencies, in public or official discourse at any rate, and the older stigmatic terms correspondingly became taboo. As the *OED* noted on *abled*: "formed in contradistinction to *disabled*; frequently used euphemistically as the second element in combinations to avoid the perceived negative connotations of the prefix *dis-*, as in *differently abled*." In an early instance, the *Washington Post* observed: "The disabled vary, like the abled" (October 30, 1981).

However, the semantic change was so rapid that the new forms attracted comment, irony, and derision. The *Oxford Dictionary of New Words* (1992) noted in its entry under *abled*: "all the forms with a preceding adverb have come in for considerable criticism." In the same year the *Los Angeles Times* commented trenchantly: "In a valiant effort to find a kinder term than *handicapped*, the Democratic National Committee has coined *differently abled*. The committee itself shows signs of being differently abled in the use of English" (April 9, 1985). The problem with *abled* is not simply its unfamiliarity: it implies a verb "to able," which does not exist. Nevertheless, both *ableism*, meaning "prejudice in favor of the able-bodied" or even "systematic oppression of the disabled" and *ableist* appeared in 1981 in a publication called *Off Our Backs*. *Disablist* joined the new glossary in 1986. These instances show the effect of semantic engineering by a pressure group. However, Robert Hughes commented with some irony in his broadside *Culture of Complaint*: "[Helms] was against racism sexism, ableism, lookism and any of the other offenses against social etiquette whose proscription by PC was already causing such mirth and laughter among the neo-conservatives" (1993, p. 162).

The ancient martial term *challenge* was also recycled, largely replacing the negative vocabulary of disability, often supplanting the broader term *problem*, and now frequently encountered in contexts like "The shortage of water represents a challenge." The difference is not simply a matter of semantic nuance: *problem* acknowledges a difficulty or deficiency requiring a solution: *challenge* implies that a response is optional. The new form *challenged* appeared as a euphemism, chiefly American, as far back as 1985 in the *New York Times*: "The disabled skiers, who Mr Kennedy prefers to call 'physically challenged' " (April 20). Once again the semantic extension was fairly extreme, since *challenged* was obviously established as the past tense of "to challenge." Although euphemisms like *mentally challenged* started to appear, in this case in the *Los Angeles Times* in 1987, the form was soon being used facetiously, derisively, and creatively, as in "hymenally challenged" for a virgin. Howard Davies, Director General of the Confederation of British Industry, described some journalists as "mostly feckless, ill-informed and otherwise unemployable people. One or two are parentally challenged" (*Daily Telegraph*, November 20, 1993).

In his *Oxford Dictionary of Euphemisms* (1995), R. W. Holder defined *challenged* as "differing from the norm in a taboo fashion," before indulging in this *tour de force*: "This usage is one of the more enduring and endearing to have proliferated, especially among the illiterate. Thus a deaf person can be *aurally challenged*, a blind person *visually*, an idiot can be *cerebrally*, *developmentally* or *mentally challenged*, an acne sufferer *dermatologically*, a bald man *follicularly*, a dwarf *horizontally*, a lame person *physically*, and so on." (The more common, not to say correct, forms are *follically* for *follicularly* and *vertically* for *horizontally*.)

While these verbal innovations were attracting comment, *basket case* was developing a steadily wider currency to refer to a person, country, or social situation so chaotic as to be without hope of resuscitation. This is surely because the origins (in the First World War) were not recognized. The original meaning was gruesomely specific, referring with black humor to a soldier with all limbs amputated, who thus had to be carried in a basket. First used literally in 1919, the designation dropped out of currency for decades, before resurfacing in the current political sense in 1967.

Over a longer time frame *disadvantaged* showed a gradual semantic shift from a general to a sociological use. The *OED* records a notable Darwinian instance by Herbert Spencer in 1879: "The uniform principle has been that the ill-adapted, disadvantaged in the struggle for existence, shall bear the consequent evils" (*Data of Ethics*). In 1934 H. G. Wells presciently condemned "This mannered ungraciousness towards disadvantaged people" (cited in *OED*). The first clear modern sociological use is recorded in *American Speech* in 1962, but Mario Pei commented in his semantic study, *Words in Sheep's Clothing*: "A 1965 Jules Feiffer cartoon shows the progression from 'poor' to 'needy' to 'deprived' to 'underprivileged' to 'disadvantaged'" (1969, p. 140).

Spastic, originally a pathological term, the adjectival extension of *spasm*, has extended its meaning from "uncoordinated" to the contemptuous senses of "clumsy," "incompetent," and "foolish." In British English it has been "a schoolchildren's vogue word from the 1960s" (Thorne, 2007), developing a wide currency of disparagement, as in "the defense was spastic," also in the abbreviation *spaz*, recorded from 1965 and increasingly current among American youth. The original *OED* contained only the medical and technical senses, but the *Supplement* (1986) added this usage note: "Although current for some fifteen years or so, it is generally condemned as a tasteless expression, and is not common in print." Virtually all dictionaries now mark it as "offensive."

An unusual manifestation of political incorrectness concerns the growth of the "sport" of dwarf-throwing. According to Simon Mort's collection,

Longman Guardian New Words (1986), it was opposed by "the Organisation of People of Restricted Growth." They would presumably have had something to say about the comment in the 2004 American Presidential election in which the Emir of Kuwait was savagely dismissed as "a chain-smoking dwarf unworthy of the shedding of one drop of Marine blood." The gentler current euphemism is *little people*, which straddles the mythological meaning of *dwarf* and reference to small people.

Mental deficiency, to use one of the older standard phrases, to some extent overlaps with what are now called *mental disorders*, which are treated separately. Some of the older and imprecise terms such as *simple, silly,* and *natural* were widely used for at least four centuries. Dr Johnson defined *idiot* in 1755 as "one whom nature debars from understanding; a fool." Words like *moron* and *cretin* were originally coined or co-opted in the modern era as precise technical terms, but have since become generalized. Thus *moron*, from an ancient Greek word meaning "foolish" or "stupid," was given a new currency in 1910 by the researcher H. H. Goddard and adopted by the American Association for the Study of the Feeble-Minded, together with *idiot* and *imbecile. Moron* referred specifically to a person with an IQ of 50–70. However, it was almost immediately adopted as a vogue word in the current contemptuous sense. All of these terms became politically incorrect, to the point that the *Encyclopaedia Britannica* (1999 edition) announced: "The once standard terms – *moron, idiot* and *imbecile* – have been abolished." *Feeble-minded* is also no longer acceptable. While this initiative is understandable, words cannot be simply "abolished," and the omissions leave researchers with a problem of precise terminology.

The essential metaphor of mental development is that of progress, so that two of the earliest terms to be co-opted were *forward* and *backward*. Thus "a very forward child" then meant one that was highly intelligent. David Hume referred, contrariwise, to "a very backward scholar" in 1777. *Backward* has tended to recede in currency as other euphemisms, discussed below, have replaced it. The only modern term to have survived with a modicum of respectability for over a century is *retarded*. Originally used of physical development, it was first recorded in the current sense in G. E. Shuttleworth's study *Mentally Deficient Children* in 1895. The formula *mentally retarded* seems to be first used in 1956, while the noun form *retard* features in American slang from about 1970, invariably used in an ironic or unsympathetic fashion, as is *brain-damaged*. The phrases *slow developer* and *late developer* date from the 1930s and have managed to preserve their neutrality.

No shortage of mocking terms exists in general parlance. In his *Slang Thesaurus* (1999) Jonathon Green lists some three hundred synonyms, ranging from archaic *addlepate* through *klutz* and *lamebrain* to *thicko* and *zipalid*. However, a new idiom has proved surprisingly creative, exemplified in the formula "two sandwiches short of a picnic." It is a classic pseudo-euphemism, a more elaborate physical metaphor than *not all there*. David Rowan's *Glossary for the 90s* includes a collection of over 60 variations, ranging from *two cards short of a full house* to *several stories short of a high-rise block* (1998, pp. 181–2). The rapid expansion of the idiom in such a short time, especially in an area where political correctness was making itself felt in artificial forms such as *differently abled* and *mentally challenged*, certainly suggests that psychological elements of schadenfreude and black humor continue to exert a spontaneous pressure.

AIDS and syphilis

AIDS is virtually unique in the nomenclature of disease since it has never had a natural name, like *malaria, Congo fever*, or *influenza*, misleading though those names are. Although the disease was known of in the 1970s, the sudden outbreak in Los Angeles presented a new condition in need of definition, and it was given a generalized descriptive name, *acquired immune deficiency syndrome*. According to the *OED* the earliest reference to the abbreviation AIDS occurs in 1982 in a statement from the US Centers for Disease Control (September 24). In an early quotation the *Observer* commented: "Across the country AIDS hysteria is being encouraged" (June 26, 1983). HIV (standing for *human immunodeficiency virus*) is similarly recorded from 1986, although the original form was HIDV, for "human immune deficiency virus." Both central terms are semantically problematic. A *syndrome* is properly a collection of symptomatic conditions, inviting the fallacious assumption or argument that AIDS, in common with other syndromes, is accordingly not infectious. On the other hand, HIV is commonly used as a semantic unit, leading to the phrase "the HIV virus," which is technically a tautology.

Attitudes towards people with AIDS and the appropriate vocabulary to describe them have been colored by a number of factors. First and foremost it is a sexually transmitted disease, with all the stigmas attached to such conditions, particularly when drastic physical deterioration is highly visible. Furthermore, all the initial patients in whom symptoms were first observed were homosexual men, exacerbating the stigmatic impact and leading to the temporary official acronym GRID (*gay-related immune deficiency*) and the more enduring unsympathetic phrase the *gay plague*, recorded from 1982. This stereotypical association continued, despite the more enlightened view of the *New Scientist* in February, 1983: "In just one year the list of people at risk from AIDS has lengthened from male homo-sexuals to include the whole population of the United States." The origin of the condition is still uncertain, but as Sander Gilman shows, it was attributed variously to Haitians, immigrants from Africa, and American biological warfare specialists (1989, p. 309–22). Susan Sontag commented incisively in *AIDS and its Metaphors*: "AIDS obliges people to think of sex as having, possibly, the direst consequences; suicide. Or murder" (1990, p. 72).

A useful comparison can be made between the naming and response to AIDS and that of syphilis, which suddenly emerged in Europe around 1500 and spread rapidly across the continent. It also had a similar history of confused terminology, since the already established word *pox* (referring to the plague) was borrowed, widely used, and extended to *pocky*. (Astonishingly, *syphilis* itself derives from the name of an allegorical poem published in 1530 by the Italian physician, astrologer, and poet Girolamo Fracastoro about a shepherd of the same name who was stricken with the disease because of his insults to Apollo.) The condition, which appeared in Europe 30 years earlier, after the return of Columbus from the New World, was blamed by each suffering nation on others, especially the French. The armies under Charles VIII of France entered the besieged city of Naples in 1495, spreading the disease as they retreated under the names of "Mal de Naples," "Morbus Gallicus," and "Franzosenkrankheit." The principal English name was the *French pox*, appearing in many slang terms such as *French goods, French gout*, and *frenchified* for "diseased." Nahum Tate translated Fracastoro's poem into English in 1686 under the title of "Syphilis: or A Poetical History of the French Disease." On the other hand, Claude Quétel's *History of Syphilis* (1990) retained the original French title of *Le Mal de Naples: histoire de la syphilis*. The attribution to Naples was not solely French, as is seen in the phrases *Neapolitan favour*, used by Robert Greene in 1591 and *Neapolitan bone-ache* in Shakespeare's *Troilus & Cressida* (1601, Act II, scene iii).

However, the differences are profound and revealing. Syphilis was widely advertised on the continent in many treatises and even depicted in gruesome woodcuts showing lesions and buboes, notably by Albrecht Dürer in 1496, and in illustrations in Sebastian Brant's *Ship of Fools* published in the same year, as well as in a French poem, *The Triumph of the High and Mighty Dame Syphilis*, published in Lyon in 1539. In his major study, *Syphilis in Shakespeare's England*, Johannes Fabricius demonstrates the enormous interest and publicity surrounding the remorseless spread of the disease. It was clearly prevalent in the English courts of Elizabeth and James I and openly commented upon. Indeed, Fabricius notes that "the court disease" was one of the names for syphilis, coined in Spain (1994, p. 154). Two notable sufferers were Robert Devereux, Earl of Essex, favorite of Queen Elizabeth, and George Villiers, Duke of Buckingham, favorite of James I. According to D. H. Lawrence's remarkable essay, "Introduction to His Paintings" (1929), syphilis generated in England "a terror, almost a horror, of sexual life . . . by the end of the sixteenth century its ravages were obvious and the shock of them had just penetrated the thoughtful and imaginative processes" (1950, p. 308).

Syphilis became a powerful factor in "name-calling." *Pox* was used for many oaths and imprecations, such as *pox on it!* or the more personal *Jack be poxed!* from Shakespeare onwards, petering out centuries later in uses by James Joyce and even Virginia Woolf, both self-consciously archaic. There were a few euphemisms, such as *blood disease*. More strikingly, there was also a strong sense of schadenfreude, manifesting itself in coarse jokes and black humor, such as the phrase "to suffer a blow over the nose with a French faggot-stick," that is, to lose one's nose, one of the extreme consequences of the disease. John Aubrey records spitefully in *Brief Lives* that William Davenant "gott a terrible clap of a Black handsome wench that lay in Axe yard Westminster . . . which cost him his Nose, with which unlucky mischance many witts were too cruelly bold."

Coded jokes about syphilis abounded on the Elizabethan, Jacobean, and Restoration stage. Virtually all Shakespeare's plays contain references of varying directness, and his *Timon of Athens* (1607) is widely regarded as dramatizing the mental disintegration which accompanies *paresis*, the third stage. There is certainly no misunderstanding Timon's hysterical tirade when he urges the whores Phrynia and Timandra to spread venereal disease, morbidly specifying its gruesome symptoms:

> Consumptions sow
> In hollow bones of man . . .
>   Down with the nose,
> Down with it flat, take the bridge quite away . . .
>   Make curled-pate ruffians bald . . .
>   Plague all,
> That your activity may defeat and quell
> The source of all erection.
>
> (Act IV, scene iii)

Troilus & Cressida (1601) ends with the syphilitic pimp Pandarus bidding an ironic adieu as he sets off for treatment, bequeathing to the audience "my diseases" (Act V, scene ix). Symptomatic terms such as *chancre*, meaning a venereal ulcer, came to be used as insults, as did *syphilitic* itself.

In essence, syphilis came to be expressed openly as a morbid condition, a fact of life and a grim joke. Francis Grose included in his slang dictionary (1785) such graphic descriptions as *pissing pins and needles* for "to have a gonorrhea." Toulouse-Lautrec depicted the medical examination of the whores of Montmartre in a cool, matter-of-fact fashion. Of Lord Randolph Churchill's terrible demise, a contemporary wrote: "There was no curtain. He died by inches in public, sole mourner at his own protracted funeral" (Rosebery, 1906, p. 72). At the onset and throughout the progress of the disease, up to its cure through the introduction of penicillin in the 1940s, nobody expressed disquiet over insensitivity or xenophobia. In the early stages there was no official policy line, no syphilis lobby, giving advice, protecting the victims, or trying to regulate the vocabulary. This is essentially because government, society, media, and information were structured quite differently from the modern practices. Comment on this sort of topic was more open then than now. In short, there were few taboos.

The historical and cultural differences between syphilis and AIDS are obviously very marked. Despite an enormous volume of research and commentary on AIDS, the modern debate in the public domain concerns, not so much the disease itself, but the rights of those who have it, proper attitudes towards them, their right to privacy, and most of all, appropriate language. These issues, widely apparent, surface in comments such as this: "These problems of nomenclature [of AIDS] disguise the question of who owns AIDS, who has the primary right to speak of it. As a cultural capital of escalating value, it has become a contested body, claimed by countries, doctors, writers, politicians, and quacks" (Koestenbaum, 1990, p. 163). Although there are parallels, it is difficult to imagine anyone writing about syphilis in this fashion. In her article "AIDS: Keywords," Jan Zita Grover discusses and analyzes the most basic terminology, from *disease, test,* and *virus* to terms like *general population, lesbian,* and *prostitute,* exploring their assumptions and nuances. She comments that Susan Sontag, in *AIDS and its Metaphors* (1990) "has called for an end to all war-metaphors. . . ." Her interest is that the term and its metaphors are used "as a second-order signifier for *fin de siècle* doom and gloom" (Grover, 1990, pp. 160–1).

A considerable semantic debate ensued over the appropriateness of the description *AIDS victim* as opposed to *living with AIDS* or *person with AIDS*, abbreviated to *PWA*. Grover quotes the statement issued at the second AIDS Forum in 1983 by the National Association of People with AIDS: "We condemn attempts to label us as 'victims,' which implies defeat, and we are only occasionally 'patients,' which implies passivity, helplessness, and dependence on the care of others. We are 'people with AIDS'" (Grover, 1990, p. 156). The earliest *OED* quotation for *PWA* is 1985. Despite this intervention, Grover notes that "the commonest usage in the media is *AIDS victim*" (p. 156). Thus the *Guardian Weekly* carried a report in 1986 referring to the Shanti Project: "a charity subsidised by the municipality to help PWAs. It makes houses available to Aids victims."

Clearly this is a very different semantic dynamic from that concerning syphilis. There is the familiar split between official, semiscientific discourse with its euphemisms, contrasted with the more direct demotic usage, with the media holding positions somewhere in the middle ground, depending on their market segment. But in addition, there is the role of pressure groups seeking to remove or reduce stigmatic denotations or connotations. Out of these different strategies arose the amalgam coined by Randy Shilts as *AIDSpeak*:

> AIDSpeak [is] a new language forged by public health officials, anxious gay politicians, and the burgeoning ranks of "AIDS activists." The linguistic roots of AIDSpeak sprouted, not so much from the truth as from what was politically facile and psychologically reassuring. . . . The language went to great lengths never to offend. (From *And the Band Played on: Politics, People and the AIDS Epidemic*, cited in Grover, 1990, p. 147)

Given the facts that AIDS, unlike syphilis, is a potentially lethal condition still without a cure, these semantic strategies seem slightly precious. By contrast, cancer patients are not referred to as "people with cancer" or *PWCs*.

Many commentators noted an initial conspiracy of official silence, which led to the slogan "Silence = Death" and the semantic development of *denial* in relation to AIDS. The original Freudian sense of *denial* (recorded from c. 1914) referred to the usually unconscious suppression of painful or embarrassing feelings, reactions, or desires. Since then more conscious states of individuals and policy makers being *in denial* and even practicing *denialism* has become familiar. The South African President Thabo Mbeki (who asserted "I honestly do not know anyone who has died of AIDS") and his Health Minister Dr Manto Tshabalala-Msimang (who notoriously recommended folk remedies of olive oil, the African potato, and other vegetables) achieved an unfortunate reputation for AIDS denialism as the disease ravaged their nation.

In popular culture, by contrast, the tragedy, horror, and insecurity of AIDS have been dealt with much more directly. Major contributions were Tony Kushner's spectacular *Angels in America*, "A Gay Fantasia on National Themes" (1991), as well as the films of *And the Band Played on* (1993), *Philadelphia* (1993), and *Love, Valor, Compassion!* (1997). On an entirely different level was the notorious 1991 Benetton advertisement showing a harrowing deathbed scene.

Addiction

The traditional substance favored for conspicuous consumption to the point of addiction among the English has been alcohol. The practice of heavy drinking partly derives from the habits of their Germanic ancestors. Even the most incurious student of *Beowulf*, the first epic poem in English, cannot fail to be impressed by the regular and copious consumption of beer, ale, and mead at all levels of society. Noting that these beverages are referred to "more than forty times in the poem, while there is no word for any item of food at all," Professor Tom Shippey even suggested that ritual drunkenness was being alluded to in places (1978, p. 9). There are certainly no disapproving comments on the practice within the poem, and modern translators face problems when drunkenness in high places and formal contexts is described. But the problem essentially derives from cultural difference in dealing with pagan practices.

By contrast, in Chaucer and Langland a more moralistic Christian attitude is clearly apparent: drunkenness is seen as a sign of depravity and corruption. The decadent Summoner in the *Canterbury Tales* is the first figure in English literature to be presented as an alcoholic who abuses his ecclesiastical office for alcoholic gain, and is regarded with authorial contempt. When the Swiss physician Thomas Platter visited London in 1599, he observed: "I have never seen more taverns and ale-houses in my whole life than in London." The theaters on the South Bank were surrounded by them, as well as by brothels. Literary treatments became more morally complex. In Shakespeare both Falstaff and his understudy Sir Toby Belch are decadent but sympathetic Dionysiac figures: the puritanical Malvolio is neither. In *Othello*, Cassio's career is ruined by a single drinking bout, and Hamlet is deeply disapproving of the supposedly excessive drinking by the new Danish régime. Flavius, the steward of Timon of Athens, condemns the orgies when "Our vaults have wept / With drunken spilth of wine" (Act II, scene ii).

For centuries "the demon drink" became a fixture, even a fixation in social mores, spectacularly depicted in Hogarth's "Gin Lane" (1751), reflecting a time when one house in three in London was involved in either the manufacture, sale, or consumption of gin. (The companion piece "Beer Lane" depicts the traditional English beverage as the source of prosperity, social cohesion, and bonhomie.) George Cruikshank produced two extensive series, "The Bottle" (1847) and its sequel, "The Drunkard's Children" (1848), both enormously popular. William Booth, founder of the Salvation Army, described "A population sodden with drink, steeped in vice, eaten up by every social and physical malady, these are the denizens of Darkest England amidst whom my life has been spent" in his dismally titled work, *In Darkest England, and the Way Out* (1880). Although *drunkenness* and *drunkard* are medieval terms, *teetotal* was coined in 1834, *alcoholism* surfaced about 1860 and the agent-noun *alcoholic* about 30 years later.

An obvious class element lies in the dictum "Drink is the curse of the working classes," subverted by Oscar Wilde as "Work is the curse of the drinking classes." A different class perspective is apparent in Evelyn Waugh's memorable description of "English county families baying for broken glass" in drunken orgies at Oxford (*Decline and Fall*, 1928, p. 14). (The work is, incidentally a compendium of political incorrectness.) Out of the realms of fiction, researchers have shown that contemporary English students spend more money on alcohol than on books in *binge drinking*. Yet the modern emphasis on alcoholism regards the condition as a disease rather than as a moral failing, a feature also apparent in such terms as *anorexia* and *bulimia*. Nevertheless, *alcoholic* has generated numerous semantic clones such as *workaholic* and *chocoholic*, which are judgmental.

Today *The Confessions of an English Opium-Eater* is a title sensational in its scandalous directness, as no doubt it was in 1821, when Thomas De Quincey's amazing self-revelation came out. Although both *addiction* and *addicted* go back to the Renaissance, the terms were not used in the modern way. They could even be positive, as when Edward Phillips commented on Shakespeare's "addiction to books" in 1675. The critical sense was more generalized. In *Twelfth Night* Olivia is "addicted to a melancholy" (Act II, scene v), while David Livingstone made the observation in 1865 that "The blacks are more addicted to stealing where slavery exists" (*Zambezi*, cited in *OED*). *Addict* in the modern sense as a noun is recorded only from the first decade of the twentieth century, always in association with drugs.

This is, of course, well after the careers of the most famous opium addicts in literature, many of whom had their curiosity aroused by De Quincey's enthusiasm for the "marvellous agency of opium," "just, subtle and all-conquering opium!", in his view the "true hero of the tale." First among the poets was Samuel Taylor Coleridge (1772–1834), who never really broke the habit and whose *Kubla Khan* (1796) is a notable but disputed case study of composition under the influence. M. H. Abrams's study *The Milk of Paradise* (1934) found clear patterns of dream-imagery in the poems of Crabbe, Coleridge, de Quincey, and Francis Thompson. Other scholars, notably Elizabeth Schneider (*Coleridge, Opium and Kubla* Khan, 1953), were less convinced of the imaginative stimulus of the opiate.

Alethea Hayter's *Opium and the Romantic Imagination* (1968) broadened the scope of her study to include Keats, Poe, Baudelaire, Berlioz, Wilkie Collins, Walter Scott, Dickens, and Elizabeth Barrett Browning. Wordsworth seems to have been the only Romantic poet who never experimented with the drug. But Hayter came to the verdict that "No clear pattern of opium's influence on creative writing . . . has emerged from this study" (1968, p. 331). Dickens describes an opium den as a scene of desolation in *The Mystery of Edwin Drood* (1870). Conan Doyle's complex detective hero Sherlock Holmes made his first appearance in 1887 in *A Study in Scarlet*. Also "addicted to melancholy," Holmes seeks escape in Chinese opium dens.

On a more mundane level, Hayter shows that "by the eighteenth century the opium addict could be met in most walks of life" (1968, p. 25). She cites the cases of the poet Thomas Shadwell, William Wilberforce, the emancipator of slaves, and Clive of India, who died of it. More astonishing was the mass consumption in the larger industrial towns, especially on Saturdays. Much of this was in the form of laudanum, a solution of opium in alcohol, which was more socially acceptable and cheaper than beer or gin, "so that in one Lancashire parish a single chemist could sell 200 lbs of opium in small packets in one year. . . . Britain imported 22,000 lbs of opium in 1830, and by 1860 the amount had more than quadrupled" (1968, pp. 33–4). In its more respectable form as *morphine* (derived from Morpheus, the classical god of dreams) it was often prescribed by doctors as an analgesic, for example to Queen Victoria in childbirth.

From its importation from America, tobacco attracted controversy. James I's famous "Counterblaste to Tobacco" (1604) is still often quoted for its orotund style and hellfire message, but there was an extensive minor literature of praise from the earliest times onwards, evidenced in such anthologies as *Smoke Rings and Roundelays*, compiled by Wilfred Partington in 1924. It contains sections such as "the Virtues of the Leaf" and "Women and the Weed." The modern social history is summed up in Allan M. Brandt's study *The Cigarette Century: The Rise, Fall and Deadly Persistence of the Product that Defined America* (2007). It contains such advertising gems from the 1930s to 1950s as "More Doctors Smoke Camel" and a seductive vamp in a red dress with the challenging caption: "Do you Inhale? Everyone's doing it" (for Lucky Strike). Although *passive smoking* is recorded from 1986, publicity has been far more recent. Today tobacco is being outlawed, while cannabis is being decriminalized. The standard politically correct formula for addiction is, of course, *substance abuse*, recorded as far back as 1975 in a reference in *US News and World Report* to "substance abuse services."

Food, Eating Disorders, and Lookism

As is the case with most of the Seven Deadly Sins, Gluttony has long been socially acceptable. In the English tradition of cookery, as many menus of previous times show, the notion of "fine eating" came to be virtually the same as gourmandizing, a practice which was seldom criticized. It was, perhaps, the first bourgeois form of conspicuous consumption.

Angela Carter was one of the earliest to criticize the modern cult of food amidst global starvation in an early politically correct broadside. In her collection mischievously mistitled *Expletives Deleted*, she quoted the epigraph of Levi-Strauss, "To eat is to fuck," before proceeding to highlight the imbalances of available food (1992, p. 75). Nevertheless, the food cult has spread, especially in the UK, with the number of "celebrity chefs" having increased dramatically to the point that they have acquired almost the status of football coaches. Books and television programs now abound. This development has occurred precisely when awareness of global poverty and dearth has intensified, leading to food riots in some less developed countries.

More specifically, *vegetarian* was coined in 1839 and *vegetarianism* was described in 1851 as "a modern term." A quotation of 1885 cited in *OED* commented: "Among ourselves vegetarianism is regarded as a harmless eccentricity." Since then vegetarianism has, of course, changed status from being a dietary régime associated with religious prohibitions to what is called a lifestyle preference based on animal rights.

Two new entrants to the semantic field are *genetically modified* and *genetically engineered*. The *OED* has quotations going back to 1968 and 1970 in scientific contexts, but the first general use is for 1995: "The new tomatoes are the first genetically modified fruit to be approved for human consumption in both the UK and the US" (*Independent*, March 21). *Genetically engineered* is recorded from 1971. *Organic* was first used in relation to fertilizers in the 1860s, but remained rare until the 1940s with quotations of this kind: "What is claimed for these organic methods of farming is that they increase the fertility of the soil, produce much better tasting crops, reduce weeds, do away with the necessity of using poisonous sprays and improve the mechanical structure of the soil" (J. I. Rodale, *Organic Methods of Farming & Gardening*, 1942, cited in *OED*).

In the vocabulary of eating there has been a typical shift in register whereby older judgmental terms such as *gluttony* and *greed* have given way to the seemingly scientific vocabulary of *eating disorders, anorexia,* and *bulimia.* Several of these turn out to have remarkably extended and interesting histories. However, new judgmental terms such as *binge* and *gorge* have also come into play, to some extent replacing the older words. A rather coy semantic arrival has been the phrase *portion control*, used typically in "I have a problem with portion control."

The long semantic history of *fat* shows the term to have been double-edged since its Anglo-Saxon origins, with various enduring positive senses such as "in a well-fed condition, plump," counterbalanced by critical uses denoting "slow-witted, indolent." Even the nickname *fatty* is recorded in a diary in 1797, cited in *OED*: "His wife is a poor miserable thing, his daughter a good looking fatty." The American authority on slang, James Farmer, noted in 1891 that *fatty* was "a jocular epithet for fat man and a comic endearment for a fat woman." A miniature social history is encapsulated in *embonpoint*. Chaucer describes his corpulent, smug Monk as "a lord ful fat and in good poynt" ("in good condition," Prologue, l. 200); the full French form was borrowed from the eighteenth century in both a complimentary and a euphemistic sense, occasionally referring to a paunch. In recent decades *fat* has become increasingly critical and steadily rendered taboo under the prohibitions of *fattism*, so that *obese* and *obesity* have rapidly changed from being rarities to common terms. At the same time "large" and "ample figure" have moved in to fill the gap. A new technical arrival was *cellulite*, borrowed from French *cellulites*, first recorded in *Vogue* in 1968.

Anorexia, broadly meaning "loss of appetite," emerged from relative obscurity to show a steadily increasing currency from the 1960s. However, it had a previous history as a rare term borrowed from French. The *OED* records *anorexie* in Joshua Sylvester's translation of *du Bartas* (1598), but *anorexic* is recorded only from 1907. Although originally intended to elicit sympathy for a psychological condition, *anorexic* is now often used unsympathetically to mean "painfully or abnormally thin."

Bulimia started its modern history in America in the late 1970s, specifically in a reference in the *Journal of the American Medical Association* to "a newly proposed disorder called bulimia" (1978). (This is also one of the first instances of *disorder* being applied to eating.) In fact, the term is previously recorded as *bulimy* from the fourteenth century in John of Trevisa. Joshua Sylvester's translation of *du Bartas* (1608) describes the contrasting symptoms: "One while the boulime, then the anorexie . . . rage with monstrous ryot" (". . . fury with alarming excess"). There are also figurative uses, such as "The French King had such a bulimy after money." The definition in the *Sydenham Society Lexicon of Medicine* (1879–99) is: "A morbid hunger, chiefly occurring in idiots and maniacs . . . the so-called canine hunger."

In the second half of the 1980s, "general diet consciousness and emphasis on physical fitness made being overweight almost into a moral issue" (*Oxford Dictionary of New Words*, 1992). A new arrival in the language was *fattism*, meaning "prejudice or discrimination against fat people," coined by the American psychologist Rita. J. Freedman. "Looksism gives birth to fatism [sic]," she observed in *Bodylove* (1988, cited in *OED*), in which she analyzed the negative perceptions and assumptions made about fat people, more especially the association with lassitude and lack of discipline, and the contrary inclination to associate thinness with prettiness and goodness. An article in *Spare Rib* chimed in: "Fatist [sic] is a refreshing new word for me, as opposed to fattest which is much more familiar" (October 1987, cited in *OED*). The spelling later changed to *fattism*; *fattist* appeared soon afterwards in 1990.

Fatness and attitudes towards the overweight became increasingly controversial issues, drawing in other political terminology. "Is Weight the New Race?" asked Rachel Cooke in an article in the *Observer* (July 9, 2006) containing phrases such as "body fascism," "fat-hate industries," and "size acceptance." "Do we demonise the obese purely on health grounds or is it a gut reaction based on prejudice?" was her opening question. She quoted Marylin Wann, director of the National Association to Advance Fat Acceptance (NAAFA), who "likes to use the word *fat*. '*Obesity* is offensive and meaningless; so is *overweight*.'" Cooke also cited Malcolm Gladwell, *The Tipping Point* (2000) and *Blink* (2005), Paul Campos, *The Obesity Myth* (2005). and Shelley Bovey, *Being Fat is Not a Sin* (1989).

Criticism of the use of the word *fat* features in news stories such as that in the *Daily Mirror* (October 16, 2005) in which the victim of a hit and run incident described the car as having been driven by "a fat woman." The police officer taking her statement said that she should withdraw the word, a spokesperson adding that Greater Manchester Police had a policy ensuring that officers used "appropriate language."

The modern emphasis and rationale for lookism is a justifiable response to the highly mediated feminine obsession with having a "perfect" body, or one which conforms to current models of beauty, more especially the assumptions and feelings of negative self-worth suffered by those who do not conform to these arbitrary or contrived standards. Coined in 1978, *lookism* was described in 1985 as "a prejudice as insidious as racism, and ageism" (*San Diego Union Tribune*, October 4). Lookism lies at the heart of the earlier feminist objections to women being presented as sexual objects in the media, especially in advertising. However, the use of pornographic images has become established in tabloid journalism, notoriously institutionalized in the UK tabloid the *Sun*'s "page 3 girl," and in the "soft porn" images which are now *de rigueur* in advertising "intimate" feminine products. Lookism has gone further, to include those with "an alternative body image," potentially an enormous category.

The Environment

Environment is a relatively new term, dating from various uses by Thomas Carlyle around 1830, such as his reference to the "picturesque environment" of Bayreuth. Since then it has increasingly been used of a general agglomeration of conditions, physical and mental. The physical environment was previously regarded as so vast as to be unchanging and unchangeable, and therefore not in need of attention or protection. It is difficult to disentangle the earlier senses, but the first *OED* citation of the modern, more contained meaning seems to surface about 1950, and the key compound *environmental pollution* is recorded from 1967. *Environment* has since become an increasingly emotive term, as opposed to *ecology* and its abbreviation *eco-*, which are more referential and scientific.

Very appropriately, *ecology* was first recorded in a letter of Thoreau dated January 1, 1858. But the term remained dormant until the early 1970s, when the compounds *eco-activist*, *eco-catastrophe*, and *ecocide* leapt into prominence, followed by the satirical terms *ecodoom*, *econut*, and *ecofreak* for alarmists. The more enduring compound *eco-friendly* dates from two decades later, in 1989, followed by the increasingly familiar formula *ecological footprint* in 1992. The use of *bio-* as a prefix has expanded enormously, as the *Oxford Dictionary of New Words* (1992) observed: "Towards the end of the decade [the 1980s] *bio-* began to be used indiscriminately wherever it had the slightest relevance . . . The prefix is sometimes even used as a free-standing adjective, meaning little more than 'biologically acceptable'." From early forms like *biosphere* (coined a century ago in 1909) there emerged *biodegradable* (1961) and the key term *biodiversity* (1989). Together with *organic*, the more recent uses are related to food.

The key word *pollution* originally meant "masturbation," before acquiring the broader sense of "defilement," but the modern sense of environmental contamination is recorded only from the 1950s. The adverse environmental impact of motor vehicles with high fuel consumption is reflected in the stigmatic term *gas guzzling* in 1968 (*Time*, August 16), followed by *gas guzzler* from 1973 (*Washington Post*). Within a few years the abbreviation *CFC* (for *chlorofluorocarbons*) became current, following a reference in 1976 in the *New Scientist*. *Ozone*, previously a largely unknown term for a gas, rapidly acquired a common currency through journalistic uses such as *ozone hole* (*New York Times*, September 23, 1989), *ozone-friendly* (*Which*, September 1989) and *ozone-depleting* (*Garbage*, November–December 1990). In the same year the concept of the *zero-emissions vehicle* or ZEV was first articulated. *Global warming*, now a basic concept-term, first surfaced in 1977 in the *Economist*. *Environmentally friendly* was, significantly, the first extension of the suffix *friendly*, now also fashionable and multipurpose, coined back in 1989. The *greenhouse effect*, widely discussed in the 1980s, is first recorded by *OED*, amazingly, in 1937 as "the so-called greenhouse effect of the atmosphere."

The environmentally favorable use of *green* developed through association with the German environmental lobby *Grüne Aktion Zukunft* ("The Green Campaign for the Future") from the early 1970s. Charles A. Reich's contemporary book, *The Greening of America* (1970) is really about rejuvenation, as is shown in the subtitle *How the Youth Revolution is Trying to make America Livable*, but the environmental sense appears in Keith Griffin's *The Green Revolution* (1972). The first reference to *Greenpeace* dates from 1971 and to the political designation *the Greens* from 1988. *Green* is now a general-purpose politically correct designation, often surfacing in unexpected places: "Spanking enthusiasts are also short of green options, since most paddles are made of leather or rubber. But Coco de Mer offers a Fairtrade spanking paddle that has been ethically made in India" (*Independent*, February 13, 2006). *Ungreen* was coined in the late 1980s in journalism: "BAT's core business is in the ungreen area of cigarettes" (*Guardian Weekly*, July 30, 1989). In the dynamics of protest, *tree house* gained a new meaning from 1995, having been preceded by *tree hugger* around 1991.

Animal Rights

The traditional Christian philosophical view that animals, lacking souls and reason, were therefore subhuman and rightly subject to humanity as beasts of burden, sources of food, and so on, was a given for centuries. Any questioning of the Great Chain of Being was dangerous. The race of rational horses mischievously created by Swift in *Gulliver's Travels* (1727) caused some outrage, but Darwin's disturbing scientific thesis in *The Origin of Species* (1859) provoked a sense of hysteria and anxiety which still reverberates. It is no coincidence that as the status of man as a rational being has increasingly been questioned, so the status of animals has correspondingly been raised.

Cruelty to animals has a long tradition in English culture, notably in the rituals of bearbaiting and cockfighting, both recorded from the fifteenth century. Thomas Platter, an observant Swiss visitor to London in 1599, noted that on every Sunday and Wednesday there were bearbaitings in theaters, such as the Bear Garden, during which sets of English mastiffs were set on the bears. Platter was impressed by the tenacity of the mastiffs, whose jaws had to be prized open by means of special sticks covered with metal. There was also cockfighting (one of the major theaters being called the Cockpit) for three quarters of the year, but this could not be continued for the last quarter because the cocks' feathers were full of blood. Platter's informant added what wonderful pleasure it was to watch the cocks fight. More surprisingly, cock fights were held in grammar schools: in 1565 the statutes for Queen Elizabeth I Grammar School in Hartlebury, Worcestershire stipulated that "The Schoolmaster shall take the profits of such cockfights as are commonly used in school." The practice went on at least until the mid-nineteenth century. Macaulay's ironic comment that "The Puritans hated bear baiting, not because it gave pain to the bear, but because it gave pleasure to the spectators," from his *History of England* (1849), is usually quoted for its anti-Puritan sentiment. He would have had in mind such figures as Philip Stubbes and his *Anatomie of Abuses* (1583). Shakespeare's most pertinent quotation is revealing: when Macbeth compares himself to a bear "tied to the stake" (Act V, scene vii), he recognizes that he now faces a desperate struggle for survival.

Only in the eighteenth century were there signs of a change of attitude, seen in William Hogarth's powerfully graphic series "The Four Stages of Cruelty" (1751). As with all his moral series, Hogarth shows that cruelty is a degrading vice which requires ever greater stimuli, leading to ruin. Contemporary was the observations of Oliver Goldsmith in 1783 that "Cock-fighting with us is declining every day." But an arresting later French painting by Jean-Léon Gérome (1847) titled "Un Combat de Coqs" is set in an idyllic Mediterranean scene. It shows a young naked couple engrossed in the combat, the woman sunning her shaved pubis and clearly flushed with excitement.

Reform started with the Society for the Prevention of Cruelty to Animals, founded in 1824, but it applied only to domestic animals, not to field and blood sports, which were covered by the Cruelty to Animals Act in 1835. Fox-hunting continued to be an elaborate society ritual, one of the most memorable criticisms being Oscar Wilde's witticism that it was "the unspeakable in full pursuit of the uneatable." The practice was finally ended, with considerable national controversy, in 2005.

The first direct reference to the concept of animal rights was E. W. B. Nicholson's *The Rights of Animals* (1879), followed by Dix Harwood's comment on "champions of animal rights" in *Love for Animals* (1928, cited in *OED*). This in turn had been preceded by a reference to "animalists and vegetablists" in 1837. (Vivisection, which had been in the language since the early eighteenth century, became a public issue with the publication of Lord Carnarvon's Vivisection Bill in 1876.) The modern currency of *animalist*, defined by the *OED* as "one who takes the animal side of the debate," seems to date from 1985. 1975 saw the publication of two ground-breaking books, *Animal Liberation* by the philosopher Peter Singer, and *Victims of Science*, by Richard D. Ryder. Both used the new word *speciesism*, defined by Ryder as "the widespread discrimination that is practised by man against other species" (1975, cited in *OED*). In his Preface, Singer provocatively compared "the tyranny of human over non-human animals" to slavery.

Since then the idea of animal rights has spread to include virtually every aspect of the inhuman treatment of animals, for fur, for food, and for laboratory testing. On another level the rather formal and whimsical *animal companion*, recorded from 1980, has become increasingly current, replacing the traditional and perhaps belittling word *pet*.

Religious Rituals and the War on Christmas

Rituals endorse the values of a whole society as well as sects within it. The festivals of Christmas, Easter, and many others reflect the Christian foundations of British society. However, all of them had pagan origins before being Christianized. Now many have regressed to become pagan exhibitions of conspicuous consumerism and consumption. A few decades ago, in protest at the way that Christmas was becoming overly commercialized, the slogan "Put Christ Back into Christmas" was coined. The first hostility to Christmas, it should be remembered, came from the Puritans, mainly on these moral grounds, as well as the doctrinal objection that the festival had no biblical justification. The fundamental issue is the extent to which a holiday should be regarded as a holy day.

As Britain has become a more self-aware multicultural society, so the primacy of these ancient rituals has come under question. "The War on Christmas," as it has come to be known, is a quintessential feature of political correctness. However, the campaign and its attendant controversies started in the 1980s in the United States, with "holiday trees" being substituted for "Christmas trees" in various states. (In some the original title has been reinstated.) Almost annually a debate surfaces on whether it is a genuine bureaucratic suppression, or kow-towing by those not wishing to appear politically incorrect, or contrived mediated exaggeration. In terms of the politics of religion, there is dispute over whether there is genuine opposition to the Christmas festival or whether the curtailing of traditional rituals is the result of local councils not wishing to appear insensitive to other religions. An early view came from Auberon Waugh, who referred in an editorial in December 1992 to "the great anti-Christmas frenzy" (*Literary Review*). An American perspective was given in the *New Yorker* of December 26, 2005:

> Chestnuts are roasting on an open fire, with Jack Frost nipping at your nose and folks dressed up as Eskimos – or to update the line for political correctness, with tots in boots just like Aleuts. . . . It's time again for the thrill that comes but one a year: the War on Christmas. The War on Christmas is a little like Santa Claus, in that it (a) comes down to us from the sky, beamed down by the satellites of cable news, and (b) does not in a boringly empirical sense, exist. What does exist is the idea of the War on Christmas. (p. 45)

Under the influence of the multiculturalist ethos, the Swahili term *kwanza* has been espoused in the US, although it really refers to a harvest festival, meaning "first fruits." An extreme effort at multiculturalism is found in the greeting "Happy Kwanhanamas," the key term being a portmanteau or blend of *Kwanza*, *Hanukka*, and *Christmas*. Currently this central Christian festival is being denamed, the commonest new usage being *Happy Holidays*, but the motives are complex. Multiculturalism is intended to encourage diversity, but often appears to favor some cultural forms over others. In a recent novel, a British headmistress explains:

> As I am sure you are aware, the school already recognizes a great variety of religious and secular events: amongst them, Christmas, Ramadan, Chinese New Year, Diwali, Yom Kippur, Hanukkah, the birth of Haile Selassie, and the death of Martin Luther King. The Harvest Festival is part of the school's ongoing commitment to religious diversity, Mr Iqbal.

This satirical sally comes from Zadie Smith's *White Teeth* (2001, p. 129).

Part IV

Cultural and Historical Issues

Chapter 7

Political Correctness in the Past

The aim of Part IV is to develop in more detail three points that have already been canvassed. The first is to show how ingrained in the past were attitudes now regarded as politically incorrect. The second is in many ways the converse, namely to trace the development of forms of enforced political correctness which developed periodically centuries ago. The third is to show that forms of humorous subversion and satire of institutions and even values were a major feature of the past. The emphasis is generally on literary models, although cartoons are naturally included (see chapter 8).

The Middle Ages

Most early medieval literature is moralistic and concerned with models of a good spiritual life. There are, however, the counterexamples of the fabliaux, comic tales celebrating immoral behavior and flaunting poetic justice. With the emergence of a more secular literature came the naturalistic expression of closely observed individual characters and plots less constrained by moral inhibitions, found in unexpected parts of Chaucer's *Canterbury Tales* (c. 1380–1400), bringing the first clear evidence of politically incorrect attitudes. Thus the majority of the ecclesiastical establishment are shown as corrupt, venal, or hypocritical. Some merely abuse their positions; others undermine the whole institution. In addition, Chaucer's *magnum opus* contains many expressions of xenophobia, racism, sexism, ageism, and lookism. In many ways these are not surprising, since they reflect the worldview, values, and prejudices of medieval society, although there are individual emphases. Others are less expected: at the height of the uproarious farce of the *Miller's Tale* the unfortunate Absolon's "misdirected kiss," directed mistakenly at Alison's posterior, classically known as *osculum in tergo*, is a parody of worshiping the Devil.

Given the social and institutional hierarchies of the times, classism can be taken for granted. But it would be a mistake to see what D. W. Robertson called "medieval society with its quiet hierarchies" (1963, p. 51). In 1381 the Peasants' Revolt severely shook the foundations of the prevailing order: the Archbishop of Canterbury was murdered and his head displayed on London Bridge like a traitor's. Preaching to the mob the renegade Lollard priest John Ball asked the famous fundamental question: "When Adam delved and Eve span, / Who was then the gentleman?" Chaucer's text is especially valuable, since the form of frame narrative contains "link passages" of dialog responding to the tales, ranging from general approval to furious denunciation.

Although not as condemning as his contemporary Langland, Chaucer is a founder of the English tradition of irony, presenting all but one of the major religious figures as if they were nobles, being ostentatiously materialistic, hedonistic, and undisciplined, flouting their vows of poverty and abusing their positions. These include the bejeweled, frenchified Prioress, the hunting, swan-eating Monk, and the flirtatious Friar. Furthermore, the bizarre couple who conclude the General Prologue, the grotesque alcoholic Summoner and vain opportunistic Pardoner, symbolize the corruption of the Last Judgment. In all these characteristics these ecclesiastics are, of course, entirely the opposite of the one true "good man of religion," the modest Parson. He loves his neighbor; the others have worldly or perverse fixations. A similar cynical mixture of business and pleasure is apparent in the *Miller's Tale*, when Absolon flirts with the women of the congregation in church:

> This Absolon, that iolif was and gay,
> Gooth with a sencer on the haliday,
> Sensyng the wyves of the parish faste;
> (Our Absolon, so jolly and entertaining,
> Proceeds with a censer on the holy days,
> Feeling up the women of the parish closely)
> (Miller's Tale, ll. 153–5)

The verbal play of *sencer* and *sensing* is a cheeky innuendo. More seriously, in the portrait of the Summoner, who when drunk would speak nothing but Latin, Chaucer adds this sly barb:

> . . . ye knowen wel how that a jay
> Kan clepen "Watte" as wel as kan the pope.
> (you know well that a jay
> can call out "Walter" as well as the Pope can.)
> (General Prologue, ll. 642–3)

Is Chaucer making a general comment about jays or a specific antiauthoritarian criticism of the papal establishment? And, since this was the period of the Great Schism, which Pope would he be referring to? Similarly, when the Host invites the Parson to tell a tale, the Shipman vehemently insists that the Parson shall not preach or "glose" (interpret) the gospel (Epilogue to the Man of Law's Tale (ll. 1178–80). Is this just a personal antagonism or a more profound criticism of dogmatic religion, a precursor of the anti-Catholic sentiments of Protestantism and of Nonconformity? Chaucer's irony is often so subtle that the reader is left with more questions than answers.

Chaucer's Knight, an idealized character according to the bulk of critical opinion, has dedicated his whole life to the war against the heathen. His portrait in the Prologue is largely a drum-roll of places where he has "foughten for oure feith" against "hethenesse" (l. 49). While Chaucer evidently endorses this martial Christianity, the same claim cannot be made for the tale of the prim and proper Prioress. Her melodramatic version of the legend of the gruesome murder of St Hugh of Lincoln, said to have been martyred by Jews in 1255, is suffused with all the stereotypes of xenophobia and especially with vicious anti-Semitism. The phrases "the cursed Jewes" and "these Jewes" are repeated at least half a dozen times in a narrative of less than two hundred lines. This hideous tale, a troubling embarrassment to modern criticism, provokes no responses from the company of pilgrims. Other expressions of xenophobia occur in the Man of Law's Tale, which is equally condemning of the Saracens.

While these can be explained as expressions of individual character, perhaps the most surprising topical reference occurs in the charming beast fable told by the Nun's Priest. In the middle of the frantic farmyard chase after Chantecleer and the fox, the genial narrator comments blandly that the pursuers made not half so loud an uproar as did Jack Straw's mob when "they wolde any Fleming kille" (ll. 774–7). The priest alludes to the massacre of Flemish immigrant weavers during the Peasants' Revolt in 1381, of which a contemporary commented: "Many lost their lives because they said *brood* and *kaas* instead of *bread* and *cheese*." (A similar xenophobic outbreak occurred on May 1, 1517, called "Evil May Day," when London apprentices attacked foreign artisans and merchants on account of their advantages and privileges.)

The whole pseudoscience of physiognomy, assuming a relationship between bodily – especially facial – appearance and character, was highly developed in the Middle Ages. Many of the pilgrims in Chaucer's Prologue are described according to this principle, with physical appearances ranging from caricature to the grotesque, presented in a coded language of significant details. The most notable and developed are the portraits of the Wife of Bath, the Miller, the Summoner, and the Pardoner. Thoroughly expounded in Walter C. Curry's major study, *Chaucer and the Mediaeval Sciences* (1960), the topic is also treated by Ruth Nevo, "Motive and Mask in the General Prologue" (1963) and Jill Mann, *Chaucer and Medieval Estates Satire* (1973).

The redoubtable Wife of Bath is a veritable compendium of politically incorrect attitudes, from both medieval and modern perspectives, as she insouciantly reveals in her extended Prologue-*cum*-confessional manifesto. Sexually omnivorous and aggressive, presented as a mixture of Venus and Mars, she alludes to the sexual significance of her buck teeth, using a casually blasphemous comparison between sacred and profane love:

> Gat-tothed I was, and that becam me weel;
> I hadde the prente of seinte Venus' seel.
> (I was goat-toothed and that suited me well;
> I had the imprint of Saint Venus.)
> (Wife of Bath's Prologue, ll. 603–4)

Openly sexist and ageist in her values, she cruelly berates her three elderly husbands, using the epithet *olde* with stinging frequency: "sire olde lecchour" (l. 242), "olde dotard" (l. 331), and "olde barrel-ful of lyes" (l. 302). She thus supplies the first recorded instances of the contemptuous use of *olde*, anticipating those given in the *OED* by over a century. Correspondingly, she adores the youthful beauty, and is attracted by the physical aggression, of her younger spouses, especially her last, Jankin, with whom she had a tempestuous relationship. This liaison with a stripling half her age started at her previous husband's funeral:

> As help me God! Whan that I saugh hym go
> After the beere, me thoughte he hadde a paire
> Of legges and of feet so clene and faire
> That al myn herte I yaf unto his hoold.
> (My God! When I saw him walking after the coffin,
> I thought he had such a shapely and desirable pair of legs and feet,
> That I gave my heart entirely into his safekeeping.)
> (Wife of Bath's Prologue, ll. 596–9)

She outrageously inverts the medieval social norm in the marriage relationship (and succeeds) by wanting, not subservience nor even partnership, but control:

An husbonde I wol have . . .
Which shal be both my dettour and my thral
(I will have a husband who is both my debtor and my slave.)
(Wife of Bath's Prologue, ll. 154–5)

In this context both *dettour* and *thral* refer to her exacting the sexual rights of marriage as a form of power. This is, of course, an inversion of the traditional feudal power structure. She is amazingly, even casually, open about what men really want: "Ye shall have queynte [cunt] right ynogh" (l. 332), and about "putting up" with men's sexual demands in order to gain power: "For wynning [profit] wolde I al his lust endure." She even admits to "faking it": "And make me a feyned appetite," even though she had no time for old flesh: "And yet in bacon hadde I nevere delit" (ll. 416–18). It is also revealing that this rather crude proto-feminist, a much-married woman who admits to being past her prime, should tell a tale which is a sexual fantasy of wish-fulfillment, about a woman who is old by day but becomes miraculously young by night.

Obviously the Wife of Bath is Chaucer's creation, a construction based on a number of stereotypical notions satirizing and criticizing unruly behavior in women in medieval texts written by men. She makes it clear from the outset of her Prologue that she is a pragmatist, believing in experience over authority in the conduct of her love life. In fact, she consistently rejects authorities who criticize women who have married more than once. Reminding us that *authority* derives from *author*, she is particularly incensed by her fifth husband's reading passages from "the book of wikked wives" (l. 685), provocatively tearing out some pages and even throwing it in the fire, thereby becoming the first book-burner in English literary history.

The very last of Chaucer's cavalcade of pilgrims are a strange couple, the Summoner and the Pardoner, both seasoned corrupters of the ecclesiastical rituals of salvation. Chaucer alludes to their homosexual partnership by means of euphemisms and ironic sexual double entendres. The Pardoner, beardless, with carefully groomed yellow locks and a goatlike voice, sings a duet, "Come hither, love to me," with his "freend and compeer [partner]," the physically revolting alcoholic Summoner who "bar to him a stif bourdoun" (gave him a strong bass accompaniment). Avoiding the more explicit terminology that was available in words such as *sodomie* and *bougrie*, Chaucer observes disingenuously that the Pardoner is no stallion: "I trowe he were a geldyng or a mare" (I imagine he was a eunuch or effeminate) (General Prologue, l. 691).

The Reformation: The Politics of Religious Conformity

The Reformation is rightly seen as seminal in the overthrow of dogmatic religion and the liberation of the individual conscience. However, English Protestantism, which developed out of a long history of opposition to papal authority, itself assumed a form of enforced political correctness when in 1534 Henry VIII proclaimed himself Head of the newly invented *Anglicana Ecclesia* or Church of England by the Act of Supremacy and commanded all subjects to take an oath of loyalty to him. Henry had already invented the idealized construct of *the body politic*: "The Realm of England is an Empire . . . governed by one Supreme Head and King . . . unto whom a Body Politick, compact of all sorts and degrees of People been bounden to bear a natural and humble obedience" (Act 24, 1532–3). The requirement of a religious oath to the King, together with the demotion of the Pope to mere "Bishop of Rome" obviously put Catholics in a deeply compromising position. While many perforce accepted the new constraints, some became what were known as "church Catholics" or what would now be called "closet Catholics." But the resolute defiance of Sir Thomas More, leading to his execution in 1535, was a moving anticipation of later objectors who found their consciences compromised by such extreme requirements of secular authority. More's death was also a significant anticipation of modern modes of managing rebels: accounts of his beheading could not be published in Henry VIII's lifetime, that is, up to 1547, and his writings were suppressed until the reign of Mary in 1553.

Changed rituals of conformity and wording were central in the whole formulation of the Anglican Prayer Book (1549) by Archbishop Thomas Cranmer. Especially in such spoken requirements as the Creed, the new work became a source of great controversy. In the same year the Act of Uniformity made it illegal to use the old "Catholic" prayer book, provoking the Prayer Book Rebellion in South-West England, in which some 4,000 people died. Through the revisions of 1552 and 1559, the rituals and formulas of the Roman Mass were changed to those of the Anglican Communion. Thus the stark symbolism of transubstantiation in the Eucharist: "This is my body" was modified first to "The Body of our Lorde Jesus Christe" and then to "Take, eat, in remembrance that Christ died for thee."

The Preamble to the Thirty-Nine Articles (agreed in 1562 and issued by the King as "Supreme Governor of the Church of England") specified their purpose as being "for the avoiding of diversities of opinions and the establishing of consent touching true religion." Furthermore, His Majesty's

Declaration issued a clear warning to those who might indulge in the "thought-crime" of unorthodox opinions:

> If any public Reader in either of Our Universities, or any Master or Head of a College . . . shall affix any new sense to any Article . . . or hold any public Disputation . . . or preach or print any thing, other than is already established . . . they shall be liable to Our displeasure . . . And We shall see there will be due Execution upon them.

Many Articles sought to clarify spiritual mysteries; others merely cleared away Catholic "baggage." Thus Article XXII, nominally on Purgatory, also removed the validity of indulgences, relics, and the invocation of Saints: "The Romish doctrine concerning Purgatory, Pardons, Worshipping, and Adoration, as well of Images as of Reliques, and also invocation of Saints, is a fond [foolish] thing vainly invented, and grounded upon no warranty of Scripture, but rather repugnant to the Word of God." This was an understandable reform. But one wonders how, 40 years later, Shakespeare conceived, and how audiences of *Hamlet* would have reacted to, the Ghost's painful evocation of the "prison-house" of Purgatory in Act I scene v, and to the terrifying prospect envisaged by Claudio in *Measure for Measure*: "Ay, but to die and go we know not where" (Act III, scene i).

All these Protestant reforms were swept away in the brief reign (1553–58) of Mary Tudor, commonly known as Bloody Mary, who reinstated Catholicism, executing some three hundred dissenters, most notably the Oxford Martyrs: Bishops Latimer and Ridley, who were burnt at the stake on October 16, 1555, and Archbishop Cranmer, who followed them on March 21, 1556. In this alarming period of oscillations in religious faith, the requirements of recantation, the formal withdrawal or renunciation of a statement or article of faith, became, literally a matter of life and death. Cranmer movingly retracted his recantation at the stake, putting his offending hand first into the fire. "Recantations usually prove the force of authority rather than the force of conviction," Isaac Disraeli shrewdly observed in 1814.

Hostility and prejudice against Catholics started to surface in the Wycliffite reformist movement in the fourteenth century. Terms like *Pope-holy* and *Rome-runner* expanded and intensified in the reign of Henry VIII with ironic glosses like that of Henry Brinklow in 1542: "Papa means pay pay." John Bale, Bishop of Ossory in Ireland, issued a pamphlet, *Yet a course at the Romyshe foxe* (1543), a hysterical broadside denouncing Catholics as "fylthye whoremongers, murtherers, thieves, raveners, idolatours, lyars, dogges, swine . . . and very devyls incarnate." Nor was this virulence the preserve of controversialists, for in the Litany of the *Book of Common Prayer* (1549), the congregation prayed to be delivered from "the tyranny of the Bishop of Rome and his detestable enormities." Hate speech was clearly alive and thriving. Guy Fawkes Day was called *Pope Day* for centuries, the last reference in the *OED* being to New England.

Later conformist requirements included the Test Act of 1673, demanding oaths of religious loyalty for applicants for the army, the universities, and other institutions. These requirements were essentially a stratagem to prevent Jews, Nonconformists, and especially Catholics from obtaining positions of power. (In addition Catholics paid double taxes and could not live within the precincts of London.) Members of the British Parliament were formally required to take the oath of allegiance "on the true faith of a Christian," exemptions being granted only from 1829 onwards. Contrariwise, under Article VI of the US Constitution, "No religious test shall ever be required as a qualification to any office or public trust under the United States."

Politics on the Renaissance Stage

In the second year of her reign, in 1559, Elizabeth commanded that no plays were to be performed "wherein either matters of religion or of the governaunce of the estate of the common weale shal be handled or treated" (Chambers, 1923, vol. IV, pp. 263–4). The ill-named Master of the Revels was increasingly given the pre-emptive right to censor plays prior to performance. Although a number of playwrights, including Ben Jonson, suffered imprisonment or other punishments, it is nevertheless true that in the reigns of Elizabeth and James playwrights explored both religion and politics with surprising daring. Despite being closely examined and often censured, the stage featured some spectacular examples of political incorrectness in its contemporary forms of xenophobia, racism, sexism, homophobia, ageism, and lookism, not to mention the less currently fashionable offense of blasphemy.

All Marlowe's heroes defy the current norms and beliefs with astonishing bravura and insouciance, even though their demise is brought about by poetic justice. Thus Tamburlane, the self-styled "Scourge of God," burns all the holy books in the library at Alexandria, defying the Almighty to respond, whereupon he is struck down by a mysterious affliction. He redefines "Nature" in his own image, rejecting the medieval model of balanced elements, replacing it with one of competition and aspiration: "Nature . . . doth teach us all to have aspiring minds." Faustus calls up the Devil (in the form of Mephistophilis) and in the course of a parody of the Catechism says provocatively "I think hell's a fable." One of the most famous images of Elizabethan drama shows Faustus at the climactic moment of this blasphemous ritual, in his magic circle, having called up the devil. Yet he is finally torn to pieces by demons when, in the spectacular stage direction, "Hell is discovered."

Marlowe's Barabbas, the Jew of Malta, is a bizarre compendium of anti-Semitic stereotypes, poisoning wells and a whole convent of nuns including even his own daughter. Contemptuous of "these swine-eating Christians, / Unchosen nation, never circumcised," he pointedly refers to "Our Messias that is yet to come." A contemporary audience might dismiss these outlandish figures as "erring barbarians," but Edward II was a Plantagenet. The King's homosexual infatuations, especially for his favorite Piers Gaveston, led to his loss of power and finally to his gruesomely symbolic murder. But in *Edward II*, Marlowe boldly includes a catalog of famous homosexual lovers from classical times (Act I, scene iv).

Heretical views attributed to Marlowe by the informer Richard Baines, although never proved, were astounding: "That Christ was a bastard and his mother dishonest . . . That Christ was the bedfellow of John the Baptist and used him after the manner of Sodom . . . That all they that love not tobacco and boyes are fools." Roma Gill notes: "Mario Praz calls him a *libertin*, using the word to mean a free-thinker and, with its accumulated secondary meaning, 'man of loose morals' " (1989, p. x). The term is instructive, showing the combination of hostility and prejudice towards those with unconventional views on religion.

Religious extremism, like any other, can effectively be dealt with by comedy. Historically Puritanism was far more powerfully ridiculed by grotesque comic characterizations, such as the hypocritical Malvolio in Shakespeare's *Twelfth Night* (1600) and the hysterical Zeal-of-the-Land Busy in Ben Jonson's *Bartholomew Fair* (1614) than by pompous sermons and serious pamphleteering. *Twelfth Night* continues to be a staple item of theater repertoire, and Jonson's comedy is still staged, whereas the scandalously successful *Marprelate Tracts* (1588–90) from the same period, anonymously satirizing contemporary ecclesiastical figures and the hypocrisy of religious politics, have now become a historical footnote. However, the authors were arrested in 1593.

Shakespeare

Where Shakespeare stood on the major contemporary issues of religion and politics is still a matter of controversy. He has been seen, or rather claimed, variously, as a royalist, a "church papist" or closet Catholic, a conservative, a radical, and a subversive. However, in terms of literal political incorrectness, that is to say the questioning or satirizing of prevailing political norms and the ideological *status quo*, Shakespeare is remarkably daring. It is true that, reflecting the instability and threats to order of his times, many of his plays show the dire consequences of division and civil strife. But others fearlessly interrogate the idea of authority, often using the guise of the Roman republic. Between "the golden round" and "the hollow crown," Shakespeare depicted kings who are ideal, some with apparently divine powers, but others temperamentally unsuited for the role, some who are mad, others who become mad, murderer kings, innocent kings, weak kings, boy kings, ill-fated princes, and embittered old queens. The idea of monarchy, glorified in some plays such as *Henry V*, is also interrogated, parodied, subverted, and occasionally rendered absurd in *Richard II*, *Henry IV* (*Parts I* and *II*), *Hamlet*, and *King Lear*. All the grandiose statements of the Divine Right are shot through with dramatic irony, while the idea of the Player King hovers mockingly in the wings.

Richard II (1595) sets up a disturbing interface between the idea of majesty and the reality. John of Gaunt's famous hymn to England as "This royal throne of kings, this scepter'd isle" ends with a lament that "this blessed plot . . . is now leased out . . . like to a tenement or a pelting [paltry] farm" (Act II, scene i). The play squarely dramatizes the unthinkable problem of a man unfit to be king, a weak, vain, materialistic, and narcissistic monarch who even in the course of his moving deposition clings vainly to the notion of divine right: "Not all the water of the rough rude sea / Can wash the balm off from an anointed king" (Act III, scene ii). Today this seems pathetic posturing in the face of a coup d'état rather than subversive drama. But the scene depicting the deposition was banned from being performed in the reign of Queen Elizabeth, and even omitted from the early printed quartos. When the Essex rebels defiantly staged the play in 1601, Elizabeth was scandalized, exclaiming "I am Richard, know ye not that?" The episode is discussed in some detail in Michael Wood's biographical study, *In Search of Shakespeare* (2003, pp. 254–7). Yet, ironically, it is Richard himself who enumerates the famous catalog of fated monarchs, "the sad stories of the death of kings," the frail mortals who briefly wear the regalia and employ the rhetoric of omnipotence, "for within the hollow crown / That round the mortal temples of a king / Keeps death his court" (Act III, scene ii).

In *Hamlet* (1601) one seminal statement of regal necessity, depicting the catastrophic results of "the cease of majesty" is put into the mouth, of all people, of Rosencrantz, a time-serving nonentity in the very act of currying royal favor. Equally ironic is the placing of another major claim for mystical support for monarchy:

> There's such divinity doth hedge a king
> That treason can but peep to what it would,
> Acts little of his will
>
> (Act IV, scene v)

This assertion of the Divine Right comes from the fratricidal ruler of a dubious northern elective monarchy. In the event, Claudius is able to bluff his way out of the crisis, but not before he has been called "a king of shreds and patches" (Act III, scene iv). In a bitter, riddling exchange Hamlet says daringly: "The king is a thing," eliciting the shocked reply of Guildenstern: "A thing, my lord!" (Act IV, scene ii). Off the stage John Selden (1584–1654), in *Table Talk*, offered the same iconoclastic opinion: "A king is a thing men have made for their own sakes, for quietness' sake. Just as in a family one man is appointed to buy the meat." These Shakespearean questionings of the doctrine come before the major statements of Divine Right, notably that of King James I, who argued before parliament in 1610 with considerable arrogance that "Kings are not only God's lieutenants upon earth and sit upon God's throne, but even by God himself are called gods."

Shakespeare's most politically correct tragedy is certainly *Macbeth* (1605). Divine Right overcomes diabolical machination throughout. One can imagine the satisfaction that the new King James must have felt watching "the Scottish play," especially at the point in Act IV when the dramatic *Show of Kings* depicts the line of Banquo stretching into the future. For the prophecy had come true, since James was indeed the descendant of the murdered Banquo. Despite the richness of the play's poetry and the psychological complexity of the Macbeths, the work is essentially a morality play, a struggle between the extremes of good and evil. Shakespeare is not so daring as to have the Devil called up on stage, as in Marlowe's *Dr Faustus*: King James, the author of *Dæmonologie* (1597) would presumably have disapproved. Evil materializes, surreptitiously and ambiguously, in the arresting stage direction *Enter three Witches*, figures later called "the weird sisters." This surprising survival of Anglo-Saxon *wyrd*, meaning "fate" prompts the unanswered question: do they control fate, as Macbeth believes, or do they simply know the future, or are they, as Banquo believes, "instruments of darkness" manipulating the ambitious and the gullible to create chaos? Believing in their supernatural powers, Macbeth becomes their agent, first a regicide, then an infanticide, massacring the innocent, finally a desperate lunatic trying to ward off Fate as all the bizarre prophecies come true.

Macbeth's murderous tyranny resting on diabolical prophecy is point-edly contrasted with the divinely ordained rule of Edward the Confessor, endowed with the miraculous gifts of healing and true prophecy. But Macbeth does recognize that he has given "his eternal jewel to the common enemy of man" (Act III, scene i), and Lady Macbeth is ultimately driven out of her mind by the sight and the smell of royal blood. However, in a man-ner typical of modern régime-change, they are simply blackened by the new order as "this dead butcher and his fiend-like queen" (Act V, scene viii).

Duncan, the twice-betrayed king, comments at the moment when he is about to reward the new traitor, Macbeth, "There's no art to find the mind's construction in the face" (Act I, scene iv). But Shakespeare's first great villain, the man popularly known as Richard Crookback, is a complex exemplar of lookism. Richard III's deformities are mocked in such cruel barbs as "poisonous bunch-backed toad" and "abortive rooting hog." He in turn harps on his afflictions in an aggressive, exhibitionist and out-rageous fashion, simultaneously claiming to be a victim of witchcraft (Act III, scene iv) and cynically rationalizing the relationship between his crippled, stunted body and his villainous mind: "Then since the heavens have shaped my body so, / Let Hell make crooked my mind to answer it" (*Henry VI, Part III*, Act V, scene vi).

King Lear (1605) can be seen as a revisiting of the theme of *Richard II*, a man no longer fit to be king, through vanity, imprudence, and senility. The insane division of the kingdom among Lear's daughters on the basis of mere protestations of love leads inexorably to Gloucester's nightmare that "machinations, hollowness, treachery and all ruinous disorders follow us disquietly to our graves" (Act I, scene ii). More profoundly, Edmund the bastard's opening soliloquy boldly questions the validity of hereditary descent, mockingly reducing legitimacy to a nominalist notion, "fine word legitimate," and provocatively asserting the rights of natural virility (Act I, scene ii). Even more cynically, Falstaff in his mock catechism, reduces "Honour" to a mere word, "air" (*Henry IV, Part I*, Act V, scene i).

In his Roman and Greek plays Shakespeare was able to explore in this ancient culture the freer rein of republican *realpolitik*, the uneasy and fra-gile compromise between patrician privilege and unwieldy plebeian force, unalloyed by mystical notions of authority, uncomplicated by connections with contemporary history and unilluminated by the Christian revelation. These plays emphasize class differences between the plebs and the patri-cians with brutal clarity, in a fashion less sharply seen in the English his-tory plays. The lower orders are regarded by the ruling class as repellent and subhuman. *Julius Caesar* opens with the tribune Marullus berating the surly tradesmen as "You blocks, you stones, you worse than senseless things!"

while Casca cruelly demeans Caesar's epileptic fit at his moment of glory by attributing it to the crowd's miasmic hysteria: "the rabblement hooted, and clapped their chop't [rough] hands, and threw up their sweaty night-caps, and uttered such a deal of stinking breath because Caesar refused the crown, that it had almost choked Caesar" (Act I, scene ii).

Coriolanus (1608) opens in uproar as a "company of mutinous citizens with staves, clubs and other weapons" erupts upon the stage. This display of riotous hunger would remind many in the audience of the peasant uprisings of the previous year in Leicestershire, Warwickshire, and Northamptonshire. The patrician Menenius seeks to assuage the mob by means of the Fable of the Belly, a lecture on the virtues of civic unity which can also be seen as a tall story of the social contract. However, it is Coriolanus, Shakespeare's most politically incorrect hero, who consistently shows a visceral hatred of the plebs. When the great war hero is absurdly condemned to banishment from Rome as "an enemy of the people," that cipher of modern political correctness, his furious scorn is withering:

> You common cry of curs! Whose breath I hate
> As reek o' th' rotten fens, whose loves I prize
> As the dead carcasses of unburied men
> That do corrupt my air – I banish you . . .
> (Act III, scene iii)

Yet his tirade is also trivial. The catalog of caustic abuse with epithets like "garlic eaters" and "apron-men" echoes through the play, reflecting an ugly intolerance of human physicality, bad breath, and body odor, attributed only to the lower classes. Caesar makes similar demeaning comments in *Antony and Cleopatra* (Act I, scene iv).

The great speech on Degree in *Troilus and Cressida* (1602) – that *locus classicus* of the Great Chain of Being – comes, not from a fine Christian king reflecting on an ideal Boethian commonwealth, but from a wily Greek general trying to get his commanders into line, and Achilles in particular out of the embraces of his catamite. Ironically, the speech fails: it is the death of Patroclus that provokes "the wrath of Achilles." On an entirely different plane, Timon of Athens, the last of the tragic heroes, dares to think the unthinkable: the dissolution of all civilized order. But Timon calls himself "misanthropos," and the audience is always aware that his views are cynical at best and deranged at worst, especially in the great curse on Athens and all its citizens which begins Act IV.

From another social perspective, Shakespeare explores the essential structure of social cohesion, the family, in a penetrating and disturbing fashion. The seemingly wholesome topic "Family Values in Shakespeare" turns out to be something of an ambush, since most of his families are dysfunctional. They commonly have a structural imbalance, with absent mothers and tyrannical fathers (Lear, Prospero, Brabantio), or absent fathers (Hamlet), tyrannical mothers (Volumnia), competitive daughters (Goneril and Regan, Katharine the Shrew and Bianca), and ambitious or adulterous wives (Lady Macbeth, Gertrude). Even those which are seemingly balanced have some paranoid parents, especially the fathers (Montagu, Capulet, Leontes).

Both Marlowe and Shakespeare also explore that fixation of modern cultural studies, the Other. Marlowe's foreign supermen are shocking in their ambition, cruelty, or decadence. Shakespeare's heroes and heroines are closer to the human scale, although their passions are extreme and obsessive. Tamburlane is a barbaric world-conqueror, Barabbas is an aggressive Semitic monster, but Shylock is a penetrating study of a Jewish outsider in Venetian mercantile society, provoking both sympathy and rejection.

The three black roles in Shakespeare all focus on the problems of outsiders. Aaron the Moor in *Titus Andronicus* is a racial, social, and psychological alien. The Prince of Morocco, suitor to Portia, is proud, but defensive about his color: "Mislike me not for my complexion, / The shadow'd livery of the burnish'd sun" (*Merchant of Venice*, Act II, scene i). When he picks the wrong casket, Portia is openly relieved: "Let all of his complexion choose me so" (Act II, scene vii). Othello, the focus of many postcolonial critical studies, is an exotic Moorish outsider in Venetian society, but uncompromising in his absolute values, and a genuine believer in the Last Judgment. Yet the construction of the "exotic" also contains dark forces: the "witchcraft in the web" of the tragic handkerchief contains *mummy*, used for embalming. The "otherness" of all three figures is underscored by such ugly stereotyping references as "thicklips" and "an old black ram." In his grand death speech Othello makes two extra-cultural references, both revealing of his assumed Venetian identity as part of the colonial power which he serves as a general. He first compares himself to the "base Indian [who] threw a pearl away richer than all his tribe," a situation with obvious resonances from America. Finally, he enacts upon himself the same punishment he once meted out in Aleppo to "a malignant and a turbaned Turk" who "beat a Venetian and traduc'd the state": "I took by the throat the circumcised dog, / And I smote him thus" [*stabs himself*] (Act V, scene ii). In this alarming fashion Othello seeks both a dignified warrior's death and to establish himself as an insider who upheld the identity and supremacy of Venice to the end. F. R. Leavis described this moment as "a superb *coup de theatre*" (1952, p. 152), but T. S. Eliot saw it as an example of *bovarysme*, meaning a self-delusion brought about by an intense desire to see oneself in a particular romantic role (1951, p. 131).

Editions of the play increasingly devote space, not simply to Othello's "ancestry" and to the psychology of colonialism, but to the actual color of the actor. There have been few major black Othellos since Ira Aldridge (1826) and Paul Robeson (1943), although Chiwetel Ejiofor won the Laurence Olivier Award for Best Actor in 2008. *The Independent* commented in 1996: "Casting a white actor as Othello is virtually unthinkable these days. But South Africa's foremost dramatist, Athol Fugard, pointedly braves the charge of political correctness in such matters" (January 10). Elsewhere, it is not assumed that Shylock should be played by a Jew, nor Macbeth by a Scot. That is what acting means.

The Age of Reason

The period saw the constitutional birth of the United Kingdom in 1707 and a number of culturally unifying institutions, such as the iconic figure of John Bull and the British National Anthem. This last arose in highly political circumstances, in 1745 when the throne of George II was threatened by the Jacobite Rebellion led by Bonnie Prince Charlie. The words, embarrassingly chauvinist to modern ears, were satirically but accurately described by E. M. Forster in *A Passage to India* as "the curt series of demands on Jehovah" (Forster, 1961, p. 27). The last verse, calling for the suppression of the Scots, has wisely been forgotten. It is uncertain who wrote the words or the music, although the names of Henry Carey and Thomas Arne have been mentioned. Arne certainly composed "Rule, Britannia!" although the poem's imperialist sentiments were the work of James Thompson in 1740.

The period was also characterized by daring and prescient satire attacking both individuals and institutions. John Dryden began his *Absolom and Achitophel* (1689) with this witty commentary on organized religion: "In pious times, ere priestcraft did begin, / Before polygamy was made a sin." He proceeded to satirize the notorious promiscuity of Charles II and the constitutional consequences: numerous bastard progeny, the source of the problems of legitimate succession. In a different vein the Earl of Rochester praised the king's famous endowments: "His sceptre and his prick are of a length." (One of the king's nicknames was Rowley, that of a famous stallion.) Alexander Pope, who terrified high society with vicious barbs, said that he was "proud to see / men not afraid of God / afraid of me." Less egotistically he criticized "The right divine of kings to govern wrong," and celebrated the Union of 1707 with the ingenious couplet on the diverse concerns of the Queen: "Here thou, great Anna! whom three realms obey, / Dost sometimes counsel take – and sometimes tea" (*The Rape of the Lock*, canto III, ll. 7–8). Tea, a newly fashionable drink, forms a resounding bathos by being juxtaposed with "counsel," Pope implying that at Hampton Court equal importance is attached to both. He also anticipates environmental protest in his observation that exotic animals are slaughtered to enhance the dressing tables and the vanity of society belles: "The Tortoise here and Elephant unite, / Transformed to combs, the speckled and the white" (*The Rape of the Lock*, canto I, ll. 135–6). More specifically, John Gay's *The Beggars' Opera* (1728) was an attack on the corrupt régime of the self-proclaimed Prime Minister Robert Walpole so transparent as to make the piece enormously and enduringly successful.

However, the most politically incorrect author in English literature and the most penetrating in his satire, Jonathan Swift, daringly slaughtered all the sacred cows in the Augustan pasture. From Chaucer onwards many had criticized the hypocrisy and venality of churchmen and the Church as an institution. But in his *Argument Against the Abolition of Christianity* (1708), Swift included the cynical connivance of the congregations (and thus the bulk of his readers) who use the church as a venue for business, matchmaking, and social advancement. In his *A Tale of Tub* (1704), satirizing the corruption of the Christian religion, the symbolically named Peter royally entertains his mystified brothers Martin and Jack with a single loaf, explaining that "Bread is the Staff of Life, in which Bread is contained . . . the Quintessence of Beef, Mutton, Veal, Partridge, Plum-pudding, and Custard." This is an elaborate, farcical parody of the sacred Christian mystery of transubstantiation in the ritual of the Mass. Swift's *Battle of the Books* (1704) dramatizes the counterclaims of ancient and modern authors to pre-eminence, anticipating the modern culture wars over "the canon" and multiculturalism. His *Modest Proposal* (1730) is a devastating attack on the ruthless tyranny of English colonial rule over Ireland, as well as the absurd cruelty which can derive from rigid adherence to utilitarian logic divorced from humanity.

Gulliver's Travels (1726) is based on the proposition, shocking to the Age of Reason, which Swift set out in a letter to Pope on September 29, 1725: "I have got Materials Towards a Treatis proving the falsity of that definition *animal rationale* [man is a rational animal]; and to show it should be only *rationis capax* [capable of reason]." Taking Defoe's *Robinson Crusoe* (1719) as a triumphalist colonial myth of success in adversity, Swift produced a grotesque but disturbing parody. Crusoe not only survived, he thrived, tamed the natives, converted the heathen, defeated mutineers, and returned rich. But in his four journeys to lands of amazing marvels,

Gulliver is variously exploited by midgets, becomes the plaything of giants, is confused by the academy of lunatics, is almost raped by an amorous Yahoo whom he detests, and, worst of all, is rejected by the rational horses, with whom he identifies. He returns home a deranged misanthrope, rejects the bosom of his family, preferring to pass his declining years in the stables talking to the horses. Crusoe was sustained by his religion; Gulliver seemingly has none, and has indeed failed to be rational. For good measure Swift also satirizes the absurd rituals of his home culture, of courts (that of Lilliput having a pointed similarity to the court of Queen Anne) and the collective insanity and cruelty of war. Gulliver's valiant attempts to convince the King of Brobdingnag of the superiority of European civilization in its courtly and military aspects provokes the shattering riposte: "I cannot but conclude the bulk of your natives to be the most pernicious race of little odious vermin that Nature ever suffered to crawl upon the surface of the earth" (Book II, chapter 6). Swift's scathing comments on the colonial enterprise are quoted in chapter 5.

The Victorian Era

The era is now generally regarded as a compendium of politically incorrect attitudes in its patriarchy, imperialism, capitalism, pollution, gluttony, sexual hypocrisy, punitive legal system, and exploitation of child labor. An iconic image of the period is Sir Edward Landseer's famous painting entitled "Windsor Castle in Modern Times" (1845), showing Albert and Victoria *en famille* as a radiant royal couple, surrounded by the bloody quarry of a hunt strewn over the carpet, with a princess fondling a dead kingfisher. Aristocratic attitudes towards hunting, traditionally upheld as a form of *droite de seigneur*, are of course now seen as brutal and politically incorrect in their violation of animal rights.

Dickens represents the schizophrenic aspect of the age with alarming clarity, as Edmund Wilson's essay "The Two Scrooges" brilliantly showed. Wholesomeness and family values struggle with crude prejudice, notoriously shown in the character of Fagin in *Oliver Twist* (1837–9). Generally called simply "the Jew," Fagin is presented as distinctly alien, epitomizing "the Other": "As he glided stealthily along, the hideous old man seemed like some loathsome reptile, engendered in the slime and darkness through which he moved" (chapter 19). In response to readers' protests, notably that of Eliza Davis in 1863, many references to "the Jew" were changed to "Fagin," together with some humanizing touches, but not until 1867. Dickens died full of honors, with the sordid secrets of his private life generally unknown, and unburdened by the weight of posthumous criticisms.

The tragedy of Oscar Wilde epitomized the period in other ways, since he was its controversial social luminary through his brilliant stage comedies and his outrageously aesthetic personality, but he became its most notorious disgrace following the scandalous homosexual revelations of his trial. Today he is seen as a martyr of the *avant garde* in his sexuality and his interest in the dark side of human nature. As Robert Ross wrote in a Wildean *mot*, "*Salomé* has made the author's name a household word wherever the English language is *not* spoken" (note to *Salomé*, my italics).

Other authors exemplify the more common transitions over time from being politically correct to becoming the obverse. Under the heading of "imperialism" are notably Kipling, whose "White Man's Burden" (1899) has now become an embarrassment, as has the triumphalist song "Land of Hope and Glory" by A. C. Benson, now familiar as Elgar's "Pomp and Circumstance March no. 1," and the hymn "Onward Christian Soldiers" by S. Baring-Gould, although the second line, "Marching *as* to war" suggests a metaphorical army. However, *Kiplingesque* and *Kiplingite* are recorded from 1894 in both a stylistic and a critical sense. Thus in 1899 the *Westminster Gazette* wrote: "Thorpe . . . is merely the primitive Kiplingesque type of man transferred from the battle-field or the plains of India to the Stock Exchange" (June 28). Even *imperialism* was used negatively from the start: Joseph Chamberlain wrote in 1878 that "This infernal Afghan business is the natural consequence of Jingoism, Imperialism [and] 'British interests'" (letter, October 15). Yet these were precisely the qualities that the British government exploited in the build-up to the Boer War, especially in the "khaki election" of 1900. Contrariwise, a powerfully Christian anti-imperialist view was created in *Trooper Peter Halkett of Mashonaland* (1897) by Olive Schreiner, a friend of Rhodes. Halkett, unwillingly involved in the oppression of Rhodesia, receives visitations from the Savior. The Frontispiece, a hideous photograph of blacks being hanged from trees, was initially suppressed.

The work which cracked the foundations of Victorian faith, was, of course, Charles Darwin's monumental and deeply controversial study, *On the Origin of Species by Means of Natural Selection* (1859), the first scientific bestseller, written by an unlikely recluse. Yet many of the literary intelligentsia would have read Arthur Hugh Clough's *Easter Day, Naples 1849*:

> Christ is not risen, no,
> He lies and moulders low;
> Christ is not risen.
> Ashes to ashes, dust to dust;
> As of the unjust, also of the just –
> Christ is not risen.

This is not only shockingly specific, but runs clean contrary to the stereo-typical notion of the Victorians as devout believers and churchgoers.

In addition, Thomas Hardy's enormously popular novels show charac-ters destroyed by a malign fate. In the most publicized and shocking pas-sage, Hardy ended the tragic story of *Tess of the D'Urbervilles* (1891) with the provocative and uncompromising conclusion that "The President of the Immortals . . . had ended his sport with Tess." This curiously executive title for the Almighty and his role as a sadist was obviously blasphemous in its mocking rejection of Divine Providence. The ensuing public uproar was sur-passed only by that which greeted the publication of *Jude the Obscure* (1895). The Bishop of Wakefield, in a letter to the *Yorkshire Post*, fulminated that he "was so disgusted by its insolence and indecency that I threw it into the fire." After this Hardy, who lived for another 33 years, wrote no more novels. It seems significant that the novel caused more public outrage than *The Origin of Species*.

Chapter 8

Culture

In the vexed debate over the canon and multiculturalism, the key term *culture* has been largely ignored. In many ways this is not surprising, since from its remote beginnings in agriculture, *culture* has acquired so many meanings that it is now difficult to define. Often thought of hierarchically, "high culture" is regarded as serious, while "popular culture" admits a greater variety of tones. For this reason, "Popular Culture, Humor and Satire" has a separate section below. As well as "national culture" there is regional culture, both using what T. S. Eliot called "the reduced sense of the word." Eliot also noted in 1948 the encouragement in Russia of " 'local culture', everything that is picturesque, harmless and separable from politics" (Eliot, 1948, p. 28). The concept now incorporates *high culture, popular culture, mass culture, alternative culture, underground culture,* and other, mainly negative uses such as "the drug culture," "yob culture," "the culture of violence," "the culture of nonpayment," and, parodying Matthew Arnold's *Culture and Anarchy* (1869), "the culture of anarchy." In his chapter on "Culture Wars," Roger Scruton has an excellent "critique of mass culture," identifying what he terms the contemporary "culture of repudiation" (2007, p. 69). And as quoted in the section on AIDS in chapter 6, Koestenbaum (1990) writes of the disease as a "cultural capital of escalating value."

This leveling down of the term is regrettable, since it gives the impression that "high" culture is entirely élitist in its interests, inaccessible to all and encouraging of conformity. Terms like *culture snobbery* (used by Aldous Huxley in 1931) and *culture vulture* (dating from 1945) tend to endorse cultural separation. Susan Sontag also took this exclusive view in her typically frank style: "The hard truth is that what may be acceptable in élite culture may not be acceptable in mass culture, that tastes which pose only innocent ethical issues as the property of a minority become corrupting when they become more established. Taste is context and the context has changed" ("Fascinating Fascism," *New York Review of Books,* February 6, 1975).

Many major Western artistic expressions are not so much élitist as politically incorrect in the sense that they shake the foundations of bourgeois order and morality in disturbing ways. So far from being anodyne, consoling or "traditional" in a dull sense, many works of ancient or classical culture are daringly illuminating of the deepest human impulses. Although the Greeks had the highest regard for rationality and order, their tragedy focuses on the violation of the profoundest taboos and the terrifying consequences, supremely evident in the stories of Oedipus, Electra, Medea, and Phædra. *The Bacchae* is a dramatization of the irrational in its collective form. Aristophanes satirized not simply the obvious targets of his society, such as politicians and lawyers, but teachers, poets, and philosophers, notably Socrates. *Lysistrata* celebrates the most powerful antiwar stratagem, whereby the wives of Athens withhold conjugal rights from their husbands until they lay down their arms. Edmund Wilson's brilliant study *The Wound and the Bow* (1941) elucidated the strange myth of Philoctetes, showing that the hero's talent as a deadly archer and his affliction, a miasmic wound causing him to be ostracized, both symbolize the artist, an unpopular but vital critic of society.

The attraction of the illicit and the transgressive clearly underlies the great tragic romances of Tristan and Isolde and Lancelot and Guinevere. This illicit quality also explains the fascination of Marlowe's supermen and several of the Shakespearean tragic figures. The Faust legend is a powerful instance. The life of the original Faust figure (c.1480–1540) acquired legendary accretions, becoming an amalgam of fortune-teller, magician, teacher, and charlatan with a reputation for supernatural powers. However, it was only the German Faust-book (1587) that introduced the basic blasphemous motif of a scholar who made a pact with the devil Mephistopheles. It had such evident appeal that it immediately took on forms in French and English literature, notably Marlowe's tragedy (1589), discussed in chapter 7. Other major versions were those by Goethe (Part I 1808, Part II 1832), operas by Spohr (1816), Berlioz (1846), Gounod (1859), Boito (1868) and Thomas Mann's great novel, *Doktor Faustus* (1948). Even more fruitful has been the legend of the libertine Don Juan, which from its Spanish origins around 1630 has generated many versions. These increasingly dispense with the original blasphemous element and the hellfire ending, focusing on the Don's obsessive erotic quest.

Two of the greatest romantic operas deal with the attraction of the illicit and of life at the margins. Carmen, the quintessential *femme fatale*, seduces Don José from both his fiancée and his soldier's profession, which he

abandons for the wild life of the gypsy and the brigand. Besotted with jealousy, José acts out Oscar Wilde's paradox: he kills the thing he loves. *La
Traviata* boldly elevates the courtesan to tragic status, but she is betrayed
by bourgeois morality. Significantly, both operas originated as highly successful novels: Prosper Merimée's *Carmen* appeared in 1845; Alexandre
Dumas's *La Dame aux Camélias* in 1848. But both initially flopped as operas,
in 1853 and 1875, respectively. This radical difference in reception no doubt
shows that what was acceptable on the page in the study could not be countenanced in public.

Much romantic opera is politically incorrect in other ways. Chauvinist
sentiments abound in numerous signature arias, famously in "La donna è
mobile" from Verdi's *Rigoletto* (1851). Mascagni's *Cavalleria Rusticana*
(1890) emphasizes the Easter Festival amidst its deadly sexual intrigue. The
bizarre decadence of Oscar Wilde's *Salomé* (1894) clearly struck a chord
with Richard Strauss, who returned with enthusiasm to the Elektra myth
in 1909. Georg Büchner's pathetic mistress-murderer *Wozzek* (1836),
resuscitated by Alban Berg in 1925, anticipates the modern tragedy of the
little violent man. Béla Bartok's *Bluebeard's Castle* (1918) studies a murderous psychotic who operates on a grand scale, while Janacek's *Jenufa*
(1916) is an alarming infanticide. Clearly Salomé, Wozzek, and Jenufa incarnate recognizable psychopathic conditions.

It is noticeable that as a consequence of the debate about culture, all
the key terms (*culture, classic, romance, hero,* and *tragedy*) have undergone semantic generalization or broadening of meaning, with reduced
implications of value.

Literature and Ideology

It would seem natural to assume that major literary works would be politically correct in the broad sense of endorsing the values of the society
in which they are generated. One can posit such a tradition, pointing to
such fundamentally Christian works as medieval mystery and morality
plays, Milton's *Paradise Lost* (1667–74), and Bunyan's *Pilgrim's Progress*
(1678). But, as was noticed in the section on "Orthodoxy in Religion and
Politics" in chapter 1, this correlation becomes a questionable proposition
because of changing orthodoxies in English history. Furthermore, there is
the problem that irony is an essential feature of numerous major authors,
from Chaucer through Pope, Defoe, Swift, Fielding, Sterne, Jane Austen,
and many modern writers. Finally, the individual creative imagination is
seldom governed by prevailing ideological or political norms, as the various

sections of chapter 7 have shown. To take one instance, the keystone values of the Victorian era were memorably exposed, satirized, and subverted by all the major novelists: Dickens, George Eliot, Thackeray, Trollope, and Hardy. Judgment on Dickens continues to be divided, since his attitudes towards many abuses such as slavery, notably in *Martin Chuzzlewit* (1844), were right, but his depiction of Fagin in *Oliver Twist* (1837–8) was certainly prejudiced, as were his intemperate remarks on "the Noble Savage" in *Household Words*, June 11, 1850. The issue is discussed further in the Conclusion. Virtually all the plays of George Bernard Shaw satirize or sabotage the accepted norms, conventions, and ideas of his time.

The divergence is sharpest in the United States. The ideology of America is essentially positive, stressing democracy, shared values, unity, progress, and success, built on powerful inspirational ideas like the American Dream, symbols like the Melting Pot, and myths like "Log Cabin to White House." Poetic justice and a happy outcome are essential. These notions are upheld, but mainly by that quintessentially American genre, the musical, by the cultural contributions of Walt Disney, and by the juvenile comic heroes Captain America, Superman, Spiderman, et al. But the major works of American literature are essentially pessimistic. *Moby-Dick*, *The Scarlet Letter*, *Uncle Tom's Cabin*, *The Portrait of a Lady*, *The Great Gatsby*, *The Sound and the Fury*, *Invisible Man*, the works of Poe, the poems of Emily Dickinson, and the plays of Eugene O'Neill, Tennessee Williams, Edward Albee, Arthur Miller, and David Mamet are quintessentially about tragedy, failure, or suffering. They deal squarely with social intolerance, injustices, outsiders, and misfits.

As Leslie Fiedler wrote provocatively in his classic study, *Love and Death in the American Novel* nearly half a century ago: "American literature is distinguished by the number of dangerous and disturbing books in its canon – and American scholarship by its ability to conceal this fact" (1966, p. 11). President Lincoln reportedly said in jest that Harriet Beecher Stowe was responsible for the Civil War, so powerful was the reaction to her novel. *Huckleberry Finn* has at its core the relationship between Huck and Jim, raising the two great problems of slavery and color. But there is a disturbingly strong religious subtext: Huck's initial decision, to turn Jim in, evokes a sense of salvation: "I felt good and all washed clean of sin for the first time I had ever felt so in my life." But his final commitment to Jim is expressed in a provocatively wicked idiom for 1885: "All right then, I'll *go* to hell" (chapter 31). In Twain's last novel, *Pudd'nhead Wilson*, Tom Driscoll is devastated by the shocking disclosure that, far from being a privileged white, he was "bawn a nigger and a slave" (chapter 9). Melville articulated the virtual blasphemy of manicheism: "That intangible malignity which has been from the beginning; to whose domination even the modern Christians ascribe one half of the world" (chapter 41). So great was the impact of Miller's tragedy *Death of a Salesman*, he was asked to address General Motors to encourage salesmen to believe in the worthiness of their occupation. No such invitation was forthcoming after *The Crucible*.

In American popular culture conspiracy theories abound, often focusing on the power of the Mafia, or – more disturbingly – that of the CIA, the FBI, and so on. They possibly spring from such unsolved political mysteries as the assassinations of President Kennedy and Malcolm X. Yet this is not a new development. For all his dreams, Gatsby has mafia connections, "the foul dust" which destroys him: the gangster Meyer Wolfsheim is casually introduced as "the man who fixed the World Series," and in Fitzgerald's "The Diamond as Big as the Ritz" (1922) a zone of rich diamond-bearing ore is concealed by the organized falsification of all the official maps of the area, and by murder.

More contentiously, Fiedler focused on the problem of "The failure of the American fictionist to deal with adult heterosexual love and his consequent obsession with death, incest and innocent homosexuality" (1966, p. 12). That is too large a topic for this treatment but, turning to Fiedler's second theme, death, let us consider the topic of war.

War and warriors

War provides an illuminating topic to explore historically the relationship between ideology and literature. As the section on "Norms and Normality" in chapter 1 shows, the warrior culture was the essential social base of Anglo-Saxon society, and the notion of a military obligation of dying for one's country continued for centuries. Subsequently the press gang coexisted with the professional soldier, before conscripted armies were instituted in the early nineteenth century, becoming the norm through both World Wars and continuing in the Draft in America. But the English literary tradition includes major explorations of the martial ethic that reveal increasingly ambivalent and even hostile attitudes.

The idea of the perfect soldier and nobleman now seems alien to us. Confronted with Chaucer's "parfit, gentil, noble knight," embodying the ancient ideal of lion on the battlefield and lamb in the hall, many readers regard him as too good to be true. Indeed, some modern critics, notably Terry Jones, have sought to see the panoply of positive epithets as an elaborate irony masking an opportunistic mercenary. This view seems to be a reflection of modern cynicism rather than the author's intention. For in the seemingly haphazard cavalcade of the Canterbury pilgrims Chaucer has clearly presented one exemplar of the three estates, the Knight as ideal nobleman, the Parson as ideal churchman, and the Plowman as ideal layman.

Moving to the less certain moral world of the Renaissance, we may start with Othello's famous line celebrating "the pride, pomp and circumstance of glorious war" (Act III, scene iii). The description seems pointedly double-edged: *pomp* and *glorious* clearly endorse the magnificence of war as a heroic enterprise (*pompous* then being a positive term), but *circumstance* undoubtedly trivializes it. The speech comes, significantly when Othello mistakenly believes that his "fair warrior" has betrayed him. He launches into the great lament: "Farewell the plumed troop and the big wars / That make ambition virtue." This is certainly a dubious rationalization, since *ambition* was then a morally questionable quality that could not simply be validated by "big wars." Shakespeare seems deliberately to set Othello's perspective in extreme terms, thereby inviting an alternative interrogating view. A similar situation occurs in *Hamlet* (Act IV, scene iv) when the hero shows an almost unbalanced admiration for the martial ethic as embodied by Fortinbras "with divine ambition puff'd," leading his army to contest a piece of land not worth "an egg-shell."

Similar opposing perspectives are given on the battlefield of Shrewsbury in the extremes of the magnificent valor of the dead Hotspur and the cynical opportunism of the ultimate survivor, Falstaff. The patriotic idealism of Henry V's rallying cry "Once more unto the breach" is immediately parodied by the parasitic Bardolph shouting "On, on, on, on, on!" (Act III, scenes I and ii). Time and again the action oscillates between the inspirational leader pursuing a dynastic claim in France, invoking "God for Harry, England and St George!" and the barflies and bawds of Eastcheap. The heroic rhetoric, ideologically correct, sounds overblown, while the camp-followers sound despicable.

One of the earliest politically incorrect war poems was Robert Southey's "After Blenheim," daringly deconstructing the great English victory of the Duke of Marlborough in 1704. "Old Kaspar" tries vainly to answer his grandchildren's simple, persistent questions, such as "what they fought each other for" and "what good came of it at last?" He cannot answer, relying on the patriotic refrain "But 'twas a famous victory." War commonly unites the nation, making poetic endorsement politically correct. As Poet Laureate, Tennyson clearly felt obliged to celebrate in his rousing effusion "The Charge of the Light Brigade" (1854) the heroism of those who obeyed orders in the face of certain death as a consequence of military and logistical incompetence. The most famous lines – "Theirs not to reason why / Theirs but to do and die" – endorse their unquestioning discipline. While it is possible to see Tennyson riding on the back of the jingoistic frenzy of the times, he makes it clear that "someone had blundered."

There were no poems from the trenches of the Crimea or Blenheim. "Drummer Hodge," poignantly lamenting a young British soldier killed in the Boer War and buried in the South African veld, was written by Thomas Hardy in old age. But the First World War bred a whole range of responses. Rupert Brooke's "The Soldier" (1915) famously embodied that patriotic loyalty which is the essence of political correctness:

> If I should die, think only this of me;
> That there's some corner of a foreign field
> That is for ever England.

Brooke's popularity subsequently declined as the full horror of the war came home to the "sad shires." Contrariwise, Wilfred Owen's reputation has steadily grown, the stark anger of his protest cutting through the propaganda of what he bluntly called "the old lie" embedded in the Horatian motto: "Dulce et decorum est pro patria mori." His "Anthem for Doomed Youth" interweaves conventional religious language with the horrific slaughter of the war machine. The bitter question, "What passing-bells for these who die as cattle?" generates terrible replies such as "the shrill demented choirs of wailing shells." Of many other poets chronicling this carnage, Lascelles Abercrombie commented savagely on the general who "Left a field of twenty thousand dead / And toddled home to die in bed."

Archibald Macleish's "Memorial Rain," reflecting on the battlefield at Ghent, is openly sarcastic about "This little field, these happy, happy dead," a bitter parody of Henry V's "we happy few" (Act IV, scene iii). American treatments changed starkly from Stephen Crane's *The Red Badge of Courage* (1895), a vivid account of the Civil War, to Joseph Heller's *Catch 22* (1961), exploring the inverted logic of sanity in qualifying for combat. Kurt Vonnegut's *Slaughterhouse-Five* (1969) is a darker allegory of the bureaucratic vacuum encountered when seeking those responsible for the fire-bombing of Dresden.

The dramatization of war has changed totally from the clearly defined struggle between the English thanes and the Danish *wælwulfas* ("slaughterous wolves") in the *Battle of Maldon* (991) to the vast incomprehensible shambles presciently imagined nearly a millennium later by Matthew Arnold, in which "ignorant armies clash by night" ("Dover Beach," 1869).

We may conclude with nostalgic militarism, which can be emotive but innocent, as in William Blake's "Bring me my bow of burning gold." Somewhat less mystical is "Awuleth' Umshini Wami" (Zulu for "Bring me my machine gun"), a martial song from the ANC's armed struggle against apartheid which from 2006 became Jacob Zuma's trademark anthem in his personal and political campaigns. A contemporary Afrikaner counterpart was the highly popular song "De la Rey, De la Rey," invoking the hero of the Anglo-Boer War and pleading for him to return. The issue raised by these and other such instances is the extent to which such invocations should be taken literally.

Contentious Texts

Out of many instances, let us consider four major cases in which controversy arose out of issues of political correctness. The first is an American play, the second a collection of letters, the third is a children's cartoon book, and the last is a South African novel.

Oleanna

Within the period that political correctness was becoming a national issue, the major theatrical event was David Mamet's play *Oleanna*. Mamet's plays have typically dealt with all-male situations in which foul language abounds as a form of macho posturing. Representing an entirely new departure, *Oleanna* was first performed in New York in 1992 and in London the following year. It is about the confused communication and ultimate conflict between John, a mediocre but basically amiable professor about to receive tenure, and Carol, a floundering student unable to understand why her assignment has been given a failing grade. It is a commonplace situation. However, outside forces come into play, redefining their language and reinterpreting their actions.

In the first act Carol has only a limited grasp of what is going on, partly because John uses obfuscating professional vocabulary. But she makes copious notes of their conversations. John is indiscreet about "the Tenure Committee" and unprofessional in offering to "make a deal" whereby Carol's grade will be given an "A" if they start the course again. When she says in desperation "I DON'T UNDERSTAND. DO YOU SEE ???" (a phrase she repeats may times), John tries to comfort her and "puts his arm around her shoulder." She rejects the gesture saying "NO" and "walks away" (Mamet, 1992, p. 36).

Surprisingly, by the next act Carol has submitted a report to the Tenure Committee "on my behalf and on behalf of my group" (p. 51). Her vocabulary has been transformed by an infusion of the current terminology of sexual politics and by the manipulation of the raw material of her notes into incriminating evidence against John. She has gained enormously in confidence and aggression. When she wants to walk out, John physically restrains her.

In the last act Carol is rampant, armed with accusations of "negligence," "flirting," "paternalism," "sexism," and finally "rape." As she explains: ". . . under the statute. I am told. It was battery . . . And attempted rape" (p. 78). This last accusation seems absurd, but not under this kind of definition: "a spectrum of incidents and behaviors ranging from crimes legally defined as rape to verbal harassment and inappropriate innuendo." (It comes from the Swarthmore College training manual, 1991.) As she leaves, the flabbergasted and ruined John is phoning his wife. Carol's parting shot, the trivial injunction "Don't call your wife baby," is the last straw, provoking in John an explosion of violence and vituperation. He attacks her, shouting "You vicious little bitch. You think that you can come in here with your political correctness and destroy my life?" (p. 79). Although the audience is aware of a case being built up against John, this is the sole use of the phrase "political correctness."

Reactions to the play were extreme. Audiences in both America and Britain were divided between applause and dispute. Feminists were scandalized. In America the reception of the piece was affected by the Senate Hearings on charges brought by Anita Hill against Judge Clarence Thomas for sexual harassment. These had taken place on October 11–13, 1991. Robin Tolmach Lakoff argues this connection fairly strongly (2000, pp. 155–7), even though the play was first staged nearly seven months after the Hill/Thomas case and dealt with a different situation. More obviously, "It was widely treated as a problem play about the ascendancy of political correctness in academia . . ." (Murphy, 2004, p. 125). Lakoff is closer to the point in her view that "Mamet intended the play as an attack on political correctness, and more specifically on feminists who illegitimately use sexual harassment as a weapon against innocent men" (2000, p. 156).

Mamet himself rejected both of these emphases. However, the transformation of Carol seems to admit two interpretations. One, in the caustic words of an early critic, is that "The bitch set him up" (Murphy, 2004, p. 125). The other is that she has been manipulated and conscientized by the mysterious "group." In an article he subsequently wrote for the *Guardian* (April 8, 2004) under the title of "Why can't I show a woman telling lies?" Mamet insisted that the real issue was the false accusation of rape. He commented on responses to a performance at Brown University, especially the question of one student: "Don't you think it's politically questionable to have the girl make a false accusation of rape?" Mamet responded, "I, in my ignorance, was stunned. I didn't realize it was my job to be politically acceptable." The wider and more insidious assumption of the accusation is that the dramatization of personal dishonesty in a woman is seen more as a political statement than a matter of morality. In the same article Mamet claimed sexist prejudice against himself as a male saying, somewhat naïvely, "The sex of an author is nobody's business."

Oleanna certainly carries another hallmark of political correctness in that the damaging verbal evidence against John derives from scouring his speech and highlighting any prejudicial or indiscreet remarks. A typical instance is John's comment "Everyone needs to expose themselves," which seems at face value to carry a clear sexual innuendo. But in context it reads quite innocently: "Everyone needs advisers. Everyone needs to expose themselves. To various points of view" (p. 55). At the National Theatre in Washington "there was a blackboard erected in the lobby after each performance to register the audience's votes under three categories "he was right," "she was wronged," and "this could really happen" (Sauer and Sauer, 2004, p. 235).

The Letters of Philip Larkin

During his lifetime (1922–85) Philip Larkin came to be regarded as England's unofficial laureate and was widely read and admired, despite acquiring a certain notoriety for being the only poet of his generation to use the most taboo four-letter words in idiomatic contexts ("They fuck you up, your mum and dad . . . ," "Books are a load of crap," etc.). Even these occasioned little adverse comment. Yet Larkin never printed a single racist epithet. Studies such as A. T. Tolley's *Larkin at Work* (1997) show that racism had no place in his poems at any stage of their development. However, his status and reputation as a major poet were seriously diminished by the posthumous publication of his *Selected Letters 1940–85* (ed. Anthony Thwaite) in 1992, since the volume contained private letters never intended for publication. Some, especially those to his close and like-minded friend, Kingsley Amis, expressed reactionary and racist views. He referred contentiously to "la divine Thatcher" and to "the successive gangs of socialist robbers who have ruled us since the war" (1992, p. 635). He also used taboo terms like *coon* and *wog* (1992, pp. 584, 690).

The first major assault came from Tom Paulin on television and in the correspondence columns of the *Times Literary Supplement*, accusing Larkin of "racism, misogyny and quasi-fascist views." Andrew Motion's biography *Philip Larkin: A Writer's Life* (1993) attracted a similar range of reviewers' condemnatory comments, such as "a foul-mouthed bigot" (Peter Ackroyd), "this provincial grotesque" (Bryan Appleyard), and "really a kind of petty-bourgeois fascist" (A. N. Wilson). An anonymous columnist in the Library Association *Record* even recommended that Larkin's works "should be banned." These views are quoted in Martin Amis's "Don Juan in Hull" (Amis, 1993), which also contains these broader observations: " 'Politically correct' is a better designation than 'bien pensant'; both bespeak a strong commitment to the herd instinct, but P.C. suggests the necessary regimentation." The fashionable condemnatory use of *fascist* by these major authors and journalists is especially revealing, since Larkin's colleagues have attested to his impeccable politeness and courtesy in the administration of his duties at Hull University Library. He also served at various times on the literature panel of the Arts Council, was chairman for several years of the Poetry Book Society, and chaired the Booker Prize judging committee for 1977.

However, not everybody joined the herd. In his review of *A Writer's Life*, Anthony Burgess made no bones about Larkin's womanizing, masturbation, and heavy drinking, but also observed that "His bigotry . . . stopped short of fascism." He even quoted some of Larkin's grosser private comments to his publisher, including a ditty sung to the tune of "Lillibulero": "Prison for strikers, / Bring back the cat, / Kick out the niggers, / How about that?" complete with the chorus: "Niggers, niggers, / Kick out the niggers" and so on. But unlike the other cited critics, Burgess separated private correspondence from published literature, concluding dryly: "Of course, it is only words. His own locutory inventions, as Kingsley Amis clearly saw, were too good not to eternise . . . Larkin belongs to the highly literate gang that could never have shed decorum in order to write Ginsberg's truly ignorant 'Howl' " (*Literary Review*, April 1993, p. 5). But few in the literary establishment and academe were as tolerant as Burgess.

Lisa Jardine, Professor of English and Dean of the Faculty of Arts at London University, gave a revealing insight into the subsequent marginalization of Larkin in her departmental syllabus in her essay, "Canon to Left of them, Canon to Right of them" (1994). This partly draws on her article in the *Guardian* in which she referred to "1950s poet Philip Larkin" and articulated "the problem of the place Larkin's poetry occupies at the heart of the canon of English literature . . . within that body of works cherished by defenders of British culture as the repository of the Best of British" (1994, p. 109). Larkin had evidently not been a canonical problem prior to the publication of the *Letters* and the *Life*. Furthermore, interpreting Larkin, the melancholy poet of the dreary, miserable, banal little lives of ordinary people in *fin de siècle* England as exemplifying "the Best of British" is in itself a bizarre miscasting.

The real problem, it was argued, was that Larkin no longer fitted the demographics and the cultural preferences of the students of Jardine's department of English. "The students in my University Department of English are for the most part neither Anglo-Saxon nor male. Furthermore, the Anglo-Saxons and the young men belong to a generation whose face is turned towards the new Europe and for whom comfortable British insularity holds no romance" (1994, p. 109). The canonical solution reached was "not to 'ban' Larkin's poetry . . . but to recontextualise him in a specialist second year course on 'Fifties British Poetry'" (1994, p. 111). While being ostensibly liberal, this appeared to be an administrative subterfuge. Even on the face of it, the "solution" was an anachronistic miscategorization, since Larkin's major collections were *The North Ship* (1947), *The Less Deceived* (1955), *The Whitsun Weddings* (1964), and *High Windows* (1974). The attempt to recast Larkin as a poet of "insular Little Englishness" and of "white British superiority," attitudes revealed by the letters but not in the poems, provoked a deluge of angry and intemperate letters to Jardine.

The Larkin affair juxtaposed two attitudes towards language: the judgmental, whereby racist vocabulary in any context whatever is regarded as an indicator of moral depravity, contrasted with the *laissez faire* or nominalist attitude regarding words as separate from ideas, things, and actions. The majority were clearly judgmental. The term *logocentric* (popularized by Jacques Derrida) is crucial in this respect: originally it was a recognition of the obsession with words and definitions which is an essential aspect of Western epistemology. (We are a long way from Francis Bacon's stricture in *The Advancement of Learning* (1605): "Here therefore, is the first distemper [sickness] of learning, when men study words and not matter.") But the term has become ambiguous, also manifesting itself in personal condemnation deriving from the use of "inappropriate" vocabulary. The witch hunts at Salem in 1693 and in the McCarthyite era in America concentrated on the names of those incriminated; in its modern form it has become a search for incriminating words.

The Larkin case shows the vital importance of using discriminating criteria discussed in the subsection on "The ethics of publication" in chapter 1. Thus the contemporary *Diaries* (1993) of Alan Clark, Minister of Trade in Margaret Thatcher's last government, were outrageously malicious about individuals and almost defiantly frank. They were enormously popular and evidently read with relish, by outsiders at any rate. There were no protests. But Larkin's letters were private, never intended for publication; indeed he gave instructions in his will for his papers to be destroyed. His wish was not respected, partly because his will was interpreted as "repugnant" or contradictory.

The racism that surfaced in Larkin's letters occurred in those to like-minded friends; it never appeared in his official published work. His offending vocabulary could be encountered in pubs and football crowds all over the country. Lisa Jardine concedes this in her essay: "Larkin's letters . . . turned out to contain offensive remarks of a puerile kind about women, about foreigners, about Asian immigrants . . . about a whole raft of things which were customarily comfortably vilified in private in postwar Britain" (1994, p. 108). It was public print that made them unacceptable, and the politically correct climate in which they were read. The difference in climate is also apparent in the example of Evelyn Waugh, whose private letters (published in 1982) are littered with politically incorrect terms, such as *nigger*, *bugger*, *coon*, and *pansy* or pseudo-euphemisms such as *Sapphist* and *blackamoor*. Although unfailingly malicious, Waugh is often amusingly sane: "All popular plays in New York are about buggers but they all commit suicide. The idea of a happy pansy is inconceivable to them" (August 18, 1949).

Posthumous quotations can be very surprising. "She is magnificently ugly – deliciously hideous . . . Yes behold me literally in love with this great horse-faced blue-stocking." Those were the sentiments of Henry James about George Eliot in a letter of May 10, 1869. "If it's the last thing I do, I'm going to do destroy every fucking grammar school in England. And Wales. And Northern Ireland." Those were the intentions of Anthony Crosland, Labour Secretary of State for Education, about 1965, as reported by his wife. Coming from a powerful public official, these sentiments, and the crudity of the language, are far more shocking than anything Larkin wrote, and had they been published at the time, would presumably have led to Crosland's dismissal. But his reputation seems to have remained unscathed.

Tintin in the Congo

Children's literature has over recent decades become a rapidly expanding field, increasingly concerned with critical awareness of the stereotypes and agendas that may be advanced. The assumption is that children absorb fiction and fantasy as if they were fact, and that their reading diet should accordingly be cleansed or regulated. Two early studies by Bob Dixon, *Catching Them Young* (1977, vols. 1 and 2) deal with sex, race, class, and political ideas in children's fiction. More dogmatic is the view that "Children and their books are ideological constructs. [publishers] perpetuate the values and cultural conceptions of the ruling group" (McGillis, 1996, p. 112). As discussed in chapter 1 (under "Textbooks and library books"), Diane Ravitch has shown that in the US children's books have become rigorously subject to publishers' guidelines. Correctness does not have a single viewpoint: several decades ago Enid Blyton's "Noddy" stories were criticized on psychological grounds because Noddy was too passive, depending on Big Ears to solve his problems. From the 1980s onwards her books faced the weightier criticism of racism, sexism, and snobbishness.

The *Adventures of Tintin* series by Hergé (Georges Remi), published from 1929, were an imaginative entrée for European children into a whole variety of cultures, including those of Russia, Egypt, Japan, Turkey, Arabia, Tibet, and Mexico. All these foreign milieux were presented in a stereotypical way with a blend of exoticism and humor. They provoked no objections. *Tintin au Congo* (1930–1) was, however, criticized in the 1960s for its depiction of the natives of the Congo. Although Hergé acknowledged the work to be a "youthful transgression" produced in "the purely paternalistic spirit of the times in Belgium," the only concession he made concerned the brutality with which some animals were killed (Thompson, 1992, p. 38). In his study, Harry Thompson argued that the work was "patronising, but by no means deliberately racist," concluding that *Tintin in the Congo* is "cautiously emerging into the light of re-acceptance as a historical curiosity" (Thompson, 1992, p. 42).

In 2007 two formal complaints were brought against the book. The first, to the British Commission for Racial Equality, elicited the judgment that "The book contains images and words of racial prejudice in which the 'savages' look like monkeys and speak like idiots." The CRE did not ban the book, but required that restrictions be placed on its sale. Shortly afterwards the booksellers Borders and Waterstones decided to reallocate it to the adult comic range. In the same month a charge of "racism and xenophobia" was brought by Bienvenu Mbutu Mondondo, a Congolese student studying in Belgium. (Both Hergé and the publishers were and are Belgian.) The burden of Mondondo's complaint is threefold: the blacks are presented according to a colonial stereotype; they cannot speak French properly; and the Belgian colonization of the Congo, which was especially brutal, has become a taboo topic (interview with *Le Figaro*, August 9, 2007, p. 4). The same article commented: "Belgium fears an epidemic of 'political correctness' in the Anglo-Saxon manner." The caricatured use of language is a basic feature of stereotyping "primitive" peoples, as is shown in chapter 5, especially in the discussion of *barbarian*. In this connection the standard French term *petit-négre* (literally "little black") refers to "basic and incorrect French" (Larousse, 2001). For the sake of cultural balance it is also perhaps worth noting that Tintin's curious ménage (all white) include the alcoholic Captain Haddock, the deaf and absent-minded Professor Tournesol, and the incompetent twin policemen Dupond.

Disgrace *and its reception*

In the New South Africa censorship was largely abolished. However, rather in the manner that Doris Lessing has described in her essay on censorship, a new political correctness surfaced in unexpected quarters. A major controversy erupted following the publication of J. M. Coetzee's *Disgrace*, for which he achieved the unique distinction of the award of a second Booker Prize in 1999. (He was to become Nobel Laureate in 2003.)

Ostensibly a work of fiction about a divorced academic (David Lurie) who has an affair with a student, is fired, and retreats to stay with his estranged daughter on her country farm where she is raped and he is brutally attacked by some neighbors, *Disgrace* is unmistakably about contemporary South Africa to a degree which is unusual in Coetzee's work. Every significant locale is named, a number of major current issues are probed, and raw nerves touched. Although the AIDS pandemic is not mentioned, there are passing references to the necessity of guns and dogs for self-protection in the country and the spread of shanty towns around Cape Town. The white academic has been displaced by "the great rationalization" from his Eurocentric specialty and consigned to a set of dumbed-down courses in "Communications." Disillusioned, unmotivated, and uncommitted to his "post-Christian, posthistorical and postliterate" students (1999, p. 32), except for casual affairs, he maintains his "irrelevant" interests, principally in the form of a chamber opera on Byron. The farm is precisely located in the Eastern Cape region where the British 1820 Settlers took up land grants. The neighbors are new settlers, black land invaders steadily encroaching on his daughter's farm, and turn out to be related to the rapists. Although the experience of the first part of the novel is relatively uncommon, the attack on the farm replicates events frequently reported in the national press.

Coetzee's Booker award was widely endorsed in the literary world, to the point that in October 2006 *Disgrace* was adjudged the "Best Novel of the Last 25 Years" by a panel of 150 British and Commonwealth authors in a poll organized by the London *Observer*. However, its publication was not universally welcomed in South Africa. As the content of the novel became more widely recognized and digested, certain prominent figures in the new élite started to register their protests. Jakes Gerwel, a noted Coloured intellectual and Director-General of the President's office under Nelson Mandela, asked the question in a leading Afrikaans newspaper, *Rapport*: "Is *this* the right image for our nation?" (February 13, 2000). The article appeared just after President Thabo Mbeki's State of the Nation address on February 4, 2000, a performance which Gerwel judged to be "outstanding and well considered." In this address Mbeki had quoted at some length an intercepted email by an unnamed white engineer who wished "to summarise what the Kaffirs have done to stuff this country since they came to power." The quoted email continued:

> Our girlfriends/wives are in constant threat of being brutally raped by some AIDS infected Kaffir (or gang of Kaffirs). Everyday someone you know is either robbed, assaulted, hijacked or murdered. . . . Half these black bastards have bought their (drivers) licences from corrupt traffic cops. . . . All I am saying is that AIDS isn't working fast enough!!! (quoted in McDonald, 2002, p. 325)

Two months later, on April 5, 2000, the ruling African National Congress party registered an official submission to the Human Rights Commission's Inquiry into Racism in the Media via Jeff Radebe, a prominent ANC minister. The submission is quoted in a publication called *A Marriage Made in Heaven or The White Man's Burden*, by Tau Y Gragramla, the *nom de plume* of some leading members of the party, Sankie Mahanyele, Smuts Ngonyama, Dumisane Makhaye, and Kgalema Motlanthe, subsequently President after the "recall" of Thabo Mbeki. The introduction ran: "Here you will see in greater depth how heavy the white man' [sic] burden is, given the savagery of the natives as faithfully reported in the media" (2001, pp. 179).

The ANC submission, some 20 pages long, deals indiscriminately with the past views of Afrikaner politicians, journalistic coverage of the transfer of power, and with *Disgrace*. It is, of course, virtually unique for a work of fiction to be categorized as part of "the media," as if it were reporting factually on current events in the manner of a newspaper. Only repressive régimes such as Communist Russia or modern Turkey do not distinguish between works of fiction and of fact. The reasons for the ANC strategy soon became apparent. After a preamble about the struggle to create a non-racial society, the statement quoted General Hertzog, "representing 'pure' Afrikaner nationalism":

> As against the European, the native stands as an eight-year-old against a man of mature experience – a child in religion, a child in moral conviction; without art and without science; with the most primitive needs and the most elementary knowledge to meet those needs . . . Differences exist in ethnic nature, ethnic custom, ethnic development and civilisation and these differences shall long exist. (2001, p. 180)

The ANC statement proceeded immediately to link Hertzog's observations, made over 50 years previously, and the novel: "This faithless, immoral, uneducated, incapacitated and primitive child is reported on by the eminent

South African novelist, J. M. Coetzee, in his 1999 novel *Disgrace*. In the novel a young white woman (Lucy) is gang-raped by three black men who, afterwards, also steal her car and household goods" (2001, p. 180). After further quotation the ANC statement continued: "In the novel, Coetzee represents as brutally as he can, white people's perception of the post-apartheid black man" (2001, p. 181). It continued with sweeping generalizations about authorial intention, the use of crude stereotypes, and the racial prejudice of whites:

> Coetzee makes the point that, five years after our liberation white South African society continues to believe in a particular stereotype of the African, defined as: immoral and amoral, savage, violent, disrespectful of private property, incapable of refinement through education, and driven by hereditary dark, satanic impulses. (2001, p. 182)

It argued:

> It is suggested that in these circumstances it might be better that our white compatriots should emigrate because to be in post-apartheid South Africa is to be in "their territory", as a consequence of which the whites will lose their cards [sic], their weapons, their property, their rights, their dignity. The white women will have to sleep with the barbaric black men. (2001, p. 181)

The ANC submission concluded by recommending that "There is a need to conduct a systematic and protracted campaign to destroy the white stereotype of black, and especially African, people and publicly to challenge the expression of this stereotype whenever it raises its head" (2001, p. 194).

The controversy provoked a number of critical studies on *Disgrace* by scholars in the field, eight of which were issued in a special number of the journal *Interventions* (vol. 4 (3), 2002). Virtually all saw the novel as reflecting other problems and issues in the New South Africa, rendering the ANC's limited and racialized interpretation simplistic and unjust. Thus Lurie's refusal to confess is seen as an analog to some responses to the Truth and Reconciliation Commission. Indeed, he makes one startling generalization: "More and more he is convinced that English is an unfit medium for the truth of South Africa" (1999, p. 117). In his contribution to *Interventions*, David Attwell points out that there is a range of fictional representation of blacks, and that the Chairman of the university disciplinary enquiry, Manas Mathabane, "is, in fact the novel's true representative of the Enlightenment" (Attwell, 2002, p. 335).

Furthermore, the black/white opposition is simplistic. The demographic history of the Cape Colony has resulted in a great range of "people of color."

David Lurie has "olive skin," we are unambiguously told, which could place him anywhere in the spectrum; his "whiteness" is an assumption deduced from his name, never a sure indicator of color, and from cultural markers and attitudes. In a discussion of "the gang rape," another academic focuses on the graphic ugliness of one participant, called "the boy": "He has a flat expressionless face and piggish eyes" (p. 92). The article concludes with the question: "Do the Coetzee texts cited here unobtrusively endorse the ancient cultural-racial hierarchy of 'European' superiority and 'African' inferiority?" (Gagiano, 2004, p. 47). "Unobtrusively" suggests "subliminal racism," the source of much discussion and accusation in the New South Africa.

Clearly, this interpretation, conflating the author with the narrator, does not accommodate three fundamental points. *Disgrace* is a work of fiction told by an unreliable narrator in the third person, and accordingly has shifting and contrasting viewpoints. More bizarrely and alarmingly, it is told in the continuous present tense as things happen unexpectedly to Lurie, so that the reader does not have the usual sense of sequence and predictability. Furthermore, at the crisis, as the father listens to his captors discussing his fate, Coetzee underscores the irony of Lurie's paranoid Eurocentric impotence: "He speaks Italian, he speaks French, but Italian and French will not save him here in darkest Africa" (p. 95). This recognition is followed by a passage of searing black humor as the narrator sees himself stereotypically as "a figure from a cartoon, a missionary in cassock and topi waiting . . . to be plunged into the boiling cauldron" (p. 95).

Even the meaning of the rape is problematic: the daughter does not react in a hysterical or a traumatized fashion, even refusing to report the crime, a much-publicized issue concerning rape statistics in South Africa. More directly, she asks "what if *that* is the price one has to pay for staying on?" (p. 158), whereas the father sees this horror as part of a process of a historical reparation or redress, making her a victim for past violations. Similarly, he reflects on the changes in the city, on the stray cows on the motorway outside Cape Town: "Soon there will be cattle again on Rondebosch Common; soon history will have come full circle" (p. 175). But personally and paternally he becomes increasingly obsessive about "[her] secret, his disgrace" (p. 109), multiplying the horror: "It happens every day, every hour, every minute, he tells himself" (p. 98).

While the official objections are understandable from the point of the more sensitive members of the new Africanist élite, many of whom, like presidents Nelson Mandela and Thabo Mbeki, are Xhosas hailing from the Eastern Cape, there is both a historical and an authorial irony in this race-based criticism of the novel. A juxtaposition of *Disgrace* with Coetzee's first work, *Dusklands* (1974) shows them to be, from colonial and postcolonial perspectives, two sides of the coin, specifically in respect of the crucial and still unresolved question of land distribution. In *Dusklands* the "Narrative of Jacobus Coetzee" describes from the point of view of a Boer pioneer the brutal acquisition of the land from the original Hottentots and Bushmen, basically by extermination. *Disgrace* describes in prescient and chilling fashion how the land is being steadily but remorselessly taken back by the natives through encroachment, occupation, and miscegenation. Jacobus Coetzee, really a civilized savage with a gun, regards the natives with total contempt: "The Hottentot is locked into the present. He does not care where he comes from or where he is going. The Bushman is a different creature, a wild animal with an animal's soul . . . Heartless as baboons they are, and the only way to treat them is like beasts" (1974, p. 62). In 1974, in the heyday of apartheid, it was possible to produce such supremacist stereotyping as a fictional reconstruction without repercussions, but 25 years later, after liberation, even a complex fictional account of relatively common criminal activity provoked a powerful public protest from the new government.

One consequence of the imbroglio over *Disgrace* was that Coetzee, born, bred, and educated in South Africa, emigrated to Australia in 2002, becoming an Australian citizen in March 2006. When he was awarded the Nobel Prize in 2003, he alluded wryly to censorship in a rare interview with a South African newspaper:

> I regard it as a badge of honour to have had a book banned in South Africa, and even more of an honour to have been acted against punitively. This honour I have never achieved, or to be frank merited. Besides coming too late in the era, my books have been too indirect in their approach, too rarified to be considered a threat to the order. (*Sunday Argus*, Cape Town, October 5, 2003)

He tactfully did not allude to *Disgrace*. When the ANC was asked in parliament whether the party's congratulations to the new Nobel Laureate would include some form of apology, the response was an emphatic refusal.

In a subsequent article under the bitter title of "Going to the Dogs," Rosemary Jolly severely criticized the ruling party: "The ANC has been negligent in its refusal to confront the extent of women's abuse in South Africa; and the ANC's desire to see fictional production conforming to a positive image of the new(ish) South Africa cannot but be read with the basest of political motives in mind" (Jolly, 2006, p. 149). Jolly's article also gives some devastating statistics of "the war on women." Coetzee himself has taken on the qualities defined by James Joyce as essential to the writer: silence, exile, and cunning.

Film

The history of film has been very different in the United States and in Britain. This brief discussion focuses principally on America, where the educational and didactic element has always been assumed: even by 1913 the National Board of Review for Motion Pictures in its "Definition of Censorship" stressed the new medium's potential for "political, social, religious propaganda . . . and for revolutionary ideas." The notorious Production Code (1930) stressed "the MORAL IMPORTANCE of entertainment" and was entirely concerned with sex and profanity, including in its banned topics "sex perversion" and "miscegenation." A recent collection, *Movies and American Society*, stresses that "Movies do more than simply show us how to dress, how to look, or what to buy. They teach us how to think about race, gender, class, ethnicity, and politics" (Ross, 2002, p. 1). No scholar or critic would write in such terms of the European or British cinema. But, of course, this simplistic prescription hardly accommodates Mel Brooks, Woody Allen, and the Coen brothers, or Spike Lee, discussed below.

D. W. Griffith's *Birth of a Nation* (1915), although silent, was the first film to arouse major protests, through its partisan treatment of the Civil War, since it glorified the role of the Ku Klux Klan and generated antiblack sentiment. The dramatic and menacing poster image of a mounted Klansman like a medieval knight but bearing a fiery cross (Figure 8.1) was obviously provocative. Although there were showings in the White House, "African Americans launched massive demonstrations to halt the exhibition of the film" (Ross, 2002, p. 7). It provoked a riposte in the form of a proposed *Birth of a Race* (1918), which flopped mainly for financial reasons.

The Western became a romanticized genre dominated by the myth of How the West was Won, avoiding the "broken promises and acts of injustice" admitted by President Hayes in 1877. Contrary to the popular image, one in four cowboys was black (Wenborn, 1991, pp. 158–9). As Marlon Brando commented at an Academy Awards ceremony, "The Indian is the forgotten man of America." In their very different ways *Dances with Wolves* (1990) and the television series *Deadwood* (2004–6) have revised the original clichés.

During World War II, propaganda films, mainly against the Japanese, proliferated, often trading on stereotypes in a very unsubtle fashion. In *Objective Burma*, for example, an American soldier surveys the ruins of a village destroyed by the Japanese and exclaims: "This was done in cold blood by people who claim to be civilized. Civilized! They are degenerate immoral idiots. Stinking little savages. Wipe them out, I say. Wipe them

Figure 8.1   Film poster for D. W. Griffith's *Birth of a Nation* (1915). Produced 50 years after the Civil War, the film's sympathetic treatment of the Southern cause and endorsement of the Ku Klux Klan provoked enormous controversy. Photo: AKG-Images, London.

off the surface of the earth" (Hamilton, 1990, p. 229). Such virulence obviously chimed in with the anti-Japanese sentiment after Pearl Harbor. After a long interval these attitudes have been corrected by revisionist films such as Clint Eastwood's *Flags of Our Fathers* and *Letters from Iwo Jima* (both 2006).

Even prior to 1968, when the Code Seal Rating Office replaced the Production Code Administration, films were becoming more daringly unconventional and politically incorrect. These included Stanley Kubrik's *Dr Strangelove* (1964), a black comedy satirizing the lunacy of nuclear strategic thinking, and Robert Altman's military farce, *MASH* (1966). Mike Nichol's *The Graduate* (1967) was a satirical exposé of the superficiality of American "family values" long before this theme became a cliché. A number of taboos were broken. The sexual initiation of anti-hero Benjamin by the predatory Mrs Robinson leads to the shocking climax when he disrupts the arranged society wedding, using a crucifix to block the church door as he and the freshly married bride elope. By ironic reversal of symbolism this action violates both the tradition of the church as a place of sanctuary and the ritual of exorcism, since by implication evil is locked in, not driven out.

War films have probed the whole morality of war and problems of loyalty in disturbing ways. David Lean's *The Bridge on the River Kwai* (1958) was followed by a whole series of films openly critical of America's role in Vietnam, notably *Apocalypse Now* (1979), *Platoon* (1986), and *Full Metal Jacket* (1987). The older gangster films such as *Little Caesar* (1930) and *Scarface* (1932) were withdrawn when the Catholic-inspired League of Decency organized a boycott (although the Mafia was actually on the rise). The Mafia returned, glamorized and institutionalized in the various *Godfather* movies (1972–90), further exploited as comedies in *Married to the Mob* (1988) and *The Whole Nine Yards* (2000).

Spike Lee

Lee is the acerbic and often politically incorrect chronicler of the contemporary "melting pot," acutely probing racial tensions, mainly concerning Blacks and Italians simultaneously struggling to make a living and to maintain a sense of identity as Italian-Americans or African-Americans.

With ironic humor and ruthless satire, *Do the Right Thing* (1989), *Get on the Bus* (1996), and *Bamboozled* (2000) show low self-esteem, lack of motivation, and confused identity among blacks, who also parade racial slurs, especially the word *nigger*, with provocative profusion. There is a great deal of self-directed irony: in *Do the Right Thing*, set in Harlem, the two key businesses are an Italian-owned pizza joint and a recently opened Korean store, a situation naturally provoking envy and hostility. One of the largely sedentary black seniors comments on the speed with which Koreans "just off the boat" have established themselves: "Either these Korean mother-fuckers are geniuses or you black asses are just plain dumb." In addition to straight racist vituperation *en passant*, the film features a protracted and stylized swearing match in which the blacks, the Koreans, and the Italians berate each other. Lee is adept at showing how moderate blacks often have to suffer in embarrassed silence when one of their own number starts swearing.

Jungle Fever (1991) begins with the best-selling number with lyrics by Stevie Wonder, including phrases like "black-boy crazy." The film made such an impact that *jungle fever* entered the American slang lexicon, defined rather coyly by the *Random House Dictionary of American Slang* (1994) as "romantic interest between a black person and a white person." The official blurb ran: "A Black architect begins an affair with his working class Italian secretary. Their relationship causes them to be scrutinized by their friends, cast out from their families and shunned by their neighbors in this moving view of inner-city life." This bromidic oversimplification belies what is a devastating exposé of racist violence and racial solidarity among ethnic groups. Lee reveals an obsession with degrees of blackness (the words *mulatto, quadroon,* and *octoroon* occur in conversation) with a simultaneous insistence on loyalty to the group. The women are open about the worthlessness of their men: "Most of them are homos or in jail." They feel bitter about the preferences of successful black men for "light-skinned girls with straightened hair." They fantasize about hunting for "tribesman" and "Zulu dick."

After a relatively casual sexual fling, the black architect is thrown out by his wife, together with all his belongings, into the street, in full view of the curious neighbors. She feels especially betrayed because her rival is only "pale": "I wasn't light enough for you. You had to get a white girl." The Italian lover (who is, ironically, virtually the same hue as the wife) is summarily beaten up by her father, who screams at her "I'd rather be stabbed in the heart with a knife than be the father of a nigger-lover!" In the end they both agree that "it's not worth it" and retreat into their racial clans.

Even while the film was being shot the sets were defaced and death-threats were received "from persons unknown" (Patterson, 1992, p. 166). On set there were differences of interpretation, Annabella Sciorra (playing the Italian girl) insisting that the role showed "genuine feelings," while Lee and Wesley Snipes (playing the black architect) felt that she undervalued the "fear of the big black dick," which Lee "had spoken of in interviews (and had even plastered all over the early promotional materials for the film)" (Patterson, 1992, p. 166). Where is Lee in all this? Only an African-American insider could make such a film, emphasizing the importance of "loyalty" among "brother" blacks, yet also showing many to be idle, insecure, or worthless drug addicts like Gator, the protagonist's bother, who is finally shot by his severe father, the Reverend Doctor Purify.

Assessments of Lee's films are obviously colored by their content and their political incorrectness. Alan Parker commented "He's not a very good filmmaker in my opinion . . . [and] what he's trying to say, I think it's very ugly – I think it's about hate, not love, it's about separatism, not integration and I cannot go along with that" (Patterson, 1992, pp. 174–5). Commenting on the fact that *Jungle Fever* was well received at Cannes, but was passed over in the Oscars, Patterson speculates: "More Thinly Veiled Racism? Maybe – or just plain old Academy stupidity" (1992, p. 177). In the film when the architect objects that his request for an African-American secretary has not been respected, one of the senior partners observes: "Sounds suspiciously like reverse racism to me." Patterson comments "Many would agree that it is – except of course that Spike believes black people are genetically incapable of racism: 'I don't think Blacks can be racist,' he said at Cannes in 1989" (1992, p. 181).

The story of Malcolm X and the racial politics of the making of Lee's film about him are alike revealing. Originally Malcolm Little, he changed his "slave-master name" first to Malcolm X, then to Malik El Shabazz, finally to El-Hajj Malik El Shabazz, following the Black Muslim route. But in the end the hero is isolated, ostracized, and finally betrayed by his fellow Muslims. Originally Norman Jewison was going to direct the film, although "James Baldwin himself had once said that 'a Malcolm movie being made by white Hollywood is unthinkable' " (Patterson, 1992, p. 195). Lee was quoted in an interview in *Playboy* in July, 1991 as saying: "I am of the opinion that only a Black man should write and direct *The Autobiography of Malcolm X*. Bottom line" (in Patterson, 1992, p. 195). Jewison responded on Canadian television in 1991: "I can't agree with Spike Lee. That's an apartheid statement" (in Patterson, 1992, p. 196).

Popular Culture, Humor, and Satire

Simultaneously with the serious cultural debate over political correctness, there was a less academic reaction consisting of caricatures and ironic parodies, as well as an upsurge in deliberate politically incorrect humor, trading on transgressions of the new codes. From relatively mild beginnings in popular culture these tended to become increasingly outrageous.

However, attitudes now regarded as politically incorrect were apparent in popular culture long before the debate itself, a point developed later in the subsection on "Jokes." In 1961 a British satirical revue made caustic fun of the nuclear holocaust, a black racist politician, an Anglican sermon, and gays, more specifically "two dreadful queens." This was *Beyond the Fringe*, the enormously successful collaboration of Peter Cooke, Alan Bennett, Dudley Moore, and Jonathan Miller, who brought the house down with the comment that he was "not really a Jew. Just Jew-*ish*. Not the whole hog."

The *National Lampoon* was launched in 1970, an offshoot of the *Harvard Lampoon*. One of its celebrated incursions into sick humor was the cover showing a revolver aimed at a cowering puppy with the threat: "If You don't Buy this Magazine We'll Kill this Dog" (January 1973). Another was a spoof advertisement for the VW Beetle illustrating its alleged abilities to float, with the caption: "If Ted Kennedy drove a Volkswagen, he'd be President today."

The Monty Python film *The Life of Brian* (1979) daringly explored the farcical possibilities of a wrongly chosen Messiah, but also satirized current issues, such as the rights to sex-change and having babies, all thwarted wishes being labeled "oppression." The importance of exact political affiliations is carried to absurdity, as when Brian (Cohen) asks, "Are you the Judean People's Front?" and is summarily corrected by Reg: "Fuck off! We're the People's Front of Judea!" The song accompanying the crucifixion, "Always Look on the Bright Side of Life," remains the major memorial of the production.

In sitcoms rebellious comic figures proliferated in farcical caricatures that had their roots in the more realistic cynicism of Johnny Speight's Alf Garnett and his American equivalent, Archie Bunker. Garnett was the reactionary, bigoted, racist, misogynistic, homophobic, and anti-Semitic antihero of *Till Death Do Us Part*, which ran from 1965 to 1975, when the "Clean Up TV" campaign of Mrs Mary Whitehouse led to Speight ending the series in protest. Bunker, a softer American version of Garnett, was the protagonist of *All in the Family*, which ran from 1971 to 1983.

British satires included *Class Act*, scripted by Michael Aitkens, sporting the redoubtable Kate Swift (played by Joanna Lumley) armed with such withering denunciations as "you obsequious little turd," "that battered slattern," "troglodytic tart," "the Fleet Street bike," and "miserable tight-fisted old cow." Much of the humor traded on pricking feminist sensibilities. But far crueler was *Absolutely Fabulous*, written by Jennifer Saunders, launched in November 1992, and still enormously popular when it ended in 2005. It starred the outrageously insensitive, decadent, idle, and alcoholic duo Patsy and Edina (Lumley and Saunders) in numerous politically incorrect exchanges, such as this from the episode "Morocco" (1994):

EDINA: Sweetie we dragged these people into the twentieth century. We gave them all the mod-cons, darling. We gave them the non-squat toilet, toilet tissue, darling. I mean, how do you think they used to wipe their bottoms before we came along . . . ?
PATSY: Old bits of hoof (Saunders, 1994, p. 62)

More sexually explicit, the American series *Sex and the City* by Candace Bushnell explored the theme of sex and the single woman, attracted by new adventures in a liberated verbal and sexual climate, but tempered by new taboos, as in the scene in where the naïve and charming Charlotte admits to some new girlfriends how much she enjoys female company, only to receive the challenging rebuff: "That's all very sweet, darling, but if you don't eat pussy, you're not a dyke" ("The Cheating Curve," 1998).

Also outrageous but more creative are the personae developed by the British comedian Sacha Baron Cohen, first popularly known as Ali G (launched on Channel 4 in 1999). Middle-class and Cambridge educated, Cohen wears his trademark costume, uses coarse Caribbean slang, grammatical solecisms, and adopts philistine and chauvinist attitudes to interview various establishment figures. Using the strategy of Socratic irony, he pretends to be an inarticulate simpleton, asking apparently naïve but actually fundamental questions, invariably trapping his expert victims into making fools of themselves. Thus he asks a bishop: "What's God done, then?" "Well, um he created the world." "And then – he just chilled?" He traps a pompous authority on the English class system by asking "What class is Pakis, then?" Most of his interviewees simply accept his sexist attitudes and routine remarks about "bitches": only two feminists and Tony Benn protested.

His alter-persona took the now notorious form of the bizarre Borat Sagdiyev, described by Steven Lee Myers of the *New York Times* as "a bumbling, boorish, anti-Semitic, homophobic, and misogynist Kazakh television reporter" (September 28, 2006). Rather than exploit the typical British targets of xenophobic satire such as the French, the Italians, or the Spaniards, Borat retailed absurd and degrading myths about life in Kazakhstan in staged interviews subsequently consolidated into a full-length film with the pidgin title *Borat: Cultural Learnings of America for Make Benefit Glorious Nation of Kazakhstan*. This was screened in November 2006 in the face of vigorous protests from the Kazakh authorities. However, the real targets of the satire, it turned out, were those Americans who naïvely revealed their racist prejudices in the course of Borat's tour of the United States.

What remains curious about the responses to Ali G and especially *Borat* is an unwillingness to criticize the grosser features of homophobia, misogyny, and especially anti-Semitism, which is astonishingly crude. There seems to be a double standard whereby critical attitudes are modified for recognized satire. More pertinently, there is also an assumption that a Jew or a black can test the boundaries more robustly and daringly than others. Thus if it were shown that Cohen was a stage name and he was not, in fact, Jewish, the critical response would be one of outrage. The reader may care to consult "Is Borat Offensive?" (*Guardian*, October 26, 2006), Joshua Muravchik's essay "Borat!" in *Commentary* (January 2007, pp. 44–7), and Charles Isherwood's "Anti-Gay Slurs: The Latest in Hilarity" (*New York Times*, December 17, 2006).

In South Africa the films of Leon Schuster are noted for their political incorrectness, using farce, reverse stereotypes, and the candid camera technique in set-up situations to probe genuine feelings beneath polite façades. In a typical instance, a white farmer is stopped at a road-block by a black policeman (Schuster in disguise) who says he is going to confiscate the vehicle because the license has expired. The enraged farmer mutters: "Dis verdomde Nuwe Suid Afrika se moer!" ("This fucking New South Africa!"). Yet Schuster's films are huge commercial successes, consistently generating more revenue than the Harry Potter series and *The Lord of the Rings*.

Jokes historical and political

Within the ambit of our topic, humor has a great range of targets and tones, incorporating xenophobia, schadenfreude, black humor, sick humor, and multifarious jokes against outgroups, condemned by the politically correct formula of "inappropriately directed laughter" or the more extraordinary *laughism*. All kinds of humor are difficult to control, since irony and connivance cannot be legislated against. The discussions on disease, crime and punishment, and disability in chapter 6 contain many examples of "laughism," some of them going back centuries. There are also unexpected social dynamics in ethnic jokes, such as the proliferation of jokes told by Jews against themselves.

There is an essential difference between popular or grass-roots jokes and those which are more artistically contrived by individuals. English jokes about traditional enemies such as the French and the Germans are a form of patriotic satire and therefore broadly politically correct. Thus Napoleon featured in much contemporary English satire, often with the nickname Boney, just as Hitler did in his time: indeed the phrase "little Hitler" for a psychotically dictatorial person dates from 1934. Less sophisticated in its macho contempt for the Nazis was the popular World War II marching song, sung to the tune of "Colonel Bogey":

> Hitler has only got one ball,
> Goering has two, but very small;
> Himmler has something similar,
> But poor old Goebbels
> Has no balls at all.

The essence of politically incorrect humor and satire is that it comes from within the society and is directed at national mores, values, the ruling class and its individuals, political or hereditary. As we have seen in chapter 7, English literature has a long tradition of such satire.

In times of war and intense political struggle or in totalitarian societies such satire requires more daring. Egon Larsen's study *Wit as a Weapon: The Political Joke in History* (1980) is a treasury of politically incorrect material, a collection of anonymous underground satire of many sorts and nationalities, especially against dictatorial or authoritarian regimes. His key quotation is from Henri Bergson, *Le Rire* (1900) on "the conspiratorial power of laughter, by which society avenges itself for the liberties taken with it . . . Laughter is always the laughter of the group; however spontaneous it seems, it always implies a kind of freemasonry, or even complicity with other laughers, real or imaginary" (1980, p. 2). Laughter is also the safety valve of people in situations of suffering, as in Gogol's comment on "Laughter under invisible tears" (1980, p. 79). This is true, but only up to a point, since laughter is also a reaction of jokes against outgroups.

Larsen's first chapter, "The People's Voice," starts with a Russian joke about a man who is paid a ruble a day to sit on the Kremlin wall waiting to blow a trumpet when the world revolution comes. When his friend protests that this is a small wage, he replies, "I know. But it's a job for life." Larsen points out that this story was widely told in Russia during the revolution, explaining that it is typical of political jokes "circulating in countries where authoritarian regimes suppress freedom of speech . . . ridiculing the professed aims of the establishment" (1980, p. 1). Similar is the question: "What was the nationality of Adam and Eve?" to which the ironic answer was: "They must have been Russians, because they had no clothes, no roof over their heads and only one apple between them – yet they insisted that they were living in Paradise" (1980, p. 82).

Many jokes dealt with queues and the unavailability of basic food, while those from the former satellite countries often expose problems of loyalty, such as the customer in a Belgrade grocer who asks for some tea. When asked to make a choice between Russian or Chinese, he hesitates and then says, "On second thoughts, make it coffee" (1980, p. 91). In Romania there are three kinds of perverse love: "sodomy, pederasty and love of the Soviet Union" (1980, p. 91). The problems facing Russian historians dealing with Krushchev's denunciation of Stalin led to the nice quip: "It's hard to predict the past accurately" (1980, p. 83). As Communism collapsed, jokes focused on key strategic points. Guarding the Berlin Wall, one GDR soldier asks his mate, "What would you do if this thing were suddenly pulled down?" "I'd climb up the nearest tree." "But why?" "I don't want to be trampled by the crowd!" (1980, p. 94). In 1977 a Budapest professor of ethnography, Imre Cotona, published some of the 3,000 political jokes he had collected over the past 30 years: One with the typical "question and answer" format ran: "How did the two German states divide the heritage of Karl Marx between them?" "The GDR has the Manifesto. The Federal Republic has the Capital" (1980, p. 96).

The Russian tradition of antiestablishment satire started in the late eighteenth century, leading to Gogol's *The Government Inspector* (1836), now a timeless global classic. Postrevolutionary satire became *de rigueur*: the weekly *Krokodil* (from 1922) thrived until it was taken over by *Pravda* and institutionalized. Other works included those by Mikhail Soshchenko, Ilf and Petrov, and Ilya Ehrenburg. Yevgeny Zamyatin's dystopia *We* (1922) is generally regarded as superior to both Huxley's *Brave New World* (1932) and George Orwell's *1984* (1949). It was never published in Russia.

In a wide-ranging discussion, Larsen includes many antiestablishment jokes across European history, starting with the anti-Catholic wisecracks of the Reformation, such as "God is everywhere on earth except Rome: only his deputy is there" and the disappointment of Pope Leo X upon arriving at the gates of heaven with his keys, only to be told that "Luther has changed the lock" (1980, p. 8). Just as the printing press disseminated Luther's 95 theses with great effect, so during the Puritan Commonwealth in England there emerged in broadsheet form in 1647 sarcastic parodies of the Creed: "I believe in CROMWELL, the Father of all Schisme, Sedition, Heresy and Rebellion" and of the Commandments: "Thou shalt have no other Gods but the LORDS and COMMONS assembled at Westminster" (1980, pp. 10–11). These attacks were, of course, unusually direct and open, whereas under the Nazi regime there emerged the genre of the *Flüsterwitze* or whispered jokes. Many focused on temporary conformity to the current regime, such as this from Italy: "The last thing an Italian wanted to be: in 1941 a soldier; in 1942 a Jew; in 1943 a Fascist" (1980, p. 57).

Larsen's conclusion is that

> Political humour has its legitimate outlet in the media. This is the reason why popular satire has declined in the democracies of the West and whispered jokes have no function to fulfil. Thus satire has been rarer in England than in other countries, and fewer political jokes have been recorded. It is almost as though satire has been regarded as an un-British activity, at least in modern times. (1980, p. 105)

The exception, he concedes, is *Private Eye*, started in 1961.

Larsen covers the modern period, not the rich legacy of satirists going back to Rowlandson, Gillray, Cruikshank, Hogarth, et al. Interestingly, the role of *Punch vis à vis* the Establishment changed completely from the Victorian era to modern times, as William Davis shows in his revealing anthology, *Punch and the Monarchy*:

> When *Punch* began in 1841, it was a low, irreverent sheet and the opposite of courtly. It was cheerfully unfair to the royal family in general and to Prince Albert in particular. But irreverence gave way, later in Victoria's

interminable reign, to a gush of sycophantic drivel. . . . For years, whenever there was an Accession or a Coronation, there was a picture of Mr. Punch bowing low to the Monarch. The contrast with the venomous drawings of men like Gillray, in the previous century, could hardly have been greater. . . . No wonder the Punch stable collected several knighthoods. (1977, p. 7)

Thus in 1917, with World War I generating xenophobic anger at Germany, King George V prudently did the politically correct thing by changing the name of the British Royal house from Saxe-Coburg-Gotha to Windsor. *Punch* immediately produced a patriotic cartoon with Mr Punch as a royal herald proclaiming "Long Live the House of Windsor!" (July 25, 1917). The change to satire came, according to Davis, in the 1960s, but even then the royal family was protected: "Mild little jokes about the royal corgis were all right, but no allusions to Prince Philip's love life, O.K.?" (1977, p. 7). However, a quarter of a century after Larsen's volume, the constricted atmosphere of political correctness has created the atmosphere of many "whispered jokes" and parodies.

South Africa has a considerable store of politically incorrect humor. In his study of the Coloured population Mohamed Adhikari retails an interracial joke concerning relative social status. In a dispute with a Coloured man over admission to a facility, an African delivers this punch line: "God made the white man, God made the black man, God made the Indian, the Chinese and the Jew – but Jan Van Riebeeck, he made the Coloured man" (2005, p. 20). Adhikari notes the altering currency of this joke, saying that in his experience "it was a very common joke often told openly to and by Coloured people during the apartheid period," adding that "the coming of the 'new' South Africa, with its heightened sensitivity to anything that might be deemed racially offensive, has caused the joke to lose much of its appeal; where still in evidence, the joke is mainly restricted to private discourse among people who share a high level of personal trust" (2005, p. 20).

Naturally, not everybody accepts this genealogy, since a valid argument can be made that the Coloured community is also descended from the original San and Khoisan people. Yet Adhikari's comment serves another purpose, essentially describing the altered status of most politically incorrect jokes. In politically correct regimes they fall into the genre of the *Flüsterwitze*, or whispered jokes. A similar demise has, curiously, affected the genre of the Van der Merwe joke, targeting the Afrikaner via the stereotype of the brutal, stupid "boer" (oaf or redneck). These jokes also thrived in the apartheid era, being told mainly by English and (to a lesser extent) Afrikaners, but have now died out completely. They became fashionable in the period of "grand apartheid" as a form of subversion, but waned as the Afrikaner lost power, even before political correctness became first fashionable and then *de rigueur*.

Sources of satire

Private Eye, which commenced publication in 1961, was a source of politically incorrect material long before the formulation of political correctness. (So, for that matter, was *Le Canard Enchainée*, founded in 1915.) Richard Ingrams' *The Life and Times of Private Eye* (1971) and Patrick Marnham's *The Private Eye Story; the First 21 Years* (1982) are rich social documents of satire. Ingenious juxtaposition of serious press photographs with ironically inappropriate captions or "bubbles" has become its hallmark. Thus a photograph of a Zulu war dance carried the caption "Verwoerd: A Nation Mourns" (September 17, 1966). That of an aide giving President Bush the devastating news of 9/11 with the words "It's Armageddon, sir" had Bush replying "Armageddon outa here." The *Eye* also published actual material under the title "Loony Feminist Nonsense," as it had done with "Pseud's Corner," and often referred to *wimmin*. The issue of "coming out" took the form of this question: " 'Is William Gay?' writes Peter Tatchell, continuing: 'Now that Prince William is 16, surely it is time for him to declare himself proud to be a homosexual' " (1998, p. 74). An earlier collection called *Private Eyesores* (1970) contained an elaborate spoof campaign for "Poove Power."

In the African ambit, exploiting the unfamiliarity of African names, the *Private Eye Annual* (Hislop, 1998, p. 53) included this fictional schedule of *Clinton in Africa*: "18:00 Visits capital of Legova to meet President Bonko Bonko. 21:00 Formal reception Chief Gobblo of the Wanafaki Tribe." These trade on one of the *Eye*'s running jokes, "Ugandan discussions" being a code term for sexual intercourse, based on an actual incident concerning a Ugandan princess. While *Private Eye* and *Punch* could make fun of African stereotypes, Alan Clark, a Conservative minister in the Thatcher government, got a bad press for his comments about "Bongo Bongo land," leaked to the press in January 1985 (Clark, 1993, p. 106).

The figure of Idi Amin underwent various fictional transformations, liberally laced with black humor. In America in the 1970s Amin featured in *Mad Magazine*, made the cover of *Time*, and was celebrated as an effigy of black power at a Harlem waxworks, a unique cultural achievement. In Britain *Punch* published for several years Alan Coren's *Bulletins of Idi Amin* (1975), presenting Amin as a figure of comic horror rather than a genocidal maniac. In a typical Coren *Punch* piece, written at the height of Amin's atrocities, he apologizes for not being "able to make de nuptials" (of Princess Anne), the illiteracy partially disguising the savagery: ". . . irrespeckertive o' de fac' dat de invite gittin' mysteriously lost in transit, an if I find de Uganda P O employee responsible, he gonna wind up with his clef' stick stuck in de middle of Amin Park an' his head wobblin' on same (Davis, 1977, p. 134).

A completely different treatment of Amin, Giles Foden's novel *The Last King of Scotland* was written between 1990 and 1996, long before the film on which it was based. It was an unusual piece of "faction," putting emphasis on a fictional character's supposed relationship with a real tyrant. Foden commented in an article in the *Guardian* (January 6, 2007): "Through a combination of lust for adventure and moral disengagement he becomes complicit in Amin's atrocities. I wanted to look at the passivity of some kinds of expatriate life, and also to look at the magnetism of a powerful person." The comments about "moral disengagement" and "passivity" smack of a new kind of political correctness, liberal guilt, and a suggestion that the colonialists were somehow complicit with Amin's tyranny. But Amin was what he was without the Scottish doctor of Foden's fiction.

Foden continued in a different vein: "As well as being a genuine historical figure, Idi Amin was a signifier, a persona. He came to represent the 'essence of dictator', perhaps even Africa itself in its troubled rather than romantic (Out of Africa) mode. He was a bloodthirsty comic nightmare." This quality of horror comedy is caught in the film's throwaway comment on cannibalism: "It's not true that I eat human flesh; I find it too salty." The film's bizarre iconic image of Amin in full Scottish regalia was developed by a number of cartoonists in depictions of the Zimbabwean tyrant Mugabe. Like Amin, Mugabe invariably exceeds the credible, denouncing the US State Department's senior diplomat for Africa as "this little American girl trotting around like a prostitute" (*Guardian*, May 26, 2008).

In the United States the first openly and consistently politically incorrect publication was the remarkable journal *Maledicta, The International Journal of Verbal Aggression*, edited by Reinhold Aman. This appeared annually from 1977 to 1989, and intermittently between 1995 and 2004, publishing articles on every conceivable taboo and embarrassing topic. True to its manifesto "They say it – we print it," *Maledicta* went far beyond the staple items on sex and evacuation, including pieces on the huge variety of obscene swearing and ethnic humor, Ethiopian jokes, and even AIDS jokes. The collection *The Best of Maledicta* (Aman, 1987) carried a "warning" on the cover: "Contains Language Offensive to Blacks, Catholics, Gays, Jews, Men, Women, and WASPs."

Varieties of modern politically incorrect humor and satire

1   *Pride and Prejudice and Niggas.* This was a one-man comic show at the London Arts Theatre in 2006. It probes the dilemma of Reginald D. Hunter, a bemused disciple of the Black Power movement, who is disturbed that, being an adherent of Black Pride means that "I should feel proud of Mugabe, Don King and Trisha." He admits "I get a lot of hate mail from black people. I've never seen so many misspelled words" (*Spectator*, December 30, 2006, p. 32).

2   Howard University Law School Final Exam

CONSTITUTIONAL LAW

A dude commit armed robbery. After he be arrested, the dude be hungry and he ax the police to get him some chicken wings and a RC Cola. The police refuse and give him a bologna sandwich and water instead. Has the dude's constitutional rights been violated? (Aman, 1987, p. 103)

In example 1 the humor is self-directed, depending on the comedian being black, but it incongruously trades on some stereotypes of blacks. In 2 the humor is other-directed, having been "submitted by P. Bernstein" to *Maledicta* and targets a noted black college. Instead of simply making fun of the supposed illiteracy of blacks, it mocks the low standards of the college, satirizes Black English by placing it in a formal context, and anticipates the fashion for Ebonics, discussed elsewhere.

3   Red Riding Hood entered the cottage and said, "Grandma, I have brought you some fat-free, sodium-free snacks to salute you in your role of a wise and nurturing matriarch" (Garner, 1994, p. 3).

4   This case involved a stand-up comic who became furious when his routine was criticized by some members of his audience. He shouted at them "There's a nigger and there's another." He paced the stage shouting "Nigger, nigger, oohh, I'm going to be arrested for saying nigger." He was the noted comic Michael Richard, a member of the *Seinfeld* team. The incident (in November 2006 at the Laugh Factory) caused a scandal, because Richard is white, those he swore at were black, and especially because he used the taboo term *nigger*, which several newspapers did not print. The incident (covered in *TLS*, December 8, 2006) showed the dangers of real racism exploding into a contrived theatrical situation.

5   "There May be Anthropological Differences That Account for Variation in Personal Lift, Though These Do Not Imply a Kinetic

Inferiority of One Ethnic Group Vis-à-Vis Another" (*Washington Post*: A parodic version of the film title *White Men Can't Jump*, 1992).

6   A Service of Condonation for the Victims of Social Deprivation in Inner-City Areas

The Archbishop of Canterbury: Dearly beloved yobboes, we are gathered here today to give thanks for the spontaneous expression of anger which took place last night on the N- or M-Estate (*here he may name Mandela or Poulson, or whomsoever shall be appropriate*)

The Blessing of On-Going Same-Sex Relationships between Meaningful Adults

Dearly and openly beloved brothers and sisters. We are gathered here today to share the sacrament of safe sex between N- and N- . . . Who giveth this condom unto this man? (*Private Eye*, 1991–93; both examples come from "Alternative Rocky Horror Services")

These parodies have echoes of some of the rituals inspired by the American militant feminist organization WITCH, especially in the publication for February, 1969 which contained a "WITCH Un-Wedding Ceremony":

> We are gathered together here in the spirit of our passion to affirm, love, and initiate our freedom from the unholy state of American patriarchal oppression.
> We promise to love, cherish and groove on each other and on all living things. We promise to smash the alienated family unit. We promise not to obey. (Morgan, 1970, pp. 546–7)

7   It is the most ridiculous country in the world, Bangladesh. It is God's idea of a *really good wheeze*, his stab at black comedy. You don't need to give out questionnaires to Bengalis. The facts of disaster are the facts of their lives. Between Aslana's sweet sixteenth birthday (1971), for example, and the year she stopped speaking directly to her husband (1985), more people died in Bangladesh, more people perished in the winds and the rain, than in Hiroshima, Nagasaki and Dresden *put together*. (Zadie Smith, *White Teeth*, 2001, p. 211)

This is obviously a far more disturbing piece of black humor, since the fictional story is interwoven with profound issues of providence and suffering, treated in a light-hearted, some would say blasphemous, fashion.

A less complex study is the collection of "Ethiopian Jokes" by Richard Christopher, in *The Best of Maledicta* (Aman, 1987, pp. 188–93).

Christopher notes the speed with which topical jokes spring up, concerning even "the holocaust of famine and death that has devastated Ethiopia" in 1985. Most of the jokes (over 50 in number) take the question and trick answer formula: Why did the chicken cross the road? He saw an Ethiopian coming after him; How many Ethiopians can you fit into a shopping cart? None. They fall through the holes.

Stephen O. Murray's foundation article "The Art of Gay Insulting" (1979) was an investigation into an unexpected variation of "sounding," played as a verbal game between homosexuals, using in-group taunts. William Leap's *Word's Out: Gay Men's English* (1996), which argues for the existence of "Gay English" as a variety, also contains some examples. There is also the overt politically incorrect genre of the AIDS joke. Introducing a collection in *The Best of Maledicta* (1987), Casper G. Schmidt quotes Gershon Legman's explanation of their rationale as being like those of dirty jokes, "to absorb and control, even to slough off, by means of jocular presentation and laughter, the great anxiety that both teller and listener feel in connection with certain culturally determined themes" (Legman, 1968, pp. 13–14). The jokes themselves, like those about syphilis, are generally characterized by irony, cruelty, and schadenfreude: "What does GAY mean? – Got AIDS Yet?"; "What does AIDS stand for? – Anally Inserted Death Sentence"; "What's the great mystery of AIDS – It can turn a fruit into a vegetable" (Schmidt in Aman, 1987, pp. 194–5).

Julie Burchill's provocative collection *Sex and Sensibility* (1992) covered most of the current politically correct bases with essays entitled "Designer Dykes," "Postures Green," "Now is the Time for All Good Men to Come to the AIDS Party," "Fags Ain't What They Used to Be," and "In Praise of the Casting Couch." Further afield, Peter Coleman noted that "The most popular play in Australian history by the country's most successful dramatist, David Williamson, was an enormously successful satire called *Dead White Males*" (Coleman, 2000, p. 11).

Humorous reclamation

The dynamic of reclamation creates a double standard in usage which works only in one direction: the stigmatic term can be used only by members of the out-group. Instances of *nigger* being used humorously have been discussed under that term. Public names like that of the rap group N.W.A (or "Niggaz With Attitude") make reclamation a more complex issue. A similar case emerges from South Africa. The term *Kaffir*, originally descriptive, is now so taboo that its use by a white person is grounds for prosecution for *crimen injuria*, an offense involving an insult or degradation of a person's dignity by action or word. However, the famous Archbishop Tutu is on record on several occasions as referring to himself in the belittling phrase of former times as "a cheeky Kaffir." Such irony is not available to whites: if ex-President F. W. de Klerk were to refer to himself as a *white boy*, no one would understand.

Reclamation is most daringly practiced by Jews. "Chaim Weizmann, the first president of Israel, would describe himself appealingly as just 'A Yid from Pinsk'" (*New York Times Book Review*, June 30, 1985). Some novels by Philip Roth, especially *Portnoy's Complaint* and *Goodbye Columbus*, contain devastating satires. In the 1970s Richard "Kinky" Friedman styled his Country and Western band "The Texas Jewboys," and included the provocative number "They Ain't Makin' Jews like Jesus Anymore." The Larsen collection contains many savagely ironic definitions such as "A Zionist is a Jew who sends another Jew to Palestine at the expense of a third Jew" (1980, p. 76). Leo Rosten's *The Joys of Yiddish* (1968) is a cornucopia of examples. Even entirely taboo topics, such as the Nazis and the Holocaust, have generated humor. A notable example features in the film *The Producers* (1967), written by Mel Brooks, which centers on the making of a deliberately offensive musical about Hitler. The show opens with the song and dance number, "Springtime for Hitler," featuring schmaltzy music counterpointed by dancing stormtroopers forming the shape of a swastika, goose-stepping showgirls, and absurd pro-Nazi lyrics.

The most surprising source is Steve Lipman's extensive collection, *Laughter in Hell: The Use of Humor during the Holocaust* (1991). Quoting Gogol's dictum that "He who fears nothing fears laughter," Lipman shows that, in common with other oppressive regimes, Nazi Germany went to considerable lengths to suppress critical humor. Yet the cabaret artist Werner Finck, who performed in a theater with members of the Nazi secret police sitting visibly in the audience, was sent briefly to a concentration camp, where he continued to entertain the inmates and the guards. The jokes, hundreds of them, are mainly of the riddle genre: "What is the difference between Christianity and National Socialism? In Christianity, one man died for everyone. In National Socialism everyone has to die for one man." Or "Before the Nazi takeover a judge would think: "He is a Jew; but he's innocent." Afterwards he would think: "He's innocent, but he's a Jew." An American GI magazine held a competition suggesting postwar punishments for Hitler. The winning entry came from a Jewish soldier stationed in Italy for this proposal: "He should live with my in-laws in the Bronx" (Lipman, 1991, p. 237).

Lipman records that Charlie Chaplin encountered many difficulties in the making of *The Great Dictator* (1940), including warnings of censorship from the film regulation organization, the Hays Office. But he was undeterred: "I was determined to go ahead, for Hitler must be laughed at." On the subject of Hitler as a caricature, Lipman quotes Freud's observation: "By making our enemy small, inferior, despicable or comic, we achieve in a roundabout way the enjoyment of overcoming him." But after the war, when the full extent of the Nazi genocide became apparent, Chaplin conceded that "Had I known of the actual horrors of the concentration camps, I could not have made 'The Great Dictator'" (1991, p. 237).

A very different tone was set by Henrik Broder, who wrote: "There's no business like Shoah business," in *Der Spiegel*, quoted by Robert S. Leventhal in an article "Romancing the Holocaust, or Hollywood and Horror: Steven Spielberg's 'Schindler's List'" (1995, available at http:// www2.iath.virginia.edu/holocaust/schinlist.html), discussing the Americanization of the Holocaust in the media.

Cartoons, caricatures, and comics

Historically the cartoon has been through many protean transformations, reflecting technical advances and differing public functions. (The idea of a private cartoon makes no sense.) The notion that it is principally a form of entertainment is a modern American emphasis, for it is one of the oldest satirical weapons against the establishment. Cartoonists are admired and feared, as are other satirists, for sailing close to the wind or cutting near the bone, for being agents provocateurs, and increasingly for being politically incorrect.

Shortly after the invention of the printing press, as part of the propaganda war of the Reformation, scurrilous images of the Papacy started to appear using scabrous visual puns. One of these (Figure 8.2) depicts Pope Leo (styled "Antichrist") as a lion and four German prelates as other animals (in Hillerbrand, 1964, p. 81).

Propaganda cartoons satirizing national enemies such as Napoleon and Hitler are typically subsumed under patriotism. More problematic are those depicting Jews by means of vicious caricatures, found all over Europe for centuries. The stereotype of the monopolistic capitalist affecting the labor politics of South Africa was encapsulated in the figure of Hoggenheimer, the creation of Daniel Boonzaier in 1903. The phonetic similarity to the name of Oppenheimer, the mining magnate, was obviously intentional, as was the caricature of Jewish features with all the accoutrements of the bloated capitalist. More daring are the contemporary satires of Zapiro

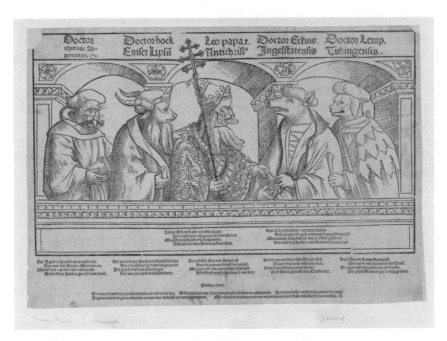

Figure 8.2 Five Opponents of Martin Luther (c. 1520). Satirical cartoon using visual puns on their names, depicting Pope Leo X as a lion also styled "Antichrist," flanked by Murner as a cat, Emser as a goat, Eck as a pig, and Lemp as a dog. (German National Museum, Nürnberg)

(Jonathan Shapiro), which dissect the current political clichés of the New South Africa, such as "the African Renaissance" (see Figure 8.3), the idiocies of the Health Minister's AIDS "remedies," the failed policy of "quiet diplomacy" with the Zimbabwean dictator Mugabe, and so on.

In the US the power of the cartoonist to create influential and stereotypical figures was epitomized in the genius of Thomas Nast (1840–1902), the creator of the Democratic donkey, the Republican elephant, the "Tammany Tiger," and a contributor to the iconic image of Uncle Sam. President Lincoln called Nast, who was strongly against slavery, "our best recruiting agent" and a contemporary journalist observed: "in losing him, *Harpers Weekly* lost its political importance" (Paine, 1974, pp. 69, 528).

English cartoonists have long satirized and lampooned politicians and public figures. While William Hogarth (1697–1764) was more social and moralistic, Thomas Rowlandson (1756–1827) and George Cruikshank (1792–1878) were often savage in their caricatures. Perhaps the nadir of this style was the vile cartoon of Alexander Pope with a deformed rat-like

Figure 8.3   "African Renaissance Gallery" (2007) by Zapiro (Jonathan Shapiro). The gallery guide is former President Mbeki, a major proponent of the "African Renaissance." The ruined statues represent the numerous "failed states" of Africa.

body and wearing a papal crown. However, these were times when sensitivities about physical appearance did not really exist. After a long period of comparative "decency," this ruthless tradition has been revived in the UK in recent decades by such cartoonists as Gerald Scarfe, Steve Bell (see Figure 8.4), Peter Brookes, and Martin Rowlands. Their cruel representations of the British Prime Ministers Tony Blair and Gordon Brown as grotesque, facially deformed idiots is matched only by their treatment of President George W. Bush with obvious affinities to an ape. (American cartoons are generally far more lenient in their physical depiction of public figures.) These British caricatures fly in the face of the new politically correct notion of *lookism*: the fact that Brown has a glass eye is often glaringly apparent, as was the blindness of David Blunkett. Yet they obviously enjoy a significant public following. Their success raises a number of issues. They continue to have an evident illicit appeal, since they blatantly transgress the taboos of political correctness.

Figure 8.4 Steve Bell cartoon of Tony Blair and David Blunkett (November 2005). Blair's half-naked appearance symbolically represents his lost credibility in the Iraq war, while Blunkett, also embroiled in scandal, retains an abject position.

These productions seem tame alongside the modern developments in the genre of the televised cartoon and comic. Cartoon characters, recognizable but not realistic, and thus always permitting greater latitude in probability and language, have been exploited to the full. *The Simpsons*, the creation of Matt Groening, launched in 1989 and winner of numerous awards, established a certain standard of satirical insight into the double standards and hypocrisy behind the façade of the American way of life, not least banal family values. There was also the staple diet of cartoon violence and crudity. In the same genre, *South Park*, created by Trey Parker and Matt Stone in 1997, is more bizarre and scatological, even more offensive and exploitative of black humor than *The Simpsons*, and equally successful. (The episode satirizing the Terri Schiavo case was aired on March 30, 2005, less than 12 hours before her highly publicized death.) *South Park, the Movie: Bigger Longer and Uncut* (1999) depicts the devastating impact of a Canadian "fart film" liberally strewn with obscenities (including the nonce-word *unclefucker*) on a quiet redneck American mountain town. This escalates phantasmagorically into a diplomatic episode, then a war, then the apocalyptic arrival of Satan on earth, accompanied by his toy-boy, Saddam Hussein. As the Canadian envoy says in a televised confrontation: "US television shows graphic violence all the time, but you get pissed off at a few swearwords." Interestingly, the *OED* even draws on the *South Park Scripts* (1999) for an instance of *gay* in the juvenile slang sense of "foolish" or "stupid."

South Park also revealed the limits of tolerance within its own production team. While certain out-groups like Jews and blacks reclaim slurs for their own ironic use, satirists do not always respond favorably when they are targeted. The catalyst for the sudden departure of Isaac Hayes from the program was explained by Matt Stone, the show's cocreator, in the following terms: "In over 150 episodes Isaac never had a problem with the show making fun of Christians, Muslims, Mormons, or Jews. He got a sudden attack of religious sensitivity when it was his religion [scientology] featured on the show" (*Times*, March 15, 2006).

In a different genre, the comic has been radically transformed from the wholesome, safe, and cosy reading matter for children by the steady rise in "adult" comics including *Zap Comix* (from 1968), and the UK comics *Viz* (from 1979), *Crisis* (1988–91), and *Brain Damage* (1989–92). These contain increasing grossness and pointed political incorrectness: *Viz* now includes a "Profanisaurus" and a homophobic spoof with the title "Robin Hood and Richard LittleJohn" featuring "Queerwood Forest," signposted as a "Public Cottaging Area" and "Strictly No Heterosexuality Allowed – £500 fine" (no. 114, May 2002, p. 36).

Antiauthoritarian and politically incorrect cartoons increasingly appear in mainstream newspapers and journals. Thus the *New Yorker* carried a cartoon about the fashion preferences of Ku Klux Klansmen (February 14/21, 2005, p. 154). A controversial cover prior to the presidential election featured Mr and Mrs Obama installed in the White House, he wearing Islamic costume, she dressed as a guerrilla, with the American flag burning in the grate. Dated July 21, 2008, it was called "the Politics of Fear." The *Spectator* depicted a "Channel 4 Alternative to the Queen's Speech" showing an Islamic woman in a burka saying "My lord and master and I . . ." (December 16/23, 2006). The study of popular culture now accommodates works on series such as *Sex and the City* (ed. Kim Akass and Janet McCabe) and *South Park* (Toni Johnson-Woods, Brian C. Anderson).

The tolerance in the West towards cartoons on virtually any topic contrasts severely with the global uproar following the 12 cartoons of Muhammad published by *Jyllans-Posten* (Jutland Post) in Denmark on

September 30, 2005. The depiction of the Prophet, while not absolutely taboo in Islam, is generally forbidden. Moreover, most of the cartoonists emphasized a stereotypical terrorist connection, further enraging the adherents of Islam who regarded this affront to the Prophet as sacrilege. The cartoons were reprinted in Belgium, France, Holland, Germany, Scandinavia, and even Egypt, but not in the USA, the UK, or Canada. Death threats were issued against some of the cartoonists and Muslim nations instituted boycotts of Danish goods.

Rap, hip-hop, and counterculture

Rap has always been a form of counterdiscourse. Originally the content was chauvinist and misogynist, in much the same manner found in "playing the dozens," a convention of verbal dueling among black youths in the USA recorded from the 1930s. Rap has since become increasingly and blatantly politically incorrect, antiauthoritarian, and homophobic. The group N.W.A put out a track called "Fuck tha Police" from the album *Straight Outta Compton*, in 1989. The group's full name (Niggaz with Attitude) is an overt form of self-identification by reclamation, emphasized by the illiterate spelling: in 1990 the *Los Angeles Times* commented on "posters promoting N.W.A . . . with the tag line 'Tha Niggaz R Back'." In recent years some rap artists have produced provocatively homophobic material. The winner of several awards including an Emmy, Eminem (Marshall Bruce Mathers III), was the first of these, and has been the object of several complaints and lawsuits by GLAAD (the Gay and Lesbian Alliance Against Discrimination). Both the British Attorney General and a former Solicitor General have taken the view that it is feasible to prosecute rappers who incite homophobic violence.

Political recidivism is also apparent. The teenage twins Lamb and Lynx Gaede of the duo Prussian Blue produced the album *Fragment of the Future* (2004), including "Road to Valhalla," praising Hitler and the Nazis, and songs of racial hatred such as "Aryan Man, Awake," encouraging him to "turn that fear to hate." In some cases rappers have become provocatively antipatriotic, vilifying their "home" culture. The French rapper Monsieur R (Richard Makela) in his album *Politikment Incorrekt* assumed the uniform of a gendarme for the video of his song "FranSSe," rapping: "France is a bitch . . . You have to treat her a like a slut, man" and "I piss on Napoleon and on General de Gaulle." Others even extol terrorism. Thus the British rappers Fun-Da-Mental produced an album called *All is War (The Benefits of G-Had)*, with one track using the words of Osama bin Laden's "statement of reason and explanation of impending conflict" and comparing him to Che Guevara. The lead singer Aki Nawaz claims the right to freedom of expression, saying "I have the right to push the boundaries as much as anyone else has" (*Guardian*, June 28, 2006).

Shock jocks

In American radio broadcasting, a new type has arisen in the form of various "shock jocks" who have acquired notoriety by testing the boundaries of political correctness and violating taboos with cultivated outrageousness and explicitly shocking verbal content. The full form *shock jock* seems to be first recorded in 1986, the second element derived from *disk jockey*. Their ancestor was Lenny Bruce, the outspoken comedian who satirized serious issues like abortion, the Ku Klux Klan, and the Roman Catholic Church. Among the new provocateurs are George Carlin, Andrew Dice Clay, and Howard Stern, self-described as "the ribald radio star." Don Imus, who had talk shows with both NBC and CBS, notoriously referred to the Rutgers women's basketball team as "nappy-headed hos" over the airwaves, provoking a national furor that led to his dismissal in April, 2007. Imus subsequently featured on the front cover of *Time* magazine (April 23, 2007), his mouth covered with an adhesive memo asking the question "WHO CAN SAY WHAT?" Clearly Imus had gone beyond what the magazine called "the boundaries of acceptable talk." However, dismissals and survivals are not governed solely by issues of principle: if advertisers abandon a program, as happened with Imus, the networks foreclose. The same economic pressures closed Ed Murrow's serious investigative program *See It Now* during its exposure of McCarthyism.

Graffiti

Historically graffiti has come to include a great range of messages of an illicit or provocative nature. Originally the medium reflected its origins in Italian *graffito*, meaning "a scratch," the message, usually of a factual or innocent nature, being scored into stone or wood. Examples have been found on houses and monuments in ancient Rome and Pompeii. Today the spray-paint can is used with the same purpose that the provocative pamphlet or broadsheet were in former times. Messages of a humorous, violent, or subversive nature are placed where the commuting public sees them unawares, and the anonymous authors are difficult to trace. Some graffiti consists of ingenious witticisms, such as "Phallic Symbolism is a lot of Cock." However, in its political dimension it has become a new sociological mode of protest, mainly of an antiestablishment or politically incorrect character, in a mode which has steadily become more intrusive, daring, and shocking.

Much political graffiti is simple sloganeering, such as "Free Tibet" or "Yankees Out!" Obscene or racist terms are exploited as in "Kill the Boers!" or plain "Fuck" and "Cunt," recorded by the British poet Tony Harrison in his poem "V" (1985), expressing outrage at the desecration of his parents' grave. Messages range from the crudest idioms like "Fuck off!" to more politically incorrect slogans like "Fuck the Pope" or even "Fuck the poor." However, the original message can become a palimpsest, vulnerable to ironic ripostes. Thus "Fuck the American Warmongers!" can invite a rejoinder like "I prefer redheads myself." Lynne Truss quotes the amusingly illiterate slogan "NIGGER'S OUT," complete with its grammatically correct rejoinder: "But he'll be back shortly" (2003, p. 51). William Leap's study of gay language, *Word's Out*, contains a chapter illustrating in a frame-by-frame fashion the evolution of actual graffiti about gays. It is a bizarre mixture of hate messages such as "Death to Fagot's [sic]" and pedantic corrections of the spelling and punctuation (1996, pp. 74–87).

Nursery rhymes and variants

These are difficult to place in the cultural spectrum, being simultaneously a common cultural foundation and a source of parody and subversion. Traditionally regarded as expressions of innocence, nursery rhymes cover a great diversity of utterance in which childishness of idiom masks adult concerns and prejudices. The classic studies of the genre are still Iona and Peter Opie's *The Lore and Language of Schoolchildren* (1959), together with their various collections of nursery rhymes. One aspect the Opies show in their wonderful compilation is the prevalence of politically incorrect expressions of many kinds. In a section on "Parody and Impropriety" are to be found such chestnuts as

> While shepherds washed their socks by night
> All seated round a tub;
> A bar of Sunlight soap came down
> And they began to scrub.

and

> We three kings of Orient are
> One in a taxi, one in a car,
> One on a scooter blowing his hooter
> Following yonder star.

But there are unexpected topical variations:

> Hark, the herald angels sing,
> Mrs. Simpson's pinched our King.

This scurrilous lyric spread so rapidly that it was being sung by schoolchildren all over the country within a few days of Edward VIII's abdication on December 10, 1936. As the discussion on censorship in chapter 1 shows, there was simultaneously in the establishment British press a conspiracy to suppress news of the developing affair. Furthermore, "Tennyson, Longfellow, Watts, and other climbers on Parnassus are brought down to street level" in such banalities as "Half an inch, half an inch, half an inch onward, into the Detention Room rode the six hundred." "The boy stood on the burning deck" has at least six variations (Opie, 1959, p. 93).

On sectarian themes the authors admit that "Our information is not extensive, for it was not thought desirable to ask about sectarian rhymes in schools" (1959, p. 344). Nevertheless, they have a considerable collection of malicious rhymes, such as this from Maryland: "Catholic, Catholic, ring the bell, / When you die you'll go to hell." To which the riposte was: "Protestant, Protestant, quack, quack, quack, / Go to the devil and never come back." Both cries "were familiar currency in the streets of Victorian England" (1959, p. 345). Instances are given of Catholic and Protestant insults chanted by children in Northern Ireland, Scotland, New Zealand, and New South Wales, many of them with a historical dimension:

> The Pope he is a gentleman,
> He wears a watch and chain;
> King Billy is a beggarman
> And lives in dirty lane.

There is, predictably, a direct inversion from the other side, running "King Billy is gentleman" (1959, p. 345). However, the military exploits of "King Billy" (William of Orange) have spread far and wide: "In Melbourne and Sydney, children used to gather round convent schools, and perhaps still do, on the anniversary of the Battle of the Boyne [1690]," chanting:

> The Irishman ran down the hill,
> The Englishman ran afther [sic],
> And mony a Pat got a bullet in his back
> At the Battle of the Boy'an Wather.
>
> (1959, p. 343)

"In London," the Opies record, "Jewish kids have long been harried by urchins running round them and shouting:

> Get a bit of pork,
> Stick it on a fork,
> And give it to a Jew boy, Jew.

According to their correspondents, "This jeer was current in 1875 . . . and probably runs back a further century, for Leigh Hunt, who went to Christ's Hospital in 1792, recalls in his *Autobiography* that there was a rhyme about pork upon a fork, concerning the Jews, chanted in his day" (1959, p. 346). They continue: "The Jewish child's traditional retaliation (London 1892, and Eastbourne, c. 1914) was:

> Get a bit of beef,
> Put it on a leaf,
> And give it to a Christian thief.

"Today," they continue, "children colloquially refer to a Jew as a Yid, Shylock or Hooknose" (1959, p. 346).

Apart from the absence of authorial comment, two points emerge from the Opies' carefully documented discussion. Firstly, and unsurprisingly, children become the bearers and maintainers of prejudice. Secondly, in some instances these British exchanges show unmistakable similarities to the verbal dueling known in the United States as "sounding" or "playing the dozens" and historically in its ancient literary British form as "flyting."

The Opies' *Oxford Nursery Rhyme Book* (1955) has amongst its "Tongue Trippers" this item from a bygone era:

> Three crooked cripples
> went through Cripplegate,
> And through Cripplegate
> went three crooked cripples.
>
> (p. 156)

Perhaps now regarded as the most politically incorrect rhyme is "Ten Little Injuns," whose remorseless diminution by various absurd means leads to the unexpected conclusion: "One little Injun living all alone; / He got married, and then there were none" (p. 193). There are also three variations of the familiar jingle

> Taffy was a Welshman
> Taffy was a thief,
> Taffy came to my house
> And stole a piece of beef.
>   (p. 91)

In the Empire there grew up some local variations. One such was *Piccanniny: South African Versions of Popular Nursery Rhymes*, compiled by Phyllis Juby in the 1930s. Among them were: "Tanzi was a Hottentot, Tanzi was a thief, / Tanzi came to my hut and stole a piece of beef," and "Ride a Cock-Horse to Niggertown Pass," and

> There was an old negro
> Who lived in a hut,
> She had so many children
> She went off her nut.

Conclusion: The Right Thing to Do? Progressive Orthodoxy, Empty Convention, or Double Standard?

We have discerned various phases in the development of political correctness: ideological, cultural, academic, literary, semantic, and behavioral, as well as different "sites of struggle," discussed in Part III. First was the historical phase of the orthodox Communist party line. With the decline of Communism, this continued, less in politics *per se*, but developed into the progressive orthodoxy first apparent in cultural and academic matters. Second was the semantic practice recognized more easily today, the proscription of taboo terms and their substitution by an approved vocabulary. Most of the terms (set out in chapter 4) are not political in the strict technical sense, but are new euphemisms referring to stigmatized groups and prejudicial practices. Third was the behavioral phase, that is, modes of lifestyle regarded as "unacceptable" or "inappropriate."

Partly reflecting these developments, the use of politically correct language has itself changed. First was the serious ideological in-group use, which then acquired a broader fashionable currency. The unfamiliar formulas, such as *correct lineism* or *political correctness* itself, and their slightly pompous tone, invited the third phase, outside the constraints of party forums, a reaction of imitation, taking on ironic and parodic forms. There then developed the open challenges of a counterculture of shock jocks and rappers provocatively adopting politically incorrect language and attitudes. But at the same time, the behavioral aspect has strengthened. This is the paradox of political correctness. Although discredited and mocked, it refuses to go away, but appears in new guises.

As *political correctness* has become more fashionable, so it has become less clearly defined, as is typical with such phrases when their currency broadens. It now covers a whole range of individual, social, cultural, and political issues, and topics as diverse as fatness, appearance, stupidity, diet, crime, prostitution, race, homosexuality, disability, animal rights, the environment, and still others. It has taken on the characteristics of a *buzzword*, becoming a fashionable phrase without a clear meaning, but one which nevertheless invokes certain clear responses, hostile or positive, depending on context. It is a semantic sign of orthodoxy with not one, but several party lines. Obviously, not all of these listed issues are of equal social importance, especially in terms of values and morality. Yet often they are accorded similar weight and seriousness. Indeed "diversity," one of the new key terms in the vocabulary, is stretched to accommodate this range of social problems and agendas.

From its first manifestations in America, political correctness has had a double agenda, being a combination of freedom and constraint. The "political" aspect involved opening up new cultural horizons, but "correctness" brought conformity in accepting new agendas, new limits on freedom of expression, and a general avoidance of certain controversial topics. The same opposing qualities are encapsulated in the formulations "progressive orthodoxy" and "positive discrimination." In his survey of 1992, Paul Berman gave a dismal picture of "an atmosphere of campus repression":

> Already the zealots of political correctness have intimidated a handful of well-respected professors into dropping courses that touch on controversial topics. They have succeeded in imposing official speech-codes on a large number of campuses. And the resulting atmosphere [is shown in] the air of caution that many people in academic settings have adopted, the new habit of using one language in private and a different and euphemistic one in public. . . . (Berman, 1992, pp. 2–3)

On a broader front, Kenneth Minogue argued that "European civilization has been attacked and conquered from within, without anyone quite realizing what has happened. We may laugh at political correctness – some people even deny that it exists – but it is a manacle round our hands" (Minogue, 2001). This view may seem melodramatic and alarmist, but consider these responses to the *fatwa* or death sentence pronounced by the Ayatollah Khomeini against Salman Rushdie in 1989: "In considered statements, the Vatican, the Archbishop of Canterbury and the Chief Sephardic Rabbi of Israel all took a stand in sympathy with – the ayatollah" (Hitchens, 2007, p. 30).

One feature of political correctness has been the replacement of cultural élitism by relativism. This is not entirely a bad thing. The days are certainly over when writers could describe themselves, as T. S. Eliot famously did, as "classicist in literature, royalist in politics, Anglo-Catholic in religion." Yet Eliot's damning comment on "the indomitable spirit of mediocrity" (from his 1949 play *The Cocktail Party*, Act I, scene ii) surely applies to much modern culture. As early as 1936, incidentally, George Orwell first referred scathingly to a 'Mickey Mouse universe'. Today we experience the "Disneyfication" of everything. Moreover, Roger Scruton has recently identified what he calls "absolutist relativism," pointing out the "deeply paradoxical nature of the new relativism. While holding that all cultures are equal and judgment between them absurd, the new culture . . . is in the business of persuading us that Western culture, and the traditional curriculum are racist, ethnocentric, patriarchal, and therefore beyond the pale of political acceptability" (Scruton, 2007, p. 84).

Double Standards

In their various ways, the observations of Berman, Minogue, Hitchens, and Scruton reveal different kinds of double standards in values and in language. Of many examples here are three. The *Guardian* objected to the Danish cartoons of Muhammad on the grounds that they gave "gratuitous offence," but often refers to Pope Benedict XVI as "God's rottweiler." The New Labour politician John Prescott was roundly condemned for his notoriously extravagant and decadent lifestyle. But he was praised for confessing (after retiring) to being a bulimic. The extreme anti-Semitism and homophobia of the Prime Minister of Iran, Mahmoud Ahmadinejad, occasioned some hostile remarks from Lee Bollinger, the President of Columbia, on his visit to the University. But Stanley Fish, himself no stranger to controversy as a department chairman, opined that "The obligation of a senior administrator is always to bring honor to the institution he or she serves . . . Columbia does not, or at least should not, stand anywhere on the vexed issues of the day, and neither should its chief executive, at least publicly" (*New York Times*, October 2, 2007).

The positive qualities of political correctness have generally given way to less attractive features. It has steadily extended the boundaries of its progressive orthodoxy to make taboo areas beyond those previously characterized by prejudicial attitudes and stigmatizing language, such as disability, sexism, and racism. It is thus something of an anomaly, since in modern Western society virtually nothing is "strictly forbidden" and traditional taboos are consistently being challenged. The point can be made by considering the following semantic alternatives:

Acceptable	Unacceptable
"rape victim"	"AIDS victim"
"rape survivor"	"AIDS survivor"
"living with AIDS"	"living with cancer"
"dying of cancer"	"dying of AIDS"

Clearly there is no longer a free choice in the use of natural language in relation to disease because of certain agendas which have developed around AIDS.

In other aspects, political correctness has increasingly become less absolute and more contextual, that is to say the emphasis is increasingly less on what is said, but more on who said it and when. This relativism is apparent in considering the following statements: "The white race is the cancer of human history"; "I don't think Blacks can be racist." Both are obviously racist generalizations of the most politically incorrect kind, the first absurdly condemnatory of "the white race", the second naïvely exculpatory of blacks. However, because the first was uttered by a noted white intellectual, Susan Sontag, and the second by a prominent black cultural figure, Spike Lee (Patterson, 1992, p. 81), neither is interpreted at face value, but benefits from contextual latitude, in this case the race and status of the speaker. If Spike Lee had uttered the first statement, he would have been roundly condemned, whereas if Susan Sontag had uttered the second, she would not have been taken seriously. What can one say of the assertions "I *know* that William Shakespeare was a black woman" uttered by Maya Angelou, or *Shylock is Shakespeare*, the title of a book by Kenneth Gross?

Individual cases of racist insult do not always have the same consequences. A British barrister Joseph Sykes, who called Philip Glah, a senior solicitor "a nigger and suggested that he returned to Ghana," was disbarred for racism (*Independent*, January 29, 2007). The Judge President of the Cape, John Hlophe was widely reported in 2005 as having called a senior advocate, Mr Greeff, "a piece of white shit," also accusing him of "being racially prejudiced and told him he should go back to Holland" (*Cape Times*, October 13, 2005). Hlophe denied making the remarks (*Cape Times*, October 6, 2005). In spite of supporting affidavits from witnesses and wide publicity, including calls for his resignation from within the profession, Justice Hlophe retained his position. The controversy is covered in the relevant Wikipedia entry.

The racist generalizations of Sontag and Lee were made several years ago. The second has been repeated often, as Dinesh D'Souza noted in *Illiberal*

Education: "You are a person of color. You cannot be a racist (1991, p. xii). It is only recently that other voices have rejected such double standards. Here is one: "Africans must guard against a pernicious, self-destructive form of racism – that unites citizens to rise and expel tyrannical rulers who are white, but excuses tyrannical rulers who are black." That was Kofi Annan in the Nelson Mandela Lecture in July 2007. Another asks: "Would African leaders have kept quiet if Mugabe were white?" That is Mamphela Ramphele (doctor, university Vice-Chancellor and World Bank director) in *Laying Ghosts to Rest*, her study of transformation in South Africa (2008, pp. 280–1). Criticism of African leaders is generally rejected as racism or disloyalty, depending on the race of the critic, and therefore avoided, with a few notable exceptions. Distinguished earlier examples were the novelists Chinua Achebe and Ngugi wa Thiong'o, both of whom had to go into exile. A more recent example was an article by Moeletsi Mbeki under the title "The African Renaissance, which surfaced in Zimbabwe, has been forcefully extinguished." The former South African president's brother argued that "The new black élites merely replaced the former white colonial élites, but the exploitation of the black masses continued as before" (*Cape Argus*, February 19, 2008).

The topic of political correctness in South Africa was first formally covered at a conference in Johannesburg on October 19, 1999. In the Preface to the proceedings Rainer Erkens was quite blunt about the social and intellectual consequences:

> This book demonstrates that political correctness, particularly the way it is used in South Africa, does not lead to a more liberal society or to more social justice. Rather it hampers open debate and the free exchange of views – the preconditions of development and progress. . . . In our view, political correctness has become a new and more sophisticated form of censorship. . . . Political correctness leaves the outer appearance of freedom, but in reality leads to a situation in which few dare utter their views freely: frankness becomes a source of isolation. (Erkens and Kane-Berman, 2000, p. 2)

Another contributor, Temba Nolutshungu, commented: "A timorous critic of politically correct positions can be cowed into silence by the mere suggestion that his or her views represent a disguised defence of the old order and show an insensitivity to the plight of back people. . . . White intellectuals are particularly susceptible to this kind of *ad hominem* attack, since political correctness preys on white guilt" (Nolutshungu, 2000, p. 23).

It seems significant that the major academic furors of recent years have concerned research into racial differences in intelligence. The contentious findings of the *Bell Curve* resurfaced in the case of James Watson, the Nobel

Prize-winning pioneer into DNA. An article written by a research assistant to publicize his book *Avoid Boring People* (2007) claimed that Watson was "inherently gloomy about the prospects for Africa" because "all our social policies are based on the fact that their intelligence is the same as ours, whereas all the testing says not really" (*The Times*, October 17, 2007). Watson was, perhaps naïvely, "mortified" and mystified, claiming that in his book he made no racist comparisons, only generalized statements: "*A priori* there is no firm reason to anticipate that the intellectual capacities of peoples geographically separated in their evolution should prove to have evolved identically. Our desire to reserve equal powers of reason as some universal heritage of humanity will not be enough to make it so." He apologized for any offense to African people. Nevertheless, on October 18 the Science Museum in London canceled a talk Watson was scheduled to give the following day, on the grounds that his comments had "gone beyond the point of acceptable debate," and he was forced to stand down as Chancellor of Cold Spring Harbor Laboratory, New York State. Such a scenario had been anticipated by Charles Murray in "The Inequality Taboo," where he argued: "The assumption of no innate differences among groups suffuses American social policy. That assumption is wrong" (*Commentary*, September 2005, p. 14).

Even when Barack Obama was elected President of the United States, the primary emphasis was on his color and race (as it had been during the campaign), less on his outstanding abilities as an orator, charismatic politician, strategist, and mobilizer of the electorate, all of which made him a deserving victor. His life story is, of course, inspirational, giving new energy to the ideals of the Melting Pot and the Land of Opportunity.

Very occasionally, racial situations elicit ironic humor: referring to the disclosure that Barack Obama and Dick Cheney are distant cousins, a spokesman for Obama made the wry observation: "Every family has its black sheep" (*Guardian*, October 18, 2007). Very different, deeper, and more daring psychological probing originated in Frantz Fanon's famous observation in *Black Skin, White Masks*: "The black man wants to be white" (1967, p. 11). There is a reprise to this observation in the Nobel Laureate Nadine Gordimer's recent collection *Beethoven Was One-sixteenth Black* (2007). The opening line of the title story is followed by a comment on the ironic reversal of values: "Once there were blacks wanting to be white. Now there are whites wanting to be black. It's the same secret."

The anniversary of Enoch Powell's so-called "rivers of blood" speech in 1968 is regularly observed by the British press, usually accompanied by editorial arguing that Powell was an irresponsible alarmist and a prophet of doom. Powell was not alone in his views. Chris Mullard later concurred in *Black Britain*: "Enoch Powell has predicted race riots in this country by 1986. For completely different reasons I see violent expressions of our position in and disgust with white society some years before that" (1973, p. 156). Forty years later these certainly seem extreme views. But current editorial does not usually accommodate widespread comment that many immigrants to Britain do not wish to assimilate, nor that in places there are pressures to introduce Sharia law, nor that some extremist Muslims have resorted to "honor killings" against their own family members and terrorism against their fellow citizens.

In recent years there have been signs of a resurrection of what Justice Holmes called the "freedom for the thought that we hate." "We must guard the right to say the unthinkable" was the title of a leader in the *Times Higher Education Supplement*, which, after discussing the Lawrence Summers (see chapter 1) and James Watson cases, concluded: "Knowledge cannot be pursued rigorously without the freedom to think the unthinkable and speak the unspeakable. And if academics cannot do that, who can?" (*THES*, October 26, 2007). The "unthinkable" and the "unspeakable," in this context, refer simply to the formulation of tenable academic generalizations about differences in human abilities and behavior. How this evidence is used is the responsibility of others.

The Efficacy and Currency of Politically Correct Language

The fundamental issue is whether linguistic changes affect underlying attitudes or are merely cosmetic. Barbara Ehrenreich argued that "If you outlaw the term 'girl' instead of 'woman,' you're not going to do a thing about the sexist attitudes underneath . . . there is a tendency to confuse verbal purification with real social change. Now I'm all for verbal uplift . . . [but] verbal uplift is not the revolution" (in Dunant, 1994, pp. 23–4). Robert Hughes made the point more strongly in his previously quoted rhetorical question about the cripple in the wheelchair (see chapter 1), asserting that "No shifting of words is going to reduce the amount of bigotry in this or any other society" (1993, p. 21). This was, admittedly, a time when cosmetic semantic changes were the order of the day: "The Union objects to the use of 'the disabled' as a collective label. The approved expression is 'people with disabilities'" (*Sunday Telegraph*, 1985). "It decided to rename the Minister for the Disabled . . . Minister for Disabled People" (*Social Work*, 1990). The comparison is often made with Orwell's artificial "Newspeak" in *1984*, designed to make "thought crime" impossible by eliminating certain crucial concept-words like "free" which Big Brother considered undesirable or subversive. It is a different matter to assume that verbal substitutions or suppressions will alter mental and political attitudes in a free society. They may, however, serve the role of "raising consciousness."

Some critics have gone further, finding intellectual intimidation and a degree of "holier than thouism." Melanie Phillips commented, "It seems to me that the main purpose of today's bowdlerism is less to protect the ostensible targets of prejudice – Black people, women or whomever – than to demonstrate the moral purity of the expurgators, their sensitivity to the evils of prejudice and discrimination" (in Dunant, 1994, p. 47). The resuscitation of *bowdlerism* (much associated with Victorian attitudes) from its predominantly sexual domain is significant. Even more condemning is the view of P. D. James: "I believe that political correctness can be a form of linguistic fascism, and it sends shivers down the spine of my generation who went to war against fascism" (*Paris Review*, 1995).

As with many notions of what constitutes "currency" in language, there is a prevailing double standard between what is acceptable in public and in private. Politically correct language is essentially public, generally confined to official discourse and in many cases artificially polite and euphemistic. Accordingly, let us consider the standard of "the dictionary" as an indicator of formal recognition of some of the major terms. In Table 9.1 the first two authorities are familiar; the less well known abbreviations are LDoCE for the *Longman Dictionary of Contemporary*

Table 9.1   Recognition of Terms by Dictionaries

Dictionary Date	OED 1989	Collins 5 2000	LDoCE 1995	MW 2003	Garner 2003	Peters 2004
Abled	✓	✓	✗	✓	✗	✓
Ageism	✓	✓	✓	✓	✓	✓
Challenged	✓	✗	✓	✓	✓	✓
Cottage (v.)	✓	✓	✓	✗	✗	✗
DWEM	✓	✓	✗	✗	✗	✗
Herstory	✓	✗	✗	✓	✗	✗
Nigga	✗	✗	✗	✗	✗	✓
Sex worker	✓	✗	✗	✓	✗	✗
Waitron	✓	✗	✗	✓	✓	✓
Wimmin	✓	✗	✗	✗	✗	✗

English, MW for *Merriam-Webster's Collegiate Dictionary*, Garner for *Garner's Modern American Usage*, and Peters for the *Cambridge Guide to English Usage*, ed. Pam Peters.

As can be seen, the only form on which there is unanimity is *ageism*, although *challenged* comes close. *Herstory, sex worker*, and *wimmin* have achieved only a marginal existence in these authorities. Out of 60 possibilities, there are as many rejections as there are inclusions. Admittedly, the authorities differ in coverage and intention, since the *OED* is comprehensive, while the Collins, Longmans, and Merriam-Webster are dictionaries on a smaller scale, and the works by Garner and Peters are usage guides.

From another perspective, consider the following dialog:

> "Charles may be from a disadvantaged background and mentally challenged, but he is an ardent multiculturalist."
> "Did I hear that his mother was a sex worker?"
> "Not at all. She was the significant other of a wealthy industrialist, but there was apparently a scandal over the size of his carbon footprint."

The point hardly needs to be labored that politically correct formulas regularly encountered in journalism and some academic studies become absurd in natural conversation. Leslie Fiedler commented on a different style of professional discourse in a *Salon* interview with Bruce Baumann: "In this department [English, at Buffalo] . . . They talk not any human language. They talk Derrida-style, Lacan or Foucault" (January 2, 2003). Was he exaggerating? James Atlas observed that "Gynocriticism . . . has become a flourishing academic field" (1992, p. 63). Maybe so, but *gynocriticism* is still not to be found in any major dictionary.

There is obviously a limit of tolerance. Forms like *greenhouse effect, zero emissions, passive smoking*, and *global warming* have become genuinely current. *Fattism, lookism*, and *speciesism* are not so secure outside protected discussion. But consider the history of *laughism* or "inappropriately directed laughter," which provoked such derision that, according to Anne Soukhanov, it "went out of currency within about five years . . . driven off the linguistic stage to the boos, hisses, catcalls, and, yes, derisive laughter of those concerned about the preservation of free speech" (1995, p. 162). This is, no doubt, because it was a solemn bureaucratic coinage originating in the University of Connecticut's presidential policy on harassment in 1988. As for *DWEM*, the racist acronym for "Dead White European Males," coined at the height of the "culture wars," it was always something of a ghost form, and has deservedly vanished.

Levels of Discourse

Just as different registers are exploited by institutions and publications, so varying degrees of political correctness tend to be present (or absent) on a hierarchical scale in levels of discourse. Thus a government communiqué or a leader in a quality newspaper will be characterized by both a formal register and a high degree of political correctness. By contrast, unofficial and underground comments, being informal or even subversive, will have a correspondingly high degree of political incorrectness, being laced with chauvinist, racist, ageist, and other belittling idioms, typically in a low register. Indeed, some recent forms of popular culture, such as chat shows presided over by "shock jocks," clearly thrive on the illicit quality of being "non-PC." Table 9.2 sets out the basic framework, but special cases should be noted.

Among special cases are religious language, idioms, and popular fiction. Although venerated and archaic, the Bible often uses what have become politically incorrect terms like *whore, abomination,* and *sodomite.* Many idioms show racism to be a traditional feature of common speech, as in "nigger in the woodpile," "doesn't stand a Chinaman's chance," and so on. Popular fiction is the most complex category, ranging from the most correct to the defiantly incorrect. Among the classics, Defoe's *Moll Flanders* (1722), Dickens's *Oliver Twist* (1837–9), and Mark Twain's *Huckleberry Finn* (1885) have become politically incorrect. Contrariwise,

Table 9.2 Framework for Levels of Discourse

	Type	*Source*	*Media*
High level of PC	Official	Government Parliament/ Congress Sermons	Quality press
			Textbooks
	Common		
	Unofficial	bar room/ locker room chat	Popular fiction
			Tabloids
	Underground	parodies jokes talk shows	
Non-PC		hip-hop, rap	

after Shakespeare, the most read, revised, and reworked standard author in modern times is Jane Austen, whose vocabulary is beyond reproach.

It is unrealistic to expect politically correct language to replace entirely the coarser established words of natural language and everyday speech. In formal contexts a government report may analyze the problems of *sex workers*, and up-market newspapers may use the term in some of their reports, but *prostitute* and *whore* maintain their vigorous demotic currencies. Frequently the double standard is apparent in that the headline of a story will use *sex worker*, but the main body of the text will use *prostitute*. The reporting of the prostitution scandal leading to the downfall of Governor Eliot Spitzer in March 2008 was a case in point: the *New York Times* report of March 13 used *prostitute* and *prostitution* four times, but *sex worker* not at all. In a quite different context, the *Guardian*'s bland euphemistic report "Austrian Father confesses to years of abuse" referred to the shocking case of incest. By contrast, the headline in the London *Times* referred directly to the "incest father" (April 29, 2008).

Furthermore, the baser instincts of schadenfreude and xenophobia naturally sustain a clandestine or suppressed currency of terms like *cripple*, *wog*, and *nigger*. But their public use is taboo, which is certainly an improvement. Political correctness thus acts as a censor, reminding people of human and communal sensitivities which should be respected. "Respect" is very much the key term. But it is one of the ironies of history that political correctness should have emerged at a time when respect is very much perceived as being on the decline.

The New Morality

Historically the most common sources of complaints about the abuse of language have concerned the proliferation of religious oaths and blasphemous insults. Significantly, these issues have not been the major focus of the political correctness debate, reinforcing the general observation that religion and blasphemy are being steadily downgraded as areas of taboo in an increasingly secularized society. Significantly, the last case of blasphemy in Britain arose in 1977 from the publication of a poem in *Gay News* implying that Christ was a promiscuous homosexual. The other instance, significantly, was the furor over *The Satanic Verses* in 1989. By contrast *Jerry Springer: The Opera* raised anger and protests among Christians, but little opposition in the wider society. A survey in 2006 revealed that the name of Jesus was familiar among the majority of British schoolchildren, but as a swearword.

With the secularization of society, the traditional canon of the Seven Deadly Sins has either diminished in force or become politicized. The Good Life is now essentially materialist, not spiritual. Thus pride has been co-opted to support previously unpopular causes as in Gay Pride, a slogan invented about 1970. (There is a "Proudly South African" campaign devised at a time when huge social problems, such as the AIDS pandemic, rising crime rates, and over 40% unemployment started to surface in the postapartheid society.) What used to be called covetousness, avarice, and envy have been harnessed as mainsprings of consumerism. Vanity is an obvious engine for the fashion and cosmetic industries. Lust, not a common word any more, is not even part of the new mechanized vocabulary of the sex drive. Most people under 50 would regard sloth as the name of a variety of slow-moving arboreal animal: the state of idleness or doing nothing has acquired an ambiguous status in terms of the work ethic, being a source of admiration or contempt. Gluttony, still celebrated in strange eating competitions, has obviously been affected, not so much by questions of morality as by the new anxieties concerning diet. Wrath is the only sin still regarded as deadly in such forms as road rage, but public spectacles of anger, such as Zinedine Zidane's notorious head-butting of an opponent in the Football World Cup of 2006, attract voyeuristic fascination.

Pope Benedict XVI's revised Seven Deadly Sins, issued on March 10, 2008, showed a marked shift from traditional spiritual values to those of political correctness and social responsibility. Now included are environmental pollution, genetic modification, and drug dealing. While the inclusion of abortion would be expected from the Pontiff, that of pedophilia showed courage. "Obscene wealth," while not in the old canon, is the clear obverse of the traditional value ascribed to poverty.

Even without such spiritual leadership, it is important to recognize that political correctness has in various ways redefined morality. A few years ago the "outing" of homosexuals was a highly controversial practice. But in an increasingly "open" dispensation, coded references concerning private matters are often dispensed with: "Organisations applying for grants from the British Arts Council are being asked to state how many board members are bisexual, heterosexual, homosexual, lesbian or whose inclinations are 'not known'." Among a whole range of hostile responses to this proposal, the playwright Christopher Hampton said: "It's bureaucracy and political correctness gone mad." The actor Simon Callow added mischievously: "I love the category of the Not Known: a despicable heresy surely, in 2008?" (London *Times*, April 2, 2008).

Callow's apposite comment about "heresy" is ironic. Yet the word takes us back to the Inquisition, the medieval split in the Christian Church, the schisms in the papacy, and the violent sectarianism in the Anglican Church during and after the Reformation. These divisions derived from fundamental matters of doctrine and authority. By contrast, the current divisions in the Anglican communion are over comparatively trivial gender issues of gay priests, women bishops, and the blessing of same-sex unions, but they are taken no less seriously.

A key semantic change is apparent in *ethical*. The traditional sense, deriving from Greek *ethika* meaning "morality," formed a whole branch of moral philosophy. Like "morals," "ethics" and "ethical" have always had positive senses. In the 1980s the concept of "ethical investment" developed, meaning investment in enterprises whose activities do not offend the moral principles of the investor, such as those involved in child labor or tobacco. From this notion the concept of "ethical living" has arisen in the past decade. This does not mean, as it would appear, conforming to norms of personal moral probity or New Testament values, but having the proper, that is, politically correct, attitudes towards climate change, fair trade, ethical investment, organic food, animal rights, and vegetarianism. It is less concerned with loving your neighbor or being a good member of the community than with "reducing your carbon footprint."

Political correctness has introduced new positive value terms such as *alternative*, *multicultural*, and *diversity*, as well as their stigmatizing opposites. Those who criticize these goals or use the wrong language do so at their risk. Thus a person may lead a life of complete probity and intellectual rigor, but be destroyed socially and professionally by being denounced for simply using "politically incorrect" language and thus labeled as a *racist*, *sexist*, *homophobe*, or *fascist*, despite the fact that these terms are problematic both in definition and specific application. Furthermore, no distinction is commonly made between fiction, dialog, and private utterance. The case of Philip Larkin's letters was discussed in chapter 8. Among many other instances, Saul Bellow's ironic but searching questions, "Where is the Tolstoy of the Zulus? . . . [and] the Proust of the Papuans?" were not answered, but resuscitated in an obituary article in *The Times* (April 18, 2005). A similar obituary in *The Guardian* focused even more basely on specific slurs in his fiction: "He was accused of racism ('niggerlove' is an unfortunate word that crept into *Herzog*) and anti-Semitism ('kikes' appears in *Humboldt's Gift*)" (April 7, 2005).

In this context it is valuable to revisit the remarks of Mary McCarthy in her review of a biography of Dickens. Comparing the current assessment of Dickens to a trial, she commented that the assailants present themselves as posthumous inquisitors. "Here, as in most inquisitions, the metonymic principle is at work – the part is substituted for the whole, and a single 'incriminating' utterance is produced in court to lay bare the man in his totality" (1962, p. 218). Those words come from "Recalled to Life," written over half a century ago, in 1953. Commenting on the selectivity and unfairness of the whole process, McCarthy added: "Dostoevsky sometimes wrote badly; he was virulently anti-Semitic, anti-Polish, anti-Catholic; but nobody seeks to indict him for it."

Literature provides a valuable and variable lens on society, since the creativity of literary artists operates in a continuum between realism and fantasy, between the conventional and the subversive. Overt censorship of the "unacceptable" and publishers' "guidelines" of "inappropriate" matter and treatment cannot guarantee the outcome once the genie is out of the bottle. As we have seen, much "high" culture is concerned with transgression, and popular culture has responded to the limitations of political correctness with some outrageous extremes.

Significantly, amongst the most highly praised literary works of recent years are to be found several with the most politically incorrect ingredients, among them J. M. Coetzee's *Disgrace* (1999), Philip Roth's *The Human Stain* (2000), and Zadie Smith's *White Teeth* (2000). Even Tarantino's *Pulp Fiction* (1994) has its champions. In the popular market the enormous success of the *Da Vinci Code* (2003) can hardly be explained by any cogency of theory, but principally by its theme of a grand conspiracy to suppress the "true" story of Jesus and Mary Magdalene, a succession of bearers of the secret of the Holy Grail, a religious sect with perverse practices, vast buried treasure, and serial ritual murders. When the basic idea was previously advanced in a more scholarly treatment, *The Holy Blood and the Holy Grail* (1978), it made little public impact, since the conspiracy was not seriously entertained and the work lacked the spice of gruesome behavior among the faithful. Both J. K. Rowling and Philip Pullman have attracted huge readerships, in spite of or perhaps because their works take unconventional views of religion and magic. In "nonfiction" as it is called, two of the best sellers in recent years are, revealingly, Richard Dawkins' *The God Delusion* (2006) and Christopher Hitchens' *God is Not Great* (2007).

The debate over the efficacy of politically correct language remains unresolved. There is little doubt that the formulas "political correctness," "politically correct," and "PC" are now basically pejorative and ironic in their use. But although there are more critics than advocates, and parodies abound, this distinct mode of language, at once "raising consciousness" and camouflaging social problems by polysyllabic obfuscation, maintains its curious semiofficial status. In its various manifestations, political correctness undoubtedly inculcates a sense of obligation in areas which should be matters of choice. But choice is the vital element of a free society. And that choice includes balancing a sense of humanity and fairness with the right to challenge what is termed "unacceptable" or "inappropriate," and on occasion to revive the injunction of Dr Johnson: "Clear your mind of cant."

Bibliography

Adhikari, Mohamed, *Not White Enough, Not Black Enough: Racial Identity in the South African Coloured Community*. Athens: Ohio University Press, 2005.

Adler, Jerry, et al., "Thought Police: Taking Offense," *Newsweek*, December 24, 1990, pp. 48–55.

Allen, Irving Lewis, *The Language of Ethnic Conflict*. New York: Columbia University Press, 1983.

Aman, Reinhold (ed.), *The Best of Maledicta*. Philadelphia: Running Press, 1987.

Amis, Kingsley, *The King's English: A Guide to Modern English Usage*. London: St Martin's Press, 1998.

Amis, Martin, "The Ending: Don Juan in Hull," *New Yorker*, July 12 1993: 74–82.

Andrews, Bert, *Washington Witch Hunt*. New York: Random House, 1948.

Asante, Molefi Kete, "Multiculturalism: An Exchange," in Paul Berman (ed.), *Debating PC: The Controversy Over Political Correctness on College Campuses*. New York: Laurel Press, 1992, pp. 299–311.

Atlas, James, *Battle of the Books*. New York: Norton, 1992.

Attwell, David, "Race in *Disgrace*," *Interventions*, 4 (3), 2002: 331–41.

Aufderheide, Patricia (ed.), *Beyond PC: Towards a Politics of Understanding*. St Paul, MN: Graywolf Press, 1992.

Ayto, John, *Twentieth Century Words*. Oxford: Oxford University Press, 1999.

Baugh, Albert C., *A History of the English Language*. London: Routledge & Kegan Paul, 1951.

Beard, Henry and Christopher Cerf, *The Official Politically Correct Dictionary and Handbook*. London: Grafton, 1992.

Beauvoir, Simone de, *The Second Sex*. Harmondsworth, UK: Penguin, 1972.

Behlmer, Rudy, *Inside Warner Brothers (1935–51)*. New York: Simon & Schuster, 1985.

Berman, Paul (ed.), *Debating PC: The Controversy Over Political Correctness on College Campuses*. New York: Laurel Press, 1992.

Berube, Michael, "Public Image Limited: Political Correctness and the Media's Big Lie," in Paul Berman (ed.), *Debating PC: The Controversy Over Political Correctness on College Campuses*. New York: Laurel Press, 1992, pp. 124–49.

Black, Jeremy, *The Slave Trade*. London: Social Affairs Unit, 2006.

Bloom, Allan, *The Closing of the American Mind*. New York: Simon & Schuster, 1987.

Bloom, Harold, *The Western Canon*. New York: Riverhead Books, 1994.

Boorstin, Daniel J. (ed.), *An American Primer*, Chicago: University of Chicago Press, 1966.

Booth, William, *In Darkest England, and the Way Out*. London: Salvation Army, 1880.

Bosman, Herman Charles, *Unto Dust*. Cape Town: Human & Rousseau, 1963.

Bradbury, Ray, *Fahrenheit 451*. London: Rupert Hart-Davis, 1954.

Bréal, Michel, *Semantics: Studies in the Science of Meaning*, trans. Mrs Henry Cust. London: Heinemann, 1900.

Brink, André, *Rights of Desire*. London: Secker & Warburg, 2000.

Britten, Sarah, *The Art of the South African Insult*. Johannesburg: 30° South Publishers, 2006.

Burchell, Jonathan and John Milton, *Principles of Criminal Law*. Cape Town: Juta, 1997.

Burchfield, Robert, *Unlocking the English Language*. London: Faber, 1989.

Burchfield, Robert (ed.), *The New Fowler's Modern English*. Oxford: Clarendon Press, 1996.

Burchill, Julie, *Sex and Sensibility*. London: Grafton, 1992.

Burgess, Anthony, *1985*. London: Hutchinson, 1978.

Butler, Guy, *Bursting World: An Autobiography, 1936–45*. Cape Town, David Philip, 1983.

Cameron, Deborah, *Verbal Hygiene*. London: Routledge, 1995.

Carter, Angela, *Expletives Deleted: Selected Writings*. London: Chatto & Windus, 1992.

Caute, David, *The Great Fear: The Anti-Communist Purge under Truman and Eisenhower*. London: Secker & Warburg, 1978.

Chambers, E. K., *The Elizabethan Stage*. Oxford: Clarendon Press, 1923.

Chapman, Robert L. *New Dictionary of American Slang*. New York: Harper & Row, 1986.

Clark, Alan, *Diaries*. London: Phoenix, 1993.

Cleaver, Eldridge, *Soul on Ice*. New York, McGraw-Hill, 1968.

Coetzee, J. M., *Dusklands*, Johannesburg: Ravan Press, 1974.

Coetzee, J. M., *Doubling the Point: Essays and Interviews*, ed. David Attwell. Cambridge, MA: Harvard University Press, 1992.

Coetzee, J. M., *Giving Offense: Essays on Censorship*. Chicago: Chicago University Press, 1996.

Coetzee, J. M., *Disgrace*. London: Penguin, 1999.

Coleman, Peter, "From Fellow Travelling to Political Correctness," in Rainer Erkens and John Kane-Berman (eds), *Political Correctness in South Africa*. Johannesburg: South African Institute of Race Relations, 2000, p. 519.

Cook, Captain James, *Voyages Round the World*, ed. M. B. Synge. London: Nelson, 1903.

Coren, Alan, *The Collected Bulletins of Idi Amin*. London: Robson Books, 1975.

Crystal, David, *The Cambridge Encyclopaedia of the English Language*. Cambridge, UK: Cambridge University Press, 1995.

Dampier, William, *Dampier's Voyages*, ed. John Masefield. London: Grant Richards, 1906.

Davis, William, *Punch and the Monarchy*. London: Hutchinson, 1977.

Dillard, J. L., *Black English*. New York: Vintage Books, 1973.

Dollard, John, *Caste and Class in a Southern Town*. New Haven, CT: Yale University Press, 1937.

Doyle, Roddie, *The Commitments*, Dublin: King Farouk, 1987.

Drabble, Margaret, *A Natural Curiosity*. London: Viking, 1989.

D'Souza, Dinesh, *Illiberal Education: The Politics of Race and Sex on Campus*. New York: Macmillan/The Free Press, 1991.

Dunant, Sarah (ed.), *The War of Words: The Political Correctness Debate*. London: Virago, 1994.

Eagleton, Terry, *Literary Theory*, 2nd edn. Oxford: Blackwell, 1996.

Ehrenreich, Barbara, "The Challenge for the Left," in Paul Berman (ed.), *Debating PC: The Controversy Over Political Correctness on College Campuses*. New York: Laurel Press, 1992, pp. 333–8.

Eliot, T. S., *After Strange Gods*. London: Faber, 1934.

Eliot, T. S., *Notes Towards a Definition of Culture*. London: Faber, 1948.

Eliot, T. S., *Selected Essays*. London: Faber, 1951.

Ellmann, Richard, *Oscar Wilde*. London: Hamish Hamilton, 1987.

Enright, D. J. (ed.), *Fair of Speech: The Uses of Euphemism*. Oxford: Oxford University Press, 1986.

Epstein, Barbara, "Political Correctness and Identity Politics," in Patricia Aufderheide (ed.), *Beyond PC: Towards a Politics of Understanding*. St Paul, MN: Graywolf Press, 1992, pp. 148–54.

Erkens, Rainer and John Kane-Berman (eds), *Political Correctness in South Africa*. Johannesburg: South African Institute of Race Relations, 2000.

Fabricius, Johannes, *Syphilis in Shakespeare's England*. London: Jessica Kingsley, 1994.

Fanon, Frantz. *Black Skin, White Masks*. London: Pluto Press, 1967.

Fiedler, Leslie, *Love and Death in the American Novel*. New York: Stein and Day, 1966.

Fish, Stanley, *There's No Such Thing as Free Speech and it's a Good Thing Too*. Oxford: Oxford University Press, 1994.

Fish, Stanley, *Professional Correctness*. Oxford: Oxford University Press, 1995.

Flexner, Stuart Berg, *I Hear America Talking*. New York: Van Nostrand Reinhold, 1976.

Forster, E. M., *A Passage to India*. Harmondsworth, UK: Penguin, 1961.

Freud, Sigmund, *Totem and Taboo*, trans. James Strachey. London: Routledge and Kegan Paul, 1950.

Fox, Celina, *Londoners*, London: Thames & Hudson, 1987.

Frost, Peter, *Fair Women, Dark Men: The Forgotten Roots of Color Prejudice*. Christchurch, NZ: Cybereditions, 2005.

Fryer, Peter, *Staying Power: The History of Black People in Britain*. London: Pluto Press, 1984.

Fussell, Paul, *Class*. New York: Ballantine Books, 1984.

Gagiano, Annie, " 'Racial' characterisation in the apartheid-period and post-apartheid writings of J. M. Coetzee," in Natasha Distiller and Melissa Steyn (eds), *Under Construction: "Race" and Identity in South Africa Today*. Johannesburg: Heinemann, 2004, pp. 38–49.

Gallie, W. B., *Philosophy and the Historical Understanding*. London: Chatto & Windus, 1964.

Garner, Bryan A., *Garner's Modern American Usage*. Oxford: Oxford University Press, 2003.

Garner, James Finn, *Political Correct Bedtime Stories*. New York: Macmillan, 1994.

Gates, Henry Louis, Jr., *Loose Canons: Notes on the Culture Wars*. New York: Oxford University Press, 1992a.

Gates, Henry Louis Jr., "Whose Canon is it, Anyway," in Paul Berman (ed.), *Debating PC: The Controversy Over Political Correctness on College Campuses*. New York: Laurel Press, 1992b, pp. 190–200.

Gill, Roma (ed.), *Doctor Faustus*. London: Benn, 1989.

Gilman, Sander L., *Sexuality: An Illustrated History*. New York: Wiley, 1989.

Goldenberg, David, *The Curse of Ham*. Princeton, NJ: Princeton University Press, 2003.

Gordimer, Nadine, *Beethoven Was One-Sixteenth Black and Other Stories*. London: Bloomsbury, 2007.

Gordon, Ted and Wahneema Lubiano, "The Statement of the Black Faculty Caucus," in Paul Berman (ed.), *Debating PC: The Controversy Over Political Correctness on College Campuses*. New York: Laurel Press, 1992, pp. 249–57.

Green, Jonathon, *New Words*, 1992. London: Bloomsbury.

Green, Jonathon, *Chasing the Sun: Dictionary Makers and the Dictionaries They Made*. London: Jonathan Cape, 1996.

Green, Jonathon, *The Slang Thesaurus*. London: Penguin, 1999.

Green, Jonathon, *The Big Book of Being Rude*. London: Cassell, 2000.

Greenblatt, Stephen (ed.), *New World Encounters*. Berkeley: University of California Press, 1993.

Greer, Germaine, *The Female Eunuch*. New York: Bantam, 1970.

Greer, Germaine, *The Madwoman's Underclothes*. London: Pan, 1987.

Grose, Francis, *A Classical Dictionary of the Vulgar Tongue*. London: S. Hooper, 1785, 1794, 1811.

Grover, Jan Zita, "AIDS: Keywords," in Christopher Ricks and Leonard Michaels (eds), *The State of the Language: 1990s Edition*. Berkeley: University of California Press, 1990, pp. 142–62.

Hamilton, Ian, *Writers in Hollywood*. London: Heinemann, 1990.

Harwood, Ronald, *All the World's A Stage*. London: Methuen, 1984.

Hayter, Alethea, *Opium and the Romantic Imagination*. London: Faber, 1968.

Hentoff, Nat, " 'Speech Codes' on the Campus and Problems of Free Speech," in Paul Berman (ed.), *Debating PC: The Controversy Over Political Correctness on College Campuses*. New York: Laurel Press, 1992, pp. 215–24.

Herrnstein, Richard J. and Charles Murray, *The Bell Curve: Intelligence and Class Structure in American Life*. New York: The Free Press, 1994.

Heywood, Christopher, *A History of South African Literature*. Cambridge, UK: Cambridge University Press, 2004.

Hillerbrand, H. J. (ed.), *The Reformation in its Own Words*. London: SCM Press, 1964.

Hislop, Ian (ed.), *Private Eye Annual 1998*. London: Private Eye Productions.

Hitchens, Christopher, "Remembering an Intellectual Heroine," *Slate*, December 29, 2004.

Hitchens, Christopher, *God is Not Great*. London: Atlantic Books, 2007.

Hoch, Paul, *The Newspaper Game*. London: Calder & Boyars, 1974.

Hoggart, Simon, "Politics," in D. J. Enright (ed.), *Fair of Speech: The Uses of Euphemism*. Oxford: Oxford University Press, 1986, pp. 174–84.

Holder, R. W., *A Dictionary of Euphemisms*. Oxford: Oxford University Press, 1995.

Holderness, Graham, Bryan Loughrey, and Nahem Yousaf (eds), *George Orwell*. London: Macmillan, 1998.

Holmes, Rachel, *The Hottentot Venus: the Life and Death of Saartjie Baartman: Born 1789 – Buried 2002*. Johannesburg: Jonathan Ball, 2007.

Howard, Philip, *New Words for Old: A Survey of Misused, Vogue and Cliché Words*. Oxford: Oxford University Press, 1977.

Hughes, Geoffrey, *Words in Time*. Oxford: Blackwell, 1988.

Hughes, Geoffrey, *Swearing*. Oxford: Blackwell, 1991.

Hughes, Geoffrey, *A History of English Words*. Oxford: Blackwell, 2000.

Hughes, Geoffrey, *Swearing: An Encyclopedia*. Armonk, NY: M. E. Sharpe, 2006.

Hughes, Robert, *The Fatal Shore*. London: Pan Books, 1988.

Hughes, Robert, *Culture of Complaint: The Fraying of America*. New York: Oxford University Press, 1993.

James, Wilmot, Daria Caliguire, Kerry Cullinan, Janet Levy, and Shauna Westcott (eds), *Now That We Are Free: Coloured Communities in a Democratic South Africa*. Boulder, CO: Lynne Rienner Publishers, 1996.

Jardine, Lisa, "Canon to Left of them, Canon to Right of them," in Sarah Dunant (ed.), *The War of Words: The Political Correctness Debate*. London: Virago, 1994, pp. 97–115.

Jespersen, Otto, *Growth and Structure of the English Language*, 9th edn. Oxford: Basil Blackwell, 1962.

Jolly, Rosemary, "Going to the Dogs: Humanity in J. M. Coetzee's *Disgrace*," in Jane Poyner (ed.), *J. M. Coetzee and the Idea of the Public Intellectual*. Athens: Ohio University Press, 2006, pp. 148–71.

Kallen, Horace M., *Cultural Pluralism and the American Idea: An Essay in Social Philosophy*. Philadelphia: University of Philadelphia Press, 1956.

Kennedy, Randall, *Nigger: The Strange Career of a Troublesome Word*. New York: Vintage Books, 2002.

Kimball, Roger, *Tenured Radicals: How Politics has Corrupted our Higher Education*. New York: Harper & Row, 1990.

Kimball, Roger, "The Periphery v. the Center: The MLA in Chicago," in Paul Berman (ed.), *Debating PC: The Controversy Over Political Correctness on College Campuses*. New York: Laurel Press, 1992, pp. 61–84.

Kinsey, Alfred C., Wardell B. Pomeroy, and Clyde E. Martin, *Sexual Behavior in the Human Male*. Bloomington: Indiana University Press, 1998.

Koestenbaum, Wayne, "Speaking in the Shadow of AIDS," in Christopher Ricks and Leonard Michaels (eds), *The State of the Language: 1990s Edition*. Berkeley: University of California Press, 1990, pp. 163–70.

Kors, Alan and Harvey Silverglate, *The Shadow University: The Betrayal of Liberty on America's Campuses*. New York: HarperPerennial, 1998.

Kramarae, Cheris and Paula Treichler, *A Feminist Dictionary*. Boston: Pandora, 1985.

Kramer, Hilton and Roger Kimball (eds), *Against the Grain*. Chicago: I. R. Dee, 1995.

Labov, William, *Language in the Inner City*. Philadelphia: University of Philadelphia Press, 1972.

Lakoff, Robin Tolmach, *The Language War*. Berkeley: University of California Press, 2000.

Larkin, Philip, *Selected Letters, 1940–85*, ed. Anthony Thwaite. London: Faber and Faber, 1992.

Larsen, Egon, *Wit as a Weapon: The Political Joke in History*. London: F. Muller, 1980.

Las Casas, Bartolomé de, *A Short Account of the Destruction of the Indes*, ed. and trans. Nigel Griffin. London: Penguin, 1992.

Lawrence, D. H., "Introduction to his Paintings," in *Selected Essays*. Harmondsworth, UK: Penguin, 1950, pp. 307–46.

Lawrence, D. H., *Lady Chatterley's Lover*, Harmondsworth, UK: Penguin, 1960.

Leap, William, *Word's Out: Gay Men's English*. Minneapolis: University of Minnesota Press, 1996.

Leavis, F. R., *The Common Pursuit*. London: Chatto & Windus, 1952.

Lee, Yueh-Ting, Lee J. Jussim and Clark R. McCauley, *Stereotype Accuracy*. Washington: American Psychological Association, 1995.

Legman, Gershon, *The Rationale of the Dirty Joke: An Analysis of Sexual Humor*. Secaucus, NJ: Castle Books, 1968.

Lessing, Doris, "Censorship," in *Time Bites*. London: Fourth Estate, 2004, pp. 72–8.

L'Estrange, Julian, *The Big Book of Insults*. London: Cassell, 2002.

Le Vaillant, François, *Travels into the Interior Parts of Africa*. London: Robinson, 1790.

Lewis, Anthony, *Freedom for the Thought that We Hate*. New York: Basic Books, 2008.

Lewis, C. S., *Studies in Words*. Cambridge, UK: Cambridge University Press, 1960.

Lipman Steve, *Laughter in Hell: The Use of Humor during the Holocaust*. Northvale, NJ and London: Jason Aronson Inc., 1991.

Liu Shao Chi, *On the Party*. Peking, Foreign Languages Press, 1951.

Loomba, Ania, *Shakespeare, Race and Colonialism*. Oxford: Oxford University Press, 2002.

Loomba, Ania, *Colonialism/Postcolonialism*, 2nd edn. London: Routledge, 2005.

Lutz, William, *Doublespeak*. New York: Harper, 1990.

Maggio, Rosalie, *The Bias-Free Word Finder: A Dictionary of Non-Discriminatory Language*. Boston: Beacon Press, 1992.

Major, Clarence, *Juba to Jive*. New York/London: Viking/Penguin, 1994.

Mamet, David, *Oleanna*. London: Methuen Drama, 1992.

Mao Tse-Tung, "On Correcting Mistaken Ideas in the Party," in *Selected Works of Mao Tse-Tung*. Peking: Foreign Languages Press, 1965.

McCarthy, Mary, *The Groves of* Academe. London: Heinemann, 1953.

McCarthy, Mary, *On the Contrary*. New York: Noonday Press, 1962.

McDonald, James, *Dictionary of Obscenity, Taboo and Euphemism*. London: Sphere Books, 1988.

McDonald, Peter D., "*Disgrace* Effects," *Interventions*, 4 (3), 2002: 321–30.

McGillis, Roderick, *The Nimble Reader: Literary Theory and Children's Literature*. New York: Twayne, 1996.

Mencken, H. L., *The American Language*, 4th edn, ed. Raven I McDavid. London: Routledge & Kegan Paul, 1963.

Mieder, Wolfgang, "Blasons Populaires," in Carl Lindahl, John McNamara, and John Lindow (eds), *Medieval Folklore*. Santa Barbara, CA: ABC-CLIO, 2000, pp. 103–5.

Miller, Casey and Kate Swift, *The Handbook of Non-Sexist Writing*. London: The Women's Press, 1981.

Mills, Jane, *Womanwords*. London: Virago, 1989.

Milosz, Czeslaw, *The Captive Mind*. New York: Vintage Books, 1955.

Minogue, Kenneth, "How Civilizations Fall," *The New Criterion*, 19 (8), 1999, p. 4.

Minogue, Kenneth, *The Concept of a University*. New Brunswick, NJ and London: Transaction Publishers, 2005.

Morgan, Robin (ed.), *Sisterhood is Powerful*. New York: Vintage, 1970.

Morison, Samuel Eliot, *The European Discovery of America*, New York: Oxford University Press, 1974.

Mphahlele, Ezekiel, *Down Second Avenue*. London: Faber, 1959.

Mugglestone, Lynda, *Lexicography and the OED. Pioneers in the Untrodden Forest*. Oxford: Clarendon Press, 2000.

Mugglestone, Lynda, *Lost for Words. The Hidden History of the Oxford English Dictionary*. New Haven, CT: Yale University Press, 2005.

Mullard, Chris, *Black Britain*. London: George Allen and Unwin, 1973.

Murphy, Brenda, "*Oleanna*: Language and Power," in Christopher Bigsby (ed.), *The Cambridge Companion to David Mamet*. Cambridge, UK: Cambridge University Press, 2004, pp. 124–37.

Murray, Charles, "The Inequality Taboo," *Commentary*, 120 (2), 2005, pp. 13–22.

Myers, Gustavus, *History of Bigotry in the United States*. New York: Random House, 1943.

Nabokov, Vladimir, *Bend Sinister*. London: Weidenfeld and Nicolson, 1960.

Nabokov, Vladimir, *Strong Opinions*, London: Weidenfeld and Nicolson, 1973.

Nash, Walter, *Jargon*. Oxford: Blackwell, 1993.

Neaman, Judith S. and Carole G. Silver, *A Dictionary of Euphemisms*. Hemel Hempstead, UK: Unwin, 1983.

Nolutshungu, Temba, "Political Correctness and the Black Intelligentsia," in Rainer Erkens and John Kane-Berman (eds), *Political Correctness in South Africa*. Johannesburg: South African Institute of Race Relations, 2000, pp. 21–7.

Opie, Iona and David Opie, *The Lore and Language of Schoolchildren*. Oxford: Clarendon Press, 1959.

Orwell, George, *Nineteen Eighty-Four*. Harmondsworth: Penguin, 1972.

Oyserman, Daphna and Kathy Harrison, "Implications of Cultural Context: African-American Identity and Possible Selves," in Janet K. Swim and Charles Stangor (eds), *Prejudice*. San Diego, Academic Press, 1998, pp. 281–300.

Paine, Albert B., *Thomas Nast, His Period and His Pictures*. Princeton: Pyne Press, 1974.

Partridge, Eric, *Words, Words, Words*. London: Methuen, 1933.

Partridge, Eric, *Shakespeare's Bawdy*. London: Routledge & Kegan Paul, 1947.

Patterson, Alex, *Spike Lee*. New York: Avon Books, 1992.

Patterson, Orlando, *Ethnic Chauvinism*. New York: Stein and Day, 1977.

Pearsall, Ronald, *The Worm in the Bud: The World of Victorian Sexuality*. Harmondsworth, UK: Penguin, 1969.

Pei, Mario, *Words in Sheep's Clothing*. New York: Hawthorn Books, 1969.

Pepper, Frank S., *20th Century Quotations*. London: Sphere, 1987.

Perry, Ruth, "A Short History of the Term *Politically Correct*," in Patricia Aufderheide (ed.), *Beyond PC: Towards a Politics of Understanding*. St Paul, MN: Graywolf Press, 1992, pp. 71–9.

Peters, Pam (ed.), *The Cambridge Guide to English Usage*. Cambridge, UK: Cambridge University Press, 2004.

Phillips, Melanie, "Illiberal Liberalism," in Sarah Dunant (ed.), *The War of Words: The Political Correctness Debate*. London: Virago, 1994, pp. 35–54.

Pine, L. G., *The Story of Surnames*. London: Country Life, 1965.

Potter, Simeon, *Our Language*. Harmondsworth, UK: Penguin, 1961.

Quinion, Michael, *Ologies and Isms*. Oxford: Oxford University Press, 2002.

Ramphele, Mamphele, *Laying Ghosts to Rest: Dilemmas of the Transformation in South Africa*. Cape Town: Tafelberg Publishers, 2008.

Rauch, Jonathan, *Kindly Inquisitors: The New Attacks on Free Thought*. Chicago: Chicago University Press, 1993.

Ravitch, Diana, "Multiculturalism: E Pluribus Plures," in Paul Berman (ed.), *Debating PC: The Controversy Over Political Correctness on College Campuses*. New York: Laurel Press, 1992, pp. 271–98.

Ravitch, Diane, *The Language Police: How Pressure Groups Restrict What Students Learn*. New York: Knopf, 2003.

Rawson, Hugh, *A Dictionary of Invective*. London: Hale, 1991.

Read, Herbert, *Art Now: An Introduction to the Theory of Modern Painting and Sculpture*, rev. 3rd edn. London: Faber and Faber.

Ricks, Christopher, *T. S. Eliot and Prejudice*. London: Faber, 1988.

Ricks, Christopher and Leonard Michaels (eds), *The State of the Language: 1990s Edition*. Berkeley: University of California Press, 1990.

Robertson, D. W., *A Preface to Chaucer*. Princeton, NJ: University of Princeton Press, 1963.

Rose, G., *Feminism and Geography*. Minneapolis: University of Minnesota Press, 1993.

Rosebery, Archibald, *Lord Randolph Churchill*. London, Humphries, 1906.

Ross, Steven J. (ed.), *Movies and American Society*. Oxford: Blackwell, 2002.

Roth, Philip, *The Human Stain*. London: Random House, 2000.

Rothenberg, Paula, "Critics of Attempts to Democratize the Curriculum are Waging a Campaign to Misrepresent the Work of Responsible Professors," in Paul Berman (ed.), *Debating PC: The Controversy Over Political Correctness on College Campuses*. New York: Laurel Press, 1992, pp. 262–8.

Rowan, David, *A Glossary for the 90s*. London: Prion Books, 1998.

Rowe, Marsha (ed.), *Spare Rib Reader*. Harmondsworth, UK: Penguin, 1982.

Roxburgh, Angus, *Pravda: Inside the Soviet News Machine*. London: Gollancz, 1987.

Rushdie, Salman, *The Satanic Verses*. London: Viking, 1988.

Safire, William, *On Language*. New York: Times Books, 1981.

Said, Edward, "The Politics of Knowledge," in Paul Berman (ed.), *Debating PC: The Controversy Over Political Correctness on College Campuses*. New York: Laurel Press, 1992, pp. 172–89.

Said, Edward, *Orientalism*. Harmondsworth, UK: Penguin, 1995.

Sartre, Jean-Paul. *What is Literature?* Methuen: London, 1950.

Sauer, David and Janice E. Sauer, "Misreading Mamet: Scholarship and Reviews," in Christopher Bigsby (ed.), *The Cambridge Companion to David Mamet*. Cambridge, UK: Cambridge University Press, 2004, pp. 220–42.

Saunders, Jennifer, *Absolutely Fabulous*. London: BBC Books, 1994.

Saussure, Ferdinand de, *Course in General Linguistics*, ed. Charles Bally and Albert Sechehaye, with Albert Reidlinger, trans. Wade Baskin. New York: McGraw-Hill, 1966.

Schlesinger, Arthur M. Jr., *The Disuniting of America*. New York: W W Norton, 1972.

Scruton, Roger, *A Dictionary of Political Thought*. London: Pan, 1982.

Scruton, Roger, *Untimely Tracts*. London: Macmillan, 1987.

Scruton, Roger, "Ideologically Speaking," in Christopher Ricks and Leonard Michaels (eds), *The State of the Language: 1990s Edition*. London: Faber, 1990, pp. 118–29.

Scruton, Roger, *Culture Counts*. New York: Encounter Books, 2007.

Searle, John R., "The Storm Over the University," *New York Review of Books*, December 6, 1990, pp. 34–42.

Shapera, I., *Khoisan Peoples of Southern Africa*. London: Geo. Routledge, 1930.

Sharpe, Tony, *T. S. Eliot: A Literary Life*. London: Macmillan, 1991.

Sheidlower, Jesse, *The F-Word: The Complete History of the Word in all its Robust and Various Uses*. New York: Random House.

Shippey, Tom, *Beowulf*. London: Arnold, 1978.

Showalter, Elaine, *Hystories: Hysterical Epidemics and the Modern Media*. New York: Columbia University Press, 1997.

Smith, Stephen A., "There's Such a Thing as Free Speech: And it's a Good Thing, Too," in Rita Kirk Whillock and David Slayden (eds), *Hate Speech*. Thousand Oaks, CA: Sage, 1995, pp. 226–63.

Smith, Edwin (ed.), *Essays and Studies: Literature and Censorship*. Cambridge, UK: D. S. Brewer, 1993.

Smith, Zadie, *White Teeth*. London: Penguin, 2001.

Sontag, Susan, *AIDS and Its Metaphors*. London: Penguin, 1990.

Soukhanov, Anne H., *Word Watch*. New York: Henry Holt, 1995.

Spears, Richard A., *Forbidden American English: A Serious Compilation of Taboo American English*. Lincolnwood, IL: Passport Books, 1990.

Steiner, George, *In Bluebeard's Castle*. London: Faber, 1971.

Steiner, George, *Language and Silence*. Harmondsworth, UK: Penguin, 1969.

Stimpson, Catharine R., "On Differences: Modern Language Association Presidential Address 1990," in Paul Berman (ed.), *Debating PC: The Controversy Over Political Correctness on College Campuses*. New York: Laurel Press, 1992, pp. 40–60.

Storr, Anthony, *Sexual Deviation*. London: Penguin, 1964.

Strachey, John, *Literature and Dialectical Materialism*. New York, Covici, Friede, 1934.

Strother, Z. S, "Display of the Body Hottentot," in Bernth Lindfors (ed.), *Africans on Stage*. Bloomington: Indiana University Press, 1999, pp. 1–61.

Sutherland, John (ed.), *The Oxford Dictionary of Literary Anecdotes*. Oxford: Oxford University Press, 1975.

Swim, Janet K. and Charles Stangor (eds), *Prejudice*. San Diego, Academic Press, 1998.

Tarantino, Quentin, *Reservoir Dogs*. London: Faber & Faber, 1994.

Tau Y Gragramla (pseudonym), *A Marriage Made in Heaven or The White Man's Burden*. Johannesburg: Native Book Club and Skotaville Publishers, 2001.

Taylor, Gary, *Reinventing Shakespeare*. London: Hogarth Press, 1990.

Teachout, Terry, "Houston Baker, Jr.: Another Sun Person Heard From," in Hilton Kramer and Roger Kimball (eds), *Against the Grain*. Chicago: I. R. Dee, 1995, pp. 101–8.

Thompson, Harry, *Tintin: Hergé and his Creation*. London: Sceptre, 1992.

Thorne, Tony, *Dictionary of Contemporary Slang*, 3rd edn. London: A & C Black, 2007.

Tolley, A. T., *Larkin at Work*. Hull: University of Hull Press and The Philip Larkin Society, 1997.

Trotsky, Leon, *Problems of the Chinese Revolution*, trans. Max Schachtman. New York: Pioneer Publishers, 1932.

Truss, Lynne, *Eats, Shoots & Leaves*. London: Profile Books, 2003.

Truss, Lynne, *Talk to the Hand*. London: Profile Books, 2005.

Tyrrell, W. B., *Amazons: A Study in Athenian Mythmaking*. Baltimore, Johns Hopkins University Press, 1984.

Ullmann, Stephen, *Language and Style*. Oxford: Basil Blackwell, 1964.

Van den Berghe, Pierre L., *The Ethnic Phenomenon*, New York: Praeger, 1981.

Walker, Alice, *In Search of Our Mothers' Gardens*, New York: Harcourt, 1983.

Walker, Samuel, *Hate Speech: The History of an American Controversy*. Lincoln: University of Nebraska Press, 1994.

Waugh, Evelyn, *Decline and Fall*. London, Chapman and Hall, 1928.

Weekley, Ernest, *The Romance of Names*. London: John Murray, 1914.

Wenborn, Neil, *The Pictorial History of the U.S.A.* London: Hamlyn, 1991.

Whillock, Rita Kirk and David Slayden (eds), *Hate Speech*. Thousand Oaks, California: Sage, 1995.

Will, George, "Radical English," in Paul Berman (ed.), *Debating PC: The Controversy Over Political Correctness on College Campuses*. New York: Laurel Press, 1992, pp. 258–61.

Williams, Gordon, *A Glossary of Shakespeare's Sexual Language*. London: Athlone Press, 1997.

Williams, Raymond, *Keywords*. London: Fontana, 1976.

Willinsky, John, *The Empire of Words: The Reign of the OED*. Princeton, NJ: Princeton University Press, 1994.

Winterson, Jeanette, *The World and Other Places*. London: Jonathan Cape, 1998.

Wood, Michael, *In Search of Shakespeare*. London: BBC Books, 2003.

Author and Subject Index

Note: Page references in italics indicate illustrations; cross-references in italic indicate Word Index.

Word Index